Educational Measurement and Evaluation

Claudio Violato
Dan McDougall
Anthony Marini

University of Calgary

 KENDALL/HUNT PUBLISHING COMPANY
2460 Kerper Boulevard   P.O. Box 539   Dubuque, Iowa 52004-0539

Contents

Preface

The field of educational measurement and evaluation has undergone rapid and extensive development in the last two decades due to numerous innovations in test theory, statistics, computer technology and changes in social and educational policy. In teaching this subject to undergraduate students preparing to be teachers, we found that current textbooks generally fail to reflect the state of the art in the area. While a number of texts have been excellent in the past, even in their current 4th, 5th, 6th editions and beyond, they tend to emphasize themes, issues, controversies and technologies of the last generation of measurement experts. Essentially, they are texts written by our professors representing the thinking of a generation ago. To better serve our students and to reflect the state of the art (and science) in educational measurement and evaluation, we decided to write our own text.

Some of the book incorporates conventional and fundamental material which is still important in a text about measurement and evaluation for prospective teachers. Chapters 3 to 6 which deal with test construction, utilizes true and tried principles of item writing together with the latest research findings supporting the writing rules that are expostulated. In the introductory chapter, we have tried to convey a sense of the history of educational measurement and evaluation and its current status together with social, legal and ethical issues surrounding testing. Chapter 2 deals with educational objectives and their role in testing. In Chapter 7, we present some elementary statistics with a focus on their meaning and significance for measurement and evaluation rather than on computational procedures. Nowadays, various statistical software is readily available as are microcomputers which can handle the computations efficiently, rapidly and without error. Accordingly, there is no need to focus on the elementary, tedious and often mind-numbing computations that have characterized so many texts in the area. We have found that little else inhibits students and makes them hostile to the area than an emphasis on statistical computations often at the expense of meaning and understanding. Accordingly, we have tried to de-emphasize rote computations and application of formulae.

Chapters 8 and 9 which deal with validity and reliability respectively, and Chapter 10 which deals with analyzing test results and item analyses, are written from the perspective of the classroom teacher. The main intent of these chapters is to deal with the issues and needs of the practitioner in the classroom. Chapter 11 is a guide for the use of standardized tests for the classroom teacher and Chapter 12 outlines sound grading and reporting procedures. Finally, Chapter 13 is a discussion of the role of computers and computer technology in educational measurement and evaluation.

To handle the needs of the student in a course for which this text was written, as well as the continuing needs of the classroom teacher, we have also developed software, CRASP and accompanying documentation which is available from the publisher, Detselig, Box G 399, Calgary, AB, Canada, T3A 2G3. This software handles the record keeping needs of teachers, the maintenance of anecdotal records and narrative reports for grading and reporting, the development of summary reports themselves, as well as producing more conventional statistical analyses, graphical analyses and reliability computations.

Many people made the writing of this book possible. In particular we would like to thank our many thousands of students over the last decade who have tried out some of the materials in the text and who provided feedback on our lectures. Of course any imperfections in the book is entirely our responsibility.

C. V.
D. M.
A. M.
Calgary, Alberta.

Chapter

Introduction

Overview

This is a text book about the science of educational testing, measurement and evaluation. This chapter provides an introduction to the field and the remainder of the book. Testing, measurement and evaluation are defined and distinguished. Subsequently we trace the origins of testing to antiquity and provide a brief history of testing to its current status. The role of testing in teaching and learning is explicated and its importance for this function is discussed. The section after that deals with the various types of tests and evaluation procedures. This chapter concludes with sections discussing current issues in testing and the likely future of educational testing and measurement.

The Science of Measurement

The science of educational measurement is more commonly known as testing. While testing has its roots in antiquity and has undergone rapid advances in the 20th century, the science of educational measurement is now only beginning to emerge as a unified field. This is because some necessary developments for the emergence of this science—statistical and mathematical theories, test theory, microcomputers and optical readers, social and political policy—have come only in the last two or so decades. Currently, the field is undergoing rapid development and change bringing exciting possibilities and challenges. Before describing the current status of educational measurement and its history, however, we must describe and distinguish testing, measurement and evaluation.

Testing, Measurement and Evaluation

Measurement involves the assignment of numbers or quantities to some dimension. Evaluation is the process of interpreting or judging the value of the measurement. Testing as used in the usual sense is a subset of measurement—it is measurement of educational or psychological outcomes.

1

Measurement instruments generally include the quantification of dimensions in many areas such as physics, biology, chemistry, medicine and so forth. Familiar examples of measurement instruments include rulers, thermometers, barometers, odometers, calipers, weight scales, chronometers (watches and clocks), and speedometers. These measurement instruments are so familiar and commonplace that you hardly attend to them at all. In psychology and education, measurement instruments include examples such as intelligence tests, achievement tests, personality inventories, spelling tests, and any classroom tests that you have taken in school. All of these are measurement instruments because they attempt to quantify (assign a number) some dimension whether it be length (ruler), time (clock), intelligence (IQ test) or scholastic aptitude (Scholastic Aptitude Test—SAT). Each assigns a number to one of a physical (length), psychological (intelligence) or educational (SAT) dimension. Tests, therefore, are measurement instruments in education and psychology.

Evaluation involves value judgements. To make an evaluation, you interpret a measurement according to some value system. If you check the outside temperature on your thermometer, for instance, and find that the temperature is 50°F, you may conclude that it is too cold to go swimming in the lake. The measurement is the actual temperature reading (50°F) while the evaluation is that it is "too cold to go swimming". As another illustration, a measurement may be a teacher reporting Jason's score on his spelling test as 19. If the teacher interprets this score and concludes that Jason is an excellent speller, then this is an evaluation. Finally, a patient may score at the 97th percentile on several scales of the Minnesota Multiphasic Personality Inventory (a personality test). The psychologist interprets this to suggest that the patient may be psychotic. This is an evaluation.

Test scores generally serve as measurements or attempts to quantify some aspect of pupil educational functioning. The letter grades (A, B, C, D, F) or adjective descriptions (Excellent, Fair, Poor) associated with these numbers are evaluations based on these test scores. Evaluation, therefore, is measurement plus value judgements. The quality of the evaluation depends on both the quality of the measurement and the care with which this result is interpreted. A careless interpretation of good quality data is likely to lead to a poor evaluation just as a careful interpretation of shoddy data would. Evaluation by teachers (or others) of pupil performance that are based on little or no data (that is, subjective evaluations) are likely to be of very poor quality. One of the main aims of this book, therefore, is to help prospective teachers develop good quality tests (measurement instruments) and to conduct careful interpretations of the results. Thus their evaluation of pupil performance will be enhanced. Later in this chapter we will explore the specific role of testing in teaching but first let us briefly examine the history of testing and its current status.

A Brief History of Testing

A chronology of some major events in testing are summarized in Table 1.1. This section is an amplification and elaboration of these major events.

The origins of testing are lost in antiquity. In China, for example, many centuries before Christ (beginning in the 12th century B.C.) there was an elaborate system of civil service examinations (Dubois, 1970). These tests were so gruelling sometimes lasting up to 72 consecutive hours, that only perhaps 3 percent passed and became mandarins and thus eligible for public office. Testing was also a normal part of the education of the ancient Greeks. Both Plato and Socrates used expert oral questioning of their students as they saw testing and teaching as

Table 1.1. Brief Chronology of Testing

12th Century B.C.	The Chinese established elaborate tests for civil service positions
1219 A.D.	Law examinations were established at the University of Bologna
1599	Rules for taking written examinations were published by the Jesuit order
1845	Horace Mann published his critique of oral testing which was in widespread use in the United States
1870's– 1880's	Sir Francis Galton did his pioneering work in statistics and anthropomorphic measurement
1890's	Karl Pearson developed his various measures of relationships: product-moment correlation, multiple R and partial r.
1897	Joseph Rice published the results of his standardized spelling tests and established norms.
1900	The College Entrance Examination Board was established.
1904	Charles Spearman's work established the foundation for the concept of test reliability and factor analysis.
1905	Alfred Binet and Theodore Simon published the first scales of intelligence.
1916	Lewis Terman published the Stanford Revision of the Binet-Simon scales that has come to be known as the Stanford-Binet.
1920's	Standardized testing was widespread in Milan for municipal civil service positions.
1931	Leon Thurstone published *The Reliability and Validity of Tests* an authoritative textbook for its time.
1935	Oscar Buros published the *Mental Measurements Yearbooks*, which contained critical reviews of the most important tests. This series continues to the present.
1937	Frederic Kuder and Marion Richardson invented the K-R 20 method of determining test reliability.
1939	David Wechsler was developing the intelligence scales which bear his name and published an initial account as, *The Measurement of Adult Intelligence.*
1940	The influential journal, *Educational and Psychological Measurement,* began publishing.
1948	Educational Testing Service (ETS) was founded at Princeton, New Jersey.
1960's	The advent of electronic computers began to influence testing through item-banking, test scoring and statistical analysis. Their accessibility was still very limited.
1965	American Congress initiated a series of hearings into testing, its use, fairness and validity.
1966	Three organizations, The American Psychological Association, the American Educational Research Association and the National Council on Measurement in Education, jointly published the *Standards for Educational and Psychological Testing.* In its third edition (1985), it still remains the standard guide for test development, use and interpretation.

1972	Lee J. Cronbach and his colleagues published the first systematic account of generalizability theory and its use for testing.
1970's	Introduction of Item Response Theory or Latent Trait Theory.
1980's	The widespread availability of microcomputers began revolutionizing item-banking, machine scoring of tests and item-analysis capacities of tests at the classroom level. The use of adaptive testing through computer administration is becoming practical at the classroom level.
1990's	The development of structural equation modelling such as Latent Variable Path Analyses or Linear Structural Relationships hold great potential in allowing scientists to break new ground in exploring the nature and structure of human abilities and achievement.

inextricably intertwined. Some of the earliest records of testing, however, can be found in the bible. Stanley and Hopkins (1981, p. 200) cite the interesting Biblical example of the oral test that was used to distinguish between men of Gilead from members of the tribe of Ephraim. The latter pronounced ''Shibboleth'' without the ''h'' following the ''S'':

> Then they said unto him, Say now Shibboleth: and he said Sibboleth: for he could not frame to pronounce it right. Then they took him, and slew him at the passages of Jordan (Judges; 12:5–6; King James Version).

This was a *final* exam indeed. Failure on this short test produced rather drastic consequences. Fortunately, failure on modern-day tests rarely produces such extreme outcomes.

The first known formal examinations in an educational institution were those in law at the University of Bologna in 1219 (Dubois, 1970). The development of written examinations in European schools followed the introduction of paper and writing materials in the thirteenth century. The Jesuits were pioneers in the systematic use of written tests for formal measurement and evaluation of educational outcomes. By 1599 they had published a document prescribing the rules of conduct of examinations including how to handle absentees, maintaining silence, preventing cheating and the disposition of incomplete papers (McGuken, 1932).

Notwithstanding the Jesuits' rules for written examinations, oral examinations still predominated in both Europe and America up to the end of last century. In 1845, Horace Mann published his critique of oral testing, presaging many of the concepts that today form the cornerstone of modern measurement theories. With the advent of inexpensive writing materials by the end of the 19th century (e.g. pencils and paper), written examinations eventually replaced the cumbersome and inept oral exams in Canada and the United States. Today, oral examinations remain in North America only in ritualistic and vestigial form as for the Masters and Doctorate degrees though they are still used widely in many other countries. Outside of the educational system forms of oral examinations such as the ''job interview'' and entertainment forms such as television game shows (e.g. *Jeopardy*) and board games (e.g. *Trivial Pursuit, Super Quiz*), still remain popular even though their measurement properties are notoriously poor. The job interview is probably the most overrated and widely misused form of the oral examination for the assessment of the candidate's suitability.

During the last two decades of the 19th century, pioneering and important work for measurement theory was carried out in statistics by Sir Francis Galton and Karl Pearson.

While Galton did extensive work in distribution theory involving anthropomorphic measurements, Pearson developed his various measures of relationships including the product-moment correlation, multiple and partial correlation. In 1904 Charles Spearman, another British statistician, published several papers which laid the foundation for the concept of reliability (see Chapter 9) and factor analysis, a statistical procedure based on correlation for identifying underlying properties of achievement and mental abilities.

At approximately the same time (1900), the College Entrance Examination Board (CEEB) was established with the purpose of developing standardized achievement tests to facilitate college admission decisions. Carl Brigham worked with the CEEB during the first decade of this century and there did pioneering work in scientific item analysis methods (Dubois, 1970). The origins of standardized testing as we know it today, however, date back to the 1890's with Joseph Rice's spelling surveys. Rice began his career as a physician but soon turned his efforts to educational research. Over the course of about two years, Rice secured spelling test results on nearly 30,000 children in 21 American cities (Rice, 1897). With these initial efforts Rice was attempting to standardize tests of spelling ability and develop what we call norms today. He devoted most of his career to making education more rational, progressive and scientific. Unfortunately, the educational leaders of the day were hostile to Rice and his work so that his ideas had very little impact on education during his lifetime.

In 1904 Alfred Binet was appointed by the French government to a committee to investigate the causes of retardation among public school pupils. As a consequence of this work, Binet saw the need to develop a screening device which could identify children who might encounter probable difficulties in their later schooling. Binet was subsequently joined by a French psychiatrist, Theodore Simon, in this work and in 1905 they published the Binet-Simon Intelligence Tests. This was a valuable contribution to measurement and test theory. In 1916, Lewis Terman, a Stanford University psychologist, used the Binet-Simon scales to produce what is now known as the Stanford-Binet Test of Intelligence. It was not until after the widespread application of standardized tests in World War I for military personnel selection, however, that testing received broad popular attention.

As the United States entered into the war in 1917, the American Psychological Association offered its services to the U.S. Army. Psychologists were called upon to develop tests and screening devices for the new recruits. This resulted in the Army Alpha Verbal Test for literates and the Army Beta NonVerbal Test for illiterates. In a very short period, these tests were administered to millions of people.

After the end of the first world war psychologists and educational researchers turned their attention to civilian testing. A variety of achievement, abilities, interest and aptitude tests were developed and standardized. The 1920's saw an unprecedented and still to be matched activity in intelligence testing. Standardized testing was in wide use elsewhere in the world. In Milan, for example, during the 1920's standardized testing was used for screening for municipal civil service positions. In the United States, standardized educational testing experienced its peak development and use between 1930 and 1950. Figure 1.1 summarizes the patterns and activities of testing in this century.

Both educational and intelligence testing decreased after the 1950s but educational testing has undergone a revival in the 1980s and 1990s. The decline of testing during the 1960s and 1970s was due in large part to social, political and educational ferment and change as well as rapid expansion of education due to the ''baby boomers'' entering school. Anti-testing sentiments were common. By the 1980s, however, state and provincial legislation as well as the

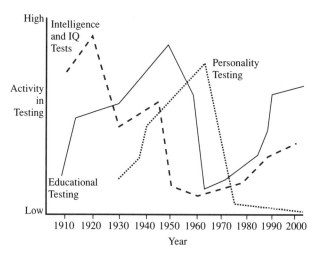

Figure 1.1. Activity in Educational, Personality and Intelligence Testing in Canada and the United States during the 20th century

demand for accountability from school systems have seen a resurgence of testing activity (see Figure 1.1). President George Bush's educational policy statements in 1991 also have stressed accountability and excellence thereby creating an environment hospitable to testing. In Canada, discussions and policy statements about a national standardized testing programme for the 1990s also portends more testing. It is estimated that several tens of millions of standardized tests are administered in Canada and the United States every year. In addition there are perhaps around 600 million classroom tests administered every year. World wide this figure no doubt exceeds 1 billion! We can anticipate as Figure 1.1 suggests that testing is likely to continue at a high rate into the next century.

Another interesting pattern evident from Figure 1.1 is the sharp rise of personality testing in the 1950s and 1960s and then its rapid decline. The initial upsurge of personality measurement in the 1960s was sufficiently large to spark public concern. In 1965 a series of congressional hearings were held into personality testing. The immediate trigger for these hearings seems to have been the use of personality tests in the federal government's personnel selection procedures (Haney, 1981). The use of the Minnesota Multiphasic Personality Inventory (MMPI) in selection of Peace Corps volunteers was subjected to particular criticism spearheaded by Senator Sam Ervin. Art Buchwald, the Washington humorist, parodied the MMPI with his own test that contained the true-false item, "A wide necktie is a sign of a disease". This item, Buchwald joked, could determine whether a person should work for the Labor Department, Peace Corps, FBI or the White House (Haney, 1981).

No direct rules or laws governing testing practices emerged from these congressional hearings. They did, however, prompt the American Psychological Association to undertake further study of testing practices. Moreover, these hearings helped to heighten sensitivities among testers for privacy rights, and increased public awareness about psychological and educational testing.

Against this background of the ebb and flow of testing during this century, a number of technical and scientific advances were occurring. In 1931 Leon Thurnstone, co-founder of *Psychometrika,* a journal of quantitative and statistical developments in psychology, published his authoritative textbook, *The Reliability and Validity of Tests* which summarized test theory up to 1931. By 1935 Oscar Buros had published the first edition of the *Mental Measurements Yearbooks* which contained critical reviews of the most important tests. This series continues to the present (Volume 10 was published in 1989). In 1937 Frederic Kuder and Marion Richardson published their KR-20 method of determining reliability (explained in Chapter 9). At about the same time, David Wechsler was developing his intelligence scales which now bear his name. His initial account was published in 1939 as the *Measure of Adult Intelligence* and he has since developed scales for children. These are now the most widely used psychological tests in the world (Lubin, Larsen, & Matarazzo, 1984). In 1940, the journal *Educational and Psychological Measurement* began publishing. It's mandate was and still is to advance the field of measurement and publish reports of research on the development and use of tests and measurements in education, industry, and government. Educational Testing Services (ETS) was founded in 1947 by the American Council on Education, the Carnegie Foundation for the Advancement of teaching, and the College Entrance Examining Board. Located in Princeton, New Jersey, the ETS was established to meet the measurement needs of American education as well as advancing measurement research.

The 1960's saw the advent of high speed electronic computers and these began to influence testing in a variety of ways. The data storage capacity of these machines allowed for the development of item-banks which are essentially test items kept in the computer memory. The main advantage of this form of storage is that the items are easily retrievable. Test scoring could now be easily mechanized with optical readers which could "read" bubble answer sheets. This information can be relayed directly into the computer and could be readily analyzed with various statistical programmes. The computers and their influence on testing, however, was very limited because the machines were very large, expensive and available only to a very few. The real, widespread impact of computers in revolutionizing testing is only beginning to be felt.

As we have already seen, there was a general public backlash against testing by the 1960s but especially against personality testing. This led to the congressional hearings of 1965 into testing generally and led to increased public sensitivity and awareness about testing and its purposes. Meanwhile, the American Psychological Association, the American Educational Research Association and National Council on Measurement in Education jointly published the *Standards for Educational and Psychological Testing* (1966) which established the standards for test development, use and interpretation. Still the standard in its third edition (1985), these guidelines establish the criteria for reliability (Chapter 9), validity (Chapter 8), and the norm group requirement for standardization (Chapter 7). Standardized published tests must meet the criteria as set out in this document governing the use of tests.

L. J. Cronbach, G. Glesser and N. Rajaratnam published the first accessible and widely available account of generalizability theory in 1972 though they had published several papers nearly 10 years earlier (1963, 1965) on the topic. These earlier papers, however, were highly technical and remained obscure. Generalizability theory was a significant departure for the "classical" test theory in that it allowed for the application of testing principles and ideas to new areas. For example, this theory allows for the study of the dependability (reliability) of the adjudication of several judges (e.g. 7) on a number of figure skaters (e.g. 12). Applying generalizability theory allows you to determine the reliability of the evaluation across both judges and skaters. Thus, generalizability theory deals with the extent to which we can generalize to a domain or "universe" of objects or events (judges, skaters, test items, etc) from a sample of them. Cronbach and his colleagues allowed us to think differently and freshly about reliability problems. Generalizability techniques have been applied to a wide range of problems including visitor satisfaction with outdoor recreation (Schomaker & Knopt, 1982), reliability of criterion-referenced tests (Kanet & Wilson, 1984) and the consistency of people's behaviour across situations (Violato & Travis, 1988).

The 1970s also saw the introduction of Item Response Theory or Latent Trait Theory. This approach departs from more traditional testing methods in that it yields a more complete picture of how an item functions across different ability levels of test-takers. It is assumed that there is a latent ("underlying") trait (human characteristics) which accounts for the response to items on a test. While this theory is quite mathematically complicated it has found several applications particularly with adaptive testing and computers.

Microcomputers flourished and became commonly available in the 1980s. What was only available on large, expensive mainframe computers in the 1960s was now becoming available to every classroom teacher (or at least every school). Combining Item Response Theory with microcomputer technology allows for the computer administered testing thus eliminating paper copies. Also, item-banking, machine scoring of tests and routine item-analysis were becoming available to the classroom teacher. Various types of software were developed for these functions.

The 1990s have already seen some important developments in statistical applications especially in structural equation modelling. The development of Latent Variable Path Analysis (LVPA) or Linear Structural Relationships (LISREL) hold great promise for breaking new ground in exploring the nature and structure of human achievement and abilities.

Current Status of Testing

The current status of testing is paradoxical. On the one hand, rapid advances in computer technology and statistical and test theory have brought impressive new capabilities to the science of educational measurement. On the other hand, most classroom testing is still very primitive. Of the 600 million or so tests given in Canada and the United States in classrooms every year, the vast majority would not meet even minimal standards of appropriate tests. How can this be?

The main reason for the poor quality of tests in most classrooms is that teachers have virtually no knowledge of basic educational measurement or test construction principles. Teachers receive virtually no education in these theories and practices in their University programmes. In the United States, most of the 50 states require no explicit training in measurement and assessment as part of teacher certification (Stiggins, 1991). Most States simply require completion of an accredited teacher education programme. A majority of teacher education programmes, however, have neither a compulsory nor an optional course in educational measurement and assessment. Indeed, many programmes have no course offering in these areas at all (Stiggins, 1988). Most American teachers have no education in this subject. The situation is similar in Canada.

There is a further irony to the situation. While as we have seen testing is on the increase and teachers as well as school administrators know little about it (Hills, 1991), the general public is very much in favour of increased testing in schools (Elam, Rose, & Gallup, 1991). In the 1991 Gallup Poll of the Public's Attitudes Toward the Public Schools, for example, 88% of respondents were in favour of using standardized testing in their community for core subjects (English, Math, Science, History and Geography), 84% favoured it for problem-solving skills, and 85% favoured it for ability to write (Elam et al, 1991, p. 46). Finally, 58% of the respondents

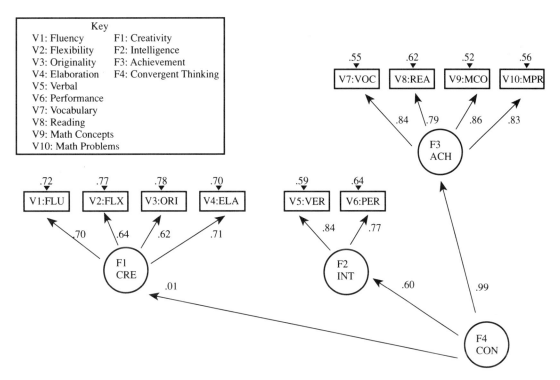

Figure 1.2. Structural Model of Achievement (ACH), Intelligence (INT), Creativity (CRE), and Convergent Thinking (CON).

were in favour of having students repeat their grade based solely on a standardized national achievement test performance. To sum up the current situation in the public schools, then, the public overwhelmingly supports testing, as does the current political climate, but most teachers who are the primary constructors and administrators of tests, know little about appropriate testing practices and standards.

The demands of classroom assessment are currently rigorous and are likely to become even more so. According to Stiggins (1988), teachers may spend as much as 20% or 30% of their professional time in assessment related activities. These include designing, developing, selecting, administering, scoring, recording, evaluating and revising tests, quizzes and daily assignments. Teachers themselves are very concerned about the quality of their tests and measurements, and lack of confidence in them. They feel frustrated by the lack of training and support. Moreover, they would welcome relevant and useful training or assistance (Stiggins & Bridgeford, 1985) in measurement.

Meanwhile, the scientific, technical and theoretical aspects of testing have made rapid advances. Violato (1991), for example, applied structural equation modelling techniques to the problem of the relationship between intelligence, achievement and creativity. In the general population, intelligence and creativity have been found to have a small to moderate relationship. In high IQ subjects, however, there is no relationship found between creativity scores and IQ scores. The "threshold" hypothesis posits that meaningful creativity is only seen in people with IQs beyond some threshold level (e.g. 120). After that point, there is no relationship between the

9

two. In his study, Violato (1991) gave a creativity test (Torrance Tests of Creative Thinking—Figural Form) which produces scores on four scales (Fluency, Flexibility, Originality, Elaboration), and an IQ test (Weshsler Intelligence Scale for Children—Revised) which produces a verbal and a performance score, and an achievement test (Canadian Tests of Basic Skills) which has four subtests (Vocabulary, Reading, Math Concepts, Math Problems), to 201 grades 5, 6, and 7 "gifted" (IQ greater than 120) elementary school children. He hypothesized that there would be a relationship between IQ and achievement scores but not between these and creativity scores. The full model specified by Violato (1991) is shown in Figure 1.2.

Four underlying factors or latent variables were predicted: F1 (Creativity), F2 (Intelligence), F3 (Achievement), and F4 (Convergent Thinking). F1, F2, and F3 are "first order" factors while F4 is a "second order" factor. This model is called a "hierarchical, confirmatory factor analysis" in the language of structural equation modelling. Violato (1991) then computed the coefficients which are summarized in Figure 1.2. These are referred to as "factor loadings" and indicate the relationships between two variables (0 means no relationship while 1.0 means a perfect relationship). Notice that the factor loadings from the three primary factors (F1, F2, F3) to their respective tests are very high (all larger than .60). Moreover, notice that the loadings from the second order factor (F4) to the two first order factors (F2, F3) are also very high but nearly 0 with F1. This outcome is just as had been predicted by the model and threshold hypothesis. Intelligence and achievement scores could be accounted for by underlying convergent cognitive processes but creativity could not. The overall fit of the data to the model was very good.

Causality can also be indicated in structural equation modelling with Latent Variable Path Analysis. Here, much like the diagram in Figure 1.2, paths are specified between variables which imply a causal link. A large path coefficient (factor loading in Figure 1.2) indicates the possibility of a causal relationship between the variables while a coefficient of 0 indicates that no such relationship is possible. Joreskog and Sorbom (1988), for example, in a re-analysis of the Head Start Data, were able to show causal paths between the intervention programmes, socio-economic status and subsequent performance on cognitive and IQ test. Previous analyses of these data had failed to conclusively establish these links and thus remained controversial.

The Role of Testing in Teaching, Learning and Education

There are essentially four categories in which testing plays a role: (1) Teaching and Learning, (2) Programme Evaluation and Research, (3) Guidance and Counselling, and (4) Administration. While these are interrelated and test results can be used in several categories, they are described in turn.

Teaching and Learning

All teaching has some goal or objective as its purpose. The objective may be implicit or explicit (see Chapter 2 for a discussion of objectives). Teaching, then, is for the purpose of having pupils reach some intended learning outcome (objective). The only sound means by which a teacher can determine the extent to which pupils have achieved the objectives is to measure performance. The outcome of the testing, therefore, is an evaluation of not only pupil performance, but the effectiveness of the teaching itself as well. The main function of testing is to measure the extent to which the instructional objectives have been met. Tests also have a number of other functions in teaching and learning.

Motivation. Tests motivate students to work and study harder than they might otherwise. With the many demands made on pupils and students, tests can motivate students to set a high priority on material that will be tested. Also frequent short testing will motivate pupils to sustain a consistently higher effort than long-term infrequent tests. Few things can motivate pupils to read a chapter or a whole textbook as a forthcoming test can. Any technique that teachers can use to motivate students is desirable.

Enhance Learning. Increasing student motivation to work will also increase their learning. When students anticipate a forthcoming test, they will attend to material more closely, increase their study time and work harder to learn the relevant material than they otherwise would (Sadler, 1983). Also the anticipation of a test improves students' learning set so that they increase their memory capacities for the material (through rehearsal, elaboration, organization). Students will make a conscious effort to improve their knowledge and understanding of material when they anticipate a test as opposed to when they do not.

Testing also promotes overlearning which occurs when you systematically study and prepare for a test. Of course some of the material learned for the test will be forgotten afterwards (hence the term overlearning) but more material will be retained in the long-run than if overlearning had not occurred. Thus testing promotes not only learning in the immediate future but results in longer more stable learning as well.

Feedback. Test scores provide feedback for both the teacher and student. The teacher can evaluate the efficacy of instruction based on the pupils' performance. If, for example, no pupil in the class was able to correctly solve the long division problems on the test, then the teacher can conclude that his teaching of long division failed. This outcome also indicates the need for review of this material.

Feedback can also be provided directly to the student. Based on performance the student can evaluate progress as a whole or in specific sub-areas measured by the test. This information can also provide insights for the student about effort. The test may indicate that effort had been adequate or that it may have to be increased.

Teaching. Giving a test itself is a form of teaching. Students may learn substantially merely from writing a test since they will have to formulate answers to questions. In a recent study Foos and Fisher (1988) gave students a short essay about the American Civil War to read. Half of the students were then given an initial test and half were not. Two days later, all the students took a final common exam—those students who took the initial test generally did better than those who did not. It may very well be that the act of retrieving the information for the original test, may have altered and strengthened it (McDaniel & Masson, 1985). In the Foos and Fisher (1988) study, then, actually taking the initial test may have taught the students about the Civil War.

Programme Evaluation and Research

Tests can also be useful to evaluate educational programmes and to conduct basic research. The data that was used to test the model about creativity, achievement and intelligence, for example, originated from an evaluation of a programme for gifted children (Violato & Blank, 1982). The test data, however, also served for basic research as it allowed for the investigation of fundamental questions about intelligence, creativity and achievement.

In the evaluation study, the efficacy of the programme in promoting creativity and achievement in gifted children was determined. This was done by comparing test scores on creativity tests and achievement tests of children in a special educational programme for the gifted with those in a control group (Violato & Blank, 1982). The programme was determined to be at least partially successful in meeting these objectives.

In another evaluation study, Violato and Odhiambo (1990) analyzed scores on the Kenyan Certificate of Primary Education (KCPE), an annually administered national examination at the end of primary education. From these data, Violato and Odhimabo (1990) concluded that while education had expanded rapidly in Kenya in recent years, there was great regional disparity in test performance. This is due to uneven distribution of resources in different parts of Kenya (e.g. trained teachers, permanent buildings for schools, books, pencils and availability of paper). Using these same data, Violato and Odhiambo (1990) were able to explore the social ecology hypothesis of literacy and achievement in a developing country—a basic research problem. With this study, then, the researchers were able to not only make an evaluation of the effects of the rapid expansion of the educational system in Kenya, but to explore a basic research problem as well.

Administration Monitoring

Administrative decisions about education from the principal to government officials can be informed and improved by test results. Standardized test results, for example, might be used by principals to monitor their school's overall performance and take appropriate action if any is required. Suppose that such results indicated that the children in a given school were performing poorly in mathematics relative to other similar schools, and relative to their own performance in language arts. This might suggest to the principal a need for a revamping of the mathematics curriculum. Similarly, a superintendent of schools might monitor the whole district's performance. Indeed, a national picture may be provided with test data as in the Violato and Odhiambo (1990) study. Kenyan government officials may develop policies to reduce regional disparities in education outcomes in Kenya as a result of the findings. Internationally, recent test results demonstrate that American and Canadian adolescents perform poorly in mathematics compared to adolescents from many other industrialized countries including Japan, Hong Kong, Finland and Sweden (McKnight, 1987). This might suggest the need for administrative action in educational policy on a national scale.

Curriculum Decisions. Results on a standardized reading test might show that children in a school are achieving better scores with reading curriculum A than other children with reading curriculum B. The principal and staff of the school may decide to adopt curriculum A as a standard. A principal in a high school may discover that students who take an elective advanced mathematics course score 75 points higher on the mathematics section of the Scholastic Aptitude Test (SAT) than students who do not take the course. He might decide to expand the course offering thereby providing other students this advantage on the SAT.

Selection and Screening. Tests are used to improve selection and screening decisions. Selection decisions for programmes for the gifted are frequently made on the basis of test data (e.g. IQ and achievement). Identification of children as learning-disabled and retarded are also made on the basis of test scores. Screening for admission to college can be based, at least in part, on the SAT, for medical school on the Medical College Admission Test (MCAT) and Law School on the Law School Admission Test (LSAT).

Certification. Virtually all professional organizations and many other groups as well have formal certification procedures involving tests. Thus to be eligible to practice as a physician, lawyer, dentist and psychologist to name a few, you must write and pass certification exams. Many organizations have moved to or are moving towards implementing certification exams as a means of determining the competency of their licensees. This is likely to increase in the future.

Guidance and Counselling

Test scores have long been used in clinical psychology and school guidance to help improve decisions. Results from intelligence, personality, interest, aptitude and achievement tests can be used by a guidance counsellor to help students make the best decisions about their future schooling, career and work. Such information can also help psychologists and psychiatrists to provide the best possible care for their clients and patients. Test scores alone, however, should never be used to make guidance and counselling decisions. Rather these should be used by the professional to assist in making the best possible decision.

Types of Tests and Evaluation Procedures. Tests and evaluation procedures are frequently classified into one or more categories. Below are some of the most commonly used categories of test types.

1. *Individual or Group Administered.* Some tests, primarily psychological ones such as IQ must be individually administered. Most educational tests, however, can be administered to a group ranging from a typical classroom to many hundreds of students simultaneously. Almost all classroom tests are of the group type.

2. *Teacher-made or Standardized Tests.* Sometimes these tests are also referred to as informal (teacher-made) or formal (standardized tests). Teacher-made tests are obviously constructed by the teacher to measure some specific aspect of achievement (e.g. reading, writing, arithmetic, social studies) relevant to that classroom. This test will likely be administered once only to this group of pupils. Standardized tests, on the other hand, are constructed by testing experts usually to measure some broad range of achievement relevant to many children (perhaps all children). Unlike teacher-made tests, the standardized test is not designed for one specific classroom or indeed school. They are intended to be used (and re-used) in broader jurisdictions such as the entire school district, or state-wide or perhaps even used nationally. Moreover, these tests are administered in formal situations according to standardized conditions. Finally, these formal tests have known statistical properties since they have been administered in advance to a peer group of those who will write the test.

3. *Speed or Power Tests.* Speeded tests obviously have time constraints on completing them. All test-takers are given a fixed amount of time designed so that many or most writers will not be able to complete the test in the allotted time. Power tests, on the other hand, do not have time as a significant constraint. While of course there is some upper limit on the time available, most test-takers can complete the test in the allotted time. Most classroom tests are power tests where time should not be a significant factor in performance. Tests should only be speeded if speed of response is a significant element in the dimension measured by the test. For most classroom learning the teacher is not so much interested in pupils speed of response but rather the accuracy and depth of response when adequate time is provided.

4. *Supply or Selection Tests.* Supply or selection refers to the type of items that make up the test. Selection items are those where pupils must select a correct answer from several options (e.g. multiple choice items). For supply items the student must provide or supply the answer or responses to a question or instructions (e.g. short-answer items). The selection item provides a much more structured task for the test-taker than does the supply item especially for essay questions. Since for supply items the pupil must provide the answer, skills such as organization, writing, fluency, and so forth play a prominent role. Supply items are also called constructed-response items and selection items are called forced choice-items.

5. *Objective or Subjective Tests.* This distinction refers to how the test is scored and graded and not to the item types. Objective tests are scored objectively by anyone in possession of the key or answer sheet. Indeed, machines (optical scanners) can score these tests. For subjective tests, only an expert in the subject matter can score these tests as expert judgement is required to evaluate the constructed answer. Selection items can be generally scored objectively. The objective-subjective distinction refers to the nature of the scoring process.

6. *Norm-referenced or Criterion-referenced Tests.* Another important way to classify tests is based on how the results are interpreted on norm group performance or against some criterion. For norm-referenced tests, an individual's performance is evaluated against the performance of a norm (peer) group. A teacher may interpret a child's spelling test score with reference to the rest of the class. It may be below average, above average or about average. For criterion-referenced tests, however, the norm group performance is irrelevant. Rather, a criterion for "passing" or "outstanding" performance is established before the test is written. Irrespective of the norm groups' performance, an individuals' score is evaluated against this standard.

Most standardized tests used in American and Canadian schools are norm-referenced. The Scholastic Aptitude Test and the Canadian Tests of Basic Skills are two tests of this type. Criterion-referenced tests are fairly rare by contrast, but are beginning to be used more widely for licensure testing by boards of professional organizations. To establish minimum performance levels for these tests usually requires a complex series of decisions by subject matter experts with the help of testing experts. While the idea of criterion-referenced measurement is appealing, its use has remained narrow largely because of the theoretical and practical difficulties of establishing standards. The test for acquiring a driver's license is an example of a common criterion-referenced test.

Another set of terms that are used synonymously with criterion-referenced and norm-referenced, are mastery tests in contrast to survey tests. For mastery tests, the pupil must exceed some pre-established standard (criterion) to have achieved mastery. By contrast, for the survey test, there is a survey of the pupils' knowledge but mastery is not evaluated against some standard.

7. *Achievement, Intelligence and Personality Tests.* Achievement tests attempt to measure the extent to which a student has "achieved" in some subject matter or on some skill. This achievement is thought to represent the level of learning due to motivation, effort, interest and work habits. A typical classroom test in social studies is an example of an achievement test. Intelligence may play a part in the outcome.

Intelligence is thought to be the potential for learning or "achieving". The actualization of this potential is achievement itself. Intelligence or this potential for learning is usually measured by IQ tests such as the Stanford-Binet.

A personality test measures that aspect of a person's psychological makeup which is not intellectual. Generally, these tests seek to measure the level of a person's adjustment, attitudes, feelings, or specific traits like introversion, sociability, and anxiety. Sometimes personality tests like the MMPI are used for clinical diagnoses to assess the degree of neuroses or psychosis of an individual.

8. *Summative, Formative, Placement and Diagnostic Evaluation.* Each of these types of evaluation refers to the use to which test results will be put.

Summative. This is a "summing up" of all assessments and measurements in order to determine final performance. Assigning the letter grade (A, B, . . . F) is a form of summative evaluation.

Formative. This is monitoring the situation. During the course of instruction, the teacher wishes to monitor if pupils are moving towards the final objectives so as to take appropriate action. This usually involves quizes, mid-term tests, etc.

Placement. Sometimes it is necessary to determine where in the educational sequence (i.e. grade) the pupil should be placed. Teachers and the principal may be uncertain, for example, in what grade to place a student coming from another country. Placement evaluation might be conducted using previous records (if any), test data, and interviews.

Diagnostic. When pupils have persistent learning problems, it may be necessary to diagnose the problem. Psychological, medical and educational data are frequently necessary to make a diagnostic evaluation.

Social Issues in Testing

As we have seen, testing is much more than a technical or scientific activity. It is very much a social and political activity as well practised on a very large scale. Most living Canadians and Americans have not only written many classrooms tests but have undoubtedly taken at least one standardized test. During this century, standardized testing had so expanded in scope and variety that it touches the life of almost every person on the North American continent. In view of this, testing has become a matter of political and social concern. We shall examine several of these in turn.

Testing and the Law. Probably no activity that educators and psychologists perform has come under as much legal scrutinizing as has testing. Since the 1950's a number of important court decisions affecting the use of tests have been handed down. Some of the most important cases affecting testing are discussed below under three issues: (1) Test bias resulting in racial discrimination, (2) Racial quotas and the "affirmative action" principle, and (3) Consumerism and test result disclosure.

Racial Discrimination. Probably the single most important case for education as a whole occurred in 1954 and is known as *Brown v. Board of Education.* In this landmark case, the Supreme Court of the United States ruled that forced segregation was unconstitutional. This decision resulted in desegregation and "bussing" which continues to be highly controversial. The implications for testings were also serious since test scores frequently result in segregation along racial lines. A number of legal challenges to testing have flowed from this case.

In 1964 the U.S. Court of Appeals overturned a decision by the Georgia State Court condoning segregation in the case of *Stell v. Hansen*. Lawyers for two white children had argued that de-segregation of the Savannah, Georgia school district would result in poorer education for all children. Their evidence consisted of test scores showing clear differences on ability tests between whites and blacks. The Court of Appeals decision in effect forced the school district to desegregate.

In *Hobson v. Hansen (1967)*, attorneys for Hobson argued that "tracking" or "streaming" in Washington D.C. schools resulted in discrimination along racial, social and economic lines resulting in blacks receiving an inferior education. Judge J. Skelly Wright agreed and prohibited the use of ability tests for tracking for differential education.

In 1979 Judge Robert Peckham of Federal District Court in California ruled that IQ scores for placing EMR (Educable Mentally Retarded) children were illegal because it discriminated against blacks. The practical effects of this ruling in *Larry P. v. Riles* was to outlaw all IQ testing for black children in California. In 1984, this decision was upheld by a Federal Appeals Court. In a 1988 U.S. Supreme Court decision, however, this position was undermined. The seven justices ruled that statistical disparity is not enough to prove discrimination. They ruled that specific decision-making practices causing discrimination against membership in a protected group (black or female) would have to be proven as well.

These rulings taken together have restricted testing when its regarded as racially discriminatory.

Affirmative Action. The affirmative action principle states that candidates for positions should be given preference over other equally qualified candidates based on race, sex or ethnicity. Allan Bakke, a caucasian, challenged this principle in the case of *Bakke v. California (1978)*. He sued the University of California at Davis because he was refused admission to the medical school. Bakke's Grade Point Average was higher than some minority students who had been admitted since 16 of the 100 places in the medical school had been set aside for minority students. The California State Supreme Court ruled in favour of Bakke because his rejection had been racially discriminatory and ordered the medical school to admit him. On an appeal, the United States Supreme Court upheld the decision but ruled that the "affirmative action" principle was legitimate. According to these decisions, it is clearly illegal to base selection decisions on racial quotas.

Test Result Disclosure. In the case of *Lora v. Board of Education (1980)*, a court ruled that test results and clinical records must be disclosed when recommendations for placements are made. The onus is on the consumer (e.g. parents of children), however, to ask for and arrange the review. In a previous contrary decision, however, a Federal Appeal Court denied a candidate access to the multiple-choice part of a screening test (*Lavash v. Kountze, 1979*). The Court argued that the candidate would have access to his essay test results because these are much more susceptible to scoring error and bias than are multiple-choice tests.

These issues are by no means settled or resolved as Court decisions are contradictory. No doubt, Courts will continue to appraise testing and thus influence its practice and help to define its legality, ethicality and scope.

Sex Bias in Testing. In the last few years there has been considerable concern for sex bias in a number of areas including testing. Critics of testing argue that tests are biased against females as they tend to use masculine pronouns, examples and illustrations. Moreover, the tests tend to depict females in traditional domestic roles. There is little doubt that in the past this was true. There is no evidence, however, to indicate that this put females at a disadvantage in test performance. Indeed, sex-typing (presenting each gender in traditional roles) is widespread throughout many segments of society and education. This applies as well to textbooks, audio-visual materials and teachers' lessons. The removal of such sex-typing from all aspects of education including tests is desirable on grounds other than test bias.

For a number of decades, boys have outperformed girls on mathematics tests. In a recent study, Benbow and Stanley (1983) found that boys outperformed girls on a standardized mathematics test and speculated that the cause was biological. There was no independent evidence of biological differences, however. Eccles and Jacobs (1986) in a series of follow-up studies found that parental attitudes especially mothers' attitudes towards their daughters' mathematics abilities explained the differences. Feingold (1988) found that a number of gender differences including mathematics performance have been narrowing over time and are likely to disappear in the future. Eccles and Jacobs (1986) concluded that parental and teacher expectation were more likely the source of gender differences than either bias in tests or biological differences. Hyde and Linn (1988), however, suggested that the continuing efforts to make test items gender neutral may also be contributing to the change in relative performance between boys and girls. Attempts to make test items gender neutral go back to the original 1916 edition of the Standford-Binet and will likely continue into the future.

Cheating. Cheating on tests is believed to be so widespread that it has become a social issue. A national newspaper recently ran a front page article about cheating (*Globe and Mail,* November 30, 1991). In it several authorities are cited claiming that 88–90% of all university students have cheated at least once on tests. In a more formal study, Cornehlsen (1965) found that 1/3 of girls and 1/2 of boys in high school cheated on tests. Even among graduate students the incidence of cheating may be as high as 40% (Zastrow, 1970). Undoubtedly, cheating among elementary school pupils is also common.

The reasons behind such widespread cheating are no doubt diverse. The fact that it is so common may legitimize it for otherwise reluctant pupils through disinhibition. Extreme competition for scarce positions in university, medical school, graduate school, etc. may be causing some students to seek every possible advantage including cheating. Indeed, many may regard cheating as a clever way of "beating the system". Still others feel that cheating may simply reflect an increase in dishonesty and immoral behaviour in all levels of society. Cheating, and other forms of dishonest, unethical, fraudulent and illegal behaviour in the business community, among professionals and others may be symptomatic of the moral decay in society generally.

Whatever the reasons for cheating on tests, testing conditions can reduce it substantially. Close proctoring of the testing and having pupils sit in alternate seats can reduce cheating substantially (Bushway & Nash, 1977). Discussions with students about cheating and its deleterious effects can alter attitudes about it. Through test design, conscientious monitoring and seating arrangements, cheating can be reduced to a minimum. It is probably unrealistic to expect, however, that cheating and especially the motivation for it can be eliminated in the near future.

Testing and the Mass Media. Testing is very much a popular topic for the mass media. Mass media presentations tend to be highly critical of testing and present extremely biased and unfair views. One of the best known popular books of this genre is called *The Tyranny of Testing* (Hoffman, 1962). In it the author argues that testing is a form of terrorizing students and stultifies learning. David Owen in a recent popular book, *None of the Above: Behind the Myth of Scholastic Aptitude* (1985), and an article in *Harpers* (May, 1983) argues like Hoffman, that objective tests tend to favour moderately intelligent and conforming testees but deny others an opportunity to demonstrate their creativity. The general argument of these authors and other popular critics is that tests are bad for education, stultify creativity, encourage conformity and generally operate to maintain the status quo in society.

Ralph Nader has recently established a journal devoted to testing called *The Fair Test Examiner*. Most of the articles have a negative anti-testing bias. News reports and documentaries on television are almost always biased against testing in one form or another. In movies and entertainment television programmes, tests and the motives behind them are frequently depicted as suspect and oppressive. In the recent popular movie *Stand and Deliver,* the representatives who come to the school from Educational Testing Services to uncover the cheating on the SAT are shown as rigid, unsympathetic and callous. Moreover, the SAT is depicted as an arbitrary barrier to pupils' success. You should always view mass media treatment of testing issues with extreme skepticism.

The Invasion of Privacy Issue

With the proliferation of personal data banks maintained by credit bureaus, and the advent of computers that can easily access such information, the public has become more and more concerned with maintaining individual privacy. In testing, this has become a major issue as well. This is especially true of personality testing where very intimate and personal questions about sexual behaviour and fantasies are sometimes asked. Such questions ask persons to make public some covert and personal aspects of the respondent's inner life. When can we justify the use of such revelations? When is the social need to know greater than an individual's right to keep his own secrets? Thorndike and Hagan (1977) have proposed that seven major questions need to be addressed in determining whether or not the social need for disclosure overrides the right to privacy (p. 611–615):

1. For whose benefit will the information be used?
2. How relevant is the information to the decisions that must be made?
3. If the information is to be gathered for a social good, how crucial is that good?
4. How "personal" is the information that is sought?
5. Has there been provision for "informed consent"?
6. To what extent may consent be assumed?
7. Is the individual's anonymity protected?

When the social or personal benefits are regarded to be high, invasion of privacy is accepted. This is very common practice in medicine for example. Countless thousands of women daily submit to gynaecological examination which certainly must be regarded as an "invasion of privacy". Similarly, countless thousands of people daily undergo surgery which also is "invasion of privacy". Nevertheless, people readily and voluntarily undergo these procedures largely because of the real or perceived benefit that accrues to them. Society as a whole benefits as well when invasive medical intervention can control or eradicate diseases. A similar principle could govern testing in education and psychology: if the benefits outweigh the right to privacy, testing is acceptable.

■ Summary and Main Points

The science of educational testing, measurement and evaluation has its origins in antiquity but is only now beginning to emerge as a unified field. This is due to developments in statistical and mathematical theory, test theory, and microcomputer advances. Testing and measurement are the acts of quantifying an educational or psychological dimension or assigning a numerical value to it. Evaluation requires a value judgement to be made based on the measurement. While the history of testing goes back to the 12th century B.C., it has emerged on a large scale only in the 20th century, coincidental with mass education. The current status of testing is paradoxical: it is on the increase and receives overwhelming public support and yet most teachers (who construct, administer and interpret the vast majority of tests) have little or no formal education in testing. Tests can be used to motivate pupils, enhance learning, provide feedback, evaluate educational programmes and for research. Other functions include curriculum revisions, selection and screening, certification and guidance and counselling. Tests can be used in a variety of ways and for several evaluation functions. A number of social issues have arisen in conjunction with the use of tests.

1. The science of educational testing, measurement and evaluation has its origins in antiquity but is only now emerging as a unified science.
2. Testing and measurement refer to assigning a numerical value to an educational or psychological dimension. Evaluation requires that a value judgement be made.
3. Testing was widespread in 12 B.C. in civil service examinations in China. It is only in the 20th century, however, that it has become a mass activity.
4. Currently there is a great deal of testing in both Canada and the United States. Besides the millions of standardized tests given in these two countries every year, there are perhaps 600 million classroom tests administered annually. World wide, this figure no doubt exceeds 1 billion! This is likely to continue.
5. Notwithstanding great amounts of activity in testing, most teachers have little or no training in testing at all.
6. Besides measurement, tests provide other functions in teaching and learning. These include motivation, enhancing learning, providing feedback and teaching itself.
7. Tests also can be employed to evaluate programmes and conduct research.
8. Administrative functions of tests include monitoring of performance of schools and districts, making curriculum decisions, use for selection and screening, and certification and licensing.
9. Tests can also be used in guidance and counselling.
10. There are several types of tests and evaluation procedures. These include the following types of tests: individual or group administered, teacher-made or standardized, speed or power, supply or selection, objective or subjective, norm or criterion referenced, achievement, intelligence and personality. There are four types of evaluation: summative, formative, placement and diagnostic.
11. A number of social issues have arisen around testing: (1) testing and the law, (2) cheating on tests, (3) mass media depiction of testing, and (4) invasion of privacy.

■ Further Readings

Dubois, P. H. (1970). *A history of psychological testing.*

Haney, W. (1981). Validity, vaudeville, and values: A short history of social concerns over standardized testing. *American Psychologist, 26,* 1021–1034.

Hernstein, R. J. (1982). IQ testing and the media. *Atlantic Monthly,* August, 68–74.

Stiggins, R. J. (1991). Assessment literacy. *Phi Delta Kappan,* March, 534–539.

Thorndike, R. M. (1990). *A century of ability testing.* Chicago: Riverside Publishing.

Chapter

2

Instructional Objectives

Overview

Instructional objectives are central to learning and teaching. When students are aware of goals, their studies may become much more organized and productive. Well organized instruction begins with a statement of objectives, accounts for the entering behavior of students and considers teaching procedures, assessment, and feedback processes. Behaviorism has strongly influenced teaching by advocating that instructional objectives be expressed as observable, student behavior. Although the behavioral objectives movement has produced much criticism, it continues to affect practice.

Educational goals are written at three levels of specificity: the ultimate goals of education, the general goals of units and programs, and the outcomes of individual lessons. Teachers organize daily instruction around the latter, third level objectives which stress student rather than teacher activities. Well written objectives specify the conditions for expression of desired behavior, the behavior itself, and the criteria of success.

We classify objectives into three taxonomies: cognitive, affective, and psychomotor. The taxonomies facilitate the writing of educational goals, the development of curricula, and the construction of tests. They are not flawless, but the taxonomies have helped education become more organized. Part of this organization results from an emphasis on measurable goals of instruction. We describe the taxonomies later in the chapter. We begin the chapter with a description of the nature of objectives and proceed to describe how to write behavioral goals as well as classify them.

The Nature of Objectives

Most behavior is goal oriented. That is, it is directed towards the achievement of particular ends some of which are more obvious than others. A casual conversation between two people, for example, may have the goal of satisfying the affiliation needs of the participants: they are talking because they want to be accepted by each other. Attendance at university, on the other hand, may be driven by the student's need for control or power. A university degree symbolizes particular knowledge and skills needed to enter a profession which may lead subsequently to influence and power in society. The elementary school child who selects a task of intermediate difficulty may be expressing a strong need to succeed. The behaviors described in the foregoing examples are aimed at attaining specific objectives.

Educational objectives are the goals to be achieved by students as they progress through school and are expressed as the desired outcomes of instruction. Objectives are based on the actual or perceived needs of students. Educators determine the knowledge and skills which will permit young people to flourish. Goals are set not only to promote self-actualization, but to facilitate the well being of the group as a whole. The group may be the child's classmates, or it may be society at large. The goals of education are stated as desired student behavior rather than teacher activities: the focus is on students and what they should be able to do at the end of lessons.

Educational objectives are expressed at different levels of specificity, facilitating the creation of programs, courses, units, or individual lessons. When curriculum developers approach a task, they have as their first item of business the statement of educational objectives. Expressed goals make explicit the direction a program, course, or lesson will take and they permit evaluation of effectiveness. In other words, a clear expression of goals is central to education.

The Basic Teaching Model

Effective teaching begins with identification of the goals of instruction, and these goals are set into the context of the entire act of teaching. What is needed is a model of teaching that provides an overview of the instructional process. In general, models are of two kinds—replica and symbolic (Chapanis, 1961). As the name implies, replica models look very much like the object they portray. For example, a globe appears to be a miniature earth. Symbolic models, in contrast, are abstractions of objects or processes. That is, symbols show elements of the environment in a nonrepresentational fashion. All models distort reality, especially through simplification. The Basic Teaching Model symbolically depicts the fundamental components of teaching in four interrelated, but oversimplified steps (Gagné, 1970; Glaser, 1965; Popham, 1965; Tyler, 1950): objectives, entering behavior, instruction, and assessment. The steps are highly generalized categories that represent complex procedures conducted by teachers.

Instructional Objectives

The first stage of the model as shown in Figure 2.1 is identification of instructional objectives. As previously stated, objectives are goals. In this case, the reference is to the goals of instruction which are sometimes called tasks or specific learning outcomes. Usually the objectives of a lesson or series of lessons are stated as the accomplishments of students in overt behavioral terms. For example, "Pupils will be able to identify correctly the place values of each of the three digits to the right of a decimal point." The overt behavior is the identification of the place values by, say, writing them above each of the specified digits.

Again, specifying overt behavior emphasizes student performance at the end of a lesson rather than teacher's activities during instruction. With this emphasis, changes in the students' behavior not the teachers' activities become the focus on instruction. After all, it is the needs of students which produce the goals of instruction in the first place (Ahmann & Glock, 1975).

22

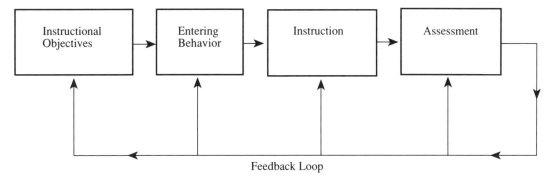

Figure 2.1. The Basic Teaching Model.

Entering Behavior

When teachers plan a course of studies, they frequently assume that the students have certain knowledge and skills related to the goals of instruction. In other words, they have the prerequisites. There are several ways to determine students' entering behavior. Analysis of the goals of instruction reveals the kinds of knowledge students will need to be successful. By way of illustration, suppose that long division is being introduced to students. Assessment of the division process suggests that pupil success depends on their subtraction, multiplication and estimation skills. From their experience with students, teachers may know that the students possess these skills. If, however, the unit is being taught at the beginning of the school year, it may be assumed that these skills were taught in the previous grades. When teachers are unsure of students' previous skill acquisition, an entering behavior test could be administered. Another approach would be to interview the students' previous teachers. In addition, cumulative records describe each pupil's past goal attainment. Finally, information about previous work can be obtained from textbooks and curriculum guides.

Instruction

This segment of the model refers to the classroom activities of teachers: how they help students acquire the knowledge and skills of a particular course of studies. A common approach to teaching, the recitation method consists of four parts: structuring, soliciting, student responding, and teacher reacting. The teacher who identifies a topic and discusses it with pupils is structuring a lesson. At the end of the discussion the teacher might solicit further responses from the pupils by having them complete an exercise on the discussion topic. The teacher reacts to the students' answers by, perhaps, assessing their work. Teachers repeat this four part pattern in many different ways. According to Gage & Berliner (1979), the recitation method has been popular for much of the twentieth century. Its popularity derives in part from its broad applicability to a range of disciplines and grades. The recitation method illustrates the kinds of activities teachers perform as they guide students towards the goals of instruction.

Assessment

As instruction proceeds, teachers monitor student progress towards the goals, and at the end of lessons achievement is usually assessed. Performance assessment includes all the methods teachers use to determine how well the students have achieved the instructional goals. These methods range from incidental observations through more formal observational techniques such as rating scales and check lists to both teacher-made and standardized achievement tests. On the basis of formal and informal assessments, teachers provide feedback to students and report their findings to parents. The results of measurement inform grouping practices and aid counseling of individual and groups of students. Assessment establishes the basis for monitoring student progress through school. As indicated by the feedback loop shown in Figure 2.1, the information generated by assessment, may lead to changes in other elements of the instructional process. For instance, student failure to reach an objective may indicate faulty instructional procedures, inadequate student entering behavior, and/or inappropriately difficult objectives. Failure might also signal problems with examinations, especially when the average score is unusually low.

With the Basic Teaching Model to guide thinking, the interrelatedness of various teaching activities becomes apparent. Suppose, for example, that analysis revealed a weakness in the entering behavior of students. Instructors might review the relevant material to help youngsters overcome the deficit. They might cover more of the basic material by starting instruction at a lower level. In addition, they might eliminate some objectives and simplify others in an attempt to match the needs of students. Similarly, other aspects of the instructional process could be altered according to the results of assessment.

The Basic Teaching Model has several advantages (De Cecco & Crawford, 1973). It represents the essential elements of instruction in a simple, easily understood manner. The model provides teachers with notions about how to begin, proceed, complete, and improve instruction. Reference to the model helps teachers explain what is currently happening in the classroom, and why their plans include certain activities. By providing a frame of reference, the basic teaching model facilitates assimilation of knowledge about teaching. With a clear understanding of this rather simple model, teachers will better understand other more complex explanations of instruction (e.g., Gagné's, 1986, model). Moreover, the basic teaching model highlights the role objectives play in the instructional process. It specifies goal statements as the first step, and each subsequent element, as we have said before, relates to the goals of instruction: entering behavior is evaluated in relation to instructional objectives; instruction proceeds towards goals; and assessment focuses on student achievement of objectives.

Behaviorism and Objectives

Advocacy of instructional objectives stated as observable behavior has it roots in behavioral psychology. That publicly observable behavior produces knowledge is an important principle underlying behaviorism. But critics point out that it may rob individuals of their freedom because such determinism places humans at the mercy of environmental forces (Morris & Pai, 1976). From the behavioral perspective, psychology is a science must focus on behavior not mentalistic phenomena such as the ego. Psychology becomes a science based on the principle of verifiability—all that is known must be verified in the public domain by direct observation of behavior. That is, facts are established by measurement of behavior accessible to more than one observer. Therefore, the study of learning and achievement becomes an investigation into the conditions of reinforced practice.

Operant Conditioning

Operant conditioning, or instrumental conditioning as it is sometimes called, refers to "the form of learning wherein the organism becomes progressively more likely to respond in a given situation with that response which, in previous similar situations, has brought about a rewarding or satisfying state of affairs" (English & English, 1958, p. 357). Operant behavior is naturally occurring behavior not under the deliberate control of others. In an experimental setting, a baseline is established by measuring behavior before introducing a treatment. The treatment, often some form of reinforcement, conditions baseline or operant behavior. For example, suppose that a teacher suspects that a young lad is avoiding work by walking aimlessly about the room too much. Baseline observations establish the legitimacy of the teacher's concern and form the basis for measuring change due to treatment.

Reinforcement, contiguity and practice produce operant conditioning. Without describing reinforcement in detail, the correct response is reinforced while other responses are ignored or punished. A correct response is any behavior that approximates the desired action. In the case of the child who is out of his seat too much, the correct behavior might be sitting in place for two minutes. This is not very long, but the response is rewarded because it is in the direction of the goal of sitting sufficiently long to complete, say, a twenty minute exercise. Contiguity refers to the timing of reinforcement. That is, reinforcement follows the correct response as closely as possible. Practice sessions permit shaping of the correct responses through reinforcement of better and better approximations of the desired behavior. For example, the child sits in his seat for longer and longer intervals. Finally, he remains seated long enough to complete an entire assignment. The goal is achieved. Reinforcement, contiguity and practice are conditions of learning that are publicly observable, and they affect the goal: overt behavior.

To make education more effective, behaviorists emphasize the reinforcement of publicly observable behavior. If a problem exists, establish a desirable outcome stated as overt behavior and apply reinforcement principles. With objectives described as over behavior, observers may verify among themselves that goals have been achieved. However, critics have challenged the behavioral objectives movement (see Focus on Research 2.1).

Value of Objectives

Starting instruction with a behavioral objectives is important for several reasons:

1. Students who are informed of the objectives will probably use them as guides to their learning.
2. Knowledge of objectives allows students to reinforce themselves when they have reached a goal. This condition is particularly significant in large group instruction where access to the teacher is necessarily limited. Students who know the goals reinforce their own achievement.
3. Lessons are developed in a systematic fashion. A task analysis of behavioral objectives, as stated earlier, produces a series of subgoals around which lessons may be organized.
4. Instructional objectives facilitate communication. When goals are explicitly stated, both teachers and students understand more clearly the process of education. With behavioral objectives as a backdrop, teachers explain to parents various aspects of children's education with greater precision. Furthermore, objectives form the foundation

Focus on Research
Criticism of Behavioral Objectives

Krathwohl and Payne (1971) discussed several criticisms of the behavioral approach. First, there is no doubt that the number of objectives increases as a result of the behavioral analysis of an instructional problem. But this is not really a drawback because teaching becomes more effective. Second, the more unimportant outcomes of a lesson will be stressed because they are easier to express behaviorally. Ease of expression is not the issue; rather it is the judgment of teachers that is being questioned. As Popham (1968) observed, trivial matters stated as behavioral objectives will be revealed as unimportant. Krathwohl and Payne recommend that teachers concentrate on the significant, more abstract goals by finding ways to state them as behavioral objectives. Third, expression of objectives as student behavior will slight the teachers' role as well as the importance of the content. Educational reformers often focus their efforts on innovations in teaching strategies and on advances in knowledge. But curriculum developed around behavioral objectives may appear to present a barrier to the reformer's efforts. For example, the behavior of scientists (the process of science) seems of more concern than the content of a scientific discipline. A balanced approach to the study of a particular science, which would not run contrary to the behavioral objectives movement, would be to observe the behavior of scientists, identify the central concepts and principles of their discipline, and then write objectives for both process and content. Fourth, prescribed objectives reduce the possibility for creative responses. Painters, for example, who are interested in children appreciating the strength of their medium, may hope that children would ex-

periment widely with paints. However, teachers who are guiding children towards specific goals may restrict the possibility of divergent responses. But this criticism seems overly pessimistic. Without specified goals, how would one recognize that a particular response was divergent? Moreover, teachers can be sensitized to the potential problem. In any event, teachers generally foster creative responses. To most teachers, the divergent response is stimulating and rewarding: it is one of the joys of teaching. Fifth, a related criticism is that teachers will permit students to pursue only the knowledge and skills identified by the objectives of a lesson. Other equally important issues which arise spontaneously during the course of instruction will be ignored (Popham, 1974). For example, a study of modern commercial fishing techniques might give rise to student interest in the Greenpeace Foundation. Teachers will differ in their responses to these instructional opportunities. Despite prespecified objectives, those who are sensitive to the needs of students will encourage unanticipated study. Sixth, critics argue that teachers rarely state objectives in behavioral terms. Nevertheless, most curriculum materials such as textbooks and the accompanying teacher's manuals as well as curriculum guidebooks are organized around behavioral objectives. Their influence is unavoidable. Seventh, behavioral objectives may be dehumanizing and mechanistic. That objectives are prespecified before the lesson begins, suggests that student interests and needs will not be adequately taken into account. However, it is possible to develop many of the goals with students thereby giving them greater control over their education.

---

for discussions among instructors, and help teachers inform school administrators and the general public about what is happening in classrooms.

5. Do instructional objectives affect achievement? Melton's (1978) answer is a qualified yes. His review of the research on objectives produced five conditions relating to the influence of objectives on achievement: (a) Students must attend to the objectives and study them carefully. (b) The objectives must be stated in clear, unambiguous language. (c) Students must perceive the goals to be relevant to their present studies. (d) Youngsters who are poorly organized and lack effective study skills are most likely to

be positively affected by objectives. The last point is probably the most important simply because goals provide structure which helps students prepare more effectively for examinations.

Levels of Objectives

Krathwohl and Payne (1971) suggested that at least three levels of objectives are required to serve the needs of youngsters. At the first and broadest level, goals exist for students who are completing secondary and post secondary education.

First Level Objectives

These objectives center around the knowledge and skills young people require to enter society as independent adults. The following statements illustrate goals related to literacy, employment, interpersonal relations and self-actualization: Students will be able to read at a level that permits them to function adequately. Students will be able to perform satisfying, productive work. Students will be able to build rewarding relations with significant others. Students will be able to participate in activities that promote their personal well being. First level objectives describe the ultimate goals of education in highly general terms, and form the basis for developing more specific objectives.

Second Level Objectives

While stated in rather sweeping terms, second level objectives are intended to serve in the development of units, courses, and programs. By way of illustration, consider the following second level objectives associated with language arts in high school: Graduates will be able to comprehend directions which describe the operation of recreational equipment such as video tape recorders. They will be able to read novels with enjoyment and insight. Students will be able to comprehend the daily newspaper and magazines. Students will be able to read general reference material to obtain information and services. The foregoing objectives were derived from the first level objective describing the ability to read at a level which allows individuals to function successfully. Second level goals aid the development of units, courses and programs.

Third Level Objectives

The individual lessons teachers present to students are based on third level outcomes which are derived from the more general, second level goals. Consider, for example, the objective about general reference material listed in the previous paragraph. In planning a lesson on the use of the dictionary, a teacher might establish the following goals: Students will be able to pronounce unfamiliar words correctly using phonology rules that are symbolized in a standard dictionary. Using dictionary definitions, students will be able to explain unfamiliar terms in their own words. Each of these objectives may require one or more lessons.

As Krathwohl and Payne (1971) suggest, third level objectives are used in test construction. That is, third stage objectives establish clearly stated tasks which are easily translated into examination questions. This level of objective particularly suits the development of short, within unit quizzes to monitor student progress. The relationship between goals and tests is explained further in Focus on Measurement 2.1.

Krathwohl and Payne note that all three levels of objectives are necessary for an effective program. In contrast to the highly specific third level objectives, the global goals at the first

Focus on Measurement
Measurement and Instructional Goals

To state instructional objectives is to imply that their achievement is measurable. At first glance, the ultimate goals of education such as "to produce a good citizen" may seem beyond the measurement capacity of educators. In one sense this may be the case, but schools can at least ensure that high school graduates have the potential to be "good citizens." Analysis of what it means to be a good citizen leads to lists of knowledge, skills, attitudes, and values that might reasonably be promoted and assessed. That is to say, analysis of first level objectives would lead to second level goals which, upon further analysis, would produce readily measurable, third level objectives.

Popham (1988) identified some objectives which need no special tests. For example, increased interest in physical fitness might be assessed by counting the frequency of participation in a sport. However, Popham goes on to say that most educational objectives require more or less formal assessment instruments. As to the answer to the question of what type of test is best, he concluded that criterion-referenced tests as compared to norm-referenced devices are preferable. This preference derives from the fact that criterion-referenced measures are closely tied to the achievement of goals according to a standard whereas norm-referenced tests are interpreted in relation to the average performance of the students' group. (We provide details about criterion-referenced tests in Chapter 11.)

stage accommodate widely disparate methodologies and curricula. They are flexible. That is, a general goal such as the promotion of the individual's well being might be achieved by children confronting moral dilemmas. But it also might be attained through studying science in order to better understand the environment. In part, well being develops when individuals clearly comprehend their surroundings and as a consequence experience less frustration in reaching goals. Educators might not agree on the content, but most would probably accept the overall objective. Beyond this flexibility, the interrelatedness of the three levels facilitates more systematic instruction. An objective of a single lesson subsumed under a unit objective which in turn relates to a program goal underscores the orderly quality of the process.

The behavioral approach to the goals of education, especially the development of three levels, tends to produce a large number of objectives of great specificity and, perhaps, triviality. While we have encountered this criticism before, Popham (1988) noted a slightly different concern that evaluators, overwhelmed by the sheer quantity of objectives, may overlook the data supporting student achievement of goals. This does not mean that behavioral objectives are to be abandoned. Rather, create third level objectives at a reasonable level of generality, covering a sensible amount of skill and knowledge. For example, the objective about the rules of phonology, which was described earlier in this section, might have been divided into subgoals relating to each rule of pronunciation such as the "schwa," or the syllabics, "l" and "n." But this increased specificity adds little to the instructional process. And undoubtedly teachers routinely incorporate these rules into lessons that are based on the more general objectives.

Preparing Behavioral Objectives

Creating behavioral objectives for a lesson, unit or program involves at least four processes: selection, classification, task analysis, and specification (Kibler, Cegala, Barker, and Miles, 1974).

Selection

Selection is concerned with the universe of tasks from which particular objectives are to be drawn. Several conditions limit the range of possible behaviors. First, student entering behavior must be considered. If inappropriately sophisticated objectives are chosen, students will experience too much failure and frustration as they begin studying a new subject. Ideally, objectives are selected that are suitably difficult. Should the curriculum guides for a course set goals which are too advanced for a group of students, teachers may alter the course by changing the objectives. Alternatively, they may help students gain the required knowledge and skills before presenting the main material. Second, the requirements of subsequent units and courses as well as the ultimate outcomes of education affect goal selection. For example, language arts teachers develop student writing skills which might conform to a sequence such as learning to write sentences, paragraphs and then essays; although, not all teachers would agree with this pattern. After young people have completed their education, they should have certain communication skills such as the ability to write personal and business letters as well as the capacity to compose technical reports. Objectives will be established to fulfill these expectations. Third, resource availability, both material and personal, influences the selection of goals. Effective science programs, for instance, require well-stocked laboratories. At the personal level, everyone has strengths and weaknesses. While overcoming weaknesses is desirable, it is not always possible. To take advantage of personal strengths, limit goals in subjects where your skills are deficient, and expand objectives in areas of expertise. Flexibility exists in most subjects so that elaboration according to the instructor's capacities and student interests and needs is possible. Nevertheless, the core content of a course must be covered.

Classification

Classification of objectives clarifies the nature and level of instruction. During the middle 1950's, Bloom and his colleagues divided the classification of educational objectives into three interrelated schemes: cognitive, affective and psychomotor domains. The group headed by Bloom concentrated on the classification of cognitive objectives and produced a taxonomy of educational outcomes (Bloom, 1956). Cognitive goals refer to problem solving, reasoning and information processing activities like retention and remembering. In other words, the cognitive domain is about thinking. Cognitive objectives range from rote memorization of facts and principles to solving problems by the application of evaluation skills. In the early 1960's, a group led by Krathwohl devised a taxonomy of affective goals (Krathwohl, Bloom, & Masia, 1964). Affective objectives include interests, attitudes, appreciations, values, and preferences. That is to say, the affective domain is about feeling. Objectives of this type vary from specific activities such as attending to particular stimuli to highly generalized value systems organized as a philosophy of life. Simpson (1972) classified psychomotor goals of education. Psychomotor outcomes emphasize physical skills, manipulation of objects, and co-ordination in the neuromuscular system. Subsequent sections of the chapter describe and illustrate each of the taxonomies.

In the present context, the significance of the classification schemes is that they facilitate preparation of objectives at the level desired. An instructor who wishes to stress abstract thinking, for example, will use the cognitive domain taxonomy to produce the preferred effect. More than this, that objectives may be classified into three different, albeit related domains enables teachers to emphasize the area that seems most appropriate: affective, cognitive, or psychomotor.

Task Analysis

Rarely are objectives in curriculum guides and other prepared lists sufficiently well defined to be directly applicable to particular lessons. Teachers refine objectives through task analysis. By asking, "What must the students do to demonstrate they have obtained an objective?" teachers identify a series of subtasks which form a path to the objective. Task analysis ends when the assumption is safely made that the students have the prerequisite knowledge. Task analysis through provision of subgoals structures lessons. Properly conducted task analysis reduces the possibility of starting instruction ahead of most students and avoids omission of important knowledge and skills.

Specification

Designation of the behavior expected of students is central to an instructional objective. To write a third level objective, specify student behavior as an infinitive denoting observable, overt action. Mager (1962) observed that words such as "to write" or "to differentiate" are open to fewer interpretations than terms like "to understand" or "to appreciate." Avoid the latter terms because they refer to processes that are not directly observable. "Understanding" and "appreciating" are indirectly measured by observation of the behavior of individuals. Indirect measurement creates greater uncertainty about what is actually being measured—it raises questions about the validity of measurement. The clarity of terms such as "to write" derives from reference to publicly verifiable behavior. The contrast between the following two examples illustrates the point:

■ **Examples**

Students will know the members of the Group of Seven.

Given a list of ten Canadian artists, the student will check all the members of the Group of Seven in the list.

Observable behavior is not specified in the first example whereas marking a list is overt behavior available for all to see. In addition, Mager advised describing the conditions under which the desired behavior would be expressed. The clause "Given a list of Canadian artists," in the second objective satisfies this requirement. Lastly, Mager added a criterion for success. This condition is met in the second objective by the stipulation that "all" the members of the Group of Seven will be identified. Criteria appropriate to the task are used (e.g., 80% correct or a time limit). To reiterate, the three characteristics of a well written instructional objective are the expected behavior, the conditions for performance, and the criteria of success. The ensuing objectives illustrate these characteristics:

■ **Examples**

Given samples of various types of wrenches, the student will be able to name each type.

In the third week of training, the team members will be able to skate at their optimum speed for three laps of the oval.

Without reference material, the students will be able to write three positive and three negative outcomes of the Vietnam War for the United States.

Problems with Mager's System. Mager's procedure for specifying objectives is not without difficulties. The criterion for success implies that all students will meet this criterion. Uniform criteria are hard to meet within traditional classrooms where norm-referenced assessment prevails. Mager's stipulation of success standards best fits criterion-referenced assessment coupled with mastery learning. (For a description of criterion-referenced assessment, see Chapter 3.) Popham (1988) cautioned that performance standards set before a program begins will be insupportable. He suggested setting acceptable performance levels after gaining experience with the program. While this suggestion seems reasonable, most experienced teachers develop insight into the achievement that might be expected from their students. Nevertheless, Good and Brophy's (1990) reminder that expectations should be appropriate for the particular students is pertinent.

A further problem develops from the description of the conditions under which the behavior will be observed. A glance at the first example in the foregoing list reveals that reference is made to specific content (in this case, wrenches). On the one hand, including content in an objective focuses attention on the materials with the result that planning is enhanced. On the other hand, reference to content may increase the number of objectives. Under Mager's system, each element of content occasions a new goal. The proliferation of goals costs extra time and energy, scarce commodities for most teachers. (See the section on criticisms of objectives in another part of the chapter.) The same objection could be made about the specificity of the designated behavior. The objective in the above list using skating as the outcome illustrates how the process would give rise to large numbers of goals: every action in a course of studies would have its own objective.

Reducing the Number of Objectives. One approach to reducing the number of objectives is to use terms which cover different kinds of specific behavior. To illustrate, consider the following objective which could refer to skating, but does not:

■ Example

In the third week of training, the team members will perform at optimum levels.

Reference to performance rather than skating permits application of this objective to other activities such as track and field, curling, and so on. The teacher writes one objective of this sort and applies it to various activities as the need arises. While savings in time and energy accrue, the loss of content distances this type of educational goal from the reality of teaching. Our preference is to maintain subject content in objectives, especially third level outcomes. With maintenance of content, objectives more directly guide instruction.

Taxonomies of Objectives

As stated earlier, taxonomies exist for each domain of behavior: cognitive, affective, and psychomotor. Division of human activity into apparently separate domains is artificial for individuals act as integrated wholes, unities. Thinking involves feeling and both often lead to action. Obviously, to separate one domain from the other is impossible, but for the classification of educational objectives each taxonomy focuses on a different aspect of behavior. The success of the taxonomies, especially in the cognitive domain, demonstrates the wisdom of classifying goals.

The Cognitive Domain Taxonomy

Bloom (1956) outlined the purposes of the taxonomy in the cognitive domain. First, clearly stated objectives, categorized according to the taxonomy, ease curriculum and lesson planning. Second, the taxonomy facilitates communication among educators. The taxonomy, for example, clarifies what it means to understand a subject. Levels of understanding are possible, and the taxonomy identifies the various levels. With the taxonomy as a backdrop, curriculum experts speak a common language, and test developers are better able to explain problems associated with examinations. Third, the taxonomy provides test item models which aid test construction at different levels of achievement. In summary, the cognitive domain taxonomy classifies tasks related to acquiring, retaining, remembering, and applying information. In other words, the central purpose is to classify behaviors associated with thinking or cognition.

The taxonomy is hierarchically organized into six categories ranging from verbatim recall of knowledge at the lowest level to the process of evaluation at the apex. Each higher category includes the behaviors at the lower levels. The tasks become increasingly more intellectually challenging as one moves up the taxonomic layers. The recall of a rule, for instance, is not as difficult as the application of the rule in assessing the worth of a particular procedure. Moreover, awareness of the processes is greater at the higher categories of the taxonomy than at the lower levels. That is, individuals are better able to describe their thinking in assessing a product as compared to recalling a specific item like a telephone number. The following sections outline the specific categories, beginning at the lowest stage.

Knowledge. The knowledge level of the taxonomy categorizes recall of specific items of information, methods of processing specific knowledge, and generalizations in the various disciplines. The cognitive process of remembering is emphasized in twelve subdivisions.

■ **Examples**

After reading a story, the children will identify the names of the main characters.
Without reference materials, the students will define terms associated with aggression.

Comprehension. Comprehension refers to understanding communications. Students demonstrate comprehension by paraphrasing a message in their own words (translation), illustrating the meaning of the communication in a form different from the original (interpretation), or drawing implications from information (extrapolation). Illustrative of comprehension are the following objectives:

■ Examples

After listening to a story, the student illustrates the main action by interpreting it in a painting.

The student will state in their own words the meaning of the central terms of the lesson.

Application. The essence of application is using knowledge to solve problems. Although students may have met the type of problem previously, the details of the situation must be new to them. The following examples are application objectives:

■ Examples

Upon studying the principles of prejudice reduction, students will be able to help people of different ethnic groups cooperate.

After studying plane geometry, students will use the theorems to solve novel, practical problems.

Analysis. Analysis of information involves separating a communication into its various parts so that the relations among the ideas are clarified. That is, analysis means discovering interrelationships. The subdivisions of this level are analysis of elements, relationships, and organizational principles. Consider the subsequent objectives as examples of analysis:

■ Examples

Given a treatise on a subject, students will identify the basic assumptions.

After reading an essay on a topic, students will provide evidence that the conclusions are consistent with the given information.

Synthesis. Synthesis is the bringing together of disparate elements to create a new entity. This high level category is subdivided into the creation of unique communications, development of plans for work, and derivation of abstract relations. Objectives suited to this level are shown below:

■ Examples

Following a field trip, students will describe their experiences in a well organized, effective way.

With advanced study in a discipline, students will derive general principles.

Evaluation. Evaluation is the qualitative and quantitative determination of the worth of processes and products in relation to internal evidence and external criteria. The following examples illustrate goals at the evaluation level:

■ Examples

Upon studying the rules of logic, students will assess the internal consistency of an argument.

According to criteria established by the average performance of a group, students will judge the value of performances by individuals.

Assessment of the Cognitive Domain Taxonomy. Bloom's taxonomy has been criticized for favoring behaviorism (Furst, 1981). For example, Furst argues that the orientation to goals that can be expressed behaviorally neglects "understanding," a primary educational outcome. But Bloom's intention was to operationalize "understanding" so that educators could agree on its meaning and how it might be measured. Perusal of the taxonomy and its many applications supports the conclusion that Bloom's group achieved their objective. Far from being a weakness, the behavioral orientation of the taxonomy is its strength.

Another criticism, according to Furst, is that specific content is omitted from the educational goals thereby producing artificiality because remembering requires content. While there is some validity to this criticism, omission of content reduces the demand for great numbers of subject specific outcomes. Moreover, the criticism is further weakened by the fact that the objectives presented in the taxonomy are not completely devoid of content, for example: "Given geometric concepts in verbal terms, the ability to translate into visual or spatial terms" (Bloom, 1956, p. 92).

Furst cites evidence that the hierarchical nature of the taxonomy has been questioned. For instance, synthesis might be placed at the same level as evaluation. The tasks at the two levels seem equally demanding.

Despite the criticisms, the cognitive domain taxonomy has been used a great deal. Noting that more than a million copies have been sold, that it has been translated into several languages and that it has been cited thousands of times in the educational literature, Furst recognized that the taxonomy supports various educational activities. After observing that the taxonomy helps planners see that a particular program focuses on cognitive rather than affective goals and that lower level outcomes are emphasized at the expense of more important, abstract cognitions, Popham (1988) concluded that the taxonomy's utility was in broad analysis rather than in finer distinctions. Nevertheless, the taxonomy opens the way to finer, content-oriented discriminations.

The Cognitive Domain Taxonomy and Writing Objectives. As an aid to specification of objectives, Table 2.1 from Metfessel, Michael & Kirsner (1969) is included. The three-column table contains levels of Bloom's (1956) cognitive domain taxonomy in the left hand column, infinitives suitable to each taxonomic level in the center column, and general, content-related terms in the right hand column. To produce an objective at a particular level, link a term in the right hand column to the appropriate infinitive in the second column. Experience with Table 2.1 should speed construction of objectives and clarify their meaning.

The Affective Domain Taxonomy

Affective objectives focus on appreciations, attitudes, beliefs, biases, emotions, interests, and values. At the lowest level affective objectives stress attending to phenomena, and progress through responding, valuing, organization of values to the development of a value complex.

Objectives in the affective domain are organized into a taxonomy according to the principle of internalization. English and English (1958) define internalization as "incorporating something within the mind or personality; adopting as one's own the ideas, practices, standards, or values of another person or of society" (p. 272). Krathwohl, Bloom and Masia (1964), authors of the affective domain taxonomy, describe internalization as a process wherein the superficial behavioral aspects of a belief are initially acquired, and eventually acceptance of the associated belief system develops. As an attitude is developed through the levels of the taxonomy, there is increased emotional involvement at the middle levels with a tapering off on

Table 2.1. Instrumentation of the Taxonomy of Educational Objectives: Cognitive Domain

Taxonomy	Classification	Key Words Examples of Infinitives	Examples of Direct Objects
1.00	Knowledge		
1.10	Knowledge of Specifics		
1.11	Knowledge of Terminology	to define, to distinguish, to acquire, to identify, to recall, to recognize	vocabulary, terms, terminology, meaning(s), definitions, referents, elements
1.12	Knowledge of Specific Facts	to recall, to recognize, to acquire, to identify	facts, factual information, (sources), (names), (dates), (events), (persons), (places), (time periods), properties, examples, phenomena
1.20	Knowledge of Ways and Means of Dealing with Specifics		
1.21	Knowledge of Conventions	to recall, to identify, to recognize, to acquire	form(s), conventions, usages, usage, rules, ways, devices, symbols, representations, style(s), format(s)
1.22	Knowledge of Trends, Sequences	to recall, to recognize, to acquire, to identify	action(s), processes, movement(s), continuity, development(s), trend(s), sequence(s), causes, relationship(s), forces, influences
1.23	Knowledge of Classifications and Categories	to recall, to recognize, to acquire, to identify	area(s), type(s), feature(s), class(es), set(s), division(s), arrangement(s), classification(s), category/categories
1.24	Knowledge of Criteria	to recall, to recognize, to acquire, to identify	criteria, basics, elements

Taxonomy	Classification	Key Words Examples of Infinitives	Examples of Direct Objects
1.25	Knowledge of Methodology	to recall, to recognize, to acquire, to identify	methods, techniques, approaches, uses, procedures, treatments
1.30	Knowledge of the Universals and Abstractions in a Field		
1.31	Knowledge of Principles, Generalizations	to recall, to recognize, to acquire, to identify	principle(s), generalization(s), proposition(s), fundamentals, laws, principal elements, implication(s)
1.32	Knowledge of Theories and Structures	to recall, to recognize, to acquire, to identify	theories, bases, inter-relations, structure(s), organization(s), formulation(s)
2.00	Comprehension		
2.10	Translation	to translate, to transform, to give in own words, to illustrate, to prepare, to read, to represent, to change, to rephrase, to restate	meaning(s), sample(s), definitions, abstractions, representations, words, phrases
2.20	Interpretation	to interpret, to reorder, to rearrange, to differentiate, to distinguish, to make, to draw, to explain, to demonstrate	relevancies, relationships, essentials, aspects, new view(s), qualifications, conclusions, methods, theories, abstractions
2.30	Extrapolation	to estimate, to infer, to conclude, to predict, to differentiate, to determine, to extend, to interpolate, to fill in, to draw	consequences, implications, conclusions, factors, ramifications, meanings, corollaries, effects, probabilities
3.00	Application	to apply, to generalize, to relate, to choose, to develop, to organize, to use, to employ, to transfer, to restructure, to classify	principles, laws, conclusions, effects, methods, theories, abstractions, situations, generalizations, processes, phenomena, procedures
4.00	Analysis		

Taxonomy	Classification	Key Words Examples of Infinitives	Examples of Direct Objects
4.10	Analysis of Elements	to distinguish, to detect, to identify, to classify, to discriminate, to recognize, to categorize, to deduce	elements, hypothesis/hypotheses, conclusions, assumptions, statements (of fact), statements (of intent), arguments, particulars
4.20	Analysis of Relationships	to analyze, to contrast, to compare, to distinguish, to deduce	relationships, interrelations, relevance, relevancies, themes, evidence, fallacies, arguments, cause-effect(s), consistency/consistencies, parts, ideas, assumptions
4.30	Analysis of Organizational Principles	to analyze, to distinguish, to detect, to deduce	form(s), pattern(s), purpose(s), point(s) of view(s), techniques, bias(es), structure(s), theme(s), arrangement(s), organization(s)
5.00	Synthesis		
5.10	Production of a Unique Communication	to write, to tell, to relate, to produce, to constitute, to transmit, to originate, to modify, to document	structure(s), pattern(s), product(s), performance(s), design(s), work(s), communications, effort(s), specifics, composition(s)
5.20	Production of a Plan, or Proposed Set of Operations	to propose, to plan, to produce, to design, to modify, to specify	plan(s), objectives, specification(s), schematic(s), operations, way(s), solution(s), means
5.30	Derivation of a Set of Abstract Relations	to produce, to derive, to develop, to combine, to organize, to synthesize, to classify, to deduce, to develop, to formulate, to modify	phenomena, taxonomies, concept(s), scheme(s), theories, relationships, abstractions, generalizations, hypothesis/hypotheses, perceptions, ways, discoveries

Taxonomy	Classification	Key Words Examples of Infinitives	Examples of Direct Objects
6.00	Evaluation		
6.10	Judgments in Terms of Internal Evidence	to judge, to argue, to assess, to decide	accuracy/accuracies, consistency/consistencies, fallacies, reliability, flaws, errors, precision, exactness
6.20	Judgments in Terms of External Criteria	to judge, to argue, to consider, to compare, to contrast, to standardize, to appraise	ends, means, efficiency, economy/economies, utility, alternatives, courses of action, standards, theories, generalizations

Note. From "Instrumentation of Bloom's and Krathwohl's Taxonomies for the Writing of Educational Objectives." by N. S. Metfessel, W. B. Michael, and D. A. Kirsner, 1969, *Psychology in the Schools, 6,* pp. 227–231. Reprinted with permission of CPPC, 4 Conant Square, Brandon, VT, 05733.

either side. That is, the emotional response associated with simple attention to a belief is rather weak, but the response becomes stronger in the middle area of the taxonomy. Gradually, as the response becomes almost automatic, the emotions that were formally aroused are dampened. With advancement up the continuum, locus of control of behavior shifts from external to internal forces.

Movement through the taxonomy is from simple to complex, concrete to abstract and conscious to unconscious processing of action. Early in the development of a value individuals simply show awareness of a process such as optical illusion in art. As experience with the art forms broadens, people may show willingness to respond by visiting galleries where "Op Art" is displayed: the value is increasing in complexity. Initially, the person may manipulate media to produce a three dimensional quality in simple geometric shapes. At a more advanced level, appreciation may be shown for more complex geometric configurations that produce, say, the effect of interior space. That is, appreciation of art has become more abstract. In the early stages of attitude development, people are aware of their responses to new phenomena such as novel processes in art. But as experience with it grows, responses become increasingly automatic. In summary, the dimensions of complexity, concreteness and awareness as well as emotionality are aspects of internalization, the formative principle of the affective domain taxonomy.

The five, interrelated categories of the affective taxonomy are described and illustrated in the following sections.

Receiving (attending). The lowest level of the taxonomy, consisting of three subsections, concerns awareness of objects or processes and willingness to respond to them as well as differentiation of stimuli. Below are examples illustrating objectives at this initial stage:

■ **Examples**

After touring the local historical buildings, students will show awareness of the architectural designs represented in the local environment.

Students note, with careful attention to detail, design features.

Responding. At this level students actively attend to phenomena. The three subdivisions characterize the students' increasing commitment to the behavior. Acquiescence in responding is the lowest stage and involves compliance to the demands of a situation which distinguishes it from the next stage, willingness to respond, where voluntary action predominates. The last subdivision refers to the response satisfaction. The subsequent list of objectives illustrates the behaviors at this level of the affective taxonomy:

■ **Examples**

Acting on the teacher's request, students will collect examples of Op Art.

Students sing in the choir with pleasure.

Valuing. Having progressed to this level, individuals see the worth of phenomena; they hold a value. Initially, individuals simply show acceptance. Later, the value takes hold and active seeking of the phenomena occurs. Internalization has progressed to commitment and conviction. The following list of objectives illustrate the category:

■ **Examples**

After viewing an exhibition of op art, students demonstrate acceptance of its value by studying the comments of art critics.

Students hold discussions extolling the merit of op art as compared to other art forms.

Organization. At this level, a value system is beginning to emerge. The two subdivisions are conceptualization of the value and its organization. Illustrative of this stage are the following objectives:

■ **Examples**

To keep abreast of developments in the local art scene, students create an acceptable pattern of visits to galleries.

Students integrate an aesthetically pleasing personal environment with the social and economic aspects of life.

Characterized by a Value or Value Complex. Internalization has advanced sufficiently so that the individual is known to hold a given value system. The two subdivisions at this level are a generalized set which represents the person's usual attitude or value structure and a philosophy of life. The following objectives are from this category:

■ **Examples**

Students approach problems at the interface of systems of art in an objective and logical manner.

Students behave in all situations in a manner consistent with an expressed philosophy of life.

Writing Affective Objectives

Lee and Merrill (1972) devised a system of writing affective objectives which parallels Mager's procedure in the cognitive domain. A well written affective objective includes a description of overt behavior, the conditions under which the behavior will be observed, and the criteria of success. In general, knowledge of people's attitudes and values are indirectly known by their approach and avoidance behavior. Most affective objectives will emphasize high probability approach behavior. The conditions will present alternative approach responses in the absence of cues so that students will be free to select among them. That is, the teacher will not attempt to control the students' choices. No indication of what behavior is desired will be given. The criteria of success includes minimum participation rates or the number of activities joined by students. An illustrative affective objective adapted from Lee and Merrill is listed below:

■ Example

Under the guidance of the teachers who refrain from promoting the program among the participants, students will establish an extracurricular, physical education program and offer it to their fellow students such that each student will participate in at least one sport.

Table 2.2, which was developed by Metfessel, Michael, and Kirsner (1969), facilitates the writing of affective objectives. The first column contains the levels of the affective taxonomy. The second column presents examples of infinitives. In the last column, content-related terms are illustrated. An affective objective may be created by linking a term from the right hand column to the selected infinitive in the second column. The infinitives and terms in Table 2.2 are to be viewed as examples for the generation of affective objectives.

The Psychomotor Domain Taxonomy

Simpson (1972) created a classification scheme for psychomotor skills which embraces muscular and motor activity. Most disciplines require this kind of activity as evidenced by the construction of laboratory equipment in a science course, but it is stressed in areas such as agriculture, art, business education, home economics, industrial education, music, physical education, and the like.

The strengths of Simpson's taxonomy are similar to those of the other taxonomies. The psychomotor domain taxonomy: informs research on teaching of psychomotor skills; promotes communication between curriculum developers and those they serve; clarifies the statement of educational goals; provides a system for ordering test items, other evaluation devices and objectives; and establishes a framework for comparing educational programs. It completes the taxonomic enterprise—the psychomotor domain has its own classification system.

Simpson organized the taxonomy around the complexity of the tasks being classified. At the higher levels of the hierarchy, the objectives refer to increasingly complex behaviors. Task difficulty increases from the lower to the upper levels. The hierarchical structure of the taxonomy is reflected in the inclusion of lower level activities by the more advanced tasks. As described below, the taxonomy has seven categories.

Table 2.2. Instrumentation of the Taxonomy of Educational Objectives: Affective Domain

	KEY WORDS	
Taxonomy Classification	**Examples of Infinitives**	**Examples of Direct Objects**
1.0 Receiving		
1.1 Awareness	to differentiate, to separate, to set apart, to share	sights, sounds, events, designs, arrangements
1.2 Willingness to Receive	to accumulate, to select, to combine, to accept	models, examples, shapes, sizes, meters, cadences
1.3 Controlled or Selected Attention	to select, to posturally respond to, to listen (for), to control	alternatives, answers, rhythms, nuances
2.0 Responding		
2.1 *Acquiescence* in Responding	to comply (with), to follow, to commend, to approve	directions, instructions, laws, policies, demonstrations
2.2 *Willingness* to Respond	to volunteer, to discuss, to practice, to play	instruments, games, dramatic works, charades, burlesques
2.3 *Satisfaction* in Response	to applaud, to acclaim, to spend leisure time in, to augment	speeches, plays, presentations, writings
3.0 Valuing		
3.1 Acceptance of a Value	to increase measured proficiency in, to increase numbers of, to relinquish, to specify	group membership(s), artistic production(s), musical productions, personal friendships
3.2 Preference for a Value	to assist, to subsidize, to help, to support	artists, projects, viewpoints, arguments
3.3 Commitment	to deny, to protest, to debate, to argue	deceptions, irrelevancies, abdications, irrationalities
4.0 Organization		
4.1 Conceptualization of a Value	to discuss, to theorize (on), to abstract, to compare	parameters, codes, standards, goals
4.2 Organization of a Value System	to balance, to organize, to define, to formulate	systems, approaches, criteria, limits
5.0 Characterization by Value or Value Complex		
5.1 Generalized Set	to revise, to change, to complete, to require	plans, behavior, methods, effort(s)

Taxonomy Classification	KEY WORDS	
	Examples of Infinitives	Examples of Direct Objects
5.2 Characterization	to be rated high by peers in, to be rated high by superiors in, to be rated high by subordinates in and	
	to avoid, to manage, to resolve, to resist	extravagance(s), excesses, conflicts, exorbitancy/exorbitancies

Note. From "Instrumentation of Bloom's and Krathwohl's Taxonomies for the Writing of Educational Objectives." by N. S. Metfessel, W. B. Michael, and D. A. Kirsner, 1969, *Psychology in the Schools,* 6, pp. 227–231. Reprinted with permission of CPPC, 4 Conant Square, Brandon, VT, 05733.

Perception. Parallel to the receiving category of the affective taxonomy, perception is the initial stage of motor activity wherein the learner senses the object of the action. Three subdivisions differentiate perception into sensory stimulation, cue selection and translation. Illustrative educational objectives at this level are as follows:

■ **Examples**

After practising the golf grip, the student will sense the feel of a correctly held club.

Students taste the presence of spices in food.

Set. One can be mentally, physically, or emotionally prepared for action. Of course, all three sets may occur simultaneously. The following objectives exemplify the tasks:

■ **Examples**

Confronted with a flat tire, the student will prepare the required tools.

In readiness to block a penalty shot in soccer, the goalie will take the proper position.

Guided response. Publicly observable responses are guided by an instructor or the memory of a model. Imitation and trial and error constitute the subdivisions of the category. Guided response is illustrated by the following two goals:

■ **Examples**

After reading the instructions and studying the diagrams, the student will be able to operate a car jack.

By attempting several methods, students will determine the best way to conduct a laboratory session.

Mechanism. At this level, the response has become automatic—it is part of the learner's response repertoire. Illustrative objectives are as follows:

Without reference to guides, the student successfully changes a tire.

Without the help of a recipe, the student cooks pancakes.

Complex overt response. The responses required at this level are a complex pattern of sub-skills proficiently and smoothly executed. The subdivisions are resolution of uncertainty and automatic performance. The objectives in the following list illustrate the category:

■ **Examples**

The student smoothly performs the golf bunker shot.

The student sets and effectively runs the power plane.

Adaptation. In new situations demanding novel reactions, learners successfully adjust their physical responses.

■ **Examples**

Confronted with a new powerplay pattern, hockey players devise successful defensive maneuvers.

Upon hearing a novel, musical piece, dancers interpret it with altered dance steps.

Organization. Students organize their knowledge and skills in order to manipulate materials in novel ways. They may produce entirely new actions.

■ **Examples**

Based on their well developed volleyball skills and knowledge, students create a new ball game involving a net.

The dancers create a new ballet in the classical tradition.

Simpson (1972) successfully applied the psychomotor domain to a unit of study on learning how to use the sewing machine to make clothing. Other taxonomies exist, for example, Kibler, Barker, and Miles (1970) produced a classification system for psychomotor behavior which was founded on developmental tasks. In the cognitive domain, Gagné (1971) classified behavior based on eight types of learning.

■ Summary and Main Points

Educational objectives are the goals of instruction that students are to achieve as they advance through school. Objectives are the first stage of a model of teaching, and they support the other parts of the instructional process. Under the influence of behavioral psychology and despite strong criticism, educators have largely accepted that goals are best stated as publicly observable, student behavior. Goals are written at three levels of specificity, the most concrete of which serves daily lesson planning and test construction. The preparation of objectives involves four processes: selection, classification, task analysis, and specification. Well developed objectives specify the conditions for the expression of the intended behavior, the behavior itself, and the criteria of success. Efforts to classify objectives produced taxonomies in three domains of behavior: cognitive, affective, and psychomotor. Although they are far from perfect, the taxonomies aid the development of objectives, curricula, and tests. The main points of the chapter are listed below:

1. Objectives are stated as overt behavior of students.
2. The first element of the Basic Teaching Model refers to the goals of instruction. The other parts of the model, entering behavior, instructional procedures, assessment, and feedback, clearly relate to instructional goals. The model stresses the integrated nature of teaching.
3. Instructional objectives, stated as overt behavior, are founded in behaviorism. Behaviorists solve instructional problems by setting desirable outcomes which are described in publicly verifiable ways and by applying the principles of operant conditioning.
4. All of the following criticisms have been levelled at behavioral objectives: (a) The behavioral approach leads to proliferation of objectives. (b) Only the trivial outcomes of instruction will be expressed behaviorally. (c) Content and the teacher's role are neglected. (d) Emphasis on behavioral outcomes restricts divergent thinking by students. (e) Under the influence of behavioral objectives, teachers narrow the knowledge and skills that students are permitted to study. (f) Teachers rarely state goals in behavioral terms. (g) Behavioral objectives dehumanize education.
5. Behavioral objectives have the following advantages: (a) Students use them to guide their learning. (b) Achievement of goals stated in behavioral terms permits self-reinforcement by students. (c) They promote systematic lesson development. (d) Behavioral objectives facilitate communication. (e) Under certain conditions, achievement is fostered by knowledge of expected outcomes.
6. Systematic education involves goals at three levels of specificity. First level objectives, the broad goals of education, focus on the knowledge and skills that students need to enter adult society successfully. Second level objectives serve development of units of study, courses, and programs. Third level goals facilitate individual lessons and test construction.
7. Preparation of instructional objectives includes selection, classification, task analysis, and specification.
8. Objectives that specify conditions of performance, overt behavior and criteria of success pose problems: (a) Under traditional norm-referenced evaluation, uniform performance standards are difficult to meet. (b) Reference to content in objectives produces too many goals. (See the criticisms of behavioral objectives in point 4 above.)
9. Terms that cover several specific behaviors reduce the number of objectives.
10. Bloom's taxonomy of educational objectives in the cognitive domain classifies the mental functions of retaining, remembering and applying information under six broad categories: knowledge, comprehension, application, analysis, synthesis, and evaluation.
11. Criticism of the cognitive domain taxonomy centers around its behavioral orientation, but the concerns are largely unfounded.
12. Besides its classificatory function, the major advantages of the cognitive domain taxonomy are that it aids development of curricula and construction of test items.

13. The affective domain taxonomy classifies goals associated with appreciations, attitudes, beliefs, biases, emotions, interests, and values under five general categories: receiving (attending), responding, valuing, organization, and characterized by a value or value complex. The organizing principle is the process of internalization.

14. Writing affective objectives follows a similar pattern to the system used in the cognitive domain. High probability approach behaviors with alternatives free from teacher influence are stressed. The usual criteria of success are frequency of participation and number of activities.

15. The psychomotor domain taxonomy classifies goals related to muscular and motor activity within seven, wide categories: perception, set, guided response, mechanism, complex overt response, adaptation, and organization. Complexity of the responses being classified provides the organizing principle.

■ Further Readings

Bloom, B. S. (Ed.). (1956). Taxonomy of educational objectives, the classification of educational goals. Handbook I: Cognitive domain. New York: David McKay

Kibler, R. J., Cegala, D. J., Barker, L. L. & Miles, D. T. (1974). Objectives for instruction and evaluation. Boston: Allyn and Bacon.

Krathwohl, D. R., Bloom, B. S., & Masia, B. B. (1964). Taxonomy of educational objectives, the classification of educational goals. Handbook II: Affective Domain. New York: David McKay.

Lee, B. N. & Merrill, M. D. (1972). Writing complete affective objectives: A short course. Belmont, CA: Wadsworth.

Mager, R. F. (1962). Preparing instructional objectives. Belmont, CA: Fearon.

National Special Media Institutes. (1972). The psychomotor domain: A resource book for media specialists. Washington, DC: Gryphon.

Popham, J. (1988). Educational evaluation (2nd ed.). Englewood Cliffs, NJ: Prentice Hall.

■ Laboratory Exercises

Part A: Cognitive Domain

1. Briefly describe the nature and purpose of the cognitive domain taxonomy.
2. Select a grade and discipline in which you might teach a lesson. In the selected discipline, outline the knowledge and skills associated with a main principle.
3. After studying Table 1 and using Mager's system, write three behavioral objectives for the selected principle at each of the knowledge, comprehension, and application (or higher) levels of Bloom's cognitive domain taxonomy of educational objectives.

Part B: Affective Domain

1. Briefly describe the nature and purpose of the affective domain taxonomy.
2. Select an age level and an attitude which you as a teacher might wish to change. Define and illustrate with appropriate educational examples the nature of the selected attitude.

3. Following careful reading of Table 2 and using Lee and Merrill's system, create one behavioral objective for the selected attitude at each of the receiving, responding, and valuing levels of the affective domain taxonomy.

Part C: Psychomotor Domain
1. Outline the nature and purpose of the psychomotor domain taxonomy.
2. Choose a grade and psychomotor skill area (e.g., basketball or another sport, shop or home economics skill). In the chosen area, describe a specific psychomotor skill.
3. After perusing the details of the psychomotor taxonomy and using Mager's system, write three objectives at each of the perception, set, and guided response levels of the psychomotor domain taxonomy.

Part D: Task Analysis
1. For the application level objective of Part A, conduct a task analysis. List the subtasks produced by the task analysis.
2. Identify the entering behavior for the main objective.

Chapter

Test Construction

Overview

The chapter begins with a general definition of a test which serves as foundation for the remainder of the discussion. To establish the main goals of test construction, we briefly consider two fundamental characteristics of tests, reliability and validity. Next we describe various types of measuring instruments relevant to education in order to expand the concept of a test.

The test development process includes the following steps: statement of goals, content outline, development of a table of specifications, item selection, item construction, composition of instructions, selection or development of answer sheets, construction of keys, test administration, and revision.

Test construction starts with a plan or table of specifications. The table includes a content outline, a list of objectives and the number of items planned for the test. Selection of the type of questions to be included on a test is affected by variables such as the time required to complete certain kinds of items, the maturity of the students, objectives, precision of response, freedom from extraneous sources of variation, number of students, and material resources.

The organization of the test should promote maximum performance by the students. Group questions according to content and by item type within content subdivisions. Since too many different kinds of items may reduce the efficiency with which students complete a test, a limited number of question types are included on any particular test. Questions that you pose should allow students to demonstrate in the best ways possible their skills and knowledge. Moreover, test format should be governed by the economical use of space and clarity of presentation.

It is important to have clear directions, uniform test administration, and consistent scoring. Instructions should describe the tasks to be completed by the students. General instructions outline the types of questions and time limits. More specific directions describe how to complete each item type. Test administration should be uniform for all students. Attention to conditions such as the physical environment and supervision of the examination are important in promoting administrative uniformity. Scoring procedures are specific to each type of test. Separate answer sheets facilitate accurate scoring, but you might wish to allow students to write answers on the test booklets. In both cases, devices such as overlay and strip keys increase scoring consistency.

In the preceding paragraphs, we outlined the test development process which is the main topic of this chapter. The initial section of the chapter provides a definition of a test and expands the concept by describing two important characteristics of tests and by briefly considering various types of tests.

Definition of a Test

While the meaning of a test may seem self-evident, there nevertheless is a need for a clear definition of the term. Within the context of educational testing, the definition should be consistent with an explanation of measurement. Educational measurement produces a number which indicates the amount a student has of a particular characteristic. For example, when Arthur a grade six student, scores six out of ten on a math quiz, the number six quantifies the amount of his knowledge in the area of arithmetic covered by the test. The accuracy of the measurement depends on the reliability and validity of the test (See Chapters 8 and 9 for detailed discussions of reliability and validity). Thus, a test consists of a task or tasks that when completed result in a number which represents the amount the examinee has of a characteristic. The tasks may range from finding answers to questions, to constructing models, or employing other devices. For instance, students might be asked in a science laboratory test to complete a series of questions requiring verbal knowledge of a particular area of biology and to create slides of materials suitable for examination under a microscope. Both tasks—answering questions and building slides— are part of the test.

Any particular test should sample all the possible items that might have been included. While a teacher may have only one version of a test with a specific number of questions, it is possible that other versions might have been constructed. The idea that a test is a sample of a larger pool of items or the universe of questions is important for understanding the concept of reliability or consistency of measurement.

Two Important Characteristics of Tests

Reliability and validity are significant characteristics of tests. While later in the book we devote entire chapters to these two aspects (Chapters 10 and 11), a brief explanation at this point extends understanding of the general nature of tests so that the overall goal of test construction is clarified.

Reliability is the consistency with which a test measures whatever it is intended to measure. When a test is administered, it is hoped that the same results would occur under slightly different conditions such as a change in the person who gives the test. That is to say, tests should yield consistent results and to do this they should be as free as possible from extraneous sources of variations in the scores. While some sources of variation such as distracting noise during testing are generally under the examiner's control, others such as the state of a student's health are not. Since all tests are more or less unreliable, you should take the following actions: attempt to minimize extraneous sources of variation, estimate how inconsistent tests are and account for this unreliability when interpreting test scores.

Validity, the most important characteristic of measuring instruments, refers to how well a test measures whatever it is supposed to measure. In other words, a test intended to measure the arithmetic skills associated with long division should measure only those skills. If it includes unfamiliar vocabulary which prevents otherwise skillful students from correctly solving the long division problems, then the test is a somewhat invalid measure of long division skills. To improve the validity of tests, you should attempt to cover the content that has been taught as well as possible. Information about the validity of tests may be gathered and considered when test results are interpreted.

Types of Tests

Tests differ in many respects. Certain tests have items that are specific to a particular course of studies while others assess general knowledge of the central ideas of a discipline. Some tests are scored with a predetermined answer key requiring no judgment while others demand judgment when they are marked. There are tests that are designed to be given to a single person at a time and others that are administered to groups of people. These and other types of tests are described in the following sections.

Teacher-made and Standardized Tests. Teacher-made tests are, as the name implies, constructed by classroom teachers specifically for their own students. The main purpose is to assess student achievement of the goals of instruction for particular study units. Of all the tests used at school, these are the most common. Teacher-made tests are valuable because they are based on the unique course of studies presented by a teacher and take into account the nature of the students who are to be examined. With appropriate training and information, teachers construct quality tests.

Standardized tests are commercially developed by teams of experts. These tests are characterized by a uniform set of questions, directions and scoring procedures. That is, standardized tests are given under fixed conditions so that the results from one group or individual may be compared with other groups or individuals. Standardized tests have usually been administered to a group of students, referred to as the norm group, which has known characteristics such as age, socioeconomic status, grade and rural or urban residence. Average scores are computed for specified subgroups of students thereby establishing a set of "norms." Norms and other pertinent psychometric data such as reliability and validity information along with directions for administration and interpretation are published in the manuals which accompany standardized tests. These tests are often classified according to their subject matter as follows: aptitude, achievement, and psychological examinations. As with all tests, the main purpose of standardized measuring instruments is to assist the education decision making process. For example, decisions regarding student placement in special programs are assisted by the results from standardized tests. See Chapter 11 for an expanded discussion of standardized tests.

Objective and Subjective Tests. This distinction among tests refers to the scoring process. Objective tests are scored in a predetermined manner such that subjective judgment is eliminated at the time of scoring. Increasingly common in the classroom, objective tests include the following types: multiple-choice, alternate-response, matching, and short-answer items, all of which are described in greater detail in subsequent chapters.

While subjective judgment is eliminated at the time of scoring, decisions about the correct answers to questions on an objective test has simply been made at an earlier time in the test development process. Consider, for example, the case of the typical multiple-choice item. When a multiple-choice question is constructed, determining the correct answer is left to the expert, and in many cases this is a highly subjective process. Nevertheless, at the time of scoring students' answers to the question, the marker uses a prepared key and mechanically marks the response right or wrong: the scoring is objective. Chapter 5 describes the construction of multiple-choice items.

Subjective tests are those which require a degree of judgment when they are scored. The essay examination is the principal example of subjective tests, but others exist such as the oral quiz. Despite the use of scoring keys, essays usually do not have a single correct answer. Responses vary in complexity and accuracy, and wide latitude in the response is usually afforded the examinees. The main purpose of the essay examination is to provide an in-depth measure of the students' knowledge which allows for an assessment of quality of thinking in problem solving. Chapter 6 outlines the nature, development and marking of essay tests.

Individual and Group Tests. When a person is separately given an examination, the instrument is called an individual test. Relatively uncommon in modern classrooms, the individual test permits assessment of the nature of the examinee's difficulties in responding. It is a highly personalized experience which requires that the examiner establish a reasonably good relationship with the student prior to administering the test. Often the results are more reliable than might be achieved with comparable group tests. When highly reliable results are required, for example, during the diagnosis of learning difficulties, individual measures such as the Wechsler Intelligence Scale for Children are administered.

A group test is given to two or more persons simultaneously. Most achievement tests in the regular classroom are group tests. Usually they are reasonably reliable and economical with respect to time and effort.

Ability, Aptitude, and Achievement Tests. Ability is the capacity to perform an act at the present time. It is the result of the interaction between genetic potential and experience. Mechanical ability, skill in manipulating objects, is an example of this concept. General ability is the capacity to solve a wide range of problems; it is synonymous with intelligence. That is, a test of general ability is an intelligence test (e.g., Wechsler Adult Intelligence Scale).

Aptitude refers to an individual's capacity to acquire certain skills in the future. It is potential for skill development. A person may have, for example, mechanical aptitude or an aptitude for a subject such as music or mathematics. Ability refers to present capacity while aptitude identifies potential. Thus, the same test may measure both capacities: an intelligence test measures present ability but also capacity for further learning.

Achievement tests assess students' ability, or past learning in a particular discipline such as geography or biology. They are subject-specific, ability tests. Since most teacher-made instruments are achievement tests, a large part of this book is dedicated to planning, constructing, analyzing and interpreting achievement tests.

Readiness and Diagnostic Tests. A test of readiness measures the individual's preparedness to profit from instruction. Reading readiness, for example, is the person's personal characteristics which allow for success in learning to read under a given teaching system. Maturation and experience affect readiness.

Diagnostic tests measure achievement in a specific aspect of a discipline with the purpose of discovering weaknesses that might be subject to remediation. This is the most useful definition, but Good (1959) lists at least one other which is relevant: a diagnostic test may be a broad examination of academic strengths and weaknesses. The latter approach is a general assessment of a student's achievement in the core subjects at school using a battery of tests. (A test battery is a group of related tests given during a relatively short period, rather than a single diagnostic instrument.)

Formative and Summative Tests. Formative tests assess the knowledge and skills that students are acquiring as they proceed towards the goals of instruction. In other words, they are used to monitor progress within a course of studies.

Summative tests assess attainment of the overall knowledge and skills represented by the terminal goals of a course of studies. Summative tests are given less frequently than formative tests, and the former type is usually longer than the latter (Bloom, Madaus, & Hastings, 1981).

Norm-referenced and Criterion-referenced Tests. Norm-referenced measurement produces results that are relative to some standard such as the average of a group's performance. When students are told that their achievement is above average in social studies, they are being given a norm-referenced interpretation of test results. This has been the most common approach to measurement and evaluation in North American schools, and remains the dominant system.

Nevertheless, Popham (1988) observed that since the 1970's, criterion-referenced interpretations have increased in popularity among educational evaluators. Criterion-referenced measurement gives rise to absolute interpretation of students' achievement. This usually means that performance is described as achievement of a known set of objectives, the criteria (Glaser, 1963).

Mastery and Minimum Competency Tests. Mastery tests have the purpose of assessing whether students have met a particular level of achievement. They are a kind of criterion-referenced test in which the criterion for success is set at a high level. Usually these tests measure achievement of the core objectives.

Minimum competency tests are similar to mastery tests and are intended to measure achievement of the knowledge and skills deemed necessary for survival. This approach is controversial in that decisions regarding standards may be arbitrarily decided rather than based on empirical evidence. Moreover, specificity of minimal competency for various occupations creates problems for test construction (Hopkins, Stanley, & Hopkins, 1990).

Power and Speed Tests. Power tests are intended to measure the maximum achievement of students. With this intention, power tests are theoretically free of time limits, but in practice, liberal time limits are imposed. After a certain point, study of a problem on a test seems to produce little benefit. In general, ninety percent or more of the examinees should complete all the questions on a power test. Achievement in the various school subjects is largely measured by power tests.

Speed tests require students to complete, within given time limits, as many questions of a uniformly low level of difficulty as possible. The questions are easy so that most pupils given sufficient time could answer all of them correctly. But with limited time, the average pupil will fail to complete the test. The purpose of speed tests is to measure the rate of work rather than the ability to do the tasks. Speed tests are reserved for measuring specific aspects of learning such as reading speed and basic skills in arithmetic.

Comparison among Test Types. In comparing the various types of tests, it is obvious that a single test might carry several different labels simultaneously. For example, the same test might be an objective, power, group test of achievement which is interpreted in a norm-referenced fashion. In other words, the various types of tests are not always mutually exclusive categories, rather they may overlap with each other. However, some of the labels cannot be applied to the same test. For instance, a test consisting of multiple-choice items is an objective test and would not be identified as a subjective test. Depending on the purpose of a test, how it is used, and the context in which it is being discussed, particular characteristics will be highlighted. The various test types are simply labels applied to tests to emphasize certain characteristics which are of interest to evaluators.

The Test Development Process: An Overview

The following steps provide an overview of the test development process.

1. Specify goals of instruction. List the general instructional objectives for a unit of study as well as the more specific goals for the individual lessons. These goals should be the starting place for test construction.
2. Outline the content of the study unit. This summary lists the actual content used to help students reach the goals of instruction.
3. Construct a table of specifications. The table of specifications is a plan for the test. As such, it brings together the objectives and the content outline. The major purpose of the table is to ensure that proper emphasis is given to all elements of a course of studies.
4. Decide on the nature of the items to be used on the test. Is a single item type to be used, or will a combination of several kinds of items (e.g., multiple-choice, true-false and matching) best meet the requirements of the testing situation? If the test is relatively short, use one type of item. With longer tests, combinations of item types are possible. An essay added to multiple-choice questions may enhance the validity of a test.
5. Construct the test items. Use a separate card for each item, write in pencil and do not number the test questions. Once all of the items have been written, the cards may be shuffled into a suitable order which may be determined by item difficulty or other variables such as type of content. The items may then be typed with the numbers. If you are using a word processor, ordering and numbering the items are the last steps before reproducing the whole test.
6. Compose the instructions. In addition to general instructions for the test, directions should be given for each item type, especially when the item type is new to the examinees.
7. Provide material for recording the students' responses. This usually means that a separate answer sheet should be supplied. With grades one and two children, however, answers should be written on the test booklet.
8. Develop the answer key. Both selection and construction-type questions should have an answer key.
9. Try the test out. Ideally, one would administer the test to a group of three or four students who are similar to those who will actually receive the test. It is seldom the case, however, that classroom teachers have the time to complete this phase of test

development. What usually happens is that the test is given to the regular classroom group with a view to revision in the future. Of course, before administration a colleague might be asked to read critically the test and suggest changes to improve it. But most teachers are so busy that they do not have time to read their colleagues' tests.

10. On the basis of the information gained from the initial administration, revise the test. Chapter 10 describes systematic procedures for test revision in the section of item analysis.

Planning Tests

A plan for a test guides the writing of individual test items and directs test development. There are several variables that must be considered in planning a test such as the course content, the instructional objectives, the interpretation of results, the kind of questions to be included, and the characteristics of students.

After teaching the course for which the test is being developed, teachers usually do not experience difficulty deciding on the content of the test. Nevertheless, an outline of the principal ideas and illustrative supporting details is required to ensure sampling validity. For example, consider a geography test on map reading skills. Table 3.1 shows a possible content outline for such a test. Since it is not a field test, but rather a paper and pencil examination, only items suitable for the latter are included. The list of concepts and facts does not cover every detail. Instead, they are only indicative of the material that will form the basis of the test.

The objectives to be achieved by the students must be part of the plan for the test. Instructional objectives stated as overt student behavior are preferable because these third level goals provide clear statements of the tasks and translate easily into test items (Chapter 2 provides a discussion of instructional objectives.). Table 3.1 contains a sample of the goals for the geography test expressed at a suitable level of generality. A goal such as "understands elevation" is too general to be of much use in writing test questions. It does not describe publicly verifiable behavior. On the other hand, "computes the difference in elevation between village A and village B" is too specific. In this example, too many objectives would be required because a new objective would be needed for each new set of points. An appropriate objective would cover all the specific instances of calculating elevation, for instance, "computes the differences in elevation between points." Obviously, skills requiring field experiences such as matching map symbols with actual geographic features cannot be assessed by paper and pencil tests, and, therefore, would be excluded from the plan.

Various instructional decisions are based on test results, and the type of decision to be made influences the character of the examination. Rank ordering students according to their relative achievement, for example, is a common assessment task. This type of decision requires a summative, norm-referenced test.

Whether the interpretation of the test results is to be norm-referenced or criterion-referenced affects test development. The main implication is that criterion-referenced tests require greater specificity in the statement of behavioral objectives than is required with norm-referenced tests. The former requires a complete list of instructional objectives which frequently includes criteria for success whereas the latter needs only more generalized statements. We are interested in the relative performance of students on norm-referenced tests, but with criterion-referenced measures interest lies in what the student is able, or unable to do. Hence, there is a need for detailed specification of criterion-referenced test objectives.

Table 3.1. Objectives and Content for a Study of Maps

Objectives
Knows common terms used in mapping
    Defines common terms.
    Reproduces symbolic representations of common terms.
Knows basic principles of mapping
    Recognizes statements of basic principles.
    Matches principles with terms
Comprehends facts and principles.
    Represents verbal facts graphically.
    Describes principles in own words.
Applies facts and principles to solving problems related to hypothetical maps.
    Interprets physical features.
    Locates places on maps.
    Determines direction relative to particular points.
    Calculates distance between points.
    Determines altitude of locations.
    Analyzes the characteristics of various types of zones (e.g., climatic, vegetation).

Content
Vocabulary related to the mechanics of mapping:

Grid	Symbols
Longitude and latitude	Standard time
Scale	Map types
Legend	

Geographical principles related to the following concepts:

Rotation	Physical features
Revolution	Altitude
Vegetation	Location
Climate	Distance
Weather	Slope

Table of Specifications

While a discussion of tables of specification appears in Chapter 8 in relation to validity, an introduction to table construction is necessary at this point. To ensure that a test measures what we want it to measure, a table of specifications is developed. This table, blueprint or behavior-content matrix, is a plan of the test that ensures representative sampling of the course content and skills. This table of specifications helps teachers write tests which have reasonable content validity. Depending on whether the test is norm-referenced or criterion-referenced, there are different ways of constructing a table of specifications.

A Table of Specifications for a Norm-Referenced Test

A table of specification for a norm-referenced test is a two-way crossbreak with the content categorized into two or three levels across the top and three or more levels of objectives identified down the left hand margin. Table 3.2 represents a table of specifications for a norm-referenced test of the geographic skills and knowledge of map reading. This content is divided into two

Table 3.2. Table of Specifications for a Norm-Referenced, Social Studies, Mapping Skills Test[a]

Objectives	Content		
	Area One, Mechanics of Map Reading (40%)	Area Two Related Geographic Principles (60%)	Total
Knowledge (25%)	5[b]	7	12
Comprehension (35%)	7	11	18
Application (40%)	8	12	20
Total	20	30	50

[a]Grade six; length of test = 60 minutes.
[b]Number of items.

areas: area one, mechanics of map reading and area two, related geographical principles. The skills associated with these content areas have been divided into three levels: knowledge, comprehension and application. In other words, the taxonomy of educational objectives, cognitive domain has been simplified so that the application level includes all the other levels above it, i.e., analysis, synthesis and evaluation. this simplification reduces the difficulty of classifying instructional objectives into the various higher level categories of the taxonomy. Moreover, it reduces the complexity of the table of specifications.

As a plan for a test, the table of specifications should include an indication of the relative importance of each of the elements related to the content and objectives. To accomplish this task, follow these steps.

(1) Determine the length of the test. The number of items varies according to a variety of factors such as the length of class periods, the type of item (Supply-type items take longer to complete than selection-type items.), age and abilities of the students. For instance, poor readers will obviously take longer to finish a test than their more skillful peers. Length is a relative matter and only through working with particular groups of students will you actually know how long it will take them to complete a test. In Table 3.2, it is intended that there will be 50 items to be completed in 60 minutes.

(2) Decide on the weight to be given to each content area. In the example, 40% of all of the items (or 20 questions) will be drawn from the mechanics of mapping while the remaining 60% (or 30 items) will be drawn from geographic principles.

(3) Decide on the weight to be given to the levels of the taxonomy. Table 3.2 indicates that 25% of the items are to be at the knowledge level, 35% at the comprehension level and 40% will be written for the application level. The relative emphasis given to the content areas and objectives is subjectively determined. The emphasis is influenced by the amount of time that a teacher has spent on each content area while teaching the unit, and the consideration that the application level is generally more important than the knowledge or comprehension levels. This importance is derived from the fact that skills at the application level are based on the information represented at the knowledge and comprehension levels. By way of illustration, solving problems about time zones depends on an understanding of standard time and the system of longitude. When assigning weights, be flexible. Remember that the table of specifications is only

a plan and as such guides the construction of a test rather than specifically determining all of the characteristics of the test.

(4) Estimate the number of items that will be constructed in each cell of the table. Previously we calculated that there would be 20 items under content area one and that 25% of these would be at the knowledge level: 25% of 20 equals five. Therefore, five items will be written for the first cell which is at the intersection of the knowledge objective and content area one. The numbers of items in the remaining cells are calculated in a similar way.

Before item writing begins, the teacher refers to the list of objectives for the unit and eliminates those goals which are not appropriate for a pencil and paper test. For example, there may be a goal related to the use of maps while hiking. Observational techniques would replace paper and pencil assessment for this type of objective.

Table of Specifications for Criterion-Referenced Testing

In general, criterion-referenced tests cover more limited areas of knowledge and skills than norm-referenced tests. To create a table of specifications for a criterion-referenced test, begin as with the table of specifications for a norm-referenced test. That is, start with the lists of content and behavioral objectives. While the content list will be similar to that created for the norm-referenced examination, the objectives should contain not only a description of the overt behavior of students but a criterion for success. Moreover, the criterion-referenced test requires a more extensive list of objectives. Here is an appropriate objective: Given examples of various kinds of maps, the student will correctly identify all the topographic maps. "Identify" is the overt behavior and the criterion for success is implied by the words "correctly" and "all." Another example would be as follows: Given a contour map of an area, the student will be able to calculate the difference in altitude between ten pairs of sites with 100% accuracy. "Calculation" is the overt behavior and "with 100% accuracy" is the criterion for success. Objectives such as these imply mastery of the skills involved and therefore lend themselves to criterion-referenced testing.

When the area being tested is highly circumscribed, a list of content and objectives may be sufficient as a plan for the test. Consider the following example in the area of map reading:

Objectives

1. Given the verbal description of five different scales, the student will be able to calculate the representative fraction for each scale.
2. Given a large-scale topographical map of a particular region, the student will be able to determine the distance to the nearest one-tenth of a kilometer between six sets of points.
3. Given a large-scale topographic map of a particular region, the student will be able to measure the distance along a road between five sets of two towns with an accuracy expressed to the nearest one-tenth of a kilometer.

Content

1. Representative fractions.
2. Measurement.
3. Scale.

Table 3.3. Table of Specifications for a Criterion-Referenced Test on Specific Map Reading Skills[a]

Content	Specific Tasks		
	Determines Values (40%)	**Calculates Differences (60%)**	**Total**
Longitude and Latitude (30%)	6[b]	9	15
Scales (30%)	6	9	15
Altitude (40%)	8	12	20
Total	20	30	50

[a]Grade six; Length of test = 50 minutes. [b]Number of items.

A highly limited list of objectives and content such as the foregoing would be easily represented on a criterion-referenced test. The test questions are implied directly from the objectives. If the teacher wishes to increase the scope of the test to include another concept such as altitude, then perhaps a table of specification such as that shown in Table 3.3 would be warranted. This table shows a plan for a 50 item objective, criterion-referenced test on specific map reading skills: the ability to determine values and calculate differences in longitude and latitude, map scales and altitude. Differential weights for the various elements of the test are indicated in parentheses. For example, the skill of determining values is weighted 40% and content for longitude and latitude has been weighted 30%. The numbers in the cells of the table indicate the combined number of items for a particular content area and behavioral objective. There will be six items, for instance, written for the task of determining values of longitude and latitude on maps. The number of items per cell, then, is calculated in the same way as previously shown for norm-referenced tests.

Selecting Item Types for Tests

In planning a test, decisions have to be made about the type of questions to be included, and the time available for testing is a major factor in selecting item types. Teacher-made tests may be classified into two general categories, subjective items (e.g., essays) and objective items (e.g., multiple-choice questions). Since subjective as compared to objective items require more time to complete, fewer items are required for any given subjective test. Nevertheless, certain kinds of objective items are rather complex and require a fair amount of reading and analysis before the student can select an answer. For example, the student might be required to read a paragraph of introductory material, study a set of alternatives and then select the correct answers to several questions. More time would obviously be required for such an item than that demanded by the usual multiple-choice item with a single statement in the stem and four or five alternatives.

Test questions that ask students to use information generally need more time to complete than items that necessitate simple recall of facts. Questions involving computation often take longer to complete than those of a verbal nature. The nature of the questions influences the time needed to complete a test.

While there are no firm rules governing the number of items per testing period, as a rough guide allow 30 to 45 seconds for simple multiple-choice or true-false questions and about 75 to 120 seconds for more complex multiple-choice questions that require more extensive problem-solving. With young children, or when the test has to be rather long to cover the material, it might be advisable to break the test into two or more parts and administer each on separate occasions.

The characteristics of the examinees affect test specification. An obvious example is the attention spans of younger pupils which are not as long as those of older students. Therefore, testing periods for younger examinees must be limited to rather short sessions. Intellectually superior students or those with more sophisticated understanding of a subject usually complete more objective items and handle more difficult questions than their less bright or unsophisticated peers. Hence, raise test length and difficulty for more advanced students. Different kinds of examinations emphasize different skills. For example, essays are necessarily reserved for older students who are able to meet the writing challenge. For young pupils, objective tests such as those containing sentence completion and multiple-choice items would be used most often.

Choice of item type should be based on a rational consideration of variables that were outlined in the previous section as well as the following selection criteria (Thorndike & Hagen, 1969):

(1) Test questions should allow students to demonstrate achievement of the objectives. Since students have learned particular knowledge and skills from a course, they should be given a chance to demonstrate their attainment level. The teacher's task in setting an examination, then, is to elicit the intended responses from pupils. Perhaps, students have learned to calculate elevation differences from a topographic map. This skill could be assessed by multiple-choice items that are based on a map. In contrast, student understanding of the variables that affect resource management might best be evaluated with an essay examination.

(2) Precision of results which varies with item type relates to the purpose of the test. If assessments of quality of thinking, organization of ideas, and argumentation are intended, then the essay is best. Assessment of breadth of knowledge is most effectively measured by multiple-choice or other objective questions.

(3) All test scores reflect variability from irrelevant sources such as reading ability. A test of mathematics that requires a reading level above that which is possessed by most of the examinees would invalidate it as a mathematics examination (See the discussion on validity in Chapter 8.). Test items must be written at the reading level of most of the examinees. Through experience, teachers will have insight into the reading skills of their students. But reference to word lists in elementary school and to basal readers and standard word lists for secondary school examinees is possible. In general, objective items are freer from irrelevant sources of variation than subjective questions. To illustrate, markers of essay examinations may be unduly influenced by the writing skills of the examinees: highly skilled writers may receive better grades than less adept peers who might actually know more about the topic but present answers less well.

Irrelevant sources of variation present a dilemma for teachers who feel that language skills are important: Should marks be deducted for spelling errors in subjects like biology? While acquisition of terminology is part of learning in any discipline, some students chronically misspell words because they may have a perceptual-motor deficit. Loss of points due to this problem seems unfair. Separate grades for knowledge in biology and spelling of terms would be more acceptable.

(4) The number of students who will take the examination influences item choice: the greater the number, the more likely it is that an objectively scored test will be used. The time taken by marking large numbers of essays might be better spent solving other instructional problems such as the remediation of faulty teaching and learning.

(5) Resources such as paper are chronically in short supply in some schools, and these shortages affect decisions about examinations. Clearly, essays need paper for student responses, and multiple-choice questions require paper for test booklets. While one set of test booklets may be used with several classes who are to take the same multiple-choice examination at different times, reusing booklets in subsequent years is precluded by the need for revision. Still, the problem of inadequate supplies is difficult to solve in a society that gives mere lip service rather than genuine commitment to education.

Oral examinations are not the answer to material shortages. Variability in listening skills and rates of work prevent the use of orals in the usual class setting where large groups of students are taught by one teacher because there would be too much time wasted in waiting for slower students to catch up to their classmates. More than this, those who work more slowly would feel pressure, and they might become targets of derision. The faster students would be frustrated by the delays.

Test Preparation

The organization of the test should not interfere with the examinees' performance. Grouping questions according to the natural subdivisions of the subject matter facilitates test completion. Questions arranged as to content allow the students to move smoothly from one item to the next without having to switch abruptly back and forth among subject areas. Within content subdivisions, group the questions according to item type, i.e., put all the matching questions together and all the sentence-completion items together. Under this format, examinees will be able to build momentum with one response style before shifting to another. Questions arranged in this manner will facilitate manual scoring because keys will be easier to follow. In general, the organization should be from less to more difficult questions so that slower students who may not reach the harder question by the end of the examination period will at least benefit from having a chance to answer the easier questions. Moreover, success with the easier questions will encourage those students who lack confidence. Gronlund (1985, p. 233) advocates the following order:

1. Alternative response items.
2. Matching items.
3. Short-answer items.
4. Multiple-choice items.
5. Interpretive exercises.
6. Essay questions.

However, limit the kinds of items in a test to as few as possible and perhaps no more than two or three item types. Each kind of question should be separated from the others by a line of symbols such as dashes or asterisks. If needed, directions introduce each set of items.

Test performance may be affected by the format of the test. While economic use of space is important, readability is essential. In general, use the full page from margin to margin, but items

Focus on Research
Item Grouping

Teachers are advised to group items according to item type within the same content areas. This seems logical in that it should facilitate student performance. Perhaps it does, but Aiken (1987) found no research evidence to support this conclusion. However, arranging the items in ascending order of difficulty affects performance under certain conditions, but not others. Performance on power tests where the students had sufficient time to devote to the more difficult items is not affected by the ordering of the items. Tests where time is short, difficulty is relatively high, or student information levels are restricted will produce a benefit to performance if the items are arranged in ascending order of difficulty (Aiken, 1987).

---

with short stems and brief alternatives may be placed in a two-column format with a vertical line separating the columns. Regardless of format, complete the questions on the page on which they were started. List alternatives one under the other rather than in paragraph form as shown in the following example:

■ **Example**

Poor: 1. **What are the findings from research on cooperative learning regarding task specialization effects on student achievement? Task specialization procedures produce (a) increased achievement, but more research is required to be certain. (b) no increase in achievement, but special circumstances should be considered. (c) about the same amount of achievement. (d) no results because no research has been conducted on their effects.**

Improved: 2. **What are the findings from research on cooperative learning regarding task specialization effects on student achievement? Task specialization procedures produce**
   (a) **increased achievement, but more research is required to be certain.**
   (b) **no increase in achievement, but special circumstances should be considered.**
   (c) **about the same amount of achievement.**
   (d) **no results because no research had been conducted on their effects.**

The improved version of the above items is easier to read and consequently students will make fewer mistakes due to confusion caused by an awkward format.

Test Instructions

Test instructions inform examinees about what is to be done and how to do it. While the written instructions should fully inform students about the requirements of the test, you should ask students to read the directions silently and at the same time read them aloud, especially with younger pupils.

Instructions may be divided into two categories, general and specific. General directions deal with the test as a whole and provide information about test type, time limits, and number of sections. General instructions are placed on the cover page, and in its absence they are set at the top of the first page. Specific directions are given for each type of question and they appear at the beginning of the separate sections. Unfamiliar item types are introduced with examples. Explain the form of the answer. For instance, problems in mathematics should have instructions that tell students how much detail is required, the nature of the units desired, whether to show their work, and where to write the answers. Special scoring procedures should be outlined. When correction formulas are to be employed, examinees should be informed. The following directions illustrate the kind of general instructions that might appear on a test cover page at the secondary school level.

■ **Example**

1. On the answer sheet and essay booklet, *print* your name, class and date.
2. This test has three parts: matching questions, multiple-choice questions and an essay question.
3. Specific directions for each of the separate parts appear at the beginning of each section.
4. Use the separate answer sheet for the matching and multiple-choice questions.
5. There is *no* correction for guessing.
6. Write your response to the essay question in the booklet provided.
7. Do not write on the test booklet.
8. The values for each section of the test paper are indicated within parentheses at the beginning of each of the sections.
9. You have 75 minutes to complete the test.
10. Are there any questions about what to do?

The following set of specific directions are for a multiple-choice section of a test.

■ **Example**

Directions: For each question, select the alternative that best completes the statement or answers the question. Blacken the space on the answer sheet by the letter of your choice. For example, if answer (c) is the best choice for question one, blacken the space next to the letter (c) opposite number one on the answer sheet.

The foregoing is an illustration of a set of specific directions for the multiple-choice section of an examination. Similar instructions appropriate to other item types would be placed at the beginning of each subdivision.

Administering a Test

The conditions under which examinations are given should be uniform for all examinees. Both the physical and social psychological conditions as far as possible should facilitate optimum performance by all students. Since the environment should be comfortable, lighting, temperature, and ventilation must be adequate. When the test booklets are about to be distributed, request that students refrain from talking to one another. Ask students to remove extraneous material from their desks and avoid conditions such as crowding desks together. Careful proctoring is part of all good testing situations. The oral instructions at the beginning of the test should be as brief as possible and interruptions during the examination avoided as far as possible. In order that they might schedule announcements on the public address system around examination sessions, inform school administrators of the periods designated for tests.

Scoring Tests

Answers can be written on the test booklet or on separate answer sheets. Answer sheets have advantages such as decreased scoring time, increased marking accuracy and reuse of the test booklets. The disadvantages are that student errors, fatigue and time needed for completion increase. With separate answer sheets, optical machine scoring is possible. Usually these machines require commercially produced answer sheets.

Scoring keys promote reliability in the marking of tests. Depending on the type of test, there are various kinds of keys. Those four essay tests will be described in Chapter 6. The various forms of objective tests require different keys. Overlay keys are best for multiple-choice tests and certain short-answer examinations. Strip keys may be used to score short-answer test questions.

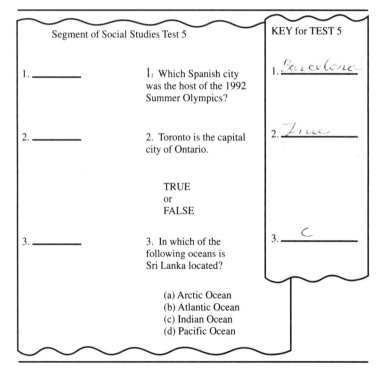

The Overlay Key. The overlay key or scoring mask for a multiple-choice test usually consists of an answer sheet with holes punched or cut over the correct alternatives so that the students' answers may be exposed. You place the key carefully over each student's answer sheet with the help of alignment marks. The answers that appear in the holes are marked right, while those that do not appear are wrong.

With short-answer tests, the possible answers to each question are written under the windows or holes as shown in Figure 3.1 where the shaded portions are the windows in the key. Writing the answers on the key facilitates quick, accurate scoring.

Figure 3.1. Example of a strip key (From Marshall, J. C. & Hales L. W. (1971). *Classroom test construction*. Reading, MA: Addison-Wesley, p. 44 (45). Reprinted by permission of the authors.)

The Strip Key. The strip key is used with short-answer tests, especially where the answers are written on the test booklet in a list format. It consists of a strip of firm paper or cardboard with the answers listed in the appropriate blanks. The key is aligned with the test questions as shown in Figure 3.2. Similar to the effects of other keys, these keys facilitate ease and accuracy of scoring.

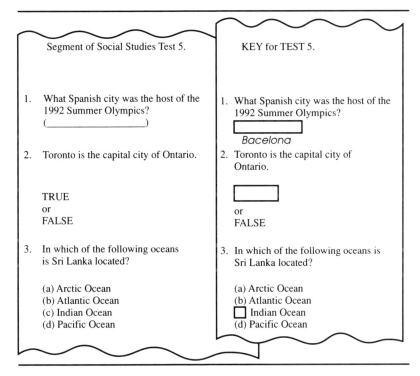

Figure 3.2. Example of an overlay key (From Marshall, J. C. & Hales L. W. (1971). *Classroom test construction*. Reading, MA: Addison-Wesley, p. 44 (45). Reprinted by permission of the authors.)

■ Summary and Main Points

Measurement produces a number which reflects the amount of a particular characteristic possessed by a student. Consistent with this view of measurement, a test may be defined as a task or tasks that when completed, quantifies the amount the examinee has of a particular trait or characteristic. Test construction should produce reliable and valid measuring instruments. Reliability refers to the consistency with which a test measures the characteristics it was designed to measure. Validity, the most important trait of any test, is the degree to which a test measures whatever it is intended to measure. A variety of tests were described. These tests appear first in the ensuing list followed by the remaining central ideas of the chapter:

1. Teacher-made tests are constructed by instructors to measure their students' achievement of the goals of instruction.

2. Standardized tests are developed by teams of experts and have uniform directions and scoring procedures. Manuals for administration and interpretation of results are created and contain norms and reliability and validity information. Similar to other tests, results from standardized tests aid the decision making process.

3. Objective tests such as multiple-choice, alternate-response, matching and short-answer questions are scored according to predetermined keys and no judgments about the correctness of the answers are needed at the time of scoring.

4. Subjective tests such as the essay examination require judgment about the value or correctness of the responses at the time of scoring.

5. Individual tests are administered to each examinee separately and generally yield more reliable results than group tests on the same subject.

6. A group test is administered to more than one person at a time. Most classroom achievement tests fall into this category.

7. Ability tests measure present capacity to perform or to complete a task. General ability tests are intelligence tests.

8. An aptitude test assesses potential in a particular area. The same test may be both an abilities test measuring current capacity and an aptitude test assessing potential in a given discipline.

9. Readiness tests produce results which indicate the pupil's preparedness to profit from instruction in a particular subject such as reading.

10. Diagnostic tests indicate weaknesses by measuring the quality of a student's achievement of the goals of instruction.

11. Formative tests assess progress towards the goals of instruction. They are given more often and they are usually shorter than summative tests which measure achievement of the terminal goals of instruction.

12. Norm-referenced examination results are interpreted in the light of a group's average scores. This is in contrast to absolute interpretations given criterion-referenced tests which measure achievement of a particular set of goals.

13. Mastery tests appraise whether students have met an established level of achievement and as such are a special form of criterion-referenced tests.

14. Minimum competency tests estimate achievement of the goals fundamental to adequate functioning.

15. Power tests gauge maximum performance in a discipline. While theoretically there should be no time limits when power is being tested, in practice generous time limits are applied.

16. Speed tests challenge examinees to complete as many questions of a uniformly easy level of difficulty as possible within set time limits.

17. A single examination may be simultaneously categorized as having the characteristics of several kinds of tests.

18. The test development process consists of the following steps: (a) List the instructional objectives. (b) Outline the content. (c) Construct a table of specifications. (d) Select the item types. (e) Develop the test questions. (f) Create the directions. (g) Establish the answer key. (h) Supply answer sheets. (i) Administer the test. (j) After analyzing the results, revise the test.

19. A table of specifications is the plan for the test. It is influenced by the course content, objectives, the kind of questions, and the traits of the examinees. The plan is to ensure representative sampling of the course content and skills.

20. Depending on whether a test is a criterion- or norm-referenced examination, the table of specifications differ. In general, criterion-referenced tests require more specific instructional objectives, than norm-referenced measuring instruments.

21. The selection of test items is influenced by several variables: the time available for testing, the characteristics of examinees, the need to allow students to show that they have achieved the goals of instruction, the precision required of the results, the need to reduce influences from irrelevant sources of variation, and the availability of material resources.

22. Test organization should facilitate student performance. One way of doing this is to group test questions according to subject matter. Within these content subdivisions, arrange questions according to item type. In addition, the less difficult questions should appear earlier in a test.

23. Organize tests so that they are easily read. Complete items on the page on which they were started. In multiple-choice items, list alternatives in columns rather in paragraphs.

24. Test instructions describe the tasks to be completed by the examinees. General directions provide information about test type, time limits, and the number of sections. Specific directions describe how to answer each separate type of test question.

25. Test administration should be uniform for all students. Establish comfortable physical and psychological conditions. Create an appropriate examination mode by requesting silence, cleared desks, and adequate spacing between desks. Supervise students during the testing period and avoid interruptions.

26. The scoring of tests is aided by the use of separate answer sheets. Scoring keys promote accuracy and consistency in marking tests. The overlay and strip key are two types of keys.

■ Further Readings

Bloom, B. S., Madaus, G. F., & Hastings, J. T. (1981). *Evaluating to improve learning*. New York: McGraw-Hill.

Good, C. V. (Ed.). (1959). *Dictionary of education* (2nd ed.). New York: McGraw-Hill.

Ebel, R. L., & Frisbie, D. A. (1986). *Essentials of educational measurement* (4th ed.). Englewood Cliffs, NJ: Prentice-Hall.

Marshall, J. C., & Hales, L. W. (1971). *Classroom test construction*. Reading, MA: Addison-Wesley.

Popham, W. J. (1988). *Educational evaluation* (2nd ed.). Englewood Cliffs, NJ: Prentice-Hall.

■ Laboratory Exercises

Before starting the following exercises, choose a subject that you know well and that is relevant to a grade that you might teach.

Part A: Table of Specifications

1. List the main concepts and principles in the selected content area.

2. Write instructional objectives at the knowledge, comprehension, and application or higher levels of Bloom's taxonomy of educational objectives, the cognitive domain.

3. Based on the content and objectives listed in items one and two, construct a three by three table of specifications as a plan for an objective, norm-referenced test. The table should include the following elements: title of the test; three levels of objectives as one way of classification, and three areas of content as the other way of classification; specify the number and percentage of items at each level of the taxonomy and each content area as well as in each cell of the table; total number of items and number and kind of items (At least two types of items are to be included.); grade; and time limit. Refer to Table 3.2 for a model of the finished product.

4. For the same subject that was identified in item one, construct a table of specifications for a criterion-referenced, objective test. Include all of the characteristics of such a table as shown in Table 3.3.

Part B: Test Instructions

1. For the test planned in Part A, develop general and specific instructions. The general instructions describe the test as a whole and explain the broad character of the examination, time limits, and number of sections. Specific directions are given for each item type.

Chapter

4

Item Construction: Objective Items I

Overview

Constructing test items is a common activity for teachers. Since teachers have information about course content, student achievement, and other variables which might influence test performance such as vocabulary development, they are usually in the best position to build a valid measure of achievement in a particular course. The quality of teacher-made tests is dependent not only on the teachers' knowledge of the subject and awareness of salient traits of students, but also on knowledge and skill it item writing.

In this chapter we begin explaining the item construction skills that teachers need to create valid and reliable measures of student achievement. Before illustrating the development of specific items, general guidelines which apply to the production of all objective items are described. These guidelines are followed by specific suggestions for the composition of alternate-response items, matching items and short-answer questions. Careful application of the rules of item writing will improve the quality of locally constructed tests.

Guidelines for Writing Objective Items

While each of the various kinds of objective items, alternate-response, matching, short-answer and multiple-choice types are written according to specific rules which will be discussed in this and subsequent chapters, there are several suggestions that apply to all objective items. Item writers who adhere to the following advice will improve the quality of their tests.

1. Construct Items at an Appropriate Difficulty Level for the Ability of the Examinees

The form and type of item may add unnecessary difficulty to a question (Mehrens & Lehmann, 1973). For instance, primary school children more easily answer matching questions where they are asked to join the two parts with a line than when they must respond on a separate answer sheet by blackening the space beside the letter of the alternative they have chosen. The latter operation is more complex than the former and, therefore, the probability of student error increases. That is, young children, who are not as advanced in their perceptual motor development as older children, may have problems handling a separate answer sheet. The errors, due to this aspect of development, obviously do not reflect student understanding of the subject covered by the item; rather the form of the item has interfered with successful performance. The type of item sometimes produces student blunders. For example, young children usually find short-answer questions easier to answer than multiple-choice items. The many comparisons required by multiple-choice items tax the abilities of young pupils thereby producing more errors. Anytime mistakes are caused by something other than student knowledge, validity suffers: the test is not measuring as well as it might that which it was intended to assess.

2. Include Items at an Appropriate Level of Difficulty for the Purpose of the Test

Achievement tests may be categorized as either norm-referenced or criterion-referenced. This categorization derives from the way test results are interpreted. Since a more detailed explanation of these categories is contained in Chapters 3 and 11, only a brief explanation is offered at this point. When a student's performance is compared to the average of the group, a norm-referenced interpretation exists whereas comparisons to achievement levels previously established by the learner indicate a criterion-referenced analysis. When test results are used to rank order individuals, most test items should be in the middle range of difficulty so that increased discrimination among the various achievement levels is attained. If the examiner's main purpose, on the other hand, is to assess mastery of certain instructional objectives then the examinees will find the items generally easier. In other words, item difficulty varies with the purpose of the test (Mehrens & Lehmann, 1973).

3. Test Significant Elements of a Course

Testing is a time consuming process which should not be wasted on gathering information about unimportant issues. Moreover, emphasis on significant aspects of a course will influence students' study practices. That is, students will more likely approach studying with the intention to learn in a meaningful way if they know that tests emphasize the central ideas of a discipline. Meaningful verbal learning facilitates retention and transfer. Testing for trivia engenders rote learning which is easily forgotten (Ausubel, Novak, & Hanesian, 1978). More than this, students are critical of tests which emphasize unimportant details, and the resulting frustration may lead to strained relationships between teachers and students.

4. Write Independent Items

In general, the answer to one question should not hinge on the answer to a previous question. As far as the content of the item is concerned, students should begin each question with the same chance at selecting the correct answer as compared to their classmates, a condition absent with related items. A case might be made for including interdependent items, especially when the content seems logically connected. For example, the calculations of the mean, standard deviation, and z-score for a group of scores are related. But separation may be achieved by using a new group of scores for each item, and supplying the values of the other measures as required for each statistic. In this way a mistake in computing the value of one statistic would not affect the calculation of the others.

While it is sometimes hard to achieve, the answer to one question should not provide clues to the answers to any other items on a test. This kind of error will tend to lower the validity of a test because testwiseness rather than knowledge of subject matter will unduly influence test results.

5. Construct Questions Free from Extraneous Reasons for Problems

When tests are based on clearly stated objectives, difficulties derived from extraneous sources are easily avoided (Wesman, 1971). For instance, suppose that understanding of statistical concepts is being assessed. To accomplish this goal, long strings of scores or even numbers larger than single digits are unnecessary. If large groups of scores of two or more digits were used, computational skills would contribute to achievement, and this would be an irrelevant cause of low achievement for some individuals.

6. Communicate the Question in Clear, Concise Language

Unless the item is testing vocabulary, the wording should not reduce a student's chance of answering the question correctly. If, for example, the item is a word problem in arithmetic, vocabulary should not interfere with finding a solution. To the degree that general vocabulary development affects solving arithmetic problems, to that degree will the test be an invalid measure of arithmetic problem solving skills. This is not to say that technical vocabulary which is part of a course of studies should be avoided. Every subject has its own vocabulary and students are responsible for acquiring the technical terminology of a discipline. Therefore, the specialized vocabulary of a subject should be used in the construction of test items. Indeed, tests in most introductory courses will have many items that assess mastery of the fundamental terminology of the discipline. The point is that inappropriately difficult words from general vocabulary should not be used.

Wesman (1971) rightly points out that clarity in item writing is a demanding task. Unlike other prose, a test item stands alone without the advantage of an elaborate context to convey meaning. A clearly stated item has a good chance of differentiating among those students who know and those who do not understand the subject. Vague, ambiguous items, on the other hand, are less likely to discriminate.

Wesman makes several suggestions for improving the clarity of test items. First, rigorous expression is important. For instance, the question "What is the meaning of the Vietnam War? is too vague. Greater precision is found in the question "What effect did the Vietnam War have on American foreign policy in the late 1970s?" Second, avoid clumsy expressions. An awkwardly worded item such as "Selective perception of what people are doing, the places where they live, and the things they own is called _____." is more clearly expressed by the following statement "Selective perception of stimuli is known as _____." Wesman further suggests that sentence structure be simple rather than complex and that complex sentences should be divided into two or more simple sentences. Moreover, state the problem early in the stem and add qualifying statements later. In this way, students will see the problem unfettered by refinements which might be confusing, especially modifiers included early in the statement of a problem. Third, qualify the question so that examinees know exactly what is required for a correct response. The above example about the effects of the Vietnam War well illustrates this point. The War's effects on foreign policy were different in the late 1960s when the War was ongoing as compared to the late 1970s which was after the American troop withdrawal. Hence, designation of the time period is important. Fourth, exclude words which serve no real purpose. If the words do not influence the selection of the correct response, then they are extraneous and can be eliminated. For example, the introductory statement "Bias is a problem when teachers use observational techniques." is unnecessary in the following item:

■ **Example**

    1. **Bias is a problem when teachers use observational techniques. What is the best term for the observation that teachers tend to rate students close to the average of the class?**
        (a) halo effect
        (b) sampling error
        (c) error of leniency
      *(d) error of central tendency

The introductory statement is an instructional aside which should be eliminated from test questions. Beyond these suggestions, clarity is aided by keeping the objectives and related content in mind while item writing. If the students' destination and how they got there are explicit, then teachers will be clear about how to test achievement.

7. In the Correct Alternatives, Paraphrase Statements from Textbooks

When creating test items, it is tempting to quote from the textbook. Mehrens and Lehmann (1973) consider this a flawed technique in that a statement removed from context may become ambiguous, particularly true-false items where a negative is added to the original statement. With short-answer items one or two key words might be omitted, but again the question may suffer from ambiguity due to loss of context. In the case of multiple-choice items, use of verbatim textbook statements in the correct response encourages rote rather than meaningful verbal learning because the task would be reduced to recognition of a previously memorized expression.

Inclusion of verbatim passages in distractors is an acceptable procedure because it helps differentiate between students who truly understand the course content and those who have relied on rote memorization. That pupils are discriminating among alternatives one of which exactly reproduces textual material, albeit applied inappropriately, avoids the criticism that this procedure relies on trickery for its effectiveness: these discriminations parallel everyday problem solving.

8. Exclude Clues to the Correct Answer

If students who would not normally give the right answer respond correctly with the help of an irrelevant clue, then student testwiseness is unduly influencing results. Various item-writing errors produce these clues: stereotypic verbal expressions, greater elaboration of correct alternatives, repetition of words or phrases in both the stem and answer, and specific determiners are some of the more usual mistakes. The subsequent examples illustrate these mistakes.

Stereotypic Verbal Expressions. This error usually takes the form of placing one segment of a common expression in the stem and the second part in the correct alternative:

■ **Example**

    1. **When describing a scene, one picture is worth more than ten thousand _____.**
        (a) books
        (b) drawings
        (c) letters
      *(d) words

The contrast in this Chinese proverb is between the visual and verbal forms of expression. Since the proverb has become a cliché, examinees would likely obtain the answer without necessarily understanding the contrast.

Elaboration of Correct Alternatives. To ensure that the correct response is the best alternative, item writers may qualify it more than the others. Testwise students who are aware of this tendency may select the correct answer without comprehension of the subject.

■ Example

1. **What is the first step in an effective demonstration?**
    (a) **Give an overview.**
    (b) **Name the new concepts.**
    *(c) **Gain students' attention because if they are not attending they cannot learn the new material.**
    (d) **Go through the process step by step.**

Removal of the qualifying clause which follows the word "attention" does not eliminate alternative (c) as the correct response, but its inclusion may be an irrelevant clue.

Repetition. The repetition of phrases in the stem and the correct alternative provides an irrelevant clue.

■ Example

1. **In Zimbardo's model prison experiment, how was the behavior of participants best explained?**
    (a) **General personality and societal factors.**
    *(b) **Power motive and the actual situation influenced the behavior of participants.**
    (c) **Experimenter effects and specific research design flaws.**

Inclusion of the phrase "behavior of participants" creates the condition where the correct alternative might be chosen without knowledge of the experiment.

Specific Determiners. Qualifiers such as "all, always, could, customarily, every, frequently, generally, mostly, never, none, sometimes, and usually" are known as specific determiners and may indicate that an expression is true or false. Words which make the statement equivocal, tend to make the statement true. Conversely, words that make the statement unequivocal, tend to make the statement false. For example, "mostly" is usually found in true statements whereas "never" is often found in false expressions. Consider the following items:

■ Examples

1. **None of the people of Montana are employed in manufacturing. (F)**

This statement might be improved as follows:

    2. **Montana's distance from markets for manufactured goods makes it difficult to develop secondary industries there. (T)**

Based on the use of the word "none," a student who is wise in the ways of writing examinations might readily identify the falsity of the first example. Specific determiners are absent from the second item, and selecting the correct alternative requires knowledge of geography and economics.

Specific determiners, repetition of words in the stem and alternatives, excessive elaboration of correct responses, and inclusion of stereotypic expressions are common mistakes made by uninformed item writers. Elimination of these unintended clues lessens the influence of student testwiseness and improves the validity of the tests.

9. Provide One Correct Answer

Construct items which have only one answer, especially where the subject matter is open to debate. When one position of a debatable issue is represented in an item, Mehrens and Lehmann (1973) suggest that the source of the position be cited to avoid confusion. The ensuing items illustrate this point:

■ **Examples**

    Poor: 1.   **Oat bran reduces the risk of heart attacks. (T)**

    Improved: 2.   **Crisp's findings indicate that regular inclusion of oat bran in the diet reduces the risk of heart attacks. (F)**

The role of oat bran in reducing the risk of heart attacks is controversial, and identifying the source of the position increases the precision of the item: since Crisp is not the source, there is only one correct answer.

10. Edit the Items

Editing will eliminate many superficial errors. First, scrutinize the correct response to ensure that it is the best answer. While good item writers routinely set their products aside for a period of twenty-four hours or more and then read them again, the correctness of the answer may best be identified by another expert in the discipline. Without the key the expert reads the test and identifies the correct answers. Discrepancies between the keyed responses and the expert's choices are studied with a view to reconciling the differences. Of course, classroom teachers seldom have the luxury of the opinion of an independent expert (Fellow teachers are generally too busy to edit their colleagues' tests.) and, therefore, they must be extra careful in reviewing items for incorrectly keyed answers. Second, if they have time, increased discrimination among alternatives may be suggested by other teachers who have taught the students and are aware of their misunderstandings. Third, study the items to ensure that they are not too difficult or easy. While this may be problematical without actually administering the test, the extreme cases: those items that are very difficult or unusually easy will be exposed. Fourth, rereading the items will remove ambiguity of expression, especially if a reasonable period of time (at least one day) has passed. Finally, the importance of each item relative to the content objectives of a course should be considered—items measuring trivia would ordinarily be discarded—although there is sometimes a place, such as the first question on a test, for an extremely easy item.

Effective item writing is a learned skill which improves with practice, especially that which incorporates the foregoing guidelines. Additional suggestions are relevant to each type of item, and it is to these that we now turn.

Alternate-Response Items

Alternate-response questions present the student with a statement requiring the selection of one of two alternatives such as true or false, yes or no, right or wrong, and other similar binary choices. These items provide a simple, straightforward approach to assessing a student's knowledge in a discipline. Ebel and Frisbie (1986) summarize the value of alternate-response items in the following four statements:

1. The essence of educational achievement is the command of useful verbal knowledge.
2. All verbal knowledge can be expressed in propositions.
3. A proposition is any sentence that can be said to be true or false.
4. The extent of students' command of a particular area of knowledge is indicated by their success in judging the truth or falsity of propositions related to it. (p. 139)

Ebel and Fresbie are implying that a student's knowledge in a subject is best measured by test questions which ask for recognition of the true application of the propositions that constitute the discipline under study. As previously noted, verbatim statements from textbooks which have been made true or false by the teacher, and then presented to students in the form of a test is not the best way to have students demonstrate their knowledge. Rote learning may be assessed this way, but meaningful learning requires that students incorporate separate propositions into coherent cognitive structures that permit transfer of learning to new situations. For instance, assessment of a student's comprehension of operant conditioning through presenting a rule as a true statement rather than asking for an analysis of an applied setting would be to misconstrue what it means to understand a subject. Consider the following example:

■ Examples
1. **A child is more likely to give a particular response in a certain situation when, in similar situations in the past, pleasure has resulted from that response.**
2. **If throwing a ball brings the child pleasure, the child is likely to throw a ball when given another opportunity.**

The first of these statements is a variation of the definition of operant conditioning whereas the second is a rough description of the principle in operation, and requires the recognition of a correct application. This second task is more difficult.

The alternate-response item takes various forms, the most common of which is the simple true–false item.

■ **Examples**

Directions: For each of the following statements, circle T if the statement is true and circle F if the statement is false.

T F Arthur upon touching a hot stove element jerks his hand away and this is called a reflex action. (T)

T F Sound is created by the vibration of a body which produces constant motion in air that radiates outward in the form of uneven waves. (T)

Differentiating between fact and opinion is another form of the alternate-response item as shown in the ensuing examples:

■ **Examples**

Directions: For the following statements, circle F when there is a statement of fact, and circle O when the statement expresses an opinion.

F O 1. C. Rogers is a proponent of client-centered therapy. (F)

F O 2. A. Einstein was the most important scientist of the 20th century. (O)

A right-wrong variety of alternate-response questions is illustrated in the subsequent examples:

■ **Examples**

Directions: For the following statements circle R if the statement is grammatically correct and circle W if the statement is wrong.

R W 1. It began to rain, the wind increased. (W)

R W 2. Where is he? (R)

Another variation is the correction type in which the student makes each false statement true by correcting an underlined word. Note that in the following examples even the true statements have a word that is underlined.

■ **Examples**

Directions: For each of the following statements, circle T if the statement is true and circle F if it is false. For each false statement change the word that is underlined so that the expression is true. Write the substitute word in the blank.

T F _____ 1. A legend defines the symbols used on a map. (T)

T F _____ 2. Meridians are lines of latitude. (F)

T F _____ 3. Roman maps were "oriented" which means that north was at the top of the maps. (F)

Guidelines for Writing Alternate-Response Items

The writing of alternate-response items is guided by a few, simple rules which are illustrated in the following section.

1. *Construct alternate-response items in pairs, one right, the other wrong.* While only one member of the pair is actually used in the test, the statement is unlikely to be a good alternate-response item if the opposite statement cannot be made. The ensuing examples from a language arts test illustrate the use of paired statements.

■ **Examples**

Pair A:	1.	After criticizing my work, I was fired. (W)
	2.	After criticizing my work, the boss fired me. (R)
Pair B:	1.	Jumping into the pool, the warmth of the water surprised me. (W)
	2.	Jumping into the pool, I was surprised by the warmth of the water. (R)

2. *When writing true-false questions, state the items so that they are wholly true or wholly false.* This usually means that the question must be qualified in such a way that most experts would agree on its truth or falsity. Both of the following statements are intended to be true, but the first, since it lacks additional qualification, is ambiguous.

■ **Examples:**

Poor:	1.	A fused sentence lacks capitals and punctuation. (T)
Better:	2.	If a sentence does not end with a punctuation mark and the subsequent one starts without a capital letter, the mistake is called a fused sentence. (T)

In the above examples, statement number one lacks sufficient detail to make it clearly true, whereas the other is adequately qualified.

3. *Include more false than true statements in any given test and vary the number of true and false statements from test to test.* There is a tendency for students to mark more statements true than false. Moreover, discrimination between those who know and those who don't know is greater for false expressions (Ebel & Frisbie, 1986). Therefore, not only vary the number of true and false items, but include more false than true statements. A related issue is that patterns within true and false items should be avoided. Students are quick to discern strings such as four true and four false items repeated several times throughout the test.

4. *Include only one main idea in each statement.* The inclusion of more than one idea in an expression may produce an item which is partially true. Students, of course, would probably mark the statement false, but they may also be confused by it. The following examples illustrate the problem:

■ **Examples**

Poor:	1.	Topic sentences are placed first and identify the subject of paragraphs.
Better:	2.	Topic sentences are brief statements of the subject of paragraphs. (T)

In the poor illustration, topic sentences are described as expressing the subject of paragraphs, but it is obviously incorrect to say that they are the first sentences of paragraphs. Topic sentences appear at the beginning, middle or end of paragraphs. Indeed, some paragraphs omit the topic sentence. Moreover, only one idea should be included in an item even if both are true.

5. *Avoid negative statements.* Under the stress of testing, students will overlook terms such as "not." While it is sometimes tempting to make a true statement false by putting it in the negative form as shown in the following example, this practice should be avoided.

■ **Examples**

Poor: 1. **Negative reinforcement does not involve the application of unpleasant stimuli such as criticism. (T)**

Better: 2. **Negative reinforcement involves the termination of unpleasant stimuli such as criticism. (T)**

In the above illustrations both statements are intended to be true, however, the improved version has the clarity of a positive expression. Research has shown that it takes more time to answer negative statements, and more errors are made (Wesman, 1971). Avoid negative statements, especially double negatives. If "not" must be used, it should be underlined.

Advantages and Disadvantage of Alternate-Response Items

Alternate-response items appear relatively easy to construct, but this may be misleading. In fact, they are challenging and time consuming to write. While they are demanding, this type of item is probably somewhat easier to write than the multiple-choice type because the latter by definition requires more distractors. A second advantage is that greater coverage of the content may be achieved on any single test because students can respond more quickly to an alternate-response item than, say, to a multiple-choice question.

On the surface alternate-response items seem to have major problems, but the difficulties may not be all that serious. One criticism is that they measure trivial elements of a course of studies. Yet some authorities argue that alternate-response items can measure students' ability to identify important applications (Ebel & Frisbie, 1986). More creativity is required in constructing application level items, but the possibility exists. Another drawback is that this type of item is often ambiguous, but this criticism is not unique to alternate-response items. Careful editing allows the item writer to create clear, concise questions. A further argument against their use is that alternate-response items are unusually open to guessing. And there is truth to this concern in that the examinee has a 50 percent chance of getting any particular item right, with an even greater probability when we acknowledge that items sometimes include clues.

Guessing, if it is based on partial knowledge, should be encouraged. When a student guesses blindly, the answer is chosen haphazardly, presumably without knowledge of the topic. Blind guessing probably does not occur very often. With greater information students are understandably more likely to guess correctly. That is, very little blind guessing is done by knowledgeable, highly motivated students, according to Ebel and Frisbie (1986), because they are more likely to approach a difficult item in a careful, problem-solving manner. Ebel and Frisbie also argue against correction formulas which compensate for the influence of blind guessing. To inform students of a correction formula will prevent timid students from guessing, but other, bolder ones will guess regardless. It

Focus on the Student

Knowledge of item construction methodology provides a basis for teaching students techniques to improve their performance on examinations. Students will develop "testwiseness" when, for example, they are taught that alternatives containing specific determiners such as "never" are frequently incorrect. Testwiseness is the skill of using the qualities of the test items and the examination conditions to improve one's score (Weitten, 1983). Since writing examinations is a large part of schooling and since students vary in the ability to take tests, they should be given instruction to improve testwiseness. With more uniform skills in this area, we will be more confident that our examinations are measuring differences in achievement.

Concerns about unduly influencing students' performance with so-called privileged, test-taking information is irrelevant, especially if teachers hone item composition skills to the point where their tests contain few extraneous clues and flaws which students might use to discover correct answers without knowledge of a subject.

is better to encourage students to guess because most of the time it will be informed by at least some knowledge. And risk taking is, after all, part of most problem solving activities.

Matching Items

To link elements from one list with those of another according to a set of instructions is the essence of matching items. The left hand list is the "premises" and usually contains longer statements such as definitions. The right hand column is the "responses" and contains shorter components such as terms. The directions are a crucial part of the matching question because they explain the basis for the matching process, and often provide limitations which tell the examinees whether or not an item can be used more than once. Topics covered by matching questions are only limited by the imagination of the item writer. While they lend themselves most easily to low level cognitive tasks, it is possible to construct matching items which require the application of knowledge and skills. Examples of two types of matching questions are shown below:

■ **Examples**

A Classification Type

Directions: The numbered items in the left hand column are examples of figures of speech, and the terms in the right hand column are the names of figures of speech. From the list of figures of speech, select the letter representing the figure of speech which is illustrated and write it in the blank next to the example. The figures of speech may be used once, more than once, or not at all.

Examples

____ 1. He ran around the room like a tornado. (C)

____ 2. To err is human; to forgive, divine.—Pope (A)

____ 3. Pleasures are like poppies spread.—Burns (C)

____ 4. All the world's a stage.—Shakespeare (A)

____ 5. At one stride comes the dark.—Coleridge (B)

Figures of Speech

A. Metaphor

B. Personification

C. Simile

■ Multiple Matching Type

Directions: Following is a list of titles of novels. For each novel, identify the author who is listed in the second column by writing the letter in the first of the two blanks next to the title. Identify the author's nationality from the third list by writing the number in the second blank opposite the title. There are more authors than titles, and authors and nationalities may be used once, more than once, or not at all.

Letters	Numbers	Titles	Authors	Nationalities
B	2	Brighton Rock	A. M. Atwood	1. American
A	3	Cat's Eye	B. G. Greene	2. British
F	2	Nineteen Eighty-Four	C. J. Jones	3. Canadian
C	1	Some Came Running	D. J. Kirkwood	
D	1	Some Kind of Hero	E. F. Mowat	
			F. G. Orwell	

Guidelines For Writing Matching Items

1. *Identify the basis for matching in the directions.* Students should have a clear understanding of how the matching is to be performed. The task is to match the responses to the premises. In the following example the teacher would like the student to match the game with the action where the latter most often occurs.

■ Examples

Poor:

Directions: Identify the game. Write the number on the line next to the action.

Actions	Games
(2) Layup shot	1. Baseball
(1) Line drive	2. Basketball
(4) Slapshot	3. Golf
(3) Slice	4. Hockey
(1) Strike	

Better:

Directions: For the following actions, identify the game in which the action is most likely to be found. Write the number of the game on the line next to the appropriate action. The games can be used once, more than once, or not at all. (The same alternatives as listed above would follow these improved directions.)

2. *Achieve as much homogeneity in the lists as possible.* Homogeneity allows a clear statement of the basis for matching. For instance, the previous example about authors and their books is restricted to novels rather than reference works and novels. Homogeneous as compared to heterogeneous lists demand finer discriminations to determine the correct answer and, therefore, are more difficult.

3. *Place the shorter items on the right and label each column.* Direct students to select answers from the right hand column. Since the lists will be read several times, labels are important when time is at a premium.

4. *Organize the list in some logical order.* A logical order will reduce the search time and avoid unnecessary errors. Numerical values arranged in order of magnitude, terms listed alphabetically, and dates arranged chronologically illustrate appropriate arrangements.

5. *Limit the length of the list.* Homogeneity will force brevity upon the test constructor. Another argument in favor of short rather than long matching items is that excessively long lists may produce errors due to extraneous variables such as clerical aptitude. For the primary grades, four or five items are sufficient. For the upper elementary, five to seven item lists are acceptable. Matching questions for secondary students should be limited to about ten items.

6. *Create an imperfect match.* Construct a different number of premises as compared to responses. Since this prevents students from achieving one mark by the process of elimination, points will not be given away.

Advantages and Disadvantages of Matching Items

The ability to associate the basic facts and generalizations in a discipline is a fundamental intellectual skill. Linking historical personages with events and dates, identifying the capital of a country, associating rules with problem situations exemplify the challenges commonly faced. Since these associations may be created within matching questions, this type of item examines the way students normally apply information.

Matching items are not without difficulties. Achieving within-list homogeneity is problematical, although thorough knowledge of the subject matter, as always, helps. On the surface it may appear as if these items are confined to testing lower level, intellectual skills, but classification type, matching questions may require students to use rather than just recognize knowledge. Finally, since matching items by their nature cover several elements of the same subject, they may restrict sampling validity of a test.

Short-Answer Items

The short-answer item is usually classified as an objective type item even though objectivity in scoring can be difficult. The three kinds of short-answer items, the question, completion and association types, are illustrated in the following examples:

■ **Examples**

Question type:
    1. **What is the name of the capital city of Texas?**
       <u>Austin</u>

Sentence completion type:
    2. **The name of the capital city of Texas is <u>Austin</u>.**

Association type:
    3. **In the blank following each city write the name of the province of Canada for which the city is the capital.**
       Victoria (<u>British Columbia</u>)
       Edmonton (<u>Alberta</u>)
       Regina (<u>Saskatchewan</u>)

The association type, also known as the identification variety, is the only one of the three requiring any further explanation. Briefly, it consists of a series of related short-answer items with common instructions.

Guidelines for Writing Short-Answer Items

1. *In general, the question form of the short-answer item leads to a more unambiguous statement of the problem.* It is easier for the beginning item writer to use questions rather than incomplete statements. In formulating questions, problems are often clarified. Moreover, students find questions a natural form in that they frequently answer teachers' questions in class.

2. *Avoid the use of too many blanks.* An item which is perforated with blanks becomes unintelligible. Therefore, restrict the number of blanks to the omission of one or two key words.

■ **Examples**

Poor: 1. If the number of _____ factors in a series of multiplications is _____, the final product is _____.

Improved: 2. If the number of negative factors in a series of multiplications is even, what form does the final product take? (<u>positive</u>).

In the first version, the student could answer positive or negative for the last blank depending on whether or not the answer to the second was odd or even. The improved version omits only the most important term. A student who is capable of correctly filling in this blank would have demonstrated knowledge of the rule.

3. *Phrase the statement so that the blank appears at the end.* When the blank appears at the end of the statement, the student's attention is directed to the meaning of the question. There is less likelihood of ambiguity and confusion as the following examples show:

■ **Examples**

Poor: 1. The final product is (<u>negative</u>) where the number of factors in a series of multiplications is odd.

Improved: 2. If the number of negative factors in the series of multiplications is odd, the final product is (<u>negative</u>).

In the examples above, the second version outlines the problem before asking for a response, a condition which helps the student understand what is required.

4. *Provide plenty of space for the answer.* If the student is asked to provide a short phrase or sentence in answering a question, sufficient space should be available. Blanks of the same length do not allow the amount of space provided for the answer to be a clue to the correct response.

5. *Where mathematical or measurement problems are posed, specify the precision and form required.* For mathematical and measurement problems, students should be told the form required in the answer. Since it is the case that there are many equivalent forms in mathematics and measurement (e.g., 0.5 equals 1/2), an indication of the form and precision demanded simply further specifies the nature of the problem: it does not reveal the answer.

■ Example

Poor:	1.	What is the area of a surface three foot six inches long by two foot six inches wide? (1260 square inches? 8.75 square feet?)
Improved:	2.	What is the area in square inches of a surface whose dimensions are three foot six inches by two foot six inches? (1260 square inches)

Avoid irrelevant hints. Test writers should avoid hints such as giving the first letter of a word at the beginning of a blank. This may be a useful teaching technique in the context of programmed instruction where incomplete statements are used, but it is out of place in a test question such as the following:

■ Example

Poor:	1.	What Canadian city was the host to "Expo 86?" *V*(ancouver)
Improved:	2.	What Canadian city was the host to "Expo 86?" (Vancouver)

The clue in the first version would encourage blind guessing.

Advantages and Disadvantages of Short-Answer Items

Short-answer items have several strengths. First, since the examinee supplies the answer as compared to other objective type questions such as multiple-choice items which are recognition tasks, blind guessing is less of a problem. Second, short-answer items are well suited to mathematics and the sciences where computational work is required. Rather than working backwards from an answer supplied, for example, in a multiple-choice item, the examinees when responding to a short-answer question must work out the answer without the help of several choices. Students actually have to produce an answer. Third, short-answer items are well suited to assessing reading vocabulary in any language.

There are at least two main disadvantages of short-answer items. Lack of scoring objectivity may present problems of bias: judgment is required to determine the value of divergent answers from students. In addition, limited as they are to brief responses, exclusive use of short-answer questions may lead teachers to emphasize lower level intellectual skills, particularly in nonmathematical areas, with the result that rote learning may be promoted. While short-answer items may lack versatility and efficiency in measuring a broad spectrum of achievement, teachers are likely to continue testing with this familiar format, especially for computational and vocabulary skills.

■ Summary and Main Points

Item writing is a learned skill which improves with guided practice. It is not enough to know the students or to understand a discipline, teachers when constructing tests must apply the methodology of item writing. After presenting general guidelines for writing objective items, suggestions for composing alternate-response, matching and short-answer items were outlined. The following list contains the main points of the chapter, beginning with the general guidelines:

1. Construct items which are at an appropriate level of difficulty for the ability of the examinees.
2. Consider the purpose of the test when constructing test items.
3. Test for important outcomes.
4. Keep items independent of one another.
5. Items should be free from extraneous sources of difficulty.
6. Express problems in clear, concise language.
7. Avoid using the language of the students' textbooks.
8. Avoid clues to the correct answer, including stereotypic expressions, excessive elaboration of the correct alternative, repetition of words in the stem and correct answer, and specific determiners.
9. Include only one correct answer.
10. After a rest period, edit items with a view to eliminating errors which include: mistakenly designating a response as correct when it is not the best alternative, incorporating inappropriately easy or difficult items, ambiguous expression, weak alternatives, and trivial items.
11. Alternate-response items ask students to distinguish between two alternatives such as true-false. Their main purpose is to test students' recognition of the true propositions of a discipline.
12. Guidelines for writing alternate-response items are as follows: (a) Construct these items in pairs, one right and the other wrong. (b) True–false items should be written so that they are either wholly true or false. (c) Include more false than true statements, and vary the number of true and false items across tests. (d) Items should contain only one main idea. (e) Avoid negative statements.
13. The advantages of alternative-response items are that they are relatively easier to construct than other forms such as the multiple-choice type and that greater coverage of the content can be achieved. The main disadvantage is that they are subject to guessing, but guessing based on partial knowledge of the subject is generally to be encouraged.
14. The task in matching items is the linkage of parts of one list with those of another according to directions.
15. Guidelines for writing matching items are as follows: (a) Identify the basis of the task in the directions. (b) Seek homogeneity within each list. (c) Place the shorter elements on the right and label each column. (d) Order the lists logically. (e) Limit the length of the lists from five to ten items. (f) Create an imperfect match by making one list longer than the other.
16. A major advantage of matching items is that the task corresponds to the way knowledge is applied, by associating, for example, an instance of a concept with its concept. Two disadvantages are that achieving homogeneity within lists is difficult and because they link several elements of the same topic, matching items tend to restrict the sampling validity of a test.
17. Three kinds of short-answer items are the question, completion, and association types.

18. Construct short-answer items according to the following suggestions: (a) To reduce ambiguity use the question type of short-answer item. (b) Avoid too many blanks. (c) The blank should appear at the end of the statement. (d) Provide adequate space for the answer. (e) In mathematical and measurement problems, specify the precision and units required. (f) Avoid irrelevant clues.

19. The strengths of the short-answer item are that: guessing is less of a problem because the student supplies the answer, they are well suited to problems where computation is required, and they are useful for testing vocabulary. Two weaknesses are that objectivity in scoring may be difficult to achieve and lower level cognitive activities may be emphasized.

◼ Further Readings

Ahmann, J. S., & Glock, M. D. (1975). *Evaluating pupil growth* (5th ed.). Boston: Allyn and Bacon.

Bloom, B. (Ed.). (1956). *Taxonomy of educational objectives, handbook 1: Cognitive domain.* New York: Longmans.

Ebel, R. L., & Frisbie, D. A. (1986). *Essentials of educational measurement* (4th ed.). Englewood Cliffs, NJ: Prentice-Hall.

Hopkins, K. D. & Stanley, J. C. (1981). *Educational and psychological measurement and evaluation* (6th ed.). Englewood Cliffs, NJ: Prentice-Hall.

Popham, W. J. (1981). *Modern educational measurement.* Englewood Cliffs, NJ: Prentice-Hall.

Thorndike, R. L. (Ed.). (1971). *Educational measurement* (2nd ed.). Washington: American Council on Education.

◼ Laboratory Exercises

Before completing the following exercises, choose a subject that you know well, list the main ideas of the subject, write instructional objectives for this content, and review the guidelines for constructing each type of item.

1. Construct five items of each of the true-false, fact-opinion, right-wrong and correction variety alternate-response questions.
2. Create one multiple matching type and one classification matching question.
3. Formulate five examples of each of the questions, completion, and association types of short-answer questions.
4. After at least one day has elapsed, edit all of the items created in this exercise.
5. Following a review of the items by a colleague, discuss the results with a view to reaching a consensus about how to improve the questions.

Chapter

Item Construction: Objective Items II, Multiple-Choice Questions

Overview

Multiple-choice items are probably the most frequently used objective test questions, but without careful construction they become trying experiences for both teachers and students. Students are frustrated by defective examination questions and this frustration may cause strained teacher-pupil relationships. The goal in constructing multiple-choice items is to have knowledgeable students select the correct answer, and at the same time to foil those who misunderstand the subject. When developing multiple-choice items, avoid ambiguity and trick questions. Various forms of the multiple-choice item may challenge examinees: the correct answer, best answer, and multiple answer types as well as the interpretive exercise are described in this chapter. We outline general guidelines for writing multiple-choice items and appropriate examples demonstrate their application. Special consideration is given to questions that contain pictorial material. We discuss advantages and disadvantages, and compare the multiple-choice format to other item types.

General Characteristics

The multiple-choice item's broad applicability makes it a highly popular test question. Skilled item writers create multiple-choice questions that measure achievement at the higher levels of cognition (thought that requires skills in analysis, synthesis or evaluation) as well as the lower levels such as comprehension. The multiple-choice item may be written for almost any subject matter, and teachers find this breadth of application highly attractive. While there are a number of variations of the multiple-choice item, it usually consists of a stem and several alternatives. The incorrect options are often referred to as distracters, but they may also be called foils, misleads, or decoys. Figure 5.1 summarizes the parts of a multiple choice item.

Distracters range in number from three to five with three being the most popular. The probability of guessing the correct answer decreases as the number of options increases.

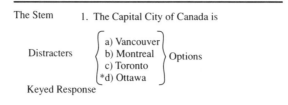

The Stem   1. The Capital City of Canada is

Distracters
- a) Vancouver
- b) Montreal
- c) Toronto
- *d) Ottawa

Keyed Response

Options

1. The stem presents the problem

2. The keyed response is the "right answer" or the one on the key that indicates the correct choice.

3. Distracters seem like reaonable answers to the examinee who doesn't know the content.

4. Options include the distracters and keyed-response.

Figure 5.1 Parts of a multiple-choice item

Nevertheless, two distracters seem to be as effective as three or more (e.g., Neidermeyer & Sullivan, 1972). Each distracter should attract examinees who do not know the answer to the question. Distracters which are not selected should be dropped from subsequent versions of the item. It is more important to have effective distracters than a uniform number of distracters throughout a particular test. Ineffective distracters obviously lower the quality of a test and waste valuable testing time. If effective distracters cannot be written, then it is probable that the question should be rephrased or deleted from the item pool.

Extrinsic and Intrinsic Ambiguity

In constructing multiple-choice items, try to build extrinsic ambiguity into the item and avoid intrinsic ambiguity. An item which has extrinsic ambiguity would seem ambiguous to the student who has faulty or inadequate knowledge. Extrinsic ambiguity is a desirable item quality, especially for measuring higher level achievement. Intrinsic ambiguity, on the other hand, should be avoided. Intrinsic ambiguity arises not from misunderstanding the subject, but from imprecise wording, inadequate framing of the items, indistinct distracters, and so forth. Ambiguity which arises from a poorly written item is intrinsic—it is "inside" the item. When ambiguity is extrinsic, it is "outside" the item. That is, the item's so-called ambiguity originates from the examinee's lack of proper comprehension of the course content. The following item has high extrinsic ambiguity:

■ **Example**

   1. Which of the following characteristics is shared by both objective tests and essay tests? They
- **a. are efficient for measuring knowledge of specific facts.**
- ***b. can measure complex achievement.**
- **c. provide for extensive sampling of content.**
- **d. have reliability of scoring.**

As mentioned, poorly worded items, ambiguous wording requiring discriminations among the options that are too fine, or "trick questions" can all lead to intrinsic ambiguity.

The following items illustrate intrinsic ambiguity:

■ **Examples**

1. **In the normal curve, the proportion of area that falls within one standard deviation of the mean is**
   a. .6811
   *b. .6826
   c. .6858
   d. .6873

2. **The Renaissance is generally thought to have begun in**
   *a. Florence
   b. Milan
   c. Rome
   d. Venice

Both of the items above require discriminations that are so fine that even knowledgeable people would have difficulty. Below is an item that has intrinsic ambiguity because it is a "trick question."

3. **If you bought two ice cream cones each costing 20¢, how much change should you receive from a dollar?**
   a. .50¢
   b. .60¢
   c. .70¢
   *d. None of the above

Generally, carefully planned, well-written items avoid intrinsic ambiguity but have extrinsic ambiguity. Ultimately, the best way to determine the degree of extrinsic ambiguity is to analyze student responses to the item as described in the item analysis section of Chapter 10.

Multiple-Choice Item Types

The multiple-choice item takes various forms: correct answer, best answer, multiple answer, and the interpretive exercise. Other types may be created as demonstrated by Wesman (1971), for example, who illustrated eight different kinds. Research shows that students prefer the standard correct or best answer form of multiple-choice items as compared to the other types (Aiken, 1987).

The correct answer type. As the title indicates, there is but one answer to this multiple-choice type.

■ **Example**

Directions: **For each question select the correct response by circling the letter of your choice.**

1. **What city is the capital of Oregon?**
   a. Oregon City
   b. Portland
   *c. Salem
   d. Springfield

The best answer form. With this type the examinees choose the alternative closest to being the best answer. That is, the students select the response which is most nearly correct from a list of partially right alternatives.

■ **Example**

Directions: For each question select the best alternative by circling the letter of your choice.
1. In the following sentences which placement of the word "only" is most appropriate?
   a. Ken told his friend that he only needed two hours.
   b. Ken told his friend that he needed two hours only.
   *c. Ken told his friend that he needed only two hours.

The multiple answer type. There is more than one correct or best answer to this form of the multiple-choice question.

■ **Example**

Directions: The following questions have more than one right answer. For each question, select the correct answers by circling the letters of your choice.
1. In which of the following sentences does a dangling gerund appear?
   *a. After patting me on the back, I was not promoted.
   b. After hitting the ball, I was called back.
   *c. After telling me off, the boss asked me to get back to work.

The interpretive exercise. The interpretive exercise is a versatile item type. It usually begins with the presentation of information in verbal, tabular or graphic form which is the basis of one or more multiple-choice questions. The interpretive exercise may challenge students at various levels of thinking. For example, students may be asked to recognize instances of a principle, resolve formulas, analyze communications, integrate disparate elements into a cohesive whole, or evaluate the worth of a product. The interpretive exercise is readily adapted to the assessment of the important outcomes of most disciplines. Creative test writers produce a wide range of tasks that are well suited to this format. The following two examples illustrate interpretive exercises.

■ **Example**

Directions: The following questions are based on the map of the imaginary place called Taurus. Select the best alternative for each question.
1. What is the location of Weston?
   (a) 135°N.; 54°W.
   (b) 54°S.; 135°E.
   (c) 135°S.; 54°W.
   *(d) 54°N.; 135°W.
2. Which city is most likely to have the highest elevation?
   (a) Core City
   (b) Placer
   *(c) Pit
   (d) Weston

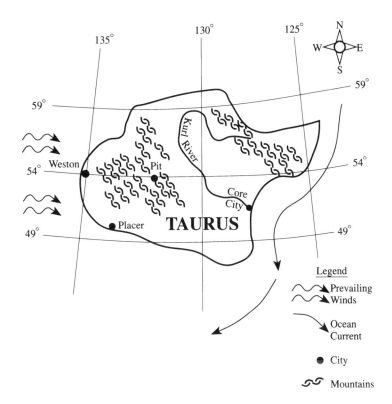

Legend

⌇⌇⌇➤ Prevailing
⌇⌇⌇➤ Winds

➤ Ocean
   Current

● City

ᗩᗡ Mountains

Note: Items 3 and 4 refer to the following paragraph.

A teacher, Ms. Gould, thinks that corporal punishment is an effective way to maintain control in the classroom. She supports her position this way: (1) "Look, I'm no ogre, but it seems to me that we've got to find a way to make these kids behave properly. (2) I've tried everything, timeout, detentions, writing lines—everything. (3) Nothing seems to work! (4) The strap's the only way. (5) The kids are afraid of it and so it'll make them behave. (6) You mark my words, a good strapping would straighten a few of these jokers up."

3. **Which of the following best represents the basic reason for Ms. Gould's belief in the effectiveness of corporal punishment?**
   - (a) "... it seems to me that we've got to find a way to make these kids behave properly." (statement 1).
   - (b) "I've tried everything, ..." (statement 2).
   - (c) "The strap's the only way." (statement 4).
   - *(d) **"The kids are afraid of it and so it'll make them behave." (statement 5).**

4. **Which of the following best illustrates exaggeration in Ms. Gould's argument?**
   - (a) "Look, I'm no ogre ..." (statement 1).
   - (b) "I've tried everything—timeout, detentions, writing lines—everything." (statement 2).
   - (c) "The kids are afraid of it ..." (statement 5).
   - (d) "... a good strapping would straighten a few of these jokers up." (statement 6).

For both of the foregoing interpretive exercises, more questions could be added. With reference to the map, you could, for example, ask about annual rainfall for the cities and natural harbors.

Guidelines for Writing Multiple-Choice Items

Begin writing multiple-choice items by creating the stem, composing the best answer and then formulating the distracters. Writing the stem first saves time because if the problem cannot be clearly stated, then there is obviously no need to continue with the other parts of the question. The best or correct alternative should be written second because it forms the basis for developing the distracters. Moreover, if a correct alternative cannot be devised, then it is pointless to create distracters.

The following guidelines develop consistency in item characteristics. However, a review of the research literature related to thcsc guidelines leads to the tentative conclusion that measurement of achievement by multiple-choice items tends to be strong even with violations of the guidelines (Aiken, 1987).

1. State the Stem in the Form of a Question

The interrogative form is a natural way of expressing test items. Since a question encourages you to formulate a specific problem, extraneous details are eliminated. Moreover, incomplete statements sometimes confuse examinees. A question, on the other hand, will more likely be meaningful on its own so that students will understand the nature of the problem. Results from empirical investigations (Dudycha & Carpenter, 1973; Violato & Harasym, 1987; Violato & Marini, 1989) support the notion that closed stems (questions) are less difficult than open stems (incomplete statements). Violato's (1991) recent study contradicts this conclusion emphasizing, thereby, the robustness of the multiple-choice item regardless of the stem construction.

■ **Example**

    Weak: 1. **Sri Lanka**
                a. **is south of Australia.**
                b. **has Thailand as its nearest neighbor.**
                c. **is located in the Pacific Ocean.**
                d. **is located in the Indian Ocean.**
  Improved: 2. **In which of the following is Sri Lanka located?**
                a. **Arctic Ocean**
                b. **Atlantic Ocean**
                c. **Indian Ocean**
                d. **Pacific Ocean**

The improved version of the preceding item states a definite problem. The interrogative statement directs the teacher to construct more homogeneous alternatives. With greater homogeneity, the quality of the item is improved, and it becomes more difficult because the student must distinguish between alternatives that are highly similar.

2. Place Most of the Subject Matter in the Stem

It is desirable that as much content as possible be placed in the stem of an item. This ensures that the stem contains a full statement of the problem. Moreover, longer stems create the possibility of shorter alternatives thereby facilitating the students' reading of the question. While it may be impossible to meet this guideline for every item, you should strive to achieve it for most items.

3. Eliminate Extraneous Material from the Stem

It is sometimes tempting to include an instructional aside in the stem. Since the objective of assessment is to measure students' achievement, do not include instructional material in stems. The time required to read the information would be better spent in answering more test questions. The example which follows illustrates the point.

■ **Example**

Poor:　1.　**The earth has seven continents. We live on North America. What is the name of the continent where China is located?**
　　　　　a.　**Africa**
　　　*b.　**Asia**
　　　　c.　**Europe**
　　　　d.　**South America**

Improved:　2.　**What is the name of the continent where China is located?**
　　　　　a.　**Africa**
　　　*b.　**Asia**
　　　　c.　**Europe**
　　　　d.　**South America**

The first two sentences of the stem in the initial version are extraneous to the purpose of the test question, and their deletion reduces the time required to read the stem. What remains is a straightforward, knowledge level question.

4. Avoid Negatively Phrased Stems

Students are sometimes confused by a negative statement which they would otherwise understand. Many students feel stress during examinations, and with stress come errors. The errors resulting from a negative qualifier reduce test validity.

There may be subject matter where it might me argued that the elimination of what not to do is important. For instance, in driver education it would seem advisable from one perspective to let trainees know what not to do as well as what to do. It could also be argued, however, that it is better to show student drivers the proper way to drive rather than the wrong way. An item with a negative stem and a positive alternative are illustrated in the following examples.

Focus on Research

Research into the effects of stem orientation has yielded inconsistent results. Some findings suggest that negatively stated stems increase the difficulty of items whereas other results contradict this conclusion. Dudycha and Carpenter (1973) showed that negatively stated stems were more difficult. Studies by Huttenlocher (1962), Wason (1961), and Zern (1967) all support Dudycha and Carpenter's findings. More recently, however, studies by Violato and Harasym (1987) and Violato and Marini (1989) do not support the inference that negatively stated stems affect item difficulty. The

earlier work, moreover, was not without flaws. For example, Violato and Marini criticized Dudycha and Carpenter for compounding the effects of stem orientation by altering the options. This problem would make it difficult to determine whether negative stem orientation was the cause of increased item difficulty. Apparently, as McMorris, Brown, Snyder and Pruzek (1972) have stated, the effectiveness of multiple-choice questions is not easily affected by violations of item writing guidelines, especially those items containing negatives.

■ **Example**

Poor: 1. When changing lanes in traffic, which of the following procedures should not be done?
   a. Look ahead, to the side and to the rear for an acceptable break in traffic.
   *b. Begin turning before signaling the intention to move right or left.
   c. Examine the blind spots in the direction of the lane change.
   d. Turn into the desired lane while adjusting speed to the flow of traffic.

Improved: 2. When changing lanes in traffic, all of the following procedures should be accomplished *except*
   a. look ahead, to the side and to the rear for an acceptable break in traffic.
   *b. begin turning before signaling the intention to move right or left.
   c. examine the blind spots in the direction of the lane change.
   d. turn into the desired lane while adjusting speed to the flow of traffic.

The improved version eliminates the negative qualification and draws attention to the irregularity through italics. Moreover, the reference to an exception is placed at the end of the stem.

Results from empirical investigations of the effects of negatively as compared to positively stated stems are inconclusive. Earlier findings indicated that negative stems were more difficult, but later results threw doubt on this conclusion. Focus 5.1 discusses this issue at greater length.

5. Ensure Similarity among the Alternate Answers in Grammatical Structure, Content, Length and Mode of Expression

Grammatical errors provide unintentional clues to the answer. The following illustration portrays inconsistent grammatical structure.

■ Example

Poor: 1. What is the shape and location of the great cordilleran belts? The cordilleran belts form
  a. disconnected sets of lengths around the Pacific Ocean.
  *b. a connected ring nearly all around the Pacific Ocean and spreading westward across Southern Asia and Southern Europe.
  c. fan out across the earth's surface in a random fashion.

Improved: 2. What is the shape and location of the great cordilleran belts? The cordilleran belts form
  a. disconnected sets of lengths around the Pacific Ocean and spread eastward towards southern Africa.

  *b. a connected ring nearly all around the Pacific Ocean and spread westward across southern Asia and Southern Europe.
  c. randomly distributed short lengths of mountains on the continents and the ocean floors.

The first version lacks parallel structure between the stem and the alternatives as well as among the alternatives. Sentence length and structure are inconsistent in the first item. The improved version does not supply the student with these structural clues to the answer.

6. With the Exception of the Multiple Answer Form, Make One of the Alternatives the Most Clearly Correct or Best Answer

At times an item will be written which mistakenly contains two correct answers. Needless to say, students will be frustrated when they attempt to answer this sort of a question, and as a consequence the teacher's credibility will suffer. A careful rereading of the test questions before they are used will help eliminate the problem.

■ Example

Poor: 1. Which of the following contains an elliptical sentence?
  a. Whose bike is this? Tony's.
  b. Thank you for the loan of your car.
  *c. Gretzky plays forward, Coffey, defence.
  d. Hoping to see you before December 1st.

Improved: 2. Which of the following contains an elliptical sentence?
  *a. Whose bike is this? Tony's.
  b. Thank you for the loan of your car.
  c. Gretzky plays forward, while Coffey plays the defence position.
  d. Hoping to see you before December 1st.

In the first version there are two elliptical sentences, alternatives "a" and "c;" the improved version has only one.

7. Make the Distracters Plausible

To be effective, distracters should be plausible which means that they must attract students who really do not know the answer to the question. There are several guidelines that will help the item writer produce likely alternatives (Ebel & Frizbie, 1986; Gronlund, 1985). (a) For any particular concept, there is usually a universe of alternatives which might be identified. Suppose, for example, that the question calls for the recognition of a specific topographic feature associated with glaciation. Given this situation, the item writer's task is to include other features of glaciation as distracters. (b) Items containing numbers might have distracters which represent separate points on the same scale as the correct answer. For instance, if a date of a particular event is in the 19th century, then the distracters would as well be drawn from the eighteen hundreds. (c) Create distracters from elements of the correct response. The correct answer to a question might be "fourth and fifth," and the distracters could be: "Third and fourth," "fourth, fifth and sixth," and "fifth and sixth." (d) Teachers usually are well aware of the kinds of mistakes students make in a subject, and these errors can be incorporated into the distracters. (e) Common expressions or standard ways of stating a principle may be used to attract uninformed examinees. A student who blindly guesses at the answer to a question may be attracted by a familiar sounding, but erroneous phrase. Do not trick the knowledgeable student into making errors, rather the intention is to distract those who really do not understand the problem posed by the item.

8. Avoid Parallel Language between the Stem and the Correct Response

Key words which appear in the stem and the correct answer will cue students to choose the right alternative. This parallelism invalidates the item as a measure of achievement. The problem is illustrated in the following items.

■ **Example**

Poor: **Which of the following associations are major subdivisions of plants?**
      a. **luxuriant growth**
    *b. **grassland associations**
      c. **semi-arid region**
      d. **vertical stratification**

Improved: **Which of the following associations are major subdivisions of plants?**
      a. **luxuriant growth**
    *b. **grassland**
      c. **semi-arid region**
      d. **vertical stratification**

The intended correct answer to both versions is the second alternative. In the first version, the word "associations" appears in both the stem and the correct alternative which is a clue to the right answer. The second version has eliminated this clue.

9. In Any Given Item, the Correct Answer Should be Randomly Distributed across the Alternative Positions

There is a tendency for inexperienced item writers "to hide" the correct answer in the middle of the list of alternatives: That is, they place it in positions "b" or "c" of a list of four alternatives. Being aware of this tendency, the testwise student who is unsure of the correct answer would tend to guess that one of these positions contains the correct answer. A solution to this problem is to arrange the alternatives in some logical order such as alphabetically for verbal material, and ascending or descending order for numerical data. Another approach is to write the letters a, b, c, and d, on separate, equal-sized cards, drop them in a hat, and shuffle them. To select the position of the correct answer for a particular item, randomly select a card from the hat.

Focus on Students

Testwiseness helps students answer examination questions, especially the multiple-choice item. Testwise students use test-taking techniques to correctly answer questions that they are uncertain about. This is not cheating. It is simply a fact of life at school: some students are better at writing examinations than others. This emphasizes the need to construct items that are as free from flaws as possible. Beyond this, all students should be given instruction in the techniques of writing examinations so that they will have an equal chance of scoring well. That is, testwiseness is a learned skill that can be taught. As noted in the previous chapter, the methodology of item construction is the basis for teaching testwiseness. Clever students notice errors of construction and other item characteristics which they use to discover the answers to questions that they might otherwise miss. Analysis of how a testwise student might produce an answer to the following two multiple-choice items illustrates the process:

Examples

1. Which of the following individuals is a behavioral psychologist?
   a. I. P. Pavlov
   b. B. F. Skinner
   c. J. B. Watson
   d. J. Wolpe
   e. all of the above

2. The Thematic Apperception Test is a
   a. abilities test
   b. inductive reasoning test
   c. intelligence test
   d. projective test

The first item illustrates analysis of a test question when "all of the above" is an option, and when the examinee is certain that at least two of the alternatives are correct. These conditions help students choose "all of the above." Even though they may be uncertain about one of the options, say, Wolpe, testwise examinees knowing that at least two of the psychologists are behaviorists would select the last alternative. The second item shows inconsistent grammatical structure between the stem and three of the alternatives: "a, b," and "c" which leads to the conclusion that option "d" is correct (Weitten, 1983).

10. Use the Alternatives ''All of the Above'' and ''None of the Above'' Sparingly

When there are several equally good answers to a question, it is tempting to list them, and then to include the alternative "all of the above." But this option is problematic. For example, whenever more than one of the alternatives is correct, the testwise student will select "all of the above" as the correct answer. Since not all of the alternatives need to be considered, the student may have arrived at the correct answer with perhaps only partial knowledge. Hence, the alternative "all of the above" should be avoided. See Focus 5.2.

When there is an absolutely correct answer to a question such as in a spelling test or an arithmetic test, it may seem appropriate to use the alternative "none of the above." But achievement in spelling and arithmetic as Gronlund (1985) points out, would more appropriately be

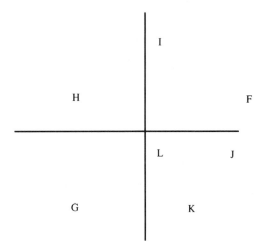

assessed by short-answer questions. The recognition of wrong answers in spelling and arithmetic seems to be an inadequate assessment.

Guidelines for Creating Pictorial, Multiple-Choice Items

Ahmann and Glock (1975) offer several suggestions for writing pictorial items. Although they appear here in the context of multiple-choice items, the guidelines may be generalized to any type of question which requires students to respond to graphics.

1. *Pictorial material should be included only when it is the best way to express the question.* In an introductory course on descriptive statistics, students learn about how correlation describes relations between variables. Since correlation is often illustrated graphically, students must learn the Cartesian rectangular co-ordinate system. This system is effectively represented by a drawing. The following item asks students to identify the parts of a graph.

■ **Example**

Directions: The drawing above represents the rectangular coordinate system for graphing relations between variables. Each part of the graph is identified by a letter. For each of the questions following the graph, identify the correct answer.

    1. **Which quadrant is represented by the letter G?**
        a. **Quadrant 1**
        b. **Quadrant 2**
      *c. **Quadrant 3**
        d. **Quadrant 4**

Other questions would ask for the identification of various parts of a graph such as the abscissa and origin.

2. *The graphics should be as simple as possible and still accurately represent the objects.* For example, the questions below which require identification of different types of fish hooks are simple, yet effective representations of the various hook types.

■ Example

1. Which of the following drawings depicts a sliced shank hook?[1]

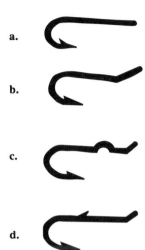

a.

b.

c.

d.

2. Which of the following drawings shows a snecked hook pattern? (Views are from the bottom.)

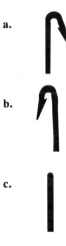

a.

b.

c.

3. *For clarity, include additional notes explaining the meaning of drawings.* Not all diagrams require explanatory notes, but some will be ambiguous without them. For instance, the drawings in the first question on fish hooks do not require further explanation, whereas the clarity of the second question is enhanced by the parenthetical explanation ("Views are from the

1. Drawings are adapted from Fly Tying and Tackle: Manual and Manufacturers' Guide (pp. 38 and 39) by G. L. Herter, 1953, Waseca, MN: Brown.

bottom.'') added immediately following the stem. The purpose of the second question is to measure students understanding of hook patterns. But without the additional note, this purpose may be foiled by student misunderstanding of the viewing angle of the drawing.

4. *The question should be closely connected to the pictorial material.* Directions, as illustrated in the question about the rectangular co-ordinate system, help set the context for the questions and the related pictorial material. Moreover, the graphic element of a test should be placed in close proximity to the related items. Suppose, for example, that several items on a geography test refer to a map. The map should appear on the page opposite to the questions. In this way, the map remains in front of the students while they read the items.

Advantages of the Multiple-Choice Item

The multiple-choice item is popular because it has many strengths. (a) It may assess achievement at any level of sophistication. That is, not only is the recall of specific facts assessed, but higher order cognitive skills such as the application and analysis of ideas may be examined. Indeed, the multiple-choice item is highly versatile: it may be used in almost any grade and with all subjects. (b) Multiple-choice items are objectively scored. It should be kept in mind, however, that judgment is involved in the selection of the correct answer during item construction. (c) The best answer form of multiple-choice questions lends itself well to assessment in disciplines such as social studies and language arts where a range of possible answers is available, rather than the existence of only one correct answer. (d) Through the analysis of the selection of options, multiple-choice items help teachers discover where students are having difficulties. This diagnosis is possible, in part, because plausible distracters indicative of common misunderstandings may be developed by knowledgeable teachers. There are other advantages, and these are discussed in a subsequent section which compares multiple-choice questions to other item types.

Disadvantages of the Multiple-Choice Item

The multiple-choice item, not being the perfect test question, has a number of disadvantages. (a) Clarity of expression in the construction of item stems is not easily obtained. While the guidelines described in earlier sections of this and the previous chapter will help, they are no substitutes for well-developed writing skills. (b) Teachers have crowded schedules, and since multiple-choice items are time consuming to construct, other less time-consuming items such as the alternate-response forms remain attractive. The mixing of item types—including some short answer and completion items along with multiple-choice questions—in any given test will relieve time pressure during test construction. (c) Effective items, particularly those assessing higher levels of cognitive activity such as analysis, require much item writing skill and diligence. (d) Anyone who has discussed the results of a test with students will realize that certain individuals, perhaps those with subtle minds, have difficulty choosing the best option. Since they often read much more into a question than was intended by the examiner or seen by their less astute peers, some students appear to be penalized for this subtlety by selecting the ''wrong'' option. The empirical support for this contention is ambiguous. For example, Aiken (1987) describes a study by Alker, Carlson and Herman (1969) of the relationship between achievement on multiple-choice tests and a number of characteristics that are normally related to profound thinking such as creativity. Confirmatory results showed that testwiseness was positively related to achievement. But disconfirmatory findings showed among other things that creativity was not significantly related to measures of verbal ability. (e) Multiple-choice items may have low face validity. Many people believe that in order to test what a student "really" knows, a free-response or constructed response type item such as the essay is needed. Even though this is not true as we have seen, this belief by many that multiple-choice items measure little more than rote learning, may affect student motivation on the test and negatively affect their attitude towards the class generally. (f) Multiple-choice items, like any pencil-and-paper test, are inappropriate for measuring learning outcomes which require skilled performance. If the learning outcome requires an interpretive dance, for example, clearly pencil-and-paper assessment is inappropriate.

Comparison of multiple-choice questions with other item types. Aiken (1987) in reviewing the empirical literature that compares multiple-choice items with other forms, concluded that multiple-choice questions, despite their disadvantages, are likely to be used increasingly more frequently. Compared to alternate-response items such as true–false questions, multiple-choice items are usually more reliable. But the alternate-response item is easier to construct and more of them can be completed during any particular testing period which gives them an advantage in content coverage. Essay, matching and short answer test questions are less versatile than the multiple-choice item. However, if the purpose is to promote retention of concepts, short-answer rather than multiple-choice items seem to be best. Reliability of the multiple-choice question is not always greater than the short answer item.

The multiple-choice test has replaced the essay question as the most popular test form. Two reasons for this situation are the difficulty of marking essay questions, and their relatively low reliability. Even though students think that they can bluff their way to higher marks, scores tend to be lower on essay tests. Aiken notes that the frequent use of the multiple-choice format has been blamed for the apparent recent decline of students' verbal skills, but he does not describe research to support this observation. Diagnosis of students' answers to essay tests may reveal strengths and weaknesses (e.g., the ability to organize a coherent response) that would go unnoticed by an analysis of answers to multiple-choice questions. (See Chapter 6 for further comparisons.)

■ Summary and Main Points

When it is poorly constructed, the popular multiple-choice item earns the derision of students who sometimes refer to bad examples as "multiple-guess" questions. Fortunately, careful adherence to the principles and practices summarized in the following list may help test makers avoid some of the more obvious errors.

1. The common variety of multiple-choice item consists of a stem stated in the interrogative form followed by a list of three to five alternatives.
2. The incorrect alternatives are usually called distracters, and they are intended to attract examinees who do not understand the subject.
3. Items that have extrinsic ambiguity, that is, those questions that are attractive to students with a poor grasp of the subject, are desirable but trick and flawed items, or those with intrinsic ambiguity, are obviously undesirable.
4. Multiple-choice items take various forms: (a) The correct answer type has only one answer. (b) The best answer form requires examinees to select the most nearly correct option. (c) The multiple answer type provides more than one right answer to the question.

(d) The interpretive exercise asks students to analyze a passage or graphic by posing one or more multiple-choice questions based on the material presented.

5. Suggestions for writing multiple-choice items are as follows: (a) Write the stem first, then compose the correct answer and finally develop the distracters. (b) State the stem in the form of a question. (c) Include as much of the content as possible in the stem. (d) Exclude nonessential material from the stem. (e) State the stem in the positive rather than the negative form. (f) Compose alternatives that are as similar as possible on relevant characteristics such as content, length and grammatical structure. (g) Except for the multiple answer type, make one alternative clearly correct. (h) Develop plausible distracters. (i) Avoid common elements such as the same words in the stem and the correct answer. (j) Throughout the test, randomly locate the keyed response among all the possible alternative positions. (k) Minimize the use of the alternatives "all of the above" and "none of the above."

6. Guidelines for constructing pictorial multiple-choice items are as follows: (a) Include pictorial material only when it is the best way to express the question. (b) Use simple graphics. (c) Explain graphics with additional notes. (d) Closely relate the question to the pictorial material.

7. Advantages of the multiple-choice item are: (a) All levels of cognition may be assessed. (b) Objectivity of scoring is present. (c) The best answer form adapts well to subjects such as psychology where a range of possible answers may exist for any given problem. (d) Student choices may be analyzed to indicate where they are having problems.

8. Disadvantages of the multiple-choice items are: (a) Clearly written stems are difficult to achieve. (b) Multiple-choice questions are time consuming to construct. (c) To create this type of item, much skill and diligence are required. (d) While the research findings are mixed, thoughtful students may have difficulty choosing the correct option. (e) Multiple-choice items may have low face validity. (f) They are limited to pencil-and-paper assessment.

9. Multiple-choice items compare favorably with other item types, and increased use is a strong possibility.

■ Further Readings

Ahmann, J. S., & Glock, M. D. (1975). *Evaluating pupil growth* (5th ed.). Boston: Allyn and Bacon.

Bloom, B. (Ed.) (1956). *Taxonomy of educational objectives, handbook I: Cognitive domain.* New York: Longmans.

Ebel, R. L., & Frisbie, D. A. (1986). *Essentials of educational measurement* (4th ed.). Englewood Cliffs, NJ: Prentice-Hall.

Educational Testing Service (1973). *Multiple-choice questions: A close look.* Princeton, NJ: Educational Testing Service.

Thorndike, R. L. (Ed.) (1971). *Educational measurement* (2nd ed.). Washington: American Council on Education.

■ Laboratory Exercises

In a subject you know well, identify the main ideas, list instructional objectives for the subject, and study the guidelines for writing multiple-choice items. With the foregoing material as a basis, complete the following exercises:

1. Construct five of each of the correct answer, best answer, and multiple answer forms of the multiple-choice item.
2. Using at least three different graphics, construct ten multiple-choice items based on these graphics.
3. Create three interpretive exercises.
4. For each of the items in the previous three exercises, identify the level of Bloom's cognitive domain taxonomy. Form a group with three classmates and discuss the statement: multiple-choice items are best suited for testing the lower levels of Bloom's taxonomy.
5. With a group of at least three other classmates, compare and contrast the multiple-choice item with other question formats, including the essay.

Chapter

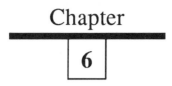

6

Essay Item Construction

Overview

The popularity of essay examinations remains strong, even though other more objective methods of testing have been developed. Undoubtedly, teachers feel comfortable with essay tests because they permit expression of solutions to problems in the students' own words. While this strength continues unchallenged, the assumption that essay tests are easy to construct may create difficulties for you and students. Ambiguous, awkwardly worded essay questions may prevent knowledgeable students from performing well. Clarity of expression is one feature of a well written essay question, and there are others. This chapter reviews the knowledge and skills necessary for proper development of essay questions.

The discussion begins with a description of the general characteristics of essays and essay examinations. The identification of two subtypes of essays, restricted- and extended-response forms, advances understanding of the nature of this important approach to testing. Guidelines present practical suggestions for the effective development of essay questions while the accompanying examples serve as models for implementation of the guidelines. Just as with all other kinds of test questions, essay examinations have strengths and weaknesses, and knowledge of these should help you avoid common pitfalls.

Essays and Essay Examinations

An essay is a written discourse of several interconnected sentences or paragraphs on a particular topic which presents a point of view in the form of a description, argument, or both. Essays are written rather than oral communications: oral communications may be stories, talks or lectures, but they are not essays. Usually an essay has several paragraphs including an introduction, body and conclusion. Some topics require long, complicated answers while others need only brief, simple replies. The essayist provides a point of view supported by descriptive detail and, perhaps, argument.

The essay examination challenges the examinee to compose a written response to a question. Much freedom is permitted and the responses usually vary in merit with no given answer is considered entirely correct (Stalnaker, 1951). Although an answer key may aid the scoring process, judgment about quality is subjectively determined at the time of scoring. Coffman (1971) added that the essay examination is commonly given under standard conditions. For example, the instructions, time and place of writing are uniform for all examinees. This standardization distinguishes the essay test from term papers which permit greater variation in the conditions under which responses are created. In summary, essay examinations are "tests in which respondents are asked to compose written statements, discussions, summaries or descriptions that are to be used as measures of knowledge, understanding, or writing proficiency" (Education Resource Information Centre, 1987, p.82).

Types of Essay Items

There are at least two types of essay questions, the restricted- and extended-response forms. This classification refers to the amount of freedom allowed students in composing their responses. The restricted-response item limits the character and breadth of the students' composition. In this type of essay question, the following conditions are present: the student is directed towards a particular type of answer, the scope of the problem is limited, and the length of the essay is sometimes specified.

■ **Example**

A restricted response essay: **How might Rogers' conditions of significant learning help teachers maintain discipline in the classroom? In answering this question, at least complete the following tasks:**
  a. **briefly describe Rogers' conditions of significant learning;**
  b. **illustrate the use of the conditions of significant learning in maintaining discipline in the classroom.**
The answer should be between one and a half and two pages long.

This example of a restricted-response essay question aims the student at the desired answer. Moreover, the scope of the essay has been circumscribed. As compared to extended essays, restricted-response questions promote greater reliability in scoring. However, they may also reduce the students' opportunity to synthesize disparate information into a coherent whole thereby curtailing divergent thinking.

The extended-response questions place limitations on discussion and the form of the answer. An example of an extended-response essay question is as follows:

■ **Example**

An extended-response essay question: **How might humanistic psychology be used to maintain discipline in the classroom? Illustrate with appropriate classroom examples the application of particular theoretical constructs from humanistic psychology in the maintenance of classroom discipline.**

In answering this essay question, students may select the particular theoretical constructs from humanistic psychology which they deem to be most important and relevant in maintaining discipline in the classroom. This is in contrast to the previous example of a restricted-response question where Rogers' concept of significant learning determined the scope of the discussion. In addition, the form of the extended-response essay remains the responsibility of the student and the length is unspecified.

Other classifications of essay tests exist and Focus 6.1 illustrates one such scheme.

Guidelines for Writing Essay Items

Allow Adequate Time for Construction of Essay Questions

It is unlikely that the first draft of essay questions will be as clear and concise as the writer had intended. Therefore, allow 24 hours or more between drafts so that you may approach the item refreshed. In editing the questions, you should be assured that: appropriate wording has been used, an important objective of the course of studies is being measured, the problem will be seen by the students to be relevant to the course of studies, and the question is one that the students can answer.

Favor Restricted-Response Essay Questions Whenever Possible

There is no doubt that restricted-response essay questions limit the latitude given examinees. However, restricted-response essay questions reduce the ambiguity of the task so that students really do know what is required of them. In stating the question, the item writer can provide a frame of reference by specifying the material covered by the item, providing particular limitations on the response, indicating the minimum number of tasks which should be covered by the answer, and using key terms that tell a student what to do in answering the question. Focus 6-2 defines a number of important words used in essay questions, and these should be taught to students to enhance their performance on examinations.

State the Problem in the Form of a Question

The interrogative form compels you to focus on the central problem at hand. As we have pointed out in relation to short-answer items, questions are a natural part of a student's everyday life in the classroom. Once the question has been stated, elaborate in such a way that the student is aimed at the answer.

■ **Example**

Another example of a restricted-response item:

1. **What are the disadvantages of two classroom punishment techniques commonly used by teachers? In answering this question, complete at least the following tasks:**
   (a) **Briefly describe and criticize the two techniques. Use real, or hypothetical examples from the classroom.**
   (b) **Describe a more acceptable punishment technique. Give an example of this technique and be sure to tell why it is more acceptable.**
   (c) **Illustrate an alternative approach to discipline which does not involve punishment.**

Focus on Practice
Six Types of Essay Tests[a]

Richard Posner (1987), a teacher of English at Sachem High School North in Lake Ronkonkoma, New York, replaced objectives tests with essays in literature composition, and vocabulary. In what follows, he provides a brief rationale and then describes the six types of essays.

In giving written tests, I wanted my students to do some thinking on paper. I wanted to see conceptualizing and connecting. What good is watching and reading *Macbeth* if you don't understand that Macbeth damns his soul to hell in return for temporal power and that this theme is an outgrowth of the medieval morality plays? Why slog through the self-pity of Holden Caulfied if you can't link his journey with the river journey of Huck Finn, another youth who becomes disgusted with the hypocrisy of "civilized" society? My goal was to go beyond trivia games. I wanted to see if my students had understood the literature, and if they had mastered language enough to write lucidly about what they understood. The purpose of the classroom test, it seemed to me, was to determine comprehension, to improve inference, and to encourage efficient reading skills. To that end, I developed six types of in-class written tests:

Literary Essay. I modelled this after the literary essay question on the New York State Comprehensive English exam since my students would be taking that exam as their final. In this test, a thesis is proposed (e.g., "In life, as in literature, some people face important decisions.") and the student must support or develop the thesis using one or two literary works. It's a basic four-paragraph expository essay, formulaic and stringent in its limitations, and, while it produces dry prose, it also provides excellent discipline in organization and documenting assertions.

Topical Composition. This is the second major essay question on the Comprehensive English exam. It's nothing more than the basic Freshman Comp theme, except that the New York State Board of Regents asks for 250 words rather than 500. A topic is proposed, deliberately vague to encourage brainstorming ("Mirrors," "Is

Anybody Listening?", "Here Comes A Jogger," etc.). Alternately, students must respond to a given situation ("Pretend you're writing a letter to your local newspaper") in which they must assume a persona and show awareness of audience.

Imitation. I saw no purpose in asking students to memorize the jaw-breaking names of the characters in *Beowulf* or to match the Canterbury pilgrims with items of their apparel. The point of teaching poetry is the poetry itself—the strong, barbaric beat of Anglo-Saxon, and the melodious lilt of Middle English. My students had to reproduce beat, rhyme (if any), and meter, and also create examples of kenning (for the Anglo-Saxon poem) and descriptive characterization (for Chaucer). They did this for up-to-date characters and situations, and, of course, they weren't required to imitate Anglo-Saxon or Middle English vocabulary or spelling. I also used the imitation test for seventeenth century Cavalier poetry (they came up with some delightfully suggestive quatrains).

Brief Answer. In this test, the student must apply knowledge in a series of short but searching questions. For example, a test on Roman Poetry began by asking students to read an attached Romantic poem they had never seen. They then had to (a) state why it was a Romantic poem, (b) state the rhyme scheme and meter and scan two lines, showing strong and weak accents, (c) cite two rhetorical devices, and (d) cite two examples of imagery. Extra points were offered if the student could guess the poet's identity from internal evidence. Another question on the same test asked the students to cite a songwriter who could be considered romantic, and to mention (a) what made his/her lyrics romantic, and (b) what poetic devices the songwriter used.

Timed Rewrites. This is an offshoot of the journal method of getting students to write more often. Students wrote for 5–10 minutes on most days, sometimes on assigned topics, sometimes on topics of their own choice. Five times per quarter, they chose one timed writing they liked best and recopied it—preferably revising—on a piece of lined paper that I provided. These timed rewrites were graded and the five grades were averaged at the end of the quarter to create a double test grade. Choosing which timed writing to hand in helped to develop critical judgment, and rewriting gave rudimentary practice in revision.

Vocabulary Tests. I dislike vocabulary books, with their arbitrary lists of words. Why learn those words and not others? So in my vocabulary lessons, I stressed etymology and connotation, sometimes with little improvised minidramas to illustrate how the words could be used. My tests asked students either to write original sentences using the words, or to write an original essay using the words. I gave five points for every word used correctly in a correct sentence, 2.5 points for a word used nearly correctly or for a word used correctly in an ungrammatical sentence, and 0 points for a misspelled word, . . . or a totally misused word. (p.36)

Posner was pleased with the results. On the independently scored New York State Comprehensive Exam, his students scored very well. Even those students who had been having difficulties improved their averages by 5 to 10 points.

---

[a] From Posner, Richard, "Life without Scan-Tron: Tests as Thinking," *English Journal*, February 1987, 76, 35–38. Copyright 1987 by the National Council of Teachers of English. Reprinted with permission.

Use several restricted-response essay items rather than a single extended-response question. A major problem with essay questions is that the test has restricted content validity. Including several short, restricted-response essay items in a single examination helps offset this validity problem. Greater reliability in scoring will probably be achieved with the restricted-response as compared to the extended-response essays.

Avoid Optional Questions

The reasons for avoiding optional questions are as follows: (a) In norm-referenced grading, performances are compared. Fairness demands that there be a common basis for these comparisons. That is, all students should have written the same question. (b) Since constructing questions of equal difficulty is problematical, and since brighter students tend to choose the more difficult questions, it is better to have a single question to which all students must respond. (c) Students differ in their ability to choose the right question to answer. The purpose of the question, however, is to measure achievement rather than ability to choose the best question to answer. Hence, when several options are provided validity may suffer.

When Asking for Students' Opinions, Demand that Students Support Their Opinions with Knowledge and Rational Argument

It is permissible to ask for student opinions, but students should be able to support their opinions with facts and logical discussion.

■ **Examples**

Poor: 1. **Was American involvement in Vietnam avoidable?**

Improved: 2. **Was American involvement in Vietnam avoidable? Take a stand. Support your stand by considering the social, economic and political factors that contributed to American involvement in Vietnam.**

Focus
Important Words in Essay Questions[a]

The following terms appear frequently in the phrasing of essay questions. You should know their meaning and answer accordingly.

Compare
Look for qualities or characteristics that resemble each other. Emphasize similarities among them, but in some cases also mention differences.

Contrast
Stress the dissimilarities, differences, or unlikenesses of things, qualities, events or problems.

Criticize
Express your judgment about the merit or truth of the factors or views mentioned. Give the results of your analysis of these factors, discussing their limitations and good points.

Define
Give concise, clear, and authoritative meanings. Don't give details, but make sure to give the limits of the definition. Show how the thing you are defining differs form things in other classes.

Describe
Recount, characterize, sketch, or relate in sequence or story form.

Diagram
Give a drawing, chart, plan or graphic answer. Usually you should label a diagram. In some cases, add a brief description.

Discuss
Examine, analyze carefully, and give reasons pro and con. Be complete, and give details.

Enumerate
Write in list or outline form, giving points concisely one by one.

Evaluate
Carefully appraise the problem, citing both advantages and limitations. Emphasize the appraisal of authorities and to a lesser degree, your personal evaluation.

Explain
Clarify, interpret, and spell out the material you present. Give reasons for differences of opinion or of results, and try to analyze causes.

Interpret
Translate, give examples of, solve, or comment on, a subject, usually giving your judgment about it.

Justify
Prove or give reasons for decisions or conclusions, taking pains to be convincing.

List
As in "enumerate," write an itemized series of concise statements.

Outline
Organize a description under main points and subordinate points, omitting minor details and stressing the arrangement of classification of things.

Prove
Establish that something is true by citing factual evidence or giving clear logical reasons.

Relate
Show how things are related to, or connected with, each other or how one causes another, correlates with another, or is like another.

Review
Examine a subject critically, analyzing and commenting on the important statements to be made about it.

State
Present the main points in brief, clear sequence, usually omitting details, illustrations, or examples.

Summarize
Give the main points or facts in condensed form, like the summary of a chapter, omitting details and illustrations.

Trace
In narrative form describe progress, development, or historical events from some point of origin.

[a]From Morgan, C.T., & Deese, J. (1957). *How to study.* New York: McGraw-Hill, pp. 78–79. Reprinted by permission of the publisher.

The first version is inadequate because it does not ask for supporting documentation and discussion, whereas the second outlines the major factors to be considered in the answer.

Create a Scoring Key for Each Question

Immediately after constructing the essay question, you should create a scoring key because the exercise of composing a scoring key may reveal ambiguities and other difficulties with the question. Due consideration should be given to the relative weighting of various parts of the question. The examiner's task is to construct a model answer in point form for the question. The use of models should promote consistency of scoring, but Hughes and Keeling (1984) found that context effects such as whether the current essay was preceded by good or poor quality papers continued despite the use of model essays. Focus 6.3 discusses context effects as well as other variables that affect the scoring of essays.

Grading essay tests. Since lack of uniformity will invalidate the test as a measure of the students' achievement, the central goal in grading is to create reliable scoring methods. To ensure uniform standards, two approaches to grading essay questions have been devised, the global method and the analytical method. Which approach is used depends on the nature of the examination.

The *global method* (sometimes called the holistic or rating method) is mainly used for extended-response essay questions. In this approach the examiner reads the essay, comes to a general conclusion, and then categorizes the essay according to a set of categories. For instance, the essays might be designated pass or fail, but more commonly letter grades are assigned. To ensure that the papers have been correctly categorized, two readings of each paper are recommended.

In the *analytical method* of marking essay papers, the teacher composes an ideal answer as a key for the test. This model answer is then analyzed into its constituent parts; each part receives a portion of the total number of points assigned to the question. The most important elements of the answer would obviously receive the most points. Each paper is then read and matched against the ideal response. The elements of the student's answer are identified and assigned points according to the predetermined allocation.

The marker adheres to the key as closely as possible, but a completely divergent response that has not been anticipated may still receive an appropriate number of points. That you began with an ideal answer should not prevent acceptance of original responses. Having a predetermined key allows you to more readily recognize divergent responses while at the same time consistently marking those papers which conform to the intended answer. In addition, you would correct any misinformation provided by students. The following example illustrates a restricted-response essay item which will be marked according to the key. Note that the subdivisions of the essay are assigned values, the presence of which should guide the student in answering the question.

■ **Example**

Sample restricted-response essay question:

Value: 30   1. **What causes forgetting and how can teachers help students remember? In answering this question, at least complete the following tasks:**

Values: **(15)** (a) **Describe three causes of forgetting.**

           (15) (b) **Suggest one appropriate way students might be helped to combat each cause of forgetting identified in part (a).**

Focus on Research
Factors Affecting Marks on Essay Tests

Research has identified a number of variables that affect the scores students receive on essay tests. Not surprisingly, for instance, essays written in good handwriting receive higher grade (Chase, 1986; Marshall & Powers, 1969). But Chase (1986) felt that many variables such as gender, ethnicity, and teacher expectations as well as penmanship may combine in unique ways to affect essay scores. He, therefore, conducted a study to investigate the interactive effects of these variables. Since results supported his contention, Chase implied that markers must consider variables such as penmanship in relation to other examinee characteristics. He found, for example, that black students who had good handwriting and for whom markers held high achievement expectations were assigned higher marks relative to white students who had good handwriting and for whom markers held high expectations. But this relationship was reversed under conditions of low expectations. It should be noted, however, that Chase's experiment was not a field study, but rather a laboratory investigation where student characteristics and essays were artificially generated.

As we noted elsewhere in the chapter, David Hughes and his colleagues conducted a series of studies to investigate context effects on essays scores (e.g., Hughes, Keeling, & Tuck, 1980; Hughes & Keeling, 1984). Huges and Keeling define context effects as those that ". . . exist in essay scoring if essays are higher when preceded by poor quality essays and lower when preceded by good quality essays" (p. 277). Variables such as analytical scoring and model answers did not eliminate context effects. Huges and Keeling concluded that context effects may be an inevitable part of marking essays, especially where quality of expression is the attribute of interest.

Norton and Hartley (1986) found other variables that affected grades obtained on essays: the more sources used the higher the grade achieved; and teachers gave higher grades to answers that reflected their own ideas. That is, it was advantageous to use lecture notes, at least in part, as a basis for answers.

Just so you don't think that the list of variables affecting essay grades is unlimited, Townsend, Kek and Tuck (1989) found that marker's mood state, positive or negative, did not generally affect scores on essay tests.

Key for analytical scoring:

The student may identify any three of the following causes of forgetting:

1. **disuse**
2. **reorganization (distortion)**
3. **repression (unconscious forgetting)**
4. **interference (retroactive inhibition, proactive inhibition, obliterative assimilation)**

Suggestions for overcoming forgetting:

Disuse:
- **overlearning**
- **repetition**
- **use variety**
- **frequent reviews of core material**

Reorganization:
- **stress meaningfulness**
- **show similarities and differences between new and old**

Repression:
- take the threat of failure out of learning, especially for high-motivation-to-avoid-failure persons
- create a supportive atmosphere in the classroom

Interference:
- overlearn and improve study habits (SQ4R: survey, question, read, reflect, recite, review)
- distributed practice
- meaningfulness (relate to previous learning, stress similarities and differences)
- use mnemonics, e.g., loci method
- active learning (act out meanings)

With this key as a guide and the required background information, you should be able to consistently and efficiently mark the students' papers. After the papers have been returned to the students and during discussion of the responses, the answer key will help to explain the grade achieved by each student. In other words, the key provides the necessary information with the result that students will identify gaps in their knowledge, and they most likely will be convinced that the marking was fair.

Establish Performances Standards which Are Realistic

Consider the grade level of the student by asking yourself, ''What level of achievement can I reasonably expect from these pupils?'' The answer to this question should avoid the problem of unrealistic expectations. The basic requirement should be that students earn the marks they receive by demonstrating their capabilities. Marks are not given by the teacher, rather they are earned by the students.

For All the Students, Mark One Question at a Time

Grading one question at a time allows you to work within the context of one answer key for all the papers. This should increase consistency because a student's achievement on the previous question will be less likely to influence the grading of present performance.

Related to this suggestion is the caution to grade all the papers, if possible, during one session. Of course, you should take short breaks, but extended breaks will reduce the reliability of the marking.

Preserve Anonymity When Grading Papers

There is no doubt that teachers will be impressed more by some students than others. Thus the overall impression of a student can influence how you evaluate that student's essay. This is called the halo effect. To avoid allowing your feelings about a student to influence the grade, mark the papers without knowing the identity of the writers. One way of doing this is to have students write their names only on the cover sheets of the answer booklet. Sometime before the grading period begins go through the papers and turn the cover page over. Mark the papers, but do not record the marks on the cover page until all questions have been graded. Of course you may recognize highly distinctive writing styles, but in general, there will be enough similarity between styles that you will be uncertain regarding the writer's identity.

Write Comments on Each Paper

Students should be informed of areas where improvement is possible. A list of omissions provides a check on the thoroughness of the student's preparation. The gaps in the student's knowledge may be due to poor study habits, or they may result from inadequate instruction. Improved methods of study and/or remedial instruction may then be implemented. Words of encouragement for particularly apt responses should also be given. The inclusion of a statement at the end of the essay which summarizes the reader's evaluation is recommended.

Advantages and Disadvantages of Essay Items

Essay examinations may readily measure higher cognitive processes such as the capacity to analyze, synthesize and judge information in a particular field of study by allowing examinees to express their thinking in unique compositions. That is, effective essay tests assess the quality of students' problem solving skills as well as their stock of information. But objective tests, especially multiple-choice items, may assess these higher skills as well. Table 6.1 compares these two approaches to assessment.

An additional advantage is that essays permit evaluation of students' communication skills. Correct use of terminology, for instance, indicates adequate performance in any discipline. Accurate use of terminology in solving problems is perhaps a better method of assessment than, say, matching terms with definitions on an objective test.

The continued popularity of essay question is rooted in the apparent ease with which questions may be created as compared to objective tests. As Mehrens and Lehmann (1973) observed, the fact that there are fewer essay questions needed as compared to objective items per unit of testing time, even though both types require careful construction, makes the essay format attractive.

Ebel and Frisbie (1986) argued that the sanctuary provided the examiners is another reason for the popularity of essay questions. That is, the freedom of response given examinees creates conditions where model answers may not be produced or defended: students may not challenge their teacher's judgment. Ebel and Frisbie also stated that essay test popularity may be based on the ease with which results are controlled. Without regard for the actual difficulty of an essay question, for instance, examiners may mark the answers so that a desired distribution of grades results.

Essays permit examinees to project their ideas onto a situation. That is to say, the examinee may reveal attitudes and beliefs, for example, about a particular environmental problem more readily in extended, written responses to essay questions than to questionnaires where social desirability (the wish to provide answers which are perceived to be acceptable to authority figures) may unduly influence responses (Mehrens & Lehmann, 1973).

Essay tests have various disadvantages. Low reliability is a major flaw (Hopkins, et al., 1990). Ebel and Frisbie concluded that low reliability of the scores is due to the restricted sampling of subject matter, the ambiguity of the task, and subjective scoring procedures. While low reliability in scoring is most apparent with extended-response essay questions, the restricted-response items suffer as well. Inconsistencies may be reduced by adhering to the suggestions for creating and scoring essay tests which were described in an earlier section of the chapter. In the main, close attention to the keyed response throughout the scoring period will improve marking consistency. Restricted-response essay questions improve sampling of the subject matter because

Table 6.1. Essay Tests Compared to Multiple-Choice Tests

Features	Essay Test	Multiple-Choice Tests
Student Related		
Type of Response	Recall: responses are constructed and organized by the student.	Recognition: students select the correct alternative.
Freedom of Response	Much freedom of content and expression given to students.	Restricted freedom: students forced to choose among limited number of alternatives.
Effects on Study	Students study for understanding.	Students study for understanding.
Skills emphasized	Writing	Reading
Levels of Cognition	All levels of Bloom's taxonomy.	All levels of Bloom's taxonomy.
Teacher Related		
Item Preparation	Few items, but questions need careful preparation.	Many items which require careful preparation.
Subjective Judgment	Although keys are prepared, judgment occurs at time of marking.	Correct response is chosen at time of item construction.
Ease of Scoring	Time consuming.	Quick: scoring is largely mechanical.
Consistency of Scoring	Relatively low.	High.
Nature of the Results	The range of grades depends on the marker.	Range of scores depends upon the traits of the test as developed by the examiner.
Content Related		
Sampling	Limited number of topics represented.	Wide scope of topics represented.

more of them can be included in any given testing period. Validity is also affected by the influence of extraneous variables such as length of the response and handwriting.

Essays require a great deal of time to score. A useful rule-of-thumb is that the teacher should spend about 15% of the time grading an essay that it took for the student to write it. For a hour essay, the teacher should spend about 8 minutes grading it. This equals 200 minutes for a class of 25 or 800 minutes (about 14 hours!) for four such classes which is not unusual for junior and senior high school teachers. Perhaps, the best solution to this problem is to combine essay questions with objective items. In this way, breadth of coverage will be achieved while at the same time allowing students to express their thoughts on a subject. The reduction in the number of essays means that the teacher will not be swamped by marking.

Summary and Main Points

Essay examinations continue to be a popular way to assess student achievement of the goals of instruction. While the need of only a few items may mislead evaluators into thinking that essay questions are easy to construct, there are pitfalls that may be avoided by developing knowledge and skill in item construction. The following points summarize the main ideas of the chapter:

1. Essays are written statements about a given subject which present a description and/or argument.
2. Essay examinations have the following characteristics: response freedom, answers that vary in merit with no single answer being entirely correct, standard conditions govern administration, and subjective judgment determines merit.
3. The restricted-response essay limits the nature, length and scope of the answers.
4. Since they are longer and broader in scope, the extended-response essay permits greater freedom for examinees.
5. Before they are presented to the examinees, essay questions should undergo several revisions.
6. The advantages of the restricted-response essay question makes them the preferred type.
7. State essay examinations as a series of questions.
8. Avoid optional questions.
9. Ask examinees to support their opinions with logical argument and factual information.
10. Score essays with the help of keys.
11. In the global method of scoring, the examiner reads the essays, draws a general conclusion about its worth, and assigns it to a category represented, perhaps, by a letter grade.
12. The analytical method relies on the matching of the student's response to a prepared model answer, the parts of which have been assigned predetermined values.
13. Hold realistic expectations for the level of sophistication to be found in students' essays.
14. Mark all the answers to one question before scoring responses to any other questions.
15. As far as possible, preserve examinee anonymity during the marking of essays.
16. Written comments inform students of the strengths and weaknesses of their efforts.
17. Several advantages of essay tests make them attractive: (a) Essays assess quality of thinking and amount of knowledge of a subject. (b) Essays provide opportunities for measuring accurate use of terminology. (c) The apparent ease of construction may be misleading because essay tests need careful development. (d) As compared to those from objective tests, examiners' essay marks are less likely to be challenged. (e) Results may be easily controlled by the marker. (f) Essays provide students with opportunities to express their attitudes and beliefs about a subject.
18. Essay tests are not without disadvantages: (a) Scoring inconsistency plagues essay examinations. (b) Restricted sampling of subject matter reduces validity. (c) Extraneous variables such as length of response, handwriting, and the halo effect affect grading. (d) Relative to other types of tests, essays take a great deal of time to mark.

Further Readings

Coffman, W.E. (1971). Essay examinations. In R.L. Thorndike (Ed.), *Educational measurement* (pp. 271–302). Washington, DC: American Council of Education.

Coker, D.R. (1988). Improving essay tests: Structuring the items and scoring responses. *Clearing House, 61,* 235–255.

Kemerer, R., & Wahlstrom, M. (1985). An alternative to essay examinations: The interpretive exercises. *Performance-Instruction, 24* (8), 9–12.

Marshall, J.C., & Hales, L.W. (1971). *Classroom test construction.* Reading, MA: Addison-Wesley.

Posner, R. (1987). Life without Scan-Tron: Tests as thinking. *English Journal, 76* 35–38.

Laboratory Exercises

In a subject where you have expertise, identify the main ideas, list instructional objectives for the subject, and study the guidelines for writing essay tests. With the foregoing material as a foundation, complete the following exercises:

1. Construct three extended-response essay questions.
2. Create five restricted-response essay items.
3. Select one of the questions from exercises one and two and develop answer keys. For the extended-response question, organize the key so that the essay may be scored by the analytical method.
4. For each of the items in exercises one and two, identify the level of Bloom's taxonomy.
5. With a group of at least two other classmates or colleagues, compare and contrast the essay examination with the interpretive exercise. (See Chapter 5 for a description of interpretive exercises.)

Chapter

Statistics and Test Score Interpretation

Overview

Virtually all professionals that work with people should have some understanding of statistics and data analysis. Descriptive statistics, the main topic of this chapter, allow you to describe the commonalities as well as the uniqueness of each person. You will study graphs and frequency distributions, particularly ungrouped and grouped frequency distributions, histograms and the frequency polygon. In descriptive statistics there are several important distributions including the normal curve as well as skewed, bimodal and rectangular distributions. A full description of any distribution requires computation of three measures of central tendency, the mode, median and mean, as well as two measures of dispersion, the range and standard deviation. Correlation, a statistical summary of the relationship between two variables, plays a very important role in statistics and test score analysis. Norms and standard scores are widely used for test score analysis and reporting score systems. This chapter concludes with a discussion of four types of standard scores, z-scores, T-scores, stanines, and percentile ranks.

Introduction: Why Statistics?

Contrary to popular belief, statistics are very simple both to understand and to calculate. Nevertheless, many students remain afraid and anxious about learning statistics perhaps because they may have already had negative experiences with statistics or heard unfavorable comments about them from their colleagues. This is unfortunate because these negative predispositions towards statistics may make it all the more difficult to learn them. Successful experiences with statistics begins with a positive attitude.

Why should prospective teachers learn about statistics? The answer to this question is very simple. Anyone who works in a professional capacity with people should learn about statistics because, as is almost an article of faith in education, each person is unique and an individual. Statistics allows you to go beyond the declaration of this truism and to quantify the uniqueness and similarity of people. This allows the teacher to make precise inferences and evaluations of pupils on the basis of numerical information and statistics. Teachers should know enough statistics to analyze and describe the results of their own tests, understand and interpret statistics in test manuals and research reports, and comprehend and discuss standard scores used in reporting pupil performance.

Before the advent of mainframe computers, hand calculators and, most importantly, microcomputers, the computations involved in statistics were tedious and prone to errors. Nowadays, however, the widespread availability of microcomputers and good software has made the computations of statistics as simple as striking a key on a keyboard. If you have entered the data correctly you can also be sure that the results of the computations will be error free. There are a number of user friendly computer programs, which will allow you to do all of the computations necessary in your measurement course and in your eventual classroom practice. Once you learn to use a program, statistical calculations will become routine and very simple.

This chapter is devoted to descriptive statistics which are essential for classroom practice. You will learn about graphs and frequency distributions, measures of central tendency, measures of dispersion and variability, measures of relationship, and norms and standard scores.

Graphs and Frequency Distributions

Graphs and frequency distributions are pictorial ways of representing data. These ways of depicting information are usually much more efficient and effective than verbal descriptions. You are probably familiar with graphs such as pie charts and bar graphs from your days in school. In this chapter we will study graphs and frequency distributions that are particularly relevant to statistics and test scores. These include ungrouped frequency distributions, grouped frequency distributions, histograms, and the frequency polygon.

Ungrouped Frequency Distributions

When test scores are first obtained they are usually in no particular order as the test scores shown in Table 7.1.

When you examine the scores on Test 1, for example, you can see that only one pupil achieved a score of greater than 45 and only one pupil got less than 21. Further study of the scores reveals that 3 pupils got 40 and 2 pupils got 36 and that scores in the 20's and 30's are quite common. You could make similar conclusions about the scores on Test 2. Keeping the scores in this haphazard arrangement and simply inspecting them, however, is quite unproductive and does not give maximum information possible about pupil performance. A first step to meaningful organization of the test scores is to arrange them in an ungrouped frequency distribution. First arrange all the score possibilities from smallest to largest and then indicate the frequency of occurrence of each score. This has been done for Test 1 for the 22 pupils and is summarized in Table 7.2.

Notice from this that there are a number of scores that have a frequency of 0 since no pupil achieved that score. Compared to the arrangement of the scores in Table 7.1, this latter arrangement is more informative because it immediately allows you to see which score occurs most frequently (4), the least frequently (all those that occur once not counting 0 frequency), and roughly which is the "average" score (perhaps 34). Despite this improvement over the haphazard arrangement in Table 7.1, however, this ungrouped frequency distribution is still quite crude and an inefficient way to represent test results.

118

Table 7.1. Raw Scores for Two Tests for Twenty-two Pupils

Pupil	Test 1	Test 2
1	36	42
2	34	35
3	44	36
4	30	29
5	27	33
6	22	24
7	20	21
8	41	42
9	40	37
10	28	30
11	36	34
12	37	35
13	48	45
14	42	44
15	29	38
16	33	34
17	40	47
18	29	34
19	35	36
20	40	44
21	26	28
22	34	37

Table 7.2. Ungrouped Frequency Distribution for Test 1

Test 1	Frequency	Test 1	Frequency
20	1	35	1
21	0	36	2
22	1	37	1
23	0	38	0
24	0	39	0
25	0	40	3
26	1	41	1
27	1	42	1
28	1	43	0
29	2	44	1
30	1	45	0
31	0	46	0
32	0	47	0
33	1	48	1
34	2	49	0

Table 7.3. Grouped Frequency Distribution of Test 1 and Test 2

Class Interval	Test 1 F(raw)	Test 1 F(%)	Test 2 F(raw)	Test 2 F(%)
20–25	2	9	2	9
26–30	6	27	3	14
31–35	4	18	6	27
36–40	6	27	5	22.5
41–45	3	14	5	22.5
46–50	1	5	1	5

Grouped Frequency Distributions

A more efficient and succint way to arrange test scores is to use a grouped frequency distribution. This has been done in Table 7.3 for both Test 1 and Test 2.

Notice that the scores have been grouped into class intervals and that the frequency of occurrence (both raw scores and percent) in each interval has been recorded. Thus on Test 1, 2 (9%) pupils achieved a score between 20 and 25, 6 (27%) between 26 and 30, and so on. Similarly, on Test 2, 2 (9%) pupils achieved scored between 20 and 25, 3 (14%) between 26 and 30, and so on. On both tests, the fewest pupils are in the extreme class intervals (the lowest and highest) and most are in the middle or "average" intervals (31–35 and 36–40). This is a property of the central tendency of scores (they tend to cluster around the center or average) which we shall return to later in this chapter.

The grouped frequency distribution provides a good summary of the results as it tells you a great deal about the scores at a glance. Some information is lost however, because in any given interval you don't know precisely what score each pupil achieved. On Test 2, for example, all you can tell from Table 7.3 is that 3 pupils achieved scores in the interval 26–30. It is impossible to tell from this information alone if all three achieved 26, or one got 26 and 2 got 28, or exactly what the results were. Nevertheless, the grouped frequency distribution is a very useful device for summarizing test data.

A problem that arises is in deciding how many class intervals you should use to construct a grouped frequency distribution. While there is no definitive answer to this problem, there is a useful rule of thumb. You should use about 4 class intervals for every 20 point range on the test. In Test 1, for example, the lowest score is 20 and the highest is 48 giving you a 28 point range. So for the first 20 points assign 4 intervals which leaves 8 points. Since this is very close to 10, assign 2 intervals to it (i.e., half as many as to 20). Thus in Table 7.3 there are 6 class intervals since there is nearly a 30 point range. Another useful strategy is to end class intervals with alternating even and odd numbers. Notice that all the intervals in Table 7.3 conform to this.

Histograms

In keeping with the old saying that "a picture paints a thousand words," it is very common in statistics to describe and depict data by "pictures" called graphs. The most common type of graphs are frequency polygons which are variations of the histogram.

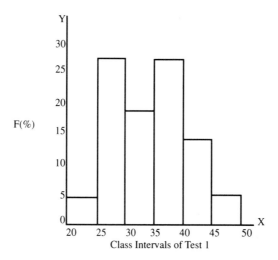

Figure 7.1. Histogram of Test 1 data

The histogram utilizes a Cartesian co-ordinate system (i.e., an x-axis and a y-axis) where the y-axis is always used for the frequency of occurrence and the x-axis has the class intervals on it. Figure 7.1 is a histogram of the Test 1 data from Table 7.3. Notice that the y-axis has the frequency of scores in percent, while the intervals of the test scores are plotted on the x-axis. Note that the exact intervals have been used so that the lines from one interval actually touch the other. At a glance, you can see that the scores on the histogram tend to cluster around the middle of the graph or have a central tendency. It is easy to see that the fewest scores (or the lowest frequency) are at the extremes of the test scale. While the histogram is a simple device to visually summarize data, the frequency polygon is much more common in statistics.

Frequency Polygons

A histogram can be easily converted to a frequency polygon by attaching the mid-points of the bars on a histogram with a line. Figure 7.2 is a converted histogram from Figure 7.1 but the bars have been left in to demonstrate the conversion. In a true frequency polygon the bars are omitted so that the line connecting the mid-points of the intervals is only visible on the graph. Figure 7.3 is a frequency polygon of the Test 2 data from Table 7.3.

Notice that the line connects the mid-points and thus presents a curve of the frequency of occurrence of scores. It is a simple pictorial representation of data and imparts information about the distribution at a glance. This is the most common and important type of graphical representation in statistics. There are several important types of frequency polygons (distributions) in common use that you should become familiar with.

Important Distributions

The term "frequency polygon" is quite cumbersome and statisticians commonly refer to this kind of graph simply as "distributions." There are four important types of frequency polygons in test data analysis. These include the following distributions: normal, skewed, bimodal and rectangular.

121

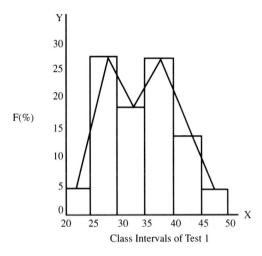

Figure 7.2. Converted histogram of
Test 1 data

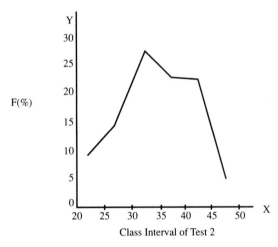

Figure 7.3. Frequency polygon of Test 2
data

The Normal Distribution

This distribution is depicted in Figure 7.4. Notice that it is a frequency polygon that has a smooth shape and is symmetrical.[1] If you were to find the center of the distribution and draw a line through it you could see that the left half of the curve is a mirror image of the right half. This property of symmetry is very important for statistical use of this curve. From the mid-point of the curve, it drops sharply as you move both to the left and right of center but the "tails" never actually touch the x-axis. Indeed, theoretically the tails are thought to extend to infinity.

122

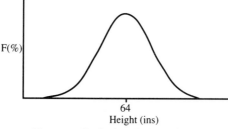

a. Frequency distribution of height of adult females (Adapted from Violato & Marini, 1988)

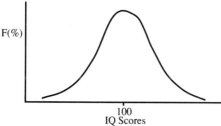

b. Frequency distribution of Children's IQs (Adapted from Terman, 1916)

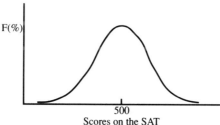

c. Frequency distribution of SAT Scores (Adapted from Crouse, 1985)

Figure 7.4. Examples of three frequency polygons which result in normal distributions

Now that you have examined the picture and noticed some important properties of it, you might wonder why it is called the **normal** distribution. Before answering this question, look at some actual examples of frequency polygons which produce a normal distribution. Three such variables are depicted in Figure 7.4.

The first variable (Figure 7.4a) is the height of adult Canadian females (19 years and older). Notice that most of the heights from this group cluster around the center and become very infrequent at the extremes of height. This is hardly surprising as most women are around an "average" height and very few are either extremely tall or extremely short.

Like the height of adult women, the distribution of the IQ of American children depicted in Figure 7.4b is also normally distributed. Again you can see that the scores have a central tendency and become very rare at the extremes of the distribution. The same is true of the Scholastic Aptitude Test (SAT) scores of American high school graduates (Figure 7.4c).

123

Clearly there is some general principle underlying the properties of the variables depicted in Figure 7.4. Indeed, this pattern (normal distribution) is widespread and does represent a general principle of variability. It is thought that variability among living things exists in this pattern and that is how things normally are. Hence, **the normal distribution.**

What is the reason for this? The explanation has to do with a principle of probability: when differences among the objects measured are due to random or chance factors, a normal distribution results. In all of the examples in Figure 7.4, the differences *between* measurements are due to chance factors and therefore a normal distribution results. For our purposes, in dealing with most physical, psychological and educational variables, you can assume an underlying normal distribution. As you may have already noticed, in practice when you get a set of scores from a class, it usually doesn't resemble a normal distribution at all. Why is this? To answer this question it is necessary to digress briefly into a distinction between samples and populations.

Populations and Samples

A population is defined as *all* of the objects (people, fish, rats, trees, rocks, or anything else that is measured) in the set that is of interest. You may define all American child in grade 6 as a set, for example, and call that a population. Then at least one or all but one child in grade six constitutes a subset or sample of the population. Populations are usually very large and samples are usually small by comparison. A single class of grade 6 children would constitute a sample while the population would be all grade six children. A teacher is usually dealing with a sample (class) which is quite small (less than 30) and perhaps idiosyncratic. Thus data from one class would not appear anything like a normal distribution. The assumption, however, is that this class is a sample from a population which itself is normally distributed.

A further complication arises because sometimes teachers treat their class as a sample and sometimes as a population. When the teacher is interested only in his particular class and not in any larger group, then that class is the whole set or population. This is the case, for example, when a teacher is deriving final grades for a class—there is no interest in comparing to other classes. Alternatively, when a teacher is interpreting scores from standardized tests, the reference group is a much larger one than only the teacher's own class which, in this case is a subset or a sample. In any case, for most purposes, these distinctions are obvious in actual practice. Using idiosyncratic or small samples like particular classes can produce skewed distributions.

Skewed Distributions

Like a hat that has gone askew, skewed distributions are off-center. There are two types of skew: one where the scores bunch up to the right and one where they bunch up to the left. When the scores pile up to the left, the distribution is referred to as a positive skew and a negative skew when the scores are at the other end (see Figure 7.5). While this may seem counter intuitive, it is the direction of the "tail" of the distribution that indicates positive or negative.

What causes a skewed distribution? If we assume that the underlying population distribution is normal, then there are two possible reasons for a skewed distribution: 1) the sample on which the data are based is biased, or 2) the test you have given is either too difficult or too easy. In most circumstances, the first possibility in not tenable. By statistical definition, 19 classes out of 20 are not biased or unusual but are "normal." That is, they represent the underlying normal distribution. When a skewed distribution occurs, then, the teacher must ask herself whether or not the class is unrepresentative such as a group of gifted children or learning disabled ones would be. If this is not true, then the second possibility is probably tenable.

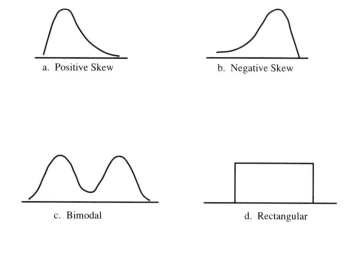

a. Positive Skew   b. Negative Skew

c. Bimodal   d. Rectangular

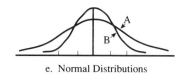

e. Normal Distributions

Figure 7.5. Examples of distributions of different shapes

When the distribution is positively skewed, the test used was too difficult for these pupils. Notice (Figure 7.5a) that the scores are piled up towards the low end of the distribution and very few pupils achieved high scores. This is called a "floor" effect as the scores are piled on the floor. For a negative skew (Figure 7.5b), this is called a "ceiling" effect as the scores bunch up on the high end or the ceiling. A negative skew indicates that the test was too easy and pupils with considerable knowledge of the subject were classified with those with only superficial knowledge (i.e., under the ceiling). In any case, whenever there is a skewed distribution, this signals the teacher that something is amiss. A bimodal distribution is also a signal that something is unusual about the class.

Bimodal Distributions

A bimodal distribution is shown in Figure 7.5c. Notice that the distribution has two "humps" with a dip between them. The lines indicate the probable underlying populations that have been combined to give this bimodal distribution. If you follow the solid line to the dip, you can see that two normal distributions have been "jammed" together. A simple example of such a bimodal distribution is a frequency polygon of the heights of adult men and women together (say 1000 of each). Of course you really have two underlying populations (with respect to height) such that when you mix them together you end up with a bimodal distribution. Anytime that you

125

have a bimodal distribution it suggests that there really are two underlying populations mixed together. Another common distribution in testing is the rectangular distribution.

Rectangular Distributions

A rectangular distribution looks like a rectangle (Figure 7.5d). This distribution may occur with very small classes (say less than 15). If you gave a class of 10 pupils, for example, on a test out 50, no two pupils might achieve the same score. Thus each score would occur only once (a frequency of 10%). When these data are plotted on a frequency polygon, a rectangular distribution results. This merely results because of the very small group involved.

To summarize then, a number of distributions can arise in practice even though the underlying population may be normally distributed. The knowledgeable teacher can usually make good inferences about the test or underlying composition of the samples based on the nature of the distribution whether it is skewed, bimodal or rectangular. Further insights into the data, however, requires statistical analysis beginning with central tendency.

Central Tendency

As has already been alluded to several times in this chapter, test scores have a central tendency or tend to cluster around the center of the distribution and produce an "average" score. In fact there are three measures of central tendency or average which shall be discussed in turn: the mode, median and mean.

The Mode

The mode (Mo) is the most popular or the modal score. To determine the mode in a distribution, you must inspect the data and find the most frequently occurring score. If you refer back to the test data in Table 7.2, for example, you can see that the mode is 40 as that score occurs the most frequently (3 times). Another example of some data is given in Table 7.4. The Mo on Quiz 1 is 14 while the Mo on Quiz 2 is 12 as they are the most frequently occurring scores on the two distributions.

It is possible of course to have more than one score occurring with equally high frequency. In that case you may have a bimodal or even a trimodal distribution. Recall that above the juxtaposition of male and female heights produced a bimodal distribution. That is, two modes (or most frequent scores) were evident; one for the height of males and one for the height of females.

The Median

The median (Md) is the score that divides the distribution in half (as the median on a boulevard divides the road in half). It is also called the counting average because in order to determine the Md, you must arrange a set or scores in rank order and then count to the point where that score divides the distribution in half. The data in Table 7.4 have been arranged in rank order and for Quiz 1, the Md has been determined to be 16. That is because there are 11 scores on Quiz 1 such that the mid-point score turns out to be 16. Half of the scores are above this point (5 scores) and half are below it (5 scores).

The matter becomes a little more complicated with the scores on Quiz 2. Here there are 12 scores so that no real occurring score constitutes the mid-point. Rather, the Md falls between two scores and is a hypothetical point. Since there are twelve scores, the mid-point occurs

Table 7.4. Measures of Central Tendency

Scores on Quiz 1	Scores on Quiz 2
10	6
14	7
14 Mo = 14	8
14	8
15	9
16 Md = 16	10 Md = 10.5
17	11
18	12
19	12 Mo = 12
21	12
<u>24</u>	13
Sum of X = 182	<u>14</u>
	Sum of X = 122

Mean = Sum of X/n

Mean for Quiz 1	Mean for Quiz 2
= 182/11	= 122/12
16.6	10.2

between score 6 and 7 (thus 6 scores are below and 6 above). The Md then, is halfway between the sixth and seventh scores (11 and 10) which is 10.5 (see Table 7.4).

A formula to compute the score which is the Md once the scores have been rank ordered is given as

$$Md_n = N + 1/2, \qquad \text{Equation 7.1}$$

where

N is the number of scores, and
Md_n is the number of the score which is the median.

If there are 25 scores in the rank ordered distribution, $Md_n = 25 + 1/2 = 13$th. The 13th score of this distribution is the median. When N is an odd number, then, the median will always be an actual score. If N = 26, for example $Md_n = 26 + 1/2 = 13.5$. Thus the score which is the median will fall between the 13th and 14th scores. When N is an even number the median will always be a hypothetical number.

The Mean

The mean (M or $\overline{X}$) is the most widely used measure of central tendency and is also known as the arithmetic average. The mean is calculated in the following manner:

Mean = Sum of all scores/Number of scores,

or

Equation 7.2

$$\overline{X} = \frac{\Sigma X}{N}$$

where

Σ is the sum of scores,
X is any score,
N is the number of scores,

Examples of how to calculate the mean are given in Table 7.4.

Comparing the Mean, Mode and Median

For any data set, the values of the three measures of central tendency can give you an indication of the nature of the underlying distribution. If all three values are identical or very similar, for example, this indicates that the underlying distribution is normal (see Figure 7.5e). If on the other hand, the mean is greater than the median which in turn is greater than the mode, this indicates a positively skewed distribution. For a situation where the mode is largest with the median next and the mean smallest, the underlying distribution is negatively skewed (Figure 7.5a and b). When there are two modes with the mean and median having the same values both intermediate between the modes, a bimodal distribution is indicated (Figure 7.5c). Finally, the measures of central tendency have little meaning in a rectangular distribution (Figure 7.5d).

Without actually plotting a frequency polygon, you can make a good estimate about the nature of the underlying distribution just by comparing the values of the mean, mode and median in any given data set. If these measures are identical or within a point or two of each other, a normal distribution is indicated. Skewed distributions can be inferred by noticing the relative values of the three measures as can a bimodal distribution. While the inferences based on the central tendency are not definitive indicators of the underlying distribution, they are useful albeit rough guidelines for classroom practice.

Which of the three measures is best? This turns out to be a nonsensical question because each measure of central tendency conveys meaning in relation to the others. It is true, however, that the mean is probably the most widely used measure of central tendency and indeed is synonymous with the term "average." Nevertheless, each measure can have a quite different numerical value (as in skewed distributions) but still be a "correct" measure of central tendency.

Astute users of statistics can convey different meaning with the same data by using different measures of central tendency. Consider a salary dispute between a school board and its teachers who are mostly young, novice teachers (the salary distribution will be positively skewed). When the teachers go out on strike, the board, in an attempt to turn public opinion against them, reports in the local newspaper that the average (mean) teacher salary is $38,500 per annum. In the same newspaper, the teachers report that the average (mode) salary is $29,800 per annum. Readers of this newspaper will undoubtedly become confused, skeptical and conclude that someone is lying. Both parties, of course, are telling the truth but in a way that supports their point of view. Newspaper readers encountering such data probably conclude that statistics are meaningless and are used for propaganda purposes. Knowledgeable persons, of course, are not likely to be taken in by these simple statistical tricks.

In addition to central tendency, accurate description of any data set must also include a description of dispersion or variability.

Dispersion and Variability

Two basic measures of dispersion, the range and standard deviation, will be discussed here. A full description of a distribution must include an indication of its dispersion or variability.

The Range

Consider two distributions as depicted in Figure 7.5e. It is obvious that both are normally distributed and have the exact same central tendencies. If all you were told was that the values of the central tendencies were identical you might conclude that the distributions are identical. From the diagram, however, it is obvious that distribution A has a greater dispersion or more variability in the scores than distribution B. This further piece of information, therefore, is required to distinguish the distributions. It is as though you had two names, both Jason, in front of you. You might conclude that they represent the same person until you discovered that one had the surname Winthrop and the other, Petrovic. Similarly, for a distribution a "surname" or measure of dispersion is required to describe it fully. If for distribution A you knew that the Range (maximum score–minimum score) is 50 (80–30) and for B it is 30 (70–40), you could conclude that they are different distributions.

While the range does convey some indication of the dispersion of a data set, it is very crude and unstable since it is based on only two scores, the maximum and the minimum. A preferred, much more stable and better measure of variability is the standard deviation which includes every score in the distribution.

The Standard Deviation

The following formula defines the standard deviation:

$$S = \sqrt{\frac{\Sigma (X - \overline{X})^2}{N}}$$

Equation 7.3

where

  S is the symbol for standard deviation (as is SD)
  $\underline{X}$ is any score
  X is the mean
  N is the number of test scores

An example of how to compute the standard deviation is given in Table 7.5.

The standard deviation, as the name implies, is a standardized deviation score. Notice from the formula (Equation 7.3) that the mean is subtracted from each score producing a deviation score. That is, each score is deviated around the mean. These are then squared, summed and averaged (i.e., divided by N; see Equation 7.3). In short the deviation scores are standardized and the resulting figure (the standard deviation) is directly interpretable as a measure of dispersion. The larger S is, the greater the dispersion of the distribution.

Returning to Figure 7.5e, it is now obvious that distribution A has a greater S than distribution B and are clearly different distributions even though both have identical central tendencies. Finally, compare the two distributions in Figure 7.5e. Notice that both have identical central tendencies but are quite clearly different distributions. This is indicated by their standard deviations.

Table 7.5. Illustration for Computing the Standard Deviation

Using the data from Quiz 1 in Table 7.4, we can demonstrate a calculation of the standard deviation. The mean = 16.6 and n = 11.

X	(X–$\overline{X}$)	(X–$\overline{X}$)^2
10	–6.6	43.56
14.	–2.6	6.76
14	–2.6	6.76
14	–2.6	6.76
15	–1.6	2.56
16	–0.6	0.36
17	1.0	1.00
18	1.4	1.96
19	2.4	5.76
21	4.4	19.36
24	7.4	54.76
		149.60 = Sum of (X–$\overline{X}$)^2

$$SD = \sqrt{149.6/11} = \sqrt{13.6} = 3.69$$

The Meaning of the Standard Deviation

Computing S is a relatively simple matter but it is much more important to understand what it means. The standard deviation is a direct measure of the group's variability or the dispersion of scores. A small S indicates that the group is quite homogeneous while a large S indicates that the group is heterogeneous.

Suppose that you gave a reading test to 3 grade 4 classes for a total of 60 pupils. You could calculate the mode, median, mean and standard deviation of this group. Now suppose you gave the same test to a group made up of grade 3s, 4s and 5s for a total of 60 pupils. Again compute the measures of central tendency as well as the standard deviation. How do you think the values will compare across the two groups? Probably the measures of central tendency will be the same (or very similar) across the two groups while the standard deviations will be quite different. The standard deviation will be greater for the second group than the first group since the former is much more heterogeneous than the latter because it is made up of grade 3, 4 and 5 pupils rather than just grade 4 pupils. Even though the measures of central tendency might be the same, comparing S gives a clear indication of the differences in homogeneity.

The standard deviation is also widely used in interpreting test scores in standard deviation units (standard scores) as we shall see later in this chapter. Finally, S is used by test publishers as well as researchers to make inferences about individual and group performance on tests and other measures.

In addition to central tendency and variability, a measure of relationship, the correlation coefficient is a very important statistic in test score analysis.

Correlation

The correlation is a statistical technique that is based on the work of the nineteenth century mathematicians and statisticians, Francis Galton and Karl Pearson and bears the latter's name, the *Pearson product-moment correlation coefficient*. Fortunately, it is common practice to refer to it by the much shorter term "correlation" or by its symbol, r.

This statistic is very easy to understand as it simply indicates the relationship between two variables. As the name implies, it is a "co-relation" between two variables. Some examples of related variables that are intuitively obvious are height and weight, effort and achievement, ages of husband and wife, and heights of fathers and sons. The correlation coefficient summarizes both the magnitude and direction of the relationship between two variables. The coefficient is given by the following

$$r = \frac{N\Sigma XY - \Sigma X \, \Sigma Y}{\sqrt{[N\Sigma X^2 - (\Sigma X)^2][N\Sigma Y^2 - (\Sigma Y)^2]}}$$ Equation 7.4

where

r is the correlation coefficient,
Σ is the summation sign,
X is any variable,
Y is any other variable,
N is the number of pupils measured.

The coefficient, r, must always take on values between +1.0 and −1.0 since it has been standardized to fit into this range (the denominator on the formula—Equation 7.4—is the product of the standard deviations of the two variables). The coefficient can also take on the value 0 which indicates that there is no relationship whatsoever between the two variables.

Equation 7.4 looks quite complex and intimidating but really only involves adding, subtracting, multiplying, dividing and taking square roots, all of which are elementary arithmetic operations. Even so, it is rare nowadays to calculate a correlation coefficient by hand since it is quite tedious and subject to arithmetic error. With the wide availability of computers it is very easy to compute the correlation coefficient. This allows you to focus on the meaning of the coefficient rather than on the tedious and unrewarding exercise of computing it. This meaning is more readily understood with graphical representations such as scatterplots.

Scatterplots and the Meaning of Correlation

The relationship between two variables can be depicted using a Cartesian co-ordinate system (i.e., X and Y axes) where one variable is plotted on the X axis and the other is on the Y axis. The intersection of the values on each variable produces a point. A number of such points produces a scatterplot which gives a picture of both the direction and magnitude of the relationship between the two variables. Some examples are given in Figure 7.6.

Perfect positive and perfect negative relationships are shown in Figure 7.6a and b respectively. Here all of the points line up on a straight line and, in Figure 7.6a, as the values increase on the X axis, they increase on the Y axis. The mutual increase makes the relationship positive while the straight line makes the relationship perfect (i.e., any unit increase in X is associated with exactly the same unit increase in Y). The decrease in Y as X increases in Figure 7.6b makes the relationship negative while the straight line makes it perfect. Figure 7.6c is a depiction of no correlation, and Figure 7.6d depicts a curvilinear relationship where not all increases in X results in increases of Y. For some increases in X, Y increases while for other increases in X, Y decreases. Equation 7.4 is inappropriate for computing such relationships and these are complex and beyond our current purposes.

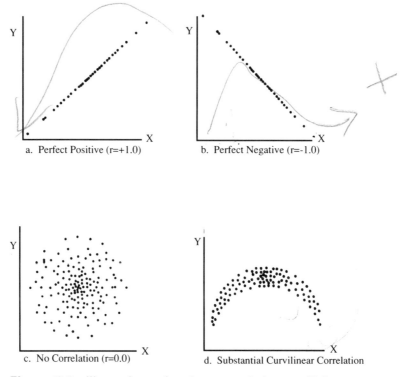

Figure 7.6. Illustrations of various correlation coefficients

Figure 7.7a, b, c and d are depictions of low, moderate, and high correlations respectively. Figure 7.7c depicts a high positive correlation while Figure 7.7d depicts a high negative one. Notice that as the correlation increases, the points become more and more aligned along a straight line as the spread becomes tighter and tighter. Conversely, when the correlation is low the points are less systematically arranged until they are scattered randomly for a 0 correlation.

There are two elements of r to attend to in interpreting it: the sign and the magnitude. The sign indicates the direction of the relationship (i.e., either positive or negative), while the magnitude indicates the strength of the relationship (weak as r approaches 0 and strong as r increases and approaches either +1.0 or –1.0).

Correlation and Causation

Cause and effect cannot be interpreted from correlation which only indicates a relationship. It is sometimes tempting to conclude that one variable causes changes in the other variable, but such inferences cannot be justified on the basis of correlation. Frequently, to make causal inferences on correlation is nonsensical. Achievement and IQ, for example, are known to be correlated (Violato & Travis, 1985) but it is nonsensical to state that IQ "causes" achievement. The height of father and sons is also correlated but it doesn't make sense to say that father's height causes son's height. Both are controlled by underlying laws of genetic inheritance and thus the two variables are correlated. Experimental evidence in addition to correlational data is required to make inferences about cause and effect of two variables.

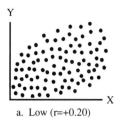

a. Low (r=+0.20)

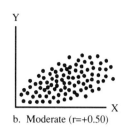

b. Moderate (r=+0.50)

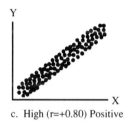

c. High (r=+0.80) Positive

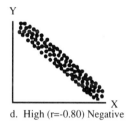

d. High (r=-0.80) Negative

Figure 7.7. Scatterplots illustrating correlations of various magnitudes

In addition to correlation, another set of important statistical concepts for analyzing and interpreting test scores and data are standard scores and norms.

Norms and Standard Scores

Norms provide information about the performance of a particular group on a specified measure. Any individual's score can thus be compared to that reference group, usually employing standard scores including z-scores, T-scores, stanines, and percentiles. In this section, we will discuss each of these standard scores and norms.

What are Norms?

Norms are statistics such as the mean and standard deviation on a norm group that give precise numerical values on some measure such as an IQ test or height measurement. Norm group is probably closest in meaning to "peer" group and its purpose is to establish a reference for comparison of a particular person.

In most educational and other kinds of performance, there are no absolute standards by which you can evaluate or judge performance. Even in athletic performance such as sprinting, for example, determination of a person's achievement must be necessarily based on a comparison to some norm or peer group values. How good a sprinter is a high school student who runs the 100 meters in 14.2 seconds? If judged in relation to the world record of approximately 10 seconds held by olympic athletes, the high school student's time seems poor. This is the wrong norm or peer group for interpreting the student's time, however. A more appropriate group for comparison is the performance of other high school students. Even more precisely, you would need to know if the student is a male or female. The main point is that the sprinter's time only makes sense in relation to some group norms, particularly a relevant group or a peer group.

Performance on standardized tests is usually interpreted on the basis of the performance of a peer or norm group (see Chapter 11). Norms, however, are not standards but only statistics that are useful for comparison. A standard is some absolute criterion against which all are judged. IQ, for example, is a norm-referenced type test since each testee is judged against the performance of their peer group. IQ makes no sense as an absolute measure.

It is imperative that the norm group be based on a representative sample which is relevant. Judging the performance of a grade three pupil on a basic skills test against the performance of junior high school pupils, for example, would violate the first requirement of representativeness. It is crucial that the norms that are established for the measure be based on a representative sample. The norms against which the sprinting achievement of the high school student above is to be judged should be based on other high school students and not olympic athletes.

Norms groups should also be relevant. It is common in Canada, for example, to use American norms for interpreting Canadian testee's scores. This is common practice on IQ tests such as the Wechsler Intelligence Scale for Children—Revised (WISC-R) even though the test and norms are clearly biased for American testees (Violato, 1986). Here the relevancy of the norms are in question as you may very well wonder how the performance of, say, rural, black children in the southern states is relevant to urban, white children living in Calgary. This norm group may be quite irrelevant for Canadian children taking the WISC-R.

Another way that norms can become irrelevant is when they become dated. The original norm group for the Wechsler Adult Intelligence Scale (WAIS) was selected in the 1950s such that testees in 1980 were judged according to those dated norms. It wasn't until 1981 that revised norms were published for the WAIS. The earlier norms had probably become inappropriate given the social, economic, and political changes that has occurred since the 1950s. In making norms relevant it is important to take into account the geographical region of the sample, its socioeconomic status, educational level, ethnic composition, gender composition, as well as other characteristics.

An individual's performance on a standardized test is usually interpreted on the basis of standard scores based on the normal distribution.

Standard Scores and the Normal Distribution

The basis for deriving standard scores is the normal distribution. This curve, as you have seen, is symmetrical and bell-shaped and has many useful mathematical properties which underlie a great deal of statistical theory. For test interpretation, one of the most useful properties is the fact that the curve can be divided into standard deviation units which define a fixed and known percentage of the area under the curve.

The normal distribution is depicted in Figure 7.8 together with the standard deviation units and the percentage of area under each unit. Notice that the curve is divided into six pieces. Imagine that the curve was rectangular. Then each of the SD units would contain an equal amount of area. Since the curve is bell-shaped, however, as you move away from the center, the amount of area bounded by an SD unit falls sharply. The first SD unit on either side of the mean, therefore, contain most area (34% each). The next two units contain approximately 13.5% of the area each while the two most extreme units have about 2.5% each. The tails of the curve

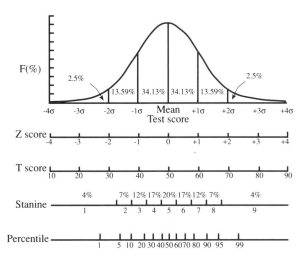

Figure 7.8. The standard normal curve with several types of standard scores

theoretically extend to infinity but for all practical purposes virtually all of the area under the curve is bounded by three SD units on either side of the mean.

The curve that is depicted in Figure 7.8 is called the *standard normal curve* because it has been transformed into standard deviation units. The mean of this curve is 0 (the mean is 0 SD units from itself), while the first value to the right of the mean is +1 (i.e., one SD above the mean). The first value to the left is –1 because it is 1 SD below the mean. The remaining values indicate how many SDs they are above (positive) or below (negative) the mean. Any normally distributed variable can be translated into the standard normal curve.

The standard normal curve is the common metric of comparing across different tests as well as comparing to a norm group. We may use world currencies as an analogy. Each country has its own peculiar currency which are not directly comparable to one another. Which is more, 10 dollars or a 1,000 lire? To the naive observer, 1,000 lire might seem more because it is numerically greater. Such comparisons are inappropriate, however, as these currencies are not directly comparable. Rather both must be translated into a common metric, the gold standard which is the standard for all world currencies. If we translate 10 dollars into the gold standard and then to lire, it turns out to be worth about 12,000 lire, the higher value.

The standard normal curve is the gold standard for test scores. Suppose that Felicia received a score of 30 on Test A and 35 on Test B. On which test did she do better? While you may be tempted to answer Test B, you have inadequate information. Test A has 40 questions while Test B has 50 questions so that Felicia received 75% on Test A but only 70% on Test B. You might be forgiven for concluding that Felicia did better on Test A but your conclusions would still be wrong. This is like directly comparing dollars to lire. You must go to the standard metric, the standard normal curve. Suppose that you now knew that the mean on Test A was 25 and the SD was 5. Therefore, Felicia scored 5 points above the mean (30–25) which is exactly 1 SD unit above the mean. On Test B, the mean was 37 and the SD was 2. Felicia, therefore, scored 1 SD below the mean (35–37/2) on Test B. Clearly, Felicia did better on Test A than she did on Test

B (see Figure 7.8). By thus standardizing a score on any test, you can compare across tests for any person, as well as across people on any test. The type of standard score (i.e., SD units) that has been described here is called a z-score. Figure 7.8 summarizes a number of standard scores under the normal distribution which will be discussed in turn.

z-Scores

The simplest standard score and the one that the others are based on is the z-score. Formalizing the computations above, the following formula defines this standard score:

$$z = X - \overline{X}/SD \qquad \text{Equation 7.5}$$

where

z is the z-score
$\underline{X}$ is the raw score
$\overline{X}$ is the mean on the test
SD is the standard deviation on the test

If you transformed any normally distributed raw scores into z-scores, you would produce the standard normal curve with a mean of 0 and an SD of 1. Thus if you were to take the IQ data in Figure 7.4 and transform all the scores into z-scores by subtracting the IQ mean from each (100) and dividing the result by the SD (15; in short applying Equation 7.5) you would produce the standard normal curve (see Figure 7.8).

The z-scores which come from raw scores less than the mean are always negative, while those coming from raw scores above the mean are always positive. This, of course, is intuitively obvious since the mean produces a z-score of 0. If the difference between the mean and a raw score is a fraction of an SD, then the resulting z-score will have a decimal value. This is illustrated by the example of a raw score of 52 on a test with a mean of 50 and an SD of 8 (z = 52 − 50/8 = .25). Locate this value in Figure 7.8.

While z-scores are well understood and readily utilized by testing experts, they can be confusing and distressing to pupils, parents and some teachers. This is because z-scores have the properties of having negative values (and 0) as well as decimal or fractional values. Most non-experts are accustomed to test scores as whole, positive numbers. A teacher may encounter difficulty trying to explain to parents that their child has a z-score of 0 (perhaps suggesting 0 knowledge to the parents), or worse yet, a z-score of −1.3 (find this value in Figure 7.8). In order to overcome these difficulties with negative and decimal values, T-scores have been developed.

T-scores

This standard score is a linear transformation of z-scores. The decimal values are eliminated by multiplying each z-score by 10 (this has the effect of moving the decimal place one to the right) and adding 50 to each result (thus setting the mean at 50 since it was previously 0) as follows

$$T = 10(z) + 50 \qquad \text{Equation 7.6}$$

Notice now that there are no negative scores (if z = −.5 then T = 10(−.5) + 50 = 45) or decimal values (always round T-scores to the nearest whole number). T-scores, then, have more intuitive appeal and are less likely to be misunderstood than z-scores, by non-experts (see Figure 7.8). Nevertheless, T-scores have shortcomings of their own.

A T-score of 50 indicates "average" performance since it is the mean of the distribution. Most people would interpret a test score of 50 as a marginal passing score since they have been exposed to years of school use where this number magically indicates a "pass." Moreover, a T-score of 60 which would indicate to these same people a passing but lackluster performance, in reality indicates quite superior performance since it is 1 SD above the mean. The problem is that most people interpret T-scores as though they are percentage test scores and thus misunderstand them. In a continuing attempt to develop simple standard scores that are not misinterpreted by the lay person, testing experts have invented the stanine.

Stanines. This standard score (from the two words standard nines) is an attempt to divide the standard normal curve into intervals rather than points so as to classify scores by categories rather than points. Notice that all T-scores between 47 and 53 receive a stanine 5 (see Figure 7.8) so that now a single digit-index of performance is used. To derive stanines you need to have either a z-score or a T-score and then read the stanine equivalent from Figure 7.8. Alternatively, you can use Table 7.6 to convert either z-scores or T-scores into stanines. The percentage of area under the curve or people in that category is also summarized in Table 7.6.

The main advantage of stanines is that a single digit reporting system is used that ranges from 1 to 9. On the surface of it, this is apparently very easy to understand. There are two main disadvantages to this system, however.

First, differences between pupils in performance are obscured. While you may be able to justify the grouping together of two pupils whose IQ's are 97 and 104 into stanine 5, you would have greater difficulty justifying putting both IQ scores of 127 and 150 into stanine 9. Similarly, IQs 72 and 43 are classified together in stanine 1. In the extreme stanines then, real differences between people are obscured. Here then, 2-digit reporting such as T-scores or z-scores is required.

Second, like T-scores and z-scores, stanines are subject to misinterpretation because of people's preconceived notions. A stanine 5, for example, indicates "average" performance as does a T-score 50 since both are means, but for many people this is marginal passing. A stanine 7 is 2 SDs above the mean and thus indicates very good performance but might mean just an adequate performance for many people.

In a continuing attempt to devise a simple, non-misleading and easy to understand reporting system, testing and measurement experts have devised the percentile.

Percentiles

This ranking system can be computed directly from z-scores. Look back momentarily at Figure 7.8. It becomes clear that if you were to score at the mean on any standard scoring system (e.g., z-score or T-score), you have scored higher than half (50%) of the norm group and thus you are at the 50th percentile. Similarly, if you score 1 SD above the mean (z = +1.0), you have scored higher than 84% of the norm group (add up all the area to the left of the z-score) and are thus in the 84th percentile. You can see then, that like z-scores, T-scores, and stanines, percentiles are just another way of reporting standard scores. It becomes a little trickier to compute the percentile rank of decimal values of z-scores.

The mathematics in computing the area under the normal curve to the left of any z-score are quite complex and require some calculus[2]. Fortunately, erstwhile mathematicians have already done this for a great number of z-scores and the results are summarized in Table 7.7. You need only look up the z-score and its associated area in this table and thus avoid complex calculations.

Table 7.6. Percent of Area under the Standard Normal Curve for Stanines

Stanine	Percent of Area	Z-Score
1	4	less than −1.75
2	7	−1.75 to −1.25
3	12	−1.25 to −0.75
4	17	−0.75 to −0.25
5	20	−0.25 to 0.25
6	17	0.25 to 0.75
7	12	0.75 to 1.25
8	7	1.25 to 1.75
9	4	more than 1.75

Table 7.7 has two columns, z-scores and the area beyond z. The area beyond z is given as a proportion rather than a percentage. In order to translate this into a percentage, merely move the decimal place 2 to the right and round to the nearest whole number. Thus for z = .30, the percentage equivalent is 38 since the proportion is .3821 (see Table 7.7). Notice, however, that the value in this column is the area to the right of z or beyond z. In order to find the area to the left of z, you merely subtract the percentage from 100. So for z = .30, the percentage of area (or people) to the left of z is 100 − 38 = 72. Thus a z-score of .30 results in a percentile of 72. A z-score of 1.10 has an associated area of .1357 (Table 7.7) which is 14%. This score, therefore, is at the 86th percentile (100 − 14 = 86).

What if the z-score is negative? This will of course result in a percentile equivalent of less than 50 since negative z-scores fall below the mean. Remember that the standard normal curve is symmetric and thus the area beyond z for scores greater than the mean (positive) is the same as the area to the left of z for z scores less than the mean (negative). A negative z-score therefore results in a percentile equivalent as listed in Table 7.7. Find the percentile equivalent for z = −.57. Ignore the sign for the moment and find z = .57 in the z column. The corresponding value in the associated column is .2843 which is 28%. This is the percentile equivalent because it is the area to the left of a negative z-score.

The rule of using Table 7.7 is simple. If the z-score is positive, subtract the percentage area in the beyond z column from 100 to give the percentile. If the z-score is negative, the percentage area in the beyond z column is the percentile equivalent.

The main advantages of percentiles is that they are accurate and easy to understand even by non-experts. There are two main disadvantages with percentiles, however. First, they are somewhat more difficult to derive than other standard scores though Table 7.7 can simplify matters. Second, not all intervals are equal on the percentile scale. A difference of 3 percentile points between 61 and 64, for example, represents a trivial difference while the same 3 points between the 96th and 99th percentile represents a huge difference in performance. Like the stanine scale, at the extreme ends of the distribution, the percentile scale distorts and obscures differences in performance.

Standard scores have strengths and weaknesses. There is no scoring and reporting system that is free of problems. Perhaps the best strategy is to use several standard scores to report to parents and pupils such as T-scores in combination with percentiles. For further clarification, the

Table 7.7. Percent of Area under the Standard Normal Curve for Z-Scores

z	area beyond z	z	area beyond z	z	area beyond z	z	area beyond z	z	area beyond z	z	area beyond z	z	area beyond z
0.00	.5000	0.48	.3156	0.95	.1711	1.43	.0764	1.91	.0281	2.40	.0082	2.88	.0020
0.01	.4960	0.49	.3121	0.96	.1685	1.44	.0749	1.92	.0274	2.41	.0080	2.89	.0019
0.02	.4920			0.97	.1660	1.45	.0735	1.93	.0268	2.42	.0078		
0.03	.4880	0.50	.3085	0.98	.1635	1.46	.0721	1.94	.0262	2.43	.0075	2.90	.0019
0.04	.4840	0.51	.3050	0.99	.1611	1.47	.0708	1.95	.0256	2.44	.0073	2.91	.0018
		0.52	.3015			1.48	.0694	1.96	.0250			2.92	.0018
0.05	.4801	0.53	.2981	1.00	.1587	1.49	.0681	1.97	.0244	2.45	.0071	2.93	.0017
0.06	.4761	0.54	.2946	1.01	.1562			1.98	.0239	2.46	.0069	2.94	.0016
0.07	.4721			1.02	.1539	1.50	.0668	1.99	.0233	2.47	.0068		
0.08	.4681	0.55	.2912	1.03	.1515	1.51	.0655			2.48	.0066	2.95	.0016
0.09	.4641	0.56	.2877	1.04	.1492	1.52	.0643	2.00	.0228	2.49	.0064	2.96	.0015
		0.57	.2843			1.53	.0630	2.01	.0222			2.97	.0015
0.10	.4602	0.58	.2810	1.05	.1469	1.54	.0618	2.02	.0217	2.50	.0062	2.98	.0014
0.11	.4562	0.59	.2776	1.06	.1446			2.03	.0212	2.51	.0060	2.99	.0014
0.12	.4522			1.07	.1423	1.55	.0606	2.04	.0207	2.52	.0059		
0.13	.4483	0.60	.2743	1.08	.1401	1.56	.0594			2.53	.0057	3.00	.0013
0.14	.4443	0.61	.2709	1.09	.1379	1.57	.0582	2.05	.0202	2.54	.0055	3.01	.0013
		0.62	.2676			1.58	.0571	2.06	.0197			3.02	.0013
0.15	.4404	0.63	.2643	1.10	.1357	1.59	.0559	2.07	.0192	2.55	.0054	3.03	.0012
0.16	.4364	0.64	.2611	1.11	.1335			2.08	.0188	2.56	.0052	3.04	.0012
0.17	.4325			1.12	.1314	1.60	.0548	2.09	.0183	2.57	.0051		
0.18	.4286	0.65	.2578	1.13	.1292	1.61	.0537			2.58	.0049	3.05	.0011
0.19	.4247	0.66	.2546	1.14	.1271	1.62	.0526	2.10	.0179	2.59	.0048	3.06	.0011
		0.67	.2514			1.63	.0516	2.11	.0174			3.07	.0011
0.20	.4207	0.68	.2483	1.15	.1251	1.64	.0505	2.12	.0170	2.60	.0047	3.08	.0010
0.21	.4168	0.69	.2451	1.16	.1230			2.13	.0166	2.61	.0045	3.09	.0010
0.22	.4129			1.17	.1210	1.65	.0495	2.14	.0162	2.62	.0044		
0.23	.4090	0.70	.2420	1.18	.1190	1.66	.0485			2.63	.0043	3.10	.0010
0.24	.4052	0.71	.2389	1.19	.1170	1.67	.0475	2.15	.0158	2.64	.0041	3.11	.0009
		0.72	.2358			1.68	.0465	2.16	.0154			3.12	.0009
0.25	.4013	0.73	.2327	1.20	.1151	1.69	.0455	2.17	.0150	2.65	.0040	3.13	.0009
0.26	.3974	0.74	.2296	1.21	.1131			2.18	.0146	2.66	.0039	3.14	.0008
0.27	.3936			1.22	.1112	1.70	.0446	2.19	.0143	2.67	.0038		
0.28	.3897	0.75	.2266	1.23	.1093	1.71	.0436			2.68	.0037	3.15	.0008
0.29	.3859	0.76	.2236	1.24	.1075	1.72	.0427	2.20	.0139	2.69	.0036	3.16	.0008
		0.77	.2206			1.73	.0418	2.21	.0136			3.17	.0008
0.30	.3821	0.78	.2177	1.25	.1056	1.74	.0409	2.22	.0132	2.70	.0035	3.18	.0007
0.31	.3783	0.79	.2148	1.26	.1038			2.23	.0129	2.71	.0034	3.19	.0007
0.32	.3745			1.27	.1020	1.75	.0401	2.24	.0125	2.72	.0033		
0.33	.3707	0.80	.2119	1.28	.1003	1.76	.0392			2.73	.0032	3.20	.0007
0.34	.3669	0.81	.2090	1.29	.0985	1.77	.0384	2.25	.0122	2.74	.0031	3.21	.0007
		0.82	.2061			1.78	.0375	2.26	.0119			3.22	.0006
0.35	.3632	0.83	.2033	1.30	.0968	1.79	.0367	2.27	.0116	2.75	.0030	3.23	.0006
0.36	.3594	0.84	.2005	1.31	.0951			2.28	.0113	2.76	.0029	3.24	.0006
0.37	.3557			1.32	.0934	1.80	.0359	2.29	.0110	2.77	.0028		
0.38	.3520	0.85	.1977	1.33	.0918	1.81	.0351			2.78	.0027	3.25	.0006
0.39	.3483	0.86	.1949	1.34	.0901	1.82	.0344	2.30	.0107	2.79	.0026	3.30	.0005
		0.87	.1922			1.83	.0336	2.31	.0104			3.35	.0004
0.40	.3446	0.88	.1894	1.35	.0885	1.84	.0329	2.32	.0102	2.80	.0026	3.40	.0003
0.41	.3409	0.89	.1867	1.36	.0869			2.33	.0099	2.81	.0025	3.45	.0003
0.42	.3372			1.37	.0853	1.85	.0322	2.34	.0096	2.82	.0024	3.50	.0002
0.43	.3336	0.90	.1841	1.38	.0838	1.86	.0314			2.83	.0023		
0.44	.3300	0.91	.1814	1.39	.0823	1.87	.0307	2.35	.0094	2.84	.0023	3.60	.0002
		0.92	.1788			1.88	.0301	2.36	.0091			3.70	.0001
0.45	.3264	0.93	.1762	1.40	.0808	1.89	.0294	2.37	.0089	2.85	.0022	3.80	.0001
0.46	.3228	0.94	.1736	1.41	.0793			2.38	.0087	2.86	.0021	3.90	.00005
0.47	.3192			1.42	.0778	1.90	.0287	2.39	.0084	2.87	.0021	4.00	.00003

actual raw score and the total percentage correct on the test should also be reported. In any case, there is no single reporting system which is devoid of problems.

■ Summary and Main Points

Some understanding of statistics and data analysis is a requirement for virtually all professionals that work with people, especially teachers. This allows for a greater appreciation of the differences and similarities between pupils, and also helps the teacher better organize and interpret test scores and other educational measures. In descriptive statistics, of great importance for teachers are graphs and frequency distributions, especially ungrouped and grouped distributions, histograms and frequency polygons. The normal curve is a particularly important distribution as are skewed, bimodal and rectangular distributions. A notable characteristic of many frequency distributions is their central tendency—the scores tend to cluster around the center. There are three measures of central tendency or average: the mode, median and mean. A full description of distributions also requires measures of dispersion, the range and standard deviation. Relationships between scores as summarized statistically by the correlation coefficient, play a large role in data analysis and understanding of test scores. Norms and standard scores are an important aspect of test score interpretation and reporting. Four types of standard scores are discussed in concluding this chapter, z-scores, T-scores, stanines, and percentiles.

1. All professionals who work with people, especially teachers, should have some understanding of statistics. This will allow them to have a better understanding of the differences as well as similarities between people.
2. Test score analysis and interpretation requires an understanding of descriptive statistics, correlation, norms and standard scores.
3. Organizing and summarizing test scores and other data begins with graphs and frequency tables, especially ungrouped and grouped distributions as well as histograms and frequency polygons.
4. There are several important frequency polygons such as the normal distribution, as well as skewed, bimodal, and rectangular distributions. These different types of distributions give insights into the nature of the scores and the underlying properties of the measurement.
5. Many frequency polygons have a central tendency; that is, the scores tend to cluster around the center or the "average" value. There are three measures of central tendency, the mode (most popular score), the median (the mid-point score), and the mean (the arithmetic average).
6. Another critical feature of distributions is their dispersion. Two measures of dispersion, the range (maximum score minus the minimum score) and standard deviation (the sum of the deviation scores squared divided by the number of scores). The range is a very crude index of dispersion while the standard deviation is a very rigorous one.
7. A very important statistic in test score analysis is the Pearson product-moment correlation coefficient, r. This is a statistical summary of the relationship between two variables which is standardized to range between –1.0 and +1.0. Negative values of r indicate an inverse relationship between two variables while positive values indicate a direct relationship. A value of r = 0.0 indicates no relationship whatsoever. A curvilinear

relationship (that is non-linear) is greatly underestimated by r and requires other statistical computations.

8. Scatterplots are Cartesian co-ordinate graphs of two variables that present a pictorial view of correlation.

9. Norms are statistical summaries of the performance of reference groups on a particular test. These can be used for research purposes or to interpret the performance of individual test takers. A norm group is closest in meaning to peer group. Norms should be relevant (reflect a meaningful peer group), up to date and representative of gender, age, socioeconomic status, geographical location, and so on.

10. There are four standard scores that are generally used to interpret test scores. All of these are based on the standard normal curve with a mean of 0 and an SD of 1.

11. Z-scores are standard deviation units ($z = X - \overline{X}/SD$) which can be compared across measures and persons. Negative and decimal values, however, make z-scores difficult to understand for the non-expert and are subject to misinterpretation.

12. T-scores are an attempt to improve on z-scores with a simple linear transformation ($T = 10(z) + 50$). The mean of the T distribution is 50 and the SD is 10.

13. Stanines are nine equal intervals (except for stanine 1 and 9) on the normal distribution that present scores as single digits rather than two-digit scores. The mean of this distribution is 5 with an SD of 2.

14. Percentiles are indices of performance that communicate the percentage of the testees that scored less than a particular z-score. Any score can be represented as a percentile once any standard score is known.

15. Each standard score has strengths and weaknesses and none is free from problems. It is recommended that scores be reported as several standard scores as well as raw scores and percentage performance.

■ Further Readings

Glass, G. V., and Hopkins, K. D. (1984). *Statistical methods in education and psychology.* Englewood Cliffs, N.J.: Prentice-Hall. Chapters 3 "Frequency Distributions", 4 "Measures of Central Tendency", 5 "Measures of Variability", 6 "The Normal Distribution and Standard Scores", and 7 "Correlation: The Measurement of Relationship".

Hays, W. L. (1988) *Statistics.* (4th ed). New York: Holt, Rinehart and Winston. Chapters 2 "Frequency and Probability Distributions", 4 "Central Tendency and Variability", 14 "Problems in Regression and Correlation".

Marascuilo, L. A., and Serlin, R. C. (1988). *Statistical methods for the social and behavioural sciences.* New York: Freeman. Chapters 3 "Graphic Methods and Pictorial Representations of Relationship", 4 "Measures of Central Tendency", 5 "Measures of Variation", 8 "Measuring Linear Relationships", 19 "The Normal Distribution".

■ Laboratory Exercises

Test Data for 25 Pupils in Science

Pupil	Test 1 (20)	Test 2 (15)	Test 3 (10)	Report (25)	Final (75)
1	19	13	10	23	60
2	16	13	9	21	61
3	11	9	6	13	33
4	18	13	9	21	66
5	10	12	5	16	50
6	16	14	8	24	58
7	18	12	8	21	62
8	16	14	10	21	58
9	12	10	6	15	39
10	10	12	5	14	49
11	16	12	9	22	59
12	10	8	5	14	44
13	7	5	4	15	38
14	16	13	8	22	57
15	15	13	8	23	59
16	7	9	6	17	47
17	8	10	6	14	43
18	5	9	3	11	32
19	19	13	10	23	58
20	16	13	9	21	63
21	13	8	8	13	33
22	7	7	6	15	38
23	12	9	7	14	46
24	10	6	5	14	41
25	17	14	10	21	63

Part A: Frequency Tables and Frequency Polygons

1. From the above data, construct grouped frequency tables for Test 1, 2, and 3. Be sure to indicate both the raw frequency and percentage frequency.
2. From the grouped frequency data in #1, construct frequency polygons for Test 1, 2 and 3. Describe the resulting frequency polygons. Are they normally distributed? Interpret the distributions.
3. Construct a grouped frequency distribution for the Final in the Science data. Plot a frequency polygon based on this table. Describe and interpret the resulting distribution.
4. The following data on index finger length and ear length were collected on adult women.

142

Length (cm)	Finger F(n)	Ear F(n)	Finger F(%)	Ear F(%)
4.1–4.5	—	30		
4.6–5.0	2	40		
5.1–5.5	6	141		
5.6–6.0	148	362		
6.1–6.5	334	623		
6.6–7.0	575	482		
7.1–7.5	445	261		
7.6–8.0	223	80		
8.1–8.5	65	40		
8.6–9.0	28	30		
9.1–9.5	18	17		
9.6–10.0	9	12		
Total	1853	2118		

Calculate the percentage frequency and complete the above table. Construct frequency polygons of finger and ear length based on the above data. Describe and interpret the distributions.

Part B: Central Tendency

5. Compute the measures of central tendency (i.e., the mode, median, and mean) for Tests 1, 2, 3, Report, and Final from the Science data. What do these measures suggest about the nature of the distributions? Are these in agreement with your interpretation in #2 and #3 above?

6. Compute the mode, median and mean for the finger and ear length data in the table in #4. What do these measures indicate about the nature of the distribution?

Part C: Dispersion and Variability

7. Calculate the range and standard deviation for all of the measures in the Science data.

8. Compute the range and standard deviation for all of the finger and ear length data above.

Part D: Correlation

9. Construct two scatterplots on graph paper. On one graph sheet, construct a scale for Test 1 on the abscissa (x axis) and a scale for Test 2 on the ordinate (y axis). Plot the paired score for each pupil on these measures. On the second graph, use the abscissa for Test 1 and the ordinate for the Final. Plot each paired score. By inspecting the scatterplots, which of the two demonstrate the strongest relationship? Explain what this relationship means.

10. Compute and report all the intercorrelations (r) between the 5 measures in the Science data. Which is the strongest relationship? Which is the weakest?

Part E: Norms and Standard Scores

11. Using all the pupils from the Science data, compute each one's z-score, T-score, stanine and percentile rank on Test 1 and the Final.

12. Below is a table of various standard scores and raw scores for a test with a mean of 65 and SD = 12. Convert each one that is given into the other scores.

z	T	Raw Score	Stanine	Percentile
1.00				
	40			
		71		
.50				
				7
	70			
		65		
	69			
				93
.75				
−1.65				

13. If a cutoff score of 125 on the Wechsler IQ tests was used to admit pupils into a program for the gifted, how many pupils would qualify in a school district with 75,000 pupils (assume a normal distribution)?

14. If all pupils who scored in the 10th percentile or less on a basic skills test were admitted into a remedial educational program, how many pupils would qualify in a school of 250 (assume a normal distribution)?

Note

1. The equation for the normal distribution is given as follows:

$$u = \frac{1}{\sigma\sqrt{2\pi}} e^{-\frac{1}{2}(X - \mu/\sigma)^2}$$

where

u = height of curve (frequency)

π = 3.14159 . . .

e = natural logarithm; = 2.71828 . . .

μ = mean of distribution

σ = standard deviation of distribution

2. To derive the area under the curve between any two points, the equation for the normal curve is integrated between these limits and this gives the desired value. Mathematicians have provided tables of these integrated values for convenient use.

Chapter

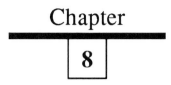

Validity

Overview

This chapter focuses on validity—the question about the extent to which a test measures whatever it is supposed to measure. Four kinds of validity are discussed: (1) Face, (2) Content, (3) Criterion-related, and (4) Construct. Face validity, the most superficial of the four types, focuses on the test's appearance: Does it appear to fit its intended purpose? Content validity deals with the issue of the adequacy of the sampling of the test: does it contain the correct content? Criterion-related validity, an empirically based concept, pertains to the correlations between a test and current performance on other relevant criteria (concurrent validity) and a test's ability to predict future performance on a relevant criterion (predictive validity). Finally, construct validity subsumes all of the other forms of validity in establishing the extent to which the test measures the hypothesized entity, process or trait. Factors which influence validity are also discussed.

Introduction

There are three critical elements of any measurement instrument, including educational tests: validity, reliability, and usability. Reliability has to do with the consistency of measurement, usability deals with the practicality of using an instrument, while validity—the main subject of this chapter—has to do with the extent to which the instrument measures whatever it is supposed to measure. That is, validity focuses on the question of how well a test carries out its intended function.

Reliability is a precondition to validity. A test must be reliable to be valid. A test which is reliable, however, is not necessarily valid. Reliability therefore, is a necessary but not sufficient condition for validity. (For a further discussion of reliability see Chapter 9). Finally, neither validity nor reliability can guarantee usability or practicality. The polygraph illustrates an instrument with low practicality under some conditions. This device measures physiological arousal on various modalities such as the electroencephalograph, Galvanic skin response, heart rate and so on. It is highly reliable and valid for measuring fear responses in the laboratory. The polygraph is not very practical or usable for the same measurement under naturalistic conditions because a person must be strapped into electrodes and other equipment. This limitation greatly reduces the use value of the polygraph.

Before we begin a detailed examination of validity, let us further illustrate the interrelations between validity, reliability, and usability. If your wristwatch is five minutes fast and you always keep it that way, it is highly reliable but lacks validity (since it produces the wrong time). Alternatively, if your watch is both consistent and tells the correct time, then it has both high reliability and validity. Finally, your watch may sometimes run fast and sometimes run slow in unpredictable ways so that it is neither reliable nor valid. In all of the above cases, however, the watch has high usability as you can strap it onto your wrist and go about your daily affairs. By contrast, a grand father clock or an atomic clock may be far more reliable and valid than your watch, but both lack practicality or usability. Similarly, the balance arm weight scales that are common in physicians' offices are probably more reliable and valid than your bathroom weight scale, but they are not as usable or practical (due to cost and size). Ultimately, the value of a measuring instrument (including educational tests) must involve a carefully balanced consideration of reliability, validity and usability.

The Nature of Validity

Does a ruler measure length? Does a clock measure time? Does a thermometer measure temperature or a speedometer measure velocity? These questions may appear trite and the answers self-evident, but they are the essence of validity. Does the Stanford-Binet (an IQ test) really measure intelligence, or the Law School Admissions Test (LSAT) measure a predilection for legal knowledge? Did the final exam in History that you wrote at the end of grade twelve really measure your knowledge of history? These questions are less trite than the first set and the answers are less evident. Indeed, these are essential questions about test validity. These questions have to do with the nature of validity.

In daily life, you are surrounded by a myriad of measurements that you rarely question. You accept automatically the information imparted by the thermometer, the wristwatch, weight scale, ruler, or many other instruments. You may not be so quick to accept without question the results of your Biology test, however. Perhaps you felt the test was unfairly difficult or didn't ask central questions about the subject mater. These are concerns about the test's validity.

Validity, however, is not an all or none phenomenon—it is not discrete. It is a matter of degree. An atomic clock is more valid than an inexpensive wristwatch but both validly measure time. Your physician's weight scale is more valid than your bathroom scale though both measure weight. Another point about validity is that it is situation specific. The validity of an instrument is clearly restricted to particular conditions. A speedometer is clearly valid for measuring velocity but not temperature. Similarly, the Stanford-Binet is valid for predicting academic achievement (to some extent) but not for predicting eventual happiness in life, economic success or leadership qualities. The central questions for the validity of a test is, "What is it valid for?" To answer this question adequately, there are four types of validity to examine.[1]

Table 8.1. Four Types of Validity

Type	Definition	Importance	Evidence	How to Establish
Face	The appearance of test	Teacher-made tests	Non-empirical	Make the test appear appropriate
Content	The adequacy with which the test samples the domain of measurement	Teacher-made tests	Non-empirical	Construct a table of specifications
Criterion related	The extent to which the test relates to some criterion of importance	Standardized tests (e.g., Scholastic Aptitude Test)	Empirical (correlation)	Correlate the test scores to some criterion of performance
Construct	The psychological mental processes that underlie performance on a test	Standardized psychological tests (e.g., IQ tests)	Empirical (correlation)	Manipulate test scores through experimental procedures and observe results

Four Types of Validity

When examining the validity of a test, there are four levels of analysis:

1. Face Validity
2. Content Validity
3. Criterion-related Validity
   a. predictive
   b. concurrent
4. Construct Validity

These levels are generally regarded as hierarchical so that a higher level includes those below it. It is not always necessary to analyze every level of validity for every situation or use of a test. Indeed there are some useful rules of thumb for classifying the validities and procedures for establishing them. These are summarized in Table 8.1.

When teachers construct classroom tests, they are primarily concerned about the first two levels of validity, face and content which are not empirical in nature. The other two levels, criterion-related and construct which are empirical in nature, are more relevant to standardized educational and psychological tests. In short, face and content validity can be established without recourse to data while criterion-related and construct validity require data for their demonstration. In the following pages, each type of validity will be discussed in more detail.

Face Validity

While some testing authorities understate the importance of face validity and even regard it as a misnomer (Gronlund & Linn, 1990; Hopkins, Stanley & Hopkins, 1990), it can play a crucial role in many testing situations. Face validity has to do with appearance—does the test *appear* to measure whatever it is supposed to measure? From the testee's perspective, does the test look right and fair? Why is this so important?

Besides providing an initial impression of what a test measures, face validity can be crucial in establishing rapport, motivation and setting classroom climate. There is little that makes a group of students hostile as quickly as a test that is perceived to be inappropriate or unfair. Students may react with poor motivation and anger towards the test and teacher. The classroom climate may become generally negative. Face validity thus plays a pivotal role in testing.

The Wechsler tests of intelligence provides examples of the importance of face validity. These tests were developed by David Wechsler at Bellvue Hospital in New York to be used with American testees. Two main tests, the Wechsler Intelligence Scale for Children—Revised (WISC-R) and the Wechsler Adult Intelligence Scale—Revised (WAIS-R), are currently widely used throughout the world to measure IQ. The Information subtest of these IQ tests contains some questions which are clearly intended for Americans. Such questions as, "Name two men who have been president of the United States since 1950", and "What are the colors of the American flag?", have clear American bias. Obviously, people in Canada, England, Australia, New Zealand and elsewhere are going to be taken aback by these and other items that are supposed to measure the respondents' general knowledge about their culture. Such items can make the respondent hostile, unmotivated, and negative towards the test and the psychologist administering the test (Violato, 1986).

Psychologists in many countries have made the tests more culturally relevant by substituting questions that are pertinent to the culture of the testee but sometimes with surprising results. In a study by Violato (1984) in Canada, for example, changing the American biased question about presidents to naming prime ministers of Canada, actually made the question *more* difficult for Canadian respondents. So while face validity was improved in this case, the properties of the test were altered in an unexpected way. Face validity, however, does play a crucial role in such testing situations.

Another useful example of the face validity problem is the *Rorschach Inkblot Test*, probably the most famous psychological test of all. This test consists of ten inkblot figures on cards that provide ambiguous forms. The testee is required to describe what the inkblots represent and the responses are analyzed for content and structure that has been "projected" onto the inkblots. This test is now so well known and has been lampooned in films, televisions programs as well as novels and stories that anyone taking this test is likely not to take it seriously. Rapport, motivation and effort may thus be seriously compromised.

In classroom and standardized educational testing, multiple-choice tests also suffer from face validity problems. Many people believe that multiple-choice items only measure rote knowledge, even though the items can be constructed to measure higher level outcomes such as comprehension, application and analysis (Violato & Marini, 1988). This general belief about multiple-choice items can influence reaction and orientation towards these type of items and undermine rapport, credibility, and general classroom climate. When using these tests, you should be aware that they have validity limitations. Alternatively, the general public probably overestimates the ability of essay tests to measure higher level cognitive outcomes such as synthesis and evaluation (Violato, 1986). While the open-ended question of the essay test provides a format for measuring outcomes requiring organization and creation of ideas, there is no guarantee that such responses will necessarily be forthcoming. Indeed, the essay test format probably overestimates the importance of saying something, but underestimates the importance of having something to say (Violato & Marini, 1988).

By way of summary then, face validity, while the most superficial sort of validity, can and does play a significant role in both educational and psychological testing. Indeed, classroom climate can be adversely or positively influenced by the face validity of a particular test. It is important therefore, for the teacher to be aware of this fact and the "public relations" role of testing. Face validity, however, plays a secondary role to content validity.

Content Validity

Content validity concerns the extent to which the test adequately samples the domain of measurement, the content. If in Grade 9 Science, for example, 175 new terms have been introduced and pupils are required to know them, then the domain of measurement refers to the definition of all the terms. You would probably not want to include all of these on a test, however, as it would be too long, tedious and exhausting. Thus you might randomly select 25 terms from the total domain of 175 terms to include in the test. The extent to which the 25 terms selected adequately represent the total number of terms, determines the content validity of the test. Content validity is usually the most important consideration in classroom tests.

Content validity, involves sampling or selecting. The domain of measurement, therefore, must be clearly defined and detailed. Not only must the content areas or subject mater be identified, but so must the cognitive processes involved. The cognitive processes refer to the levels of Bloom's Taxonomy (knows, comprehends, applies, analyzes, synthesizes, evaluates). You must determine not only the subject matter to be tested, but as well the cognitive outcomes that have been specified by the instructional objectives. Enhancing content validity may be achieved most directly through the use of a table of specifications.

Table of Specifications. A table of specifications is a blueprint of the test. While this topic was introduced in Chapter 3, here it is discussed to clarify its role in relation to validity. Just as an engineer develops a detailed plan of a bridge that is to be built and an architect draws a blueprint of the building that is to be erected, so to the teacher begins with a plan for the test. This plan *specifies* the content areas to be tested as well as the cognitive outcomes that are to be measured. Thus it is called a Table of Specifications. Constructing a test without a table of specifications results in the same quality product as does constructing a bridge or building without blueprints.

The table of specifications is a chart where, by convention, the content area to be measured is itemized along the vertical axis, while the cognitive outcomes are specified along the horizontal axis. Use the following steps to construct the table of specifications:

1. Prepare a heading on a blank sheet of paper. Write the subject, date and grade level of the test.
2. Identify all of the content areas to be tested and list these on the left hand margin in the order they were taught.
3. Across the horizontal, specify the levels of learning outcomes specified in the instructional objectives.

149

4. Determine the total number of items that will be on the test.
5. In the right-hand margin, write the number and percentage of items that will be devoted to each specified content area and do the same for the objectives.
6. In each cell (intersection of content area and level of learning outcome) write the number of items and percentage of the total test that these items represent (some cells may be blank).
7. Carefully consider the percentage of test items in each cell and ensure that this accurately reflects the emphasis and time spent in the teaching and learning of this content. If only 10% of the total time was spent learning names of scientists and their discoveries, then only 10% of the test items should be devoted to this.
8. Each item should be carefully checked to ensure that it indeed measures at the intended cognitive outcome (Chapters 3, 4, 5 and 6 contain detailed discussions of item construction). If, for example, an arithmetic problem intended to measure application outcomes is given but the problem has been previously presented in class, then the item probably only measures at the knowledge level since the pupils may have simply memorized the answer.

A well-designed and carefully developed table of specifications will provide a sound plan for your test. The closer the match between the test in its accurate sampling of both the content and learning outcomes, the higher the content validity. If a teacher develops a test with high content validity, then a good test usually results. Examples of tables of specifications are presented in Tables 8.2 and 8.3. Table 8.4 is the table of specifications from a standardized test battery, the *Metropolitan Achievement Tests* (Reading Diagnostic Test). Notice that it is called a "scope and sequence chart" but essentially specifies the content of the test (left-hand margin) and the difficulty levels (horizontal) together with the number of items in each cell.

Table 8.2. Table of Specifications for Grade II Biology Test

		Level of Understanding				
Content		**Knowledge**	**Comprehension**	**Application**	**Higher**	**Total**
1.	History	1	1	—	1	(3)6%
2.	Cells	3	2	—	—	(5)10%
3.	Development	2	2	—	—	(4)8%
4.	Ecology	1	2	2	2	(7)14%
5.	Evolution	1	1	2	1	(5)10%
6.	Heredity	2	2	1	—	(5)10%
7.	Morphology	3	2	1	—	(6)12%
8.	Physiology	3	1	—	—	(4)8%
9.	Ethology	1	1	3	1	(6)12%
10.	Taxonomy	2	2	1	—	(5)10%
	Total	(19)38%	(16)32%	(10)20%	(5)10%	(50)100%

Table 8.3. Table of Specifications for Grade 6 Geography Test of Canada

Content	Knowledge	Comprehension	Application	Higher	Total
1. Climate and Landscape	2	2	—	—	(4)10%
2. Natural Resources	2	2	1	—	(5)12%
3. Waterways	2	3	—	—	(5)12%
4. Energy and Transportation	3	3	1	—	(7)18%
5. Population	2	2	2	1	(7)18%
6. Industries	2	2	1	1	(6)15%
7. Farming	2	2	1	1	(6)15%
Total	(15)37%	(16)40%	(6)15%	(3)8%	(40)100%

Table 8.4. Scope and Sequence Chart for the Metropolitan Achievement

	Primer Grades K.5–1.9		Primary 1 Grades 1.5–2.9		Primary 2 Grades 2.5–3.9		Elementary Grades 3.5–4.9		Intermediate Grades 5.0–6.9		Advanced 1 Grades 7.0–9.9	
	Items	Min.	Items	Min.	Items	Min.	Items	Min.	Items	Min.	Items	Min.
Visual Discrimination	24	15										
Letter Recognition	26	15*										
Auditory Discrimination	24	25*	20	20*								
Sight Vocabulary	30	5*	30	5*	30	5*						
Phoneme/Graph-Consonants	30	19*	27	20*	27	20*	24	20*	24	20*		
Phoneme/Grapheme: Vowels			30	17	36	20	42	25	42	25		
Vocabulary in Context	15	10	22	15	22	15	22	15	24	15	24	15
Word Part Clues			21	22	24	20	24	19	18	10		
Rate of Comprehension							33	5	35	4	31	4
Skimming and Scanning									20	20	20	20
Reading Comprehension	38	44	53	43	55	40	60	40	60	40	60	40
Total Diagnostic Battery	**187**	**2 hrs. 13 min.**	**203**	**2 hrs. 22 min.**	**194**	**2 hrs.**	**205**	**2 hr. 4 min.**	**223**	**2 hrs. 14 min.**	**135**	**1 hr. 19 min.**

*Test is dictated or partially dictated.

Content validity, then, is central to teacher-made as well as standardized tests and can be enhanced by using a table of specifications. The next type of validity, criterion-related, is a form of empirical validity.

Criterion-related Validity

When we are interested in how performance on a test correlates with performance on some other criterion, we are concerned about criterion-related validity. The criterion may be any performance on some other measure. There are two subcategories of criterion-related validity: (1) predictive, and (2) concurrent. Predictive validity refers to how current test performance correlates with some *future* performance on a criterion and thus involves the problem of prediction. Concurrent validity refers to how test performance correlates *concurrently* (at the same time) with some criterion. If you develop a test which will be used for screening and hiring management personnel, you are dealing with a prediction problem because it is the future performance of the candidate as manager that is at question. A pencil-and-paper test of knowledge of computers represents a concurrent validity problem where the simultaneous criterion is actual skills in computer use. Since the empirical procedures used in both predictive and concurrent validity are essentially the same (correlation), and since each involve a criterion external to the test, they are classified together under criterion-related validity and involve the use of validity coefficients.

Validity Coefficients. Evaluating the criterion-related validity of a test requires examining the magnitude of the correlation coefficient, which is referred to as the validity coefficient. Validity coefficients are merely correlations that are interpreted within the context of validity. Interpretations can be aided further by using the coefficient of determination (r^2) and then determining the percentage of variance (a statistical summary of the total differences in test scores—see Chapter 7) that is accounted for in the criterion by the test. The percentage of variance accounted for is derived by multiplying the coefficient of determination by one hundred ($r^2 \times 100$ = percent of variance accounted for).

When the correlation is used within the context of predictive validity, it is called the predictive validity coefficient. In the context of concurrent validity, it is called the concurrent validity coefficient. We will now expand on these notions, beginning with predictive validity.

Predictive Validity

How well does test performance predict some future performance? Figure 8.1 schematically represents this problem. Generally, a criterion and a predictor are identified and their intercorrelation is called the predictive validity coefficient. The arrow in the Figure which points from the predictor to the criterion indicates that interest is unidirectional from the predictor to the future. Five examples are given in Part A of Figure 8.1.

In the Law School Admissions Test (LSAT) example, the correlation between this predictor and law school Grade Point Average (GPA) which is the criterion, is approximately r = .50. This indicates that 25% of the variance ($.50^2 \times 100 = 25\%$) in law school GPA is accounted for by performance on the LSAT. Referring to Figure 8.1, how much of the variance in college GPA is accounted for by the SAT?

The correlation between the Reading Readiness Test (given to preschool children) and performance on a standardized reading achievement test given at the end of grade one is r = .60 (Hopkins, Stanley & Hopkins, 1990). Therefore, 36% of the variance ($.60^2 \times 100 = 36\%$) in reading achievement is accounted for by reading readiness before children begin school. Finally,

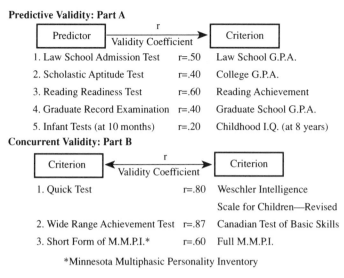

Predictive Validity: Part A

Predictor		r Validity Coefficient		Criterion

1. Law School Admission Test   r=.50   Law School G.P.A.

2. Scholastic Aptitude Test   r=.40   College G.P.A.

3. Reading Readiness Test   r=.60   Reading Achievement

4. Graduate Record Examination   r=.40   Graduate School G.P.A.

5. Infant Tests (at 10 months)   r=.20   Childhood I.Q. (at 8 years)

Concurrent Validity: Part B

Criterion		r Validity Coefficient		Criterion

1. Quick Test   r=.80   Weschler Intelligence Scale for Children—Revised

2. Wide Range Achievement Test   r=.87   Canadian Test of Basic Skills

3. Short Form of M.M.P.I.*   r=.60   Full M.M.P.I.

*Minnesota Multiphasic Personality Inventory

Figure 8.1. Schematic Representation of Criterion-related Validity

in example five of Figure 8.1, Infant Tests (vocalization, locomotion, manipulatory skills of hands and fingers, attention span, goal directedness) correlate with childhood IQ at approximately r = .20. This accounts for 4% ($.20^2 \times 100 = 4\%$) of the variance (McCall, Hogarty & Hurlburt, 1972). Given the above data, are the predictors good, moderate or poor? How large does the predictive validity coefficient have to be?

Interpreting the Predictive Validity Coefficient. It is quite rare to derive a predictive validity coefficient greater than r = .60. This is because the criterion we wish to predict is extremely complex (e.g., achievement, IQ, marital satisfaction, managerial skills), and because people and situations are continuously changing (Violato & Travis, 1989). As Cronbach (1984) has noted, the factors determining whether or not a validity coefficient is large enough depends on the benefits obtained by making the predictions, the cost of testing, and the cost and validity of alternative methods of prediction. Obviously, the higher the predictive validity coefficient the better. In some circumstances, a validity coefficient of r = .60 may not justify an extremely expensive and time consuming examination while in others, a coefficient of r = .20 may make an appreciable difference (Cronbach, 1984).

In the predictive validity examples in Figure 8.1, the LSAT, SAT, RRT, and GRE are moderate to good predictors of their respective criteria (16% to 36% of the variance is accounted for). The Infant Tests, however, are poor predictors of childhood IQ as only trivial amounts of the variance is accounted for (4%). Determining the efficacy of a predictor, therefore, is based on a number of factors including the magnitude of the validity coefficient, the variance accounted for in the criterion, the cost of testing, and the financial and social costs of alternative procedures.

So far the discussion has focussed on judging the overall predictive validity of the test. But how can we predict an *individual's* score on the criterion, given a score on the predictor?

Focus on Research

The Scholastic Aptitude Test: A Predictive, Criterion-related Validity Problem

The Scholastic Aptitude Test (SAT) which was created by the College Entrance Examination Board (CEEB), was first given in 1926. Its main purpose was to create a common metric or standard on which all college bound students could be compared. Because grade averages vary dramatically from school to school and district to district, colleges found it difficult to use these as the sole basis for selection decisions. A student with a grade average of A in a school with liberal standards might have received a grade average of B in a school with more rigorous standards. How can a college admissions committee equate these averages for two students from different schools in different regions of the country? Such equating, of course, cannot be done. The SAT plays a role here. Irrespective of the grade averages, the two students can now be compared on the common standard of the SAT.

The SAT which purports to measure "scholastic aptitude" should, then, predict differential performance in college. Students who achieve low SAT scores should not do as well in college as those who achieve high scores on the SAT. Quite clearly, this is a predictive validity problem. Surprisingly, despite more than 60 years of use and research, the predictive validity of the SAT remains in question and is a controversial issue.

The SAT was standardized beginning when it was first administered through the period to 1941. Since that time, it has undergone continual re-standardization and extensive research. Indeed, so much effort has gone into the SAT that one expert concluded that "it exemplifies the most sophisticated procedures in modern psychometrics" (Wallace, 1972). Ann Anastasi (1982) a leading authority on testing similarly concluded that "the SAT has undergone continuing development and extensive research of high technical quality" (p. 316). Notwithstanding these conclusions, some continue to challenge the predictive validity of the SAT.

James Crouse (1985) writing in the *Harvard Educational Review* concluded that the SAT does not improve the selection decisions made by colleges above and beyond high school grade averages. Crouse (1985) arrived at these conclusions based on data from the National Longitudinal Study (NLS) of the class of 1972. In this study, 19, 144 seniors from 1,069 high schools were surveyed in the spring of 1972. They were followed up in the fall of 1973, 1974 and 1976. Eventually, SAT scores and other data for 5,873 of these seniors were incorporated into an analysis. According to Crouse (1985), the results showed that using high school records plus SAT scores increases the correct admission forecast (students who will pass first year college) only 2.7 for each 100 forecasts over using high school rank alone. This is a proportional increase of only 29.3% correct admission decisions. Thus, Crouse (1985) concluded that the use of the SAT is not justified.

Hanford (1985), however, noted that Crouse's analysis is based on a misunderstanding and over-simplification of the actual admission process into college. Crouse assumed that colleges use high school class ranks and SAT scores to compute predicted GPA indices. All applicants are ranked by these indices and only those with GPAs above a predicted cutoff are admitted. Hanford (1985) pointed out that few colleges use prediction formulae in such mechanistic ways. In fact, a study by the College Board (1980) showed that only 11% of public, four-year colleges and 3% of private, four-year colleges use such computations. Sixty percent of the private colleges make no computations of this sort. Both high school marks and SAT scores are used in varying ways together with interviews, letters, statements of interest, courses taken and so on. Accordingly, the SAT provides a useful contribution to admission decisions and predictions of success (Hanford, 1985).

The SAT has had a number of critics in the past (Allen Nairn and Associates, 1980; Owen, 1985) and will undoubtedly continue to have them in the future. The question, of course, focuses on the SAT's predictive validity and this will likely continue to concern educators and researchers.

Regression—Predicting Individual Scores. When the correlation between two variables is known, as in the case of predictive validity, a person's outcome on the criterion can be predicted using Regression techniques. The simplest way to carry out the prediction is using standard scores. Thus:

$$Z_{criterion} = r \times Z_{predictor} \qquad \text{Equation 8.1}$$

where

$Z_{criterion}$ = z score on the criterion
r = validity coefficient
$Z_{predictor}$ = Z score on the predictor

Suppose for example, that you wish to predict a student's first year college GPA given a SAT score of 570. The SAT has a mean of 500 and a standard deviation of 100 while the GPA mean is 2.50 and the standard deviation is 0.7. The predictive validity coefficient in this case is $r = .40$ (see Figure 8.1). Therefore, using Equation 7.5 the z score (see Chapter 7) on the SAT (predictor) is

$$Z_{SAT} = 570 - 500/100 = .70$$

employing Equation 8.1,

$$Z_{GPA} = .40 \times .70 = .28$$

This student's predicted GPA is .28 standard deviations above the mean. To calculate his actual GPA, rearrange Equation 7.5

$$X = \overline{X} + ZS \qquad \text{Equation 8.2}$$
$$X = 2.5 + (.28 \times .70)$$
$$= 2.70$$

Such predictions also have classroom applications. Suppose that a Chemistry teacher knows that the correlation between a Quiz (Mean = 15; S = 2) given in September and the Final exam (Mean = 68; S = 10) given in January is $r = .72$. If Jason achieves a score of 8 on the Quiz, what is his predicted score on the final? Employing Equation 7.5, Bob's Z score on the Quiz is

$$Z = 8 - 15/2 = -3.5$$

Now using Equation 8.1, the Z score on the Final is

$$Z = .72 \times -3.5 = -2.52$$

To derive Bob's predicted score on the Final, use Equation 8.2

$$X = 68 + (-2.52)10 = 43$$

All things remaining equal, Bob's predicted score on the Final may mean that he will fail the course. Now is the time, of course, for the teacher to intervene and make sure "that all things do not remain equal". The prediction has allowed the teacher to identify Bob as a student at risk.

Concurrent Validity

A similar problem to predictive validity is that of concurrent validity. Part B of Figure 8.1 depicts the concurrent validity problem. Compared to predictive validity (Part A), concurrent validity has no predictor. Both variables are called criteria. The line with an arrow at both ends is used to indicate a simultaneous, reciprocal relationship. The two tests or measures are taken simultaneously. In predictive validity on the other hand, time (months or years) separate the two measures.

The concurrent validity problem arises most frequently when we wish to substitute a quicker, less expensive test for a more elaborate one. Three such examples are given in Part B of Figure 8.1. The Quick Test (see Focus on Research 8.2) has been devised as a quick and inexpensive way to measure IQ. In some circumstances, this test may be a suitable substitute for more elaborate and expensive tests such as the Stanford-Binet and the WISC-R. The Wide Range Achievement Test (WRAT) is similarly a shortened and quicker test of general achievement batteries, and the Short Form of the Minnesota Multiphasic Personality Inventory (MMPI) which consists of 71 items is a much shortened version of the Full Scale MMPI (544 items). The underlying idea is that both the WRAT and Short Form MMPI may be adequate for some purposes.

To determine the validity of these substitute tests, research must be carried out. The tests must be given simultaneously (within hours or a few days at most) to determine their intercorrelation. Used in this context, the correlation is called a concurrent validity coefficient.

Based on the data on the Quick Test (QT) (Figure 8.2 and Focus on Research 8.2), the concurrent validity of the Quick Test can be summarized. First, notice the correlations between the Quick Test and more conventional IQ measures (the WISC-R and the Stanford-Binet) are very high (r = .89 and r = .82 respectively). Thus the validity coefficients are considered to be high. Second, notice that the correlation between the Quick Test and achievement is r = .57. This is approximately the same correlation between the WISC-R and the S-B which are well established. Third, the correlation of the QT with memory is r = .42 which again is about the same as the correlations between the WISC-R and memory and the S-B and memory (Figure 8.2). Based on the above data then, there is substantial support for the concurrent validity of the QT as a measure of IQ since it correlates highly with more conventional measures of IQ. Moreover, it correlates at about the expected level with other criteria (achievement, memory). How high does a concurrent validity coefficient have to be?

Interpreting the Concurrent Validity Coefficient. When examining the correlation between the shorter test and the one that it will replace, the higher the correlation the better. The actual magnitude required, however, depends on the cost and time saving and efficiency of the new test over the old one. If the saving of time, resources and money are great, and if the efficiency is greatly enhanced, a somewhat reduced validity coefficient may be acceptable (perhaps as low as r = .55). Alternatively, if little is gained and important decisions are to be made based on the test results, very high validity coefficients are required (perhaps greater than r = .90).

The correlations between the new test and an external criterion should be about the same as those between that criterion and the original test. This suggests that the new test is measuring the same variable as the old test. In the example of the QT, the correlations fall into the expected pattern and support the concurrent validity of the QT. Ultimately then, the magnitude of

156

Focus on Research

The Quick Test: A Concurrent, Criterion-related Validity Problem

As the name implies, the Quick Test (QT) was developed to provide a fast and simple measure of IQ (Ammons & Ammons, 1962). Most individually administered IQ tests are very time consuming and expensive to give. Moreover, highly specialized skills are frequently required to administer these tests. The Wechsler Intelligence Scale for Children (WISC) and the Stanford-Binet (S-B) are common examples of such tests. R. B. Ammons and C. H. Ammons wondered if it would be possible to develop a quick and easy measure of IQ that could be easily used by psychologists, pediatricians, teachers, and counsellors. Taking the Full-Range Picture Vocabulary Test (FRPV) as their starting point, Ammons and Ammons (1962) developed three cardboard plates, each with four drawings on it (see Figure 8.3). The exmainee is shown the plate and a word is read aloud. The testee must then point to the correct picture (based on previous research, thousands of subjects have agreed on the "correctness" of the answer). There are 50 words for each plate (Forms 1, 2 and 3) arranged in a hierarchy of difficulty. The number of correct answers are matched to norms to derive the subject's mental age and subsequently the IQ. The QT can be administered in 5–7 minutes.

Does the QT really measure IQ? This is clearly a concurrent, criterion-related validity problem that requires empirical analysis. The first research task is to establish a correlation between the QT and other more established measures of IQ such as the WISC, S-B, FRPV, and so on. A number of such studies have now been conducted.

The correlations between the QT and FRPV, for example, are commonly higher than $r = .85$ and as high as $r = .96$ (Ammons & Ammons, 1962, p. 129). In a group of mentally retarded adults, Lambirth and Panek (1982) found a correlation of $r = .71$ between the QT and S-B, while Carlisle (1965) found a correlation of $r = .64$ between the QT and Wechsler Adult Intelligence Scale (WAIS) with a similar sample. Zimmerman, Schroll, Ackles, Barrett and Auster (1978) studying both institutionalized retarded children and adults found correlations between the QT and WISC of $r = .63$, and the WAIS of $r = .60$, and the S-B of $r = .63$. Marini (1990) found correlations of $r = .66$ between scores on the QT and the WISC-R Verbal Scale with a sample of gifted subjects.

In normal subjects the correlations tend to be even higher. Pless, Snider, Eaton and Kearsely (1965) found the correlation between the QT and the WISC to be $r = .84$. Traub and Spruill (1982) found $r = .64$ between the QT and WAIS-R. Joesting and Joesting (1972) found QT and S-B scores to correlate at $r = .79$.

For a psychiatric sample of adults, Husband and DeCata (1982) found QT and WAIS scores to correlate at $r = .89$, while Ciula and Cody (1978) found $r = .91$ with the same tests for a similar sample. For neuropsychiatric patients, Quattlebaum and White (1969) found $r = .86$ between the WAIS and QT and Ogilvie (1965) found $r = .75$ with the same measures and similar sample. In schizophrenic subjects, Dizzone and Davis (1973) found the QT to correlate with the WAIS at $r = .80$.

The QT also correlates with criteria other than intelligence tests. Violato, White and Travis (1984), for example, found correlations of $r = .54$ with a standardized achievement test, while Burgess and Wright (1962) found $r = .57$ for the same variables. O'Malley and Bachman (1967) found $r = .59$ between the QT and SAT scores. For reading ability, Mednick (1969) found the QT to correlate at $r = .66$ with the Gates Reading Test and $r = .57$ between the same variables in a separate study (Mednick, 1967). Finally, Violato *et al* (1984) found the QT to correlate with memory for narrative material in children at $r = .40$.

The above data clearly show that there is considerable evidence for the concurrent, criterion-related validity of the QT as a measure of IQ. Nevertheless, the QT has a number of limitations. First, because of its extreme brevity, it should be employed with caution. Second, the QT is unsuitable for diagnostic purposes since it does not include subtests of cognitive functioning. Third, it is of little help in planning remedial educational programs for underachievers. Fourth, it cannot be used with confidence for making important decisions about people (such as institutionalization or classification into remedial education) since it samples only perceptual-motorskills. These limitations notwithstanding, and given its substantial concurrent, criterion-related validity, however, the QT is quite useful as a measure of IQ.

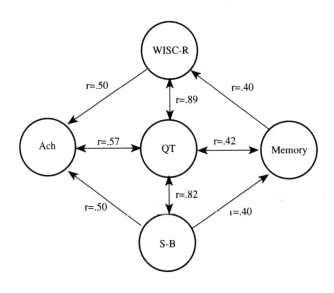

Legend:
    WISC-R=Weschler Intelligence Scale for Children—Revised
    S-B=Stanford-Binet
    Ach=Achievement as measured by standardized tests
    QT=Quick Test

Figure 8.2. Concurrent, Criterion-related Validity Data for the Quick Test.

the concurrent validity coefficient must be examined with reference to the theoretical framework and the pattern of expected correlations.

In the other two examples of concurrent validity in Figure 8.1, the WRAT has acceptable concurrent validity coefficients (r = .87) and is recommended as a replacement for longer test batteries when circumstances warrant it (Anastasi, 1982). The concurrent validity coefficient of the Short Form of the MMPI (r = .60), however, is too low to be acceptable and the Short Form is not generally recommended for use (Graham, 1987).

Construct Validity

Construct validity focuses on the truth or correctness of a construct and the instruments that measure it. What is a construct? A construct is an *"entity, process,* or *event* which is itself not observed" but which is proposed to summarize and explain facts, empirical laws and other data (MacCorquodale & Meehl, 1948, p. 95–96). In the physical sciences, gravity and energy are two examples of hypothetical constructs. Gravity has been proposed to explain and summarize facts such as planets in orbit, the weight of objects, and mutual attraction between masses. Gravity, defined as a process or force, itself cannot be directly observed or measured; only its effects can be identified and quantified. Energy, also an abstraction or construct, is used to explicate such disparate phenomena as photosynthesis in plants, illumination from a light bulb, and the engine that propels a jet liner.

Figure 8.3. One of the Stimulus Plates for the Quick Test (Ammons, R. B. & Ammons, C. H. The Quick Test. Missoula, MT: Psychological Test Specialists, 1962. Copyright Psychological Test Specialists.)

In psychological and educational measurement, examples of constructs include intelligence, scholastic aptitude, anxiety, honesty, impulsivity, verbal fluency, and creativity. These constructs have been proposed to explain, summarize and organize empirical relationships and response consistencies (Cronbach & Meehl, 1955). Intelligence, like gravity, cannot be directly observed or measured; its existence must be inferred from behavioral measurements. Similarly, anxiety is indicated by behavioral and physiological markers, while creativity is indexed by products (e.g., paintings, novels, inventions) though it is thought to be a process. In any case—whether gravity, energy, intelligence, or anxiety—construct validity requires the gradual accumulation of information from a variety of sources. In effect, it is a special instance of the general procedure of validating a theory in any scientific endeavour. The ultimate purpose of validation is explanation, understanding and prediction.

Cronbach (1984) has proposed that *all* forms of validity are really construct validity. Content and criterion-related evidence are pieces of the puzzle on which we can focus our attention. In many tests, it follows that all forms of validity should be considered and synthesized to produce an explanation and understanding. Therefore, all data from the test or data relevant to it, are pertinent to its construct validity. There are, however, specific procedures that contribute to construct validity. These are explicated below.

In general, several important steps and procedures are central to establishing construct validity. These may be summarized as follows:

1. Identify and describe the meaning of the construct.
2. Derive theoretical support for the construct.
3. Based on the theory, develop items, tasks or indicators of the construct.
4. Develop a theoretical network for the construct that can be empirically established by correlation. If, for example, the test is to measure neuroticism, then it should correlate with clinical ratings of neuroticism made by psychologists and psychiatrists. A test of mechanical aptitude as another instance, should correlate with measures such as ability to fix an engine or assemble machinery.
5. Conduct research to obtain the data necessary to investigate the correlations between the variables in the theoretical framework.
6. Design experiments based on the construct, theory, and correlations to test for causal relationships.
7. Evaluate all of the relevant evidence and revise the theory, construct and measures if necessary.
8. Fine tune the measures of the construct by eliminating items and revising the tasks.
9. Return to step 3 and proceed again.

Probably the best developed, most widely researched and readily measurable construct in psychology and education is intelligence. The process of establishing construct validity of intelligence will be summarized here since it serves as an excellent illustration.

The Construct Validity of Intelligence. The concept of intelligence has its roots in antiquity. The early Greek philosophers such as Plato and Aristotle speculated about and debated the nature of intelligence. More recently, Charles Darwin offered an analysis of intelligence in his book, *The Descent of Man* (1871), as did his cousin, Sir Francis Galton in his book, *Hereditary Genius* (1869). These original but crude conceptions involved equally crude measures such as reaction time and attention span.

With the work of Alfred Binet in France at the beginning of the twentieth century, understanding of intelligence and its measurement underwent considerable advances. In 1904 Binet was appointed by the French government to a committee to investigate the causes of retardation among public school children. Binet decided to refine the concept on intelligence and develop a test which measured important aspects of it. Based on rational and logical analyses (procedures for establishing content validity), Binet constructed a test which measured verbal and numerical reasoning. By giving the test to large numbers of children at different ages, Binet was able to develop norms of mental age (MA). Binet then identified various criteria (school performance, reading ability) that were relevant to the test and gathered data to see if the test correlated with these. These early tests did show impressive results, both as concurrent and predictive measures. It was the German psychologist Wilhelm Stern who took the next logical step and divided mental age (as determined by the test) by chronological age and multiplied this quotient by 100 to produce the familiar Intelligence Quotient (IQ). That is,

$$IQ = MA/CA \times 100$$

The French psychiatrist, Theodore Simon, joined Binet in his later work and revision of the test to produce the Binet-Simon Intelligence Tests. These were valuable beginnings in the measurement of intelligence.

In 1916, the Stanford University psychologist Lewis Terman, using the Binet-Simon test as a model, produced a test for use in the United States. This is now called the Stanford-Binet Tests of Intelligence. Terman and his colleagues gave the tests to many thousands of subjects and studied the nature of the distribution of the scores, correlations between the scores and other criteria (school success, memory ability, reading ability, etc.), and the internal consistency of the subtests across different populations. In addition, Terman launched a longitudinal study (which is still ongoing) that has produced important data relevant to the stability/instability of intelligence over the life span. Many thousands of other researchers have since administered the tests to many millions of people and have empirically studied its relationships to other theoretically relevant variables.

A number of other measures of intelligence have since been developed by other psychologists such as David Wechsler (the Wechsler Intelligence Scales) as well as others (e.g., the Otis-Lennon, Full-Range Picture Vocabulary Test).

The data that has accumulated over the course of this century involving thousands of scientists, millions of subjects, and many different measures, are all relevant to the construct validity of IQ, intelligence, and the tests which are used to measure it. Based on this research and these data the following general conclusions can be made:

1. Mental age (as measured by the original Binet scales) increases steadily until cognitive maturity is reached in late adolescence or early adulthood (Siegler & Richards, 1982). Thereafter, it stabilizes. This is in keeping with the general principles of growth (height for example).

2. People who score poorly on IQ tests generally also have difficulties in theoretically related tasks such as reading, memory, arithmetic, and abstract reasoning. Conversely, those who achieve high scores on IQ tests do well on these tasks (Estes, 1982).

3. Children who achieve high scores on IQ tests tend to do well in school; those who achieve low scores tend to do poorly (Snow & Yallow, 1982).

4. Subjects with clinical abnormalities affecting brain growth and organization (e.g., Down's Syndrome, Phenylketoneuria), do very poorly on IQ tests (Campione, Brown & Ferrara, 1982).

5. IQ scores show stability over a number of years and even over the entire life span (Siegler & Richards, 1982).

6. The IQs of identical twins show very high correlations even when the siblings are raised apart (Bouchard & McGue, 1981).

7. Experiments to alter or increase IQ have yielded inconsistent results (Scarr & Carter-Saltzman, 1982). While this last conclusion still remains controversial, some psychologists have concluded that intervention attempts have demonstrated that IQ is not very malleable and represents a stable trait (Violato, 1990).

The above results are in substantial agreement with logical, theoretical and empirical expectations of intelligence. Thus current evidence provides support for the construct validity of intelligence and some tests which measure it (Wechsler tests, Stanford-Binet). Even so, the construct of intelligence as it is currently formulated and operationalized, is constantly undergoing critical scrutiny and is the center of much controversy (e.g., Gardner, 1984; Sternberg, 1985) in the continuing process of construct validation.

Factors that Influence Validity

A number of test characteristics, administration and other factors can seriously affect the validity of a test. Twelve such factors are summarized below.

1. Directions of the test. If the directions are vague, misleading or unclear, this can have detrimental effects on test performance. Pupils may run out of time to complete the test, for example, if the directions about the time allotted are unclear or misleading. Long complicated directions may similarly distract and confuse test-takers and reduce validity.
2. Reading level. If many of the testees cannot understand the questions because the reading level is too difficult, validity is compromised. A reading level that is appropriate for grade six pupils may be too difficult for grade four pupils.
3. Item Difficulty/Ease. If the items on a test are either too difficult or too easy for the students in question, then validity is compromised.
4. Test items inappropriate for the instructional objectives. If the items fail to correspond to the objectives, content validity is undermined. Items that measure synthesis are inappropriate for comprehension level objectives. Conversely, items that measure knowledge are not appropriate for application objectives.
5. Time problems. Insufficient time to write the test will reduce its validity. This is because pupils may fail to complete some portion of the test or because they may be so rushed that they give only superficial attention to some items.
6. Test length. A test which is too short will fail to sample adequately the domain of measurement and thus reduce content validity. Essay tests frequently suffer from this problem because a few essay items may not adequately sample the relevant domain.
7. Unintended clues. Wording of questions which provide clues to the answer reduces test validity. These can take the form of word associations, grammatical errors, plural-singular connections, and carryovers from previous questions.
8. Improper sampling of content/outcomes. Even when the test length is adequate, there may be improper sampling of content and outcomes such as too much emphasis on a content area (or too little). This will reduce content validity.
9. Noise or distractions during test administration. External noise or distractions within the examination room can affect performance and thus validity.
10. Cheating and copying. Students who cheat or copy from others do not provide their own performance and thus invalidate their results.
11. Scoring of the test. Careless or global scoring strategies by the teacher can influence test validity in a negative fashion.
12. The criterion problem. Tests which are to predict some future performance or which are to relate to some other measure of performance concurrently, must correlate with some measure called the criterion. Frequently, the criterion is very difficult to define, operationalize and measure. This is called the criterion problem. Consider, for example, a test which is to predict future performance as a manager. How can this criterion be defined, operationalized and measured? What content and processes should be included

on this test? How do you determine the relevant aspects of managerial performance to correlate the test to?

These interrelated issues constitute the criterion problem. When the criterion is general and abstract, it is difficult to construct a test which will show correlations to the criterion. Conversely, the more specific and precise the criterion is, the easier it is to sample on a test. The problem is one of criterion-related validity.

The particular kind of validity that is of interest will depend on the specific use of a test. An illustration of validity concerns for the various purposes of a verbal reasoning test is given in Table 8.5.

Table 8.5. Validity of a Verbal Reasoning Test for Various Purposes

Purpose of Test	Validity	Type of Information Rendered
Achievement test in elementary school reading	Content	Amount of verbal learning that Ashley has achieved
Aptitude test to predict performance in high school	Criterion-related: predictive	Jason's potential for future learning literature course
A procedure for diagnosing learning disabilities	Criterion-related: concurrent	Specific disabilities of Jerrod's performance
A measure of verbal reasoning	Construct	The nature of Trista's cognitive processes

■ Summary and Main Points

Validity—the extent of which a test measures whatever it is intended to measure—is usually classified into four types: (a) face, (b) content, (c) criterion-related, and (d) construct. Face and content which are the most important types on teacher made tests, are non-empirical forms of validity. Criterion-related and construct validity both require empirical evidence (primarily correlational) for their support. Criterion-related validity involves concurrent and predictive forms both of which require validity coefficients. Construct validity subsumes *all* forms of validity plus a further determination of the psychological processes involved in the construct. Finally, there are a number of factors, some inherent to the test and some due to the administration which affect validity.

1. Three critical factors characterize educational tests: validity, reliability, and usability.
2. Validity, at its most general level, is the extent to which the test measures whatever it is supposed to measure.
3. There are four main types of validity: (a) Face, (b) Content, (c) Criterion-related, and (d) Construct.
4. Face validity has to do with the appearance of the test. It can affect classroom climate and mood, as well as influence testees' motivation.

5. Content validity, usually the most important consideration in classroom tests, is defined as the extent to which the test adequately samples the domain of measurement. this form of validity can be enhanced by the use of a table of specifications.

6. When we are interested in how performance on a test correlates with performance on some other criterion, we are concerned about criterion-related validity. There are two categories of this kind of validity: (a) predictive (How well does a test predict some future performance), and (b) concurrent (How well do two tests intercorrelate concurrently).

7. The determination of a test's criterion-related validity requires empirical evidence in the form of correlation coefficients (r). Interpreted in the context of validity, r is called a validity coefficient. Then validity coefficient can be transformed into the coefficient of determination (r^2) which in turn is used to determine the percentage of variance in the criterion that is accounted for by the test.

8. In predictive validity, individual scores on the criterion can be estimated using regression techniques. This strategy allows the prediction of individual scores on some future criterion.

9. Construct validity focuses on the truth or correctness of a construct and the instruments that measure it. A construct is defined as an entity, process or event which is itself not observed and can be measured only indirectly. Establishing the validity of constructs also requires determination of the validity of relevant instruments. Establishing construct validity is a complex process.

8. One of the most widely researched and readily measurable constructs in education and psychology is intelligence. Systematic measurement and research in the area has been going to nearly one hundred years beginning with the work of Alfred Binet in France. Much controversy, however, continues to surround the validity of the construct of intelligence.

9. A number of factors influence the validity of tests. Some of these factors are internal to the tests such as the directions on the test. Others such as noise or distractions during test administration are external to the test. We summarized twelve such factors in this chapter.

■ Further Readings

American Psychological Association (1985). *Standards for Educational and Psychological Measurement.* Washington, DC: APA Press.

Anastasi, A. (1988). *Psychological Testing* (6th ed.). New York: Macmillan.

Cronbach, L. J. (1984). *Essentials of Psychological Testing.* (4th ed.) New York: Harper & Row.

Cronbach, L. J., and Meehl, P. (1955). Construct validation in psychological tests. *Psychological Bulletin, 52,* 281–302.

Violato, C. (1986). Canadian versions of the information subtests of the Wechsler Tests of Intelligence. *Canadian Psychology, 27,* 69–74.

Laboratory Exercises

Part A: Face Validity

1. Briefly define face validity.
2. Why is it so important that educational tests have high face validity.
3. Construct four questions at the application level of knowledge that measures basic concepts in arithmetic (e.g., area, percentage). Write several versions of each question so that it has face validity for four groups of people (e.g., carpenters, mechanics, bank tellers, teachers, carpet layers, etc.). A particular question should measure the same concept for everyone but should be stated so as to have face validity for each group (e.g., If 12 cm. are cut from a board 80 cm. long, what percentage is removed—application for carpenters. If six pupils leave a class of 40 pupils, what percentage has left the class?—application for teachers).
4. Discuss the aspects of the test that you would examine to improve face validity when developing a grade six social studies test.

Part B: Content Validity

1. Briefly define content validity.
2. How can a table of specifications be used to enhance content validity?
3. Construct a table of specifications for a test in a subject area in which you have some expertise. Make the test 50 items long and use at least four levels of learning outcomes from Bloom's taxonomy. Break the content areas into appropriate subdivision.
4. Identify two psychological tests that may have content validity problems. Specify what these shortcomings are.

Part C: Criterion-related Validity

1. From the Science data (Exercises, Chapter 7), compute the validity coefficient (i.e., r) for Quiz 1 as a predictor of the Final. Treat the Final as the criterion and Quiz 1 as the predictor.
2. Compute the validity coefficient for a composite predictor (sum of Quiz 1, 2, and 3) of the Final. Is there a significant increase in predictive efficiency by combining the results of Quiz 1, 2 and 3 rather than just Quiz 1? Explain your answer.
3. Compute the predicted scores on the Final for students who achieve the following scores on Quiz 1: 12, 17, 8, 10, 14, 16, 9, 15, 7, 11.
4. A psychologist developed a new test of intelligence, the Cognitive Processes Test (CPT). This test consists of two subscales, Verbal and Nonverbal, and provides a Total score as well. In order to determine the validity of the CPT, the psychologist gave the test to 40 grade 7 pupils. He also gave the subjects the WISC-R and obtained their cumulative GPA. These data are summarized below. Is there any evidence of the criterion-related validity of the CPT? What kinds? Explain your answer.

Data Set From the Cognitive Processes Test (CPT), GPA and Wechsler
Intelligence Scale for Children Revised (WISC-R)

Subject	CPT Total Raw Score	CPT Verbal Raw Score	CPT Nonverbal Raw Score	GPA	WISC-R IQ
1	70	35	35	3.0	112
2	80	40	40	2.0	93
3	65	27	38	2.2	98
4	64	32	32	3.1	114
5	55	26	29	2.0	95
6	62	34	28	2.5	106
7	58	34	24	2.5	107
8	73	43	30	3.3	132
9	67	35	32	3.5	123
10	62	36	26	3.3	127
11	68	34	34	3.9	136
12	60	31	29	2.6	102
13	64	36	28	2.1	92
14	59	28	31	2.5	98
15	52	27	25	1.8	87
16	63	35	28	2.0	90
17	69	35	34	3.8	134
18	58	24	34	1.7	83
19	47	22	25	3.4	133
20	65	33	32	3.4	124
21	56	29	27	2.5	104
22	53	33	20	2.4	110
23	59	30	29	2.7	109
24	52	22	30	2.3	104
25	60	33	27	3.0	111
26	62	31	31	3.2	109
27	49	28	21	2.4	100
28	52	31	21	2.1	97
29	52	23	29	2.6	103
30	75	42	33	3.1	110
31	53	24	29	2.9	103
32	59	29	30	2.4	96
33	57	26	31	2.3	95
34	54	31	23	3.4	117
35	51	33	18	2.9	100
36	66	37	29	2.4	101
37	69	40	29	2.5	96
38	59	25	34	2.0	88
39	71	37	34	1.8	85
40	56	27	29	2.0	90

5. From the CPT data set, is there any evidence for the validity of the GPA as a measure of academic achievement? What kinds of validity? Explain your answer.

Part D: Construct Validity

1. Briefly describe the general procedure for determining construct validity.
2. From the CPT data set, is there any evidence of the construct validity of the CPT? Discuss.

Notes

1. In conventional discussions, three forms of validity are generally recognized (content, criterion-related, and construct). Face validity is not regarded as a form of validity *per se*. A joint committee of the American Psychological Association, National Council on Measurement in Education, and the American Educational Research Association has prepared a document, *Standards for educational and Psychological Testing* (Washington, D.C.: American Psychological Association, 1985), which describes validity and sets standards for test use. In this treatment, face validity is not regarded as a form of validity. Many textbook writers also do not discuss this form as a separate kind of validity. Nevertheless, in the present text, it is discussed as a separate type of validity because it influences classroom climate or rapport between psychologist and testee. Therefore, for present purposes, face validity is considered a form of validity.

Chapter

9

Reliability

Overview

After validity, probably the most important characteristic of a test is reliability. This chapter deals with reliability and its nature. Four ways to derive reliability estimates or coefficients are described. These are test-retest, parallel forms, split-half, and internal consistency. Another method of interpreting reliability, the standard error of measurement is described and discussed as is the concept and application of true scores. This chapter concludes with a discussion of several factors that influence reliability.

Introduction

Reliability has to do with the consistency of measurement. It is a necessary condition for validity. While reliability is a precondition for validity, it does not guarantee it. That is, a measurement instrument which is reliable, is not necessarily valid. A clock which always runs ten minutes fast is reliable since it is consistent but it is not valid since it gives the incorrect time. It is evident then, that reliability is a necessary but not sufficient condition for validity. Alternatively, an instrument which is valid must be reliable. The focus of this chapter is on reliability and its nature.

The Nature of Reliability

What is meant by the consistency of measurement? What factors can lead to the inconsistency of measurement? How can you tell if some measurement is consistent or not? These questions are at the heart of the concept of reliability. A simple example can help to clarify the nature of reliability.

Suppose that you measured the length of your kitchen table with a ruler and it turned out to be 50 inches long. Later that day, you began to doubt this measurement so next morning you measured the table again. This time it turned out to be 46 inches long. Which is correct? To settle the matter you measured the table a third time and this time it was 53 inches long. Still unsure you measured the table several more times with a different result each time. What is the problem here? There are two possibilities: (1) the table keeps changing length every time it is measured, or (2) something is wrong with your measurement instrument.

Under normal conditions, of course, tables do not change length so in this case the problem must be the measurement instrument. Upon closer examination you discover that your ruler is made of rubber and the differential results are due to the inconsistency of the measurement. This is why of course, rulers are made from wood, plastic or metal so that they don't stretch and shrink from time to time.

This example is not merely unlikely or trite, though, as many psychological and educational tests do in fact behave like rubber rulers, as they produce inconsistent results or unreliable measurements. The concern with reliability in educational and psychological measurement is paramount because of the difficulty of producing consistent measures of achievement and psychological constructs. In measuring physical properties of the universe, reliability is usually not a big problem (For example, think of measuring height, velocity, temperature, weight, and so on), while it is a central problem for measuring psychological or educational characteristics of people.

Reliability is a multifaceted concept rather than a singular idea. Indeed, there are several ways of thinking about and discussing reliability. Four methods of establishing reliability are usually recognized. These are discussed in turn in the following section.

Four Methods for Establishing Reliability

The four methods or techniques for determining the reliability of a measurement instrument are listed below.

1. Test-retest
2. Parallel Forms
    a. given at the same time
    b. given at different times
3. Split-Half
4. Internal Consistency

These techniques are not only different methods for establishing reliability, but each type produces a somewhat different type of reliability as well. While all forms of reliability focus on consistency, there are different aspects of the testing to which the consistency is relevant. The consistency on the test-retest method, for example, focuses on time. That is, does the test produce consistent results from one measurement to another at a different time?

A second type of reliability is estimated by parallel forms or equivalent forms method as it is also called. Here the focus is on the consistency of measurement across different forms (parallel or equivalent) of the same test. Because the different forms can be given either simultaneously or at different times, stability of the test over time can also play a role in this method.

The third type of reliability that is estimated both by split-half method and the internal consistency method, deals with the internal consistency of the test or the consistency of measurement across different items within the test. Thus neither time nor form equivalence is relevant here. Split-half as we shall see in more detail later, is a special version of internal consistency.

Here we are concerned about the extent to which each item (or group of items) consistently measures in the direction of the other items on the test. Let us examine each method and type of reliability in more detail.

The Test-retest Method

Probably the simplest way to understand reliability is to think of it as consistency over different measurements. This is estimated by the test-retest method. In this method, a teacher gives a test today, for example, and exactly one week later, the teacher gives the same test to the same pupils. Suppose that Jaden, one of the students that took the test, is a very good student, studies diligently and works hard, and so scored very well on the test. By contrast, Tracy is a lackadaisical student and thus scored poorly on the test. All things remaining equal, how would you expect Jaden and Tracy to score on the second administration of the test (assume no practice effects or further studying)? The most obvious answer is that Jaden should score well on the second administration and Tracy should score poorly on the second administration of the test.

Test-retest rests on the ensuing assumption. Suppose that 25 pupils had taken the test in the above example. Those who did well on the first administration should do well on the second and those who did poorly on the first should do poorly on the second. Of course the mediocre students are also expected to remain about the same. The idea is that there should be consistency of performance across the two administrations.

We determine the degree of consistency in the test-retest method by using correlation (See Chapter 7 for a discussion of correlation). Since in our example, 25 pupils took the test, each one will have two scores (one on the first administration and one on the second). By treating each set of scores as a variable (say, X for time 1 and Y for time 2), we can compute the correlation (using the Pearson-product moment correlation computations) between the two sets of scores. This will be the estimate of the consistency or reliability of the test. This correlation, because it is interpreted within the context of reliability, is now called a reliability coefficient.

Reliability Coefficients. Like validity coefficients, reliability coefficients are correlations but are now interpreted in the context of reliability. The reliability coefficient is computed using exactly the same procedures as for computing the validity coefficient. The interpretation, though, has some important differences.

In validity, the proportion of variance (Refer to Chapter 8 for a discussion of variance and validity.) accounted for is derived by employing the coefficient of determination (r^2). This is because two different variables are correlated (e.g., SAT with GPA) and thus, r must be squared in order to derive the proportion of variance accounted for in one variable by another. In reliability on the other hand, the exact same variable is correlated with itself (the same test at different times) and thus there is no need to square r to derive the proportion of variance accounted for in the two measurements. The correlation coefficient r is a direct measure of the amount of variance accounted for in the measurement over two times. To distinguish it from a general correlation coefficient, the reliability coefficient is written as r with xx subscripts, r_{xx}, meaning a variable (test) correlated with itself. The difference from unity $(1 - r_{xx})$ is the amount of inconsistency in the measurement over two occasions. The magnitude is a direct indication of the consistency or reliability of the test. Thus the size of r_{xx} tells how good the reliability of the test is. How large must a reliability coefficient be?

Interpreting the Reliability Coefficient. As in interpreting the validity coefficient, there are no fixed and firm rules for interpreting the reliability coefficient. To some degree, contextual factors need to be taken into account. There are however, several useful rules of thumb which can help you to interpret the reliability coefficient. Different standards apply to different testing situations.

For standardized tests (achievement, reading, IQ), reliability coefficients are generally expected to exceed $r_{xx} = .90$. This means that 90% of the variation in repeated measurements ($[1 - r_{xx}] \times 100 = 90\%$) is due to consistent and stable measurements. The remaining 10% is due to errors of measurement. A standardized test with a reliability of less than $r_{xx} = .85$ is considered inadequate as 15% of the variance is due to errors of measurement.

Different standards though, must guide the adjudication of teacher made tests. Generally, any test, teacher made or otherwise is considered poor if r_{xx} is less than .50. This means that only 50% of the variance in the measurement is consistent and a true measure while 50% is error. A test with $r_{xx} = .40$ has 60% error of measurement and only 40% consistent measurement. Teacher made tests with reliabilities of .50 to .60 are adequate, of .61 to .70 are good, and with .71 and greater are very good and excellent. When r_{xx} exceeds .70, the error or measurement is less than 30%. Most teachers can realistically aim for reliabilities for their tests in the order of $r_{xx} = .65$. On the other hand, technically sound tests like the WISC-R have reliabilities of around $r_{xx} = .97$.

As you may have guessed by now, the test-retest method is impractical for classroom purposes and is hardly ever used. There are several reasons for this. First, giving the exact same test twice is a waste of precious classroom time. Second, pupils will consider this to be an odd practice and may react unfavourably to taking the same test twice. Thus classroom climate may be affected adversely. Third, if pupils know that they will receive the test again (even if not told by the teacher they will anticipate it if test-retest becomes routine practice) some will study and practice the items during the interval. The result will indicate highly unstable performance and suggest an unreliable test (even though the reliability hasn't actually been determined). Fourth, it is simply inefficient practice to use test-retest methods for classroom testing purposes. Other methods for determining the reliability of classroom tests should be employed.

The Parallel Form Method

The main problem with the test-retest method is that pupils receive *exactly* the same items on both testing occasions. The solution to this problem might be to construct several different forms or versions of the test called parallel forms or equivalent forms. This means that on testing occasion two the pupils would receive different items that measured the same thing as the test which was given on testing occasion one. The analogy here would be to measure the length of an object with one ruler on occasion one and a different ruler on occasion two and compare the results. The rulers are considered to be parallel or equivalent measures of length. The degree to which they produce equivalent results is an indication of their reliability (consistency across different forms or rulers).

To create parallel forms, the teacher might proceed in the following way. First, the universe or domain of measurement is defined. This domain is defined by the instructional objectives that are to be assessed or by the table of specifications. (See Chapters 3 and 8 for discussions of tables of specifications.) Thus the content area and the level of understanding of the content areas are defined. Second, for each cell in the table of specifications, the teacher constructs a number of items. Many more items than will appear on any form of the test need to be constructed (perhaps 10 times as many). Third, the teacher randomly selects the desired number of items from each cell in the table of specifications to make up the whole test. This is called Form A. Fourth, the teacher, using the same procedure, selects another set of items to make up Form B. Following the above steps, more forms can be constructed until the item pool is depleted. Forms A, B and any other forms are called parallel or equivalent forms.

Suppose that Mr. Cooney, a grade six teacher, wanted to construct parallel forms of the geography test of Canada that is outlined in the table of specifications in Table 8.3 (See Chapter 8). In this table of specifications there are four levels of understanding and seven content areas for a total of twenty-eight cells. The test is to consist of forty items. This defines the universe or domain of measurement.

Mr. Cooney now constructs 400 items, 10% of which (40 items) deal with climate and landscape, 12% (50 items) with natural resources, 12% (50 items) with waterways, and so on. (See Table 8.3.) To make Form A, Mr. Cooney now randomly selects 2 items from the climate and landscape at the knowledge level cell, 2 from the comprehension level cell, 2 from the natural resources at the knowledge level cell, 2 from comprehension level cell, 1 from the application level call, and so on until all forty items have been selected. A test has now been constructed according to the table of specifications and therefore samples the universe or domain of measurement. Using the same procedures, Mr. Coney can select another forty items to construct Form B. Further forms can be constructed if necessary.

There are two options now available to Mr. Cooney. He can administer Forms A and B at the same time or with a time interval of, say, one week. These two procedures will yield somewhat different estimates of reliability. Let us examine both procedures beginning with administration at the same time.

Parallel Forms Administered at the Same Time. In this condition, Mr. Cooney has all his 24 grade 6 pupils write both forms at one sitting. Half of the pupils (12) are randomly selected to write Form A first and the other half will write Form B first. When they are finished, those that wrote Form A will write Form B, and those that wrote Form B will write Form A. This procedure is to remove the possibility of order effects (doing one thing will have an effect on the thing that is to be done immediately after). Each pupil will now have two scores, one on Form A and one on B.

Mr. Cooney can now correlate the two sets of scores using the Pearson correlation to derive a reliability coefficient, r_{xx}. This is an indicator of form equivalence. That is, it tells the extent to which the two test forms indeed measure the same thing. A very high index (close to 1.0) means that the two forms are highly equivalent, while a low index (close to 0.0) means that they are not at all equivalent. The second method is to administer the forms with a time interval.

Parallel Forms Administered at Different Times. The second option which Mr. Cooney had was to administer Form A first and one week later to administer Form B (as before to eliminate order effects, half of the pupils receive Form A and half Form B on testing occasion one, and vice versa on occasion two). As before, each pupil will have two scores, one on Form A and one on Form B.

Using the Pearson correlation as before, Mr. Cooney can compute a reliability coefficient, r_{xx}. In this case, the reliability tells not only about form equivalence (since two forms are compared) but also about the stability of the forms since a time interval has lapsed between administration of the two forms. All things remaining equal then, we would expect the coefficient that was computed using the second method to be smaller than the one computed using the first method. Only one source of error of measurement is introduced in the first procedure (lack of item equivalence), while two sources are introduced in the second situation (lack of item equivalence and instability of the test over time). The second method is the most rigorous measure of the test's reliability since both sources of measurement error are sampled. It is also more rigorous than the test-retest method, since in the parallel forms method only instability over time contributes to measurement error (the items are identical so there is no issue of equivalence) in that condition.

It probably has become obvious that the parallel form method (either at the same time or at different times) is highly impractical for classroom use. This is true for a number of reasons. First, twice the testing time is required compared to a single administration of the test. Second, a tremendous amount of effort goes into test construction by the teacher since large number of items are required for this method. Third, pupils may anticipate the second administration and so may prepare or study the material sampled by the first form. Given these limitations, the parallel form method is rarely used in classroom practice. Nevertheless, the parallel form method is widely used in standardized testing.

Such well known tests as the LSAT, SAT, MCAT and so on, come in multiple forms. These and many other tests have been developed, standardized, and are scored by Educational Testing Services (ETS) in Princeton, New Jersey. For several decades, this organization has been the foremost educational test developer in the world. As well, ETS is responsible for conducting research into testing and test development and has huge resources at its disposal such as a large campus-like physical plant, large high speed mainframe computers, and many hundreds of employees, many of which are psychologists and other specialists in testing and psychometrics.

With these abundant resources at their disposal, ETS can obviously do what the classroom teacher cannot. The SAT, for example, has multiple forms on any given testing each of which has known form equivalence reliability. In its computer banks, ETS has many thousands of items that are designed for the SAT according to the general procedures described above. As well, new items are constantly developed, added to the tests and tried out on forms of the test. The item bank, therefore, is constantly being replenished. Each form of the SAT is unique and will never be given as it is again. While these procedures employed by ETS approximate the ideal for test construction and development, they require such huge resources that it is not practical for classroom use, or at least hasn't been until recently.

Presently, test banks and test development software for personal and microcomputers are widely available. Many of these software packages have the capabilities to store up to 10,000 items. Teachers, therefore, can build item banks over time from which they can generate multiple forms of the same test by issuing a few simple commands to their computers. The ideal of the practice of ETS then, is now becoming a real possibility for individual teachers or at least groups of teachers in schools. Even so, however, the limitations of the parallel form method which were described above still hold. Thus other methods for establishing the reliability of classroom tests have been developed. An important such method is the split-half technique.

The Split-Half Method

Suppose that instead of giving his pupils Form A and then Form B of his test, Mr. Cooney simply had a single test made up of all of the items from the two forms. As far as the pupils are concerned, they received just one test. After the test was written, Mr. Cooney could *split the test in half* and derive a score for each pupil on each half. Then using the correlation procedures, he could compute the correlation between the scores on the two halves. This correlation is the basis for determining the reliability of the test. This procedure is the split-half method.

There are many ways of splitting a test in half. For a 50 item test, for example, items 1–25 could constitute the first half and items 26–50 could constitute the second half. Alternatively, items 1–7, 16–23, 32–43 could constitute the first half and the remaining items the second half. Indeed, the possibilities for splitting the test in half are staggering.[1] For a 25 item test, for example, there are 300 unique split-halves. A rule of thumb that has been developed is to use an **odd-even split.** In other words, the first half is made up of all the odd items (1, 3, 5, etc.) and the second half has all the even items (2, 4, 6, etc.).

This easy to remember rule allows for equivalent forms to be constructed. Each pupil then, receives a score on the even half and the odd half. These paired scores can now be correlated. Of course, you don't actually split the test but derive two scores for each pupil by, say, marking the odd items with a red pen and recording this score on the right-hand corner of the test, and the even half with a blue pen and recording this score on the left-hand corner. These scores can then be recorded and subsequently entered on the computer for analysis. A Pearson correlation can be computed for these scores although the result is not yet the actual reliability of the test. This is because the reliability of the test is based on test length and by splitting the test in half, the correlation that has been computed underestimates the actual reliability.

Test Length and Reliability. There is a relationship between the length of a test and its reliability. Generally, the longer the test, the more reliable it is. This is because a longer test samples more of the behavior of interest than does a short test. Each item on the test can be thought of as a sampling of the behavior—the more the behavior is sampled, the more reliable the results.

Consider an analogy of meeting new people to illustrate this principle of test length. When you meet a person for the first time for, say, one minute, you form an impression about that person. This impression is probably not very reliable since the sampling of behavior that you have is highly limited. Now suppose that you meet that person again for another minute, your impression is likely to be more reliable than the first one but still is probably poor. The more you interact with that person the more reliable your impression becomes—up to a certain point. Once you know someone very well, further interactions are not likely to change your impression of them very much. This is the same with tests. One item will not produce a very reliable measurement. Two items produce more reliability than one but still the reliability is low. As the number of items increases, so does the reliability. After a certain point, however, adding more items and thus sampling more behavior will not make much difference to the reliability just as your impression of a friend is unlikely to change with one further meeting once you have a very large sampling of their behavior. The relationship between test length and reliability is depicted in Figure 9.1.

Notice that as test length increases on short tests, the reliability increases sharply. When the test is longer, however, further increases in the length has little effect on the reliability. In fact, the "saturation" point on most tests is reached at about 75–80 items and there is little increase in reliability after this. As far as reliability is concerned, this is the point of diminishing returns (see Figure 9.1). The relationship between test length and reliability is not linear but rather is geometric and is described by a mathematical relationship, the Spearman-Brown formula.

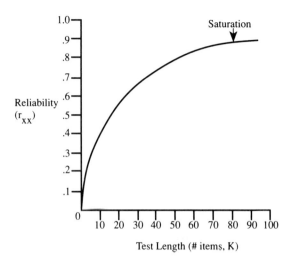

Figure 9.1. The relationship between test length and reliability

The Spearman Brown-Prophecy Formula. This formula "prophesizes" the change in reliability in a test given a change in the test's length. Thus we can equally determine the new reliability whether we increase the length of the test or decrease it. The formula is as follows:

$$r'_{xx} = \frac{Lr_{xx}}{1 + (L-1)r_{xx}}$$

Equation 9.1

where

> r'_{xx} is the adjusted reliability
> L is the ratio in change in length of the test
> r_{xx} is the known reliability

Suppose for example, Ms. Wong's arithmetic test had a reliability of $r_{xx} = .60$ with 20 items. Ms. Wong wants to know what the reliability will be if she doubles the test length to 40 items for next year. Using Equation 9.1,

> L = 40/20 = 2
> $r_{xx} = .60$

Thus,

$$r'_{xx} = \frac{2 \times .60}{1 + (2-1).60} = \frac{1.2}{1.6} = .75$$

Doubling the test length, therefore, will increase r_{xx} from .60 to .75, a substantial improvement. This is based on the assumption that the new items added are of equal quality to the original items. If the items are of better quality, the increase in reliability will be greater. If the items are of poorer quality the increase will be less.

The Spearman-Brown formula as given above is in its most general form and can be used to compute the change in reliability to a test for any item number change whether an increase or a decrease. All you need to know is the original reliability, r_{xx}, and L, the ratio change in length. L can be more precisely defined as k_2/k_1 where k_1 is the original test length and k_2 is the new test length (k always refers to the number of items). Thus if you wished to add 10 items to a 30 item test, the original test length, $k_1 = 30$ and $k_2 = 40$:

$$L = k_2/k_1 = 40/30 = 1.33$$

Alternatively, if you had a test of 50 items and you wished to shorten it to 40 items,

$$L = k_2/k_1 = 40/50 = .80$$

In the split-half computations, however, we always want to know the result when we double the test length and so L is always 2. Substituting 2 for L, the special version of Equation 9.1, then is

$$r'_{xx} = \frac{2 \times r_{oe}}{1 + r_{oe}} \qquad \text{Equation 9.2}$$

where

> r'_{xx} is the adjusted reliability as before
> r_{oe} is the correlation between the scores on the odd and even half of the test

The general split-half method and especially the odd-even split, is based on the assumption that the two halves of the test are equivalent. This assumption tends to be supported in most cases. If it is not, however, the reliability will be incorrect. This might happen, for example, if you were to give all of the items measuring knowledge level outcomes an even number and all items measuring higher level outcomes an odd number. In this case an odd-even split would not result in equivalent forms since the even half would be measuring at a lower cognitive level than the odd-half.

To summarize, the split-half method of determining reliability involves the following steps:

1. Determine a score for each pupil on the odd items of the test.
2. Determine a score for each pupil on the even items of the test.
3. Correlate the two sets of scores.
4. Using the special instance of the Spearman-Brown Prophecy formula (Equation 9.2), adjust the correlation between the odd and even halves to give the reliability of the test.

An example of the determination of the split-half reliability of a test is given in Table 9.1.

The split-half method of determining reliability, despite its strengths, is somewhat impractical and labor intensive for classroom use. In their continuing efforts to develop simple and practical methods for determining reliability, statisticians have invented several internal consistency methods.

The Internal Consistency Methods

The odd-even split is just one of many possible split-halves. Indeed, there are a great many possible split-halves as we have seen, with a 25 item test producing 300 unique combinations. If you computed a correlation for each split-half, then you would have 300 correlations that would not be identical to each other. Taking the mean of these correlations, r, and adjusting this with

177

Table 9.1. An example of computing the split-half reliability.

Ms. Yen gave her grade 6 class a 40 item Social Studies test and got the following odd-even split results:

Pupil	Even Score	Odd Score	Total Score
1	19	15	34
2	11	12	23
3	16	14	30
4	8	9	17
5	7	8	15
6	14	12	26
7	8	10	18
8	15	14	29
9	15	20	35
10	8	6	14
11	6	10	16
12	12	15	27
13	9	11	20
14	13	10	23
15	14	16	30

Ms. Yen correlated the even scores with the odd scores and got, r_{oe} = .74. She also computed descriptive statistics for the total test scores and got the following: mean = 23.79, s^2 = 45.72, s = 6.72. Using the special version of the Spearman-Brown prophecy formula (Equation 9.2), Ms. Yen did the following calculation

$r_{xx} = 2r_{oe}/1 + r_{oe}$
$= 2 \times .74/1 + .74$
$= .85$

Ms. Yen, therefore, concluded that the split-half reliability of her entire test was r_{xx} -= .85. The test has good reliability.

the Spearman-Brown formula (Equation 9.2), will produce a reliability estimate, r_{xx}, which is called KR20. This reliability computation was invented by G. F. Kuder and M. W. Richardson in 1937, and there is a shortcut computation which fortunately avoids the necessity of calculating correlations at all. The formula is

$$KR20 = \left(\frac{k}{k-1} \quad 1 - \frac{\Sigma_{pq}}{s^2} \right)$$
Equation 9.3

where

p is the proportion passing an item
q is the proportion not passing an item (i.e., 1 – p)
k is the number of items on the test
s^2 is the variance of the test

Computing the KR20 by hand is very tedious and impractical so that Kuder and Richardson proposed another formula, KR21. While it is not as accurate as KR20, this second formula is much simpler to compute and therefore it is the recommended formula for classroom applications. It requires that we only know the mean ($\overline{X}$) of the test, the variance (s^2), and the number of items (k). Thus,

Table 9.2. An example of how to compute KR21 reliability.

Mr. Francs gave his grade three class a 30 item test and got the following test scores: 26, 8, 14, 14, 21, 23, 17, 14, 10, 11, 29, 11, 15, 14, 20, 18, 22, 12, 9, 9. He wanted to derive an internal consistency reliability measure so decided on KR21. Using his statistical program, he derived the following results: Mean = 15.94, s^2 = 32.84, s = 5.73, and he knew that k = 30. Using Equation 9.4, Mr. Francs did the following computations:

$$KR21 = \frac{30}{30-1}(1 - \frac{15.94(30-15.94)}{30 \times 32.84})$$

$$=.79$$

Therefore, Mr. Francs concluded that the internal consistency of his test was, r_{xx} = .79.

$$KR21 = \frac{k}{k-1}(1 - \frac{\overline{X}(k-\overline{X})}{ks^2}) \qquad \text{Equation 9.4}$$

The KR21 formula also assumes that each item on the test is of equal difficulty, which we know not to be true. Nevertheless, this method gives adequate results for most classroom applications even though not all the assumptions are met. KR21 will slightly underestimate KR20 for any test but produces acceptable results.

Another more general internal consistency measure of reliability was developed by L. J. Cronbach (1951) and is called Cronbach's alpha or coefficient alpha. Both KR20 and KR21 are specific cases of alpha which is the most general reliability coefficient. It too, however, is very tedious and impractical to compute for classroom purposes and is rarely used in such circumstances. Of the internal consistency measures, the one recommended for classroom use is KR21. An example for computing KR21 is given in Table 9.2.

For different purposes, different methods of estimating reliability are appropriate. For typical classroom purposes, however, two factors are of overriding importance: (1) practicality, and (2) ease of computation. The method which best fits both of these criteria is KR21. And even while it is not as elegant and precise as some of the other methods, it is preferable to nothing at all which is what most teachers will have if other computations or procedures are recommended. The other methods for deriving reliability (test-retest, parallel forms, split-half, KR20, coefficient alpha) are too complex, time consuming, tedious and impractical for most classroom use although they are in wide use for research purposes and for standardized tests. The various ways of estimating reliability and the procedures involved are summarized in Table 9.3.

Another way of thinking about reliability and utilizing the test data is the standard error of measurement.

Standard Error of Measurement

The unreliability of the test $(1 - r_{xx})$ is due to errors of measurement. In other words, the difference between the reliability coefficient and 1 is due to errors. This can tell you the percentage or proportion of the variance in pupil performance that is due to error and not real differences in pupil performance.

If, for example, the variance in performance on a test is 200, how much of this is due to real differences in performance among the pupils and how much is due to errors of measurement? This

179

Table 9.3. Various Methods of Estimating Reliability

Method	Reliability Measure	Procedure
Test-retest	Stability over time	Give the exact same test to the same group of pupils at different times (interval of hours, days, months, years, etc.)
Parallel Forms (same time)	Form equivalence	Give two forms of the same test to the same group at the same time
Parallel Forms (different time)	Form equivalence and stability over time	Give two forms of the same test with a time interval between the two forms
Split-half	Internal consistency	Split the test into odd-even halves and correlate the resulting scores. Adjust with the Spearman-Brown formula
KR20, KR21, Cronbach's alpha	Internal consistency	Give the test once and apply the Kuder-Richardson formula or Cronbach's alpha coefficient formula

question can be answered by using the reliability coefficient. A test with a reliability of r_{xx} = .70 leaves .30 due to errors of measurement $(1 - r_{xx})$. That is, 30% of the variance is due to errors of measurement. Therefore, 60 units of the variance $(200 \times 30/100)$ arise as a direct result of measurement error and not real differences in pupil performance.

These concepts and data can be used more importantly to interpret individual test scores as well as group performance. What is of interest is how many points on the test are actually due to errors of measurement. This is called the standard error of measurement and is a direct function of the reliability of the test. The formula for the standard error of measurement is

$$S_e = S_t \sqrt{1 - r_{xx}} \qquad \text{Equation 9.5}$$

where

S_e is the standard error of measurement
S_t is the standard deviation of test scores
r_{xx} is the reliability of the test

Thus for a test with r_{xx} of .80 and S_t of 10,

$$S_e = 10 \sqrt{1 - .80}$$
$$= 10 \sqrt{.20}$$
$$= 4.47$$

If a pupil received a score of 67 on this test (k = 100), this pupils' real or *true* score on this test could be at least 4.47 points higher or 4.47 points lower because these are how many test points are due just to errors of measurement. The S_e then, is most useful for interpreting raw scores and deriving true scores.

True Scores. When you write a test, you receive an obtained or raw score which is mixed with error. It is assumed that at the moment of writing the test you have a theoretical entity called a true score which is your error free, measured level of performance. Since it is not possible to ever measure anything completely free of error, true scores cannot be measured directly. You can only estimate the range within which the true score falls at a particular level of probability. This idea is based on the fact that errors of measurement are normally distributed (See Chapter 7 for a description of the normal distribution.) with a mean of zero. (This is the definition of error of measurement—random fluctuation.)

For a test that has S_e = 5, the distribution of its errors of measurement is normal with a mean of 0 and standard deviation of 5. Therefore, 68% of the time that this test is applied, it will produce raw scores that fluctuate within 1 standard deviation (S = 5) of the mean (0). Actual raw scores will fluctuate 10 points (0 ± 5) 68% of the time. Of course, 95% of the time it will produce raw scores that fluctuate 20 points (0 ± 10; i.e. ± 2S) and 99% of the time, the raw scores will fluctuate 30 points (0 ± 15; i.e. ± 3S). These facts can be used in a slightly different version to help interpret test scores.

When a pupil receives a raw score of 54 on the above test, you can be confident at the 68% level that his true score fluctuates between 49 and 59 (54 ± 5; i.e., 54 ± 1S_e). While you can never know his true score (since true scores are error free theoretical entities), you can construct confidence intervals around the raw score within which the true score falls. The relationship between raw score, true score and error is given as

$$R = T + e \qquad\qquad \text{Equation 9.6}$$

where

    R is the raw score
    T is the true score
    e is error of measurement

The error of measurement in any given test is estimated by S_e and R is a known quantity for any given pupil. The three confidence intervals that are commonly used are defined by the standard deviations of the normal distribution (± 1S, ± 2S, ± 3S), 68%, 95% and 99%. For true score estimation, the confidence level and true scores are given as

Confidence level	True Score interval
68%	± 1S_e
95%	± 2S_e
99%	± 3S_e

True scores, reliability and standard error of measurement are all interrelated. Notice too that as the level of confidence increases (you are more confident about the range of true score), the range of the true score becomes larger. Of course if you were to encompass the whole range of the test, you would be 100% confident that the true score falls in that range. The idea is to increase confidence without increasing the range of the true score interval. This can only be done by increasing the reliability of the test and therefore decreasing S_e. There are a number of factors that influence the reliability of tests.

Factors That Influence Reliability

Six main factors influence reliability.

1. Test Length. As already described, the length of the test is directly related to its reliability. A longer test not only provides a better sampling of the content area and cognitive outcomes of interest, but it also tends to reduce the effects of chance factors such as guessing. If you had a test with only one true-false question, for example, the probability of selecting the correct answer by chance alone is 50%. Thus a pupil who guesses wrong, receives a 0 and is thought to know absolutely nothing about the content. Alternatively, a pupil who guesses correctly receives a perfect score. Neither of the results, however, are indicative of any true knowledge because the test is far too short to produce reliable results.

In general, teachers should strive for the longest tests possible because of the reliability concern. Test length, however, reaches the point of diminishing returns as discussed previously (see Figure 9.1). Moreover, many other factors such as time available for testing, the amount of content to be covered by the test, the grade level of the pupils, and so on will influence the determination of test length. Even taking all of these into account, a long test is usually more desirable then a short one.

2. Time Interval. In the test-retest and parallel form methods of estimating reliability, the time interval between testing sessions can vary from hours to days to months and even to years. The longer the time interval, the lower the reliability tends to be. This is because the more time has elapsed between testing periods, the changes in the phenomenon that is measured (e.g., math achievement, IQ) are likely to increase. Thus the scores will likely be inconsistent across the testing periods producing low reliability estimates.

When teachers are using tests whose reliability is based on the test-retest or parallel form method, it is crucial that the time interval between the first and second administrations of the test is known. This is especially important when pupils' progress is measured using the same test (or parallel forms of it) over time. It is very common, for example, to administer standardized achievement tests in every grade in elementary school as a way of monitoring pupil progress. If you give a child a basic skills test in grade 3 and then again one year later in grade 4, it is crucial that you know the reliability of the test over a one year time span. Interpretations in the absence of this knowledge are likely to be incorrect. The test may be quite reliable over the period of a month but not at all reliable over a year.

3. Heterogeneity of Test Takers. The greater the heterogeneity of a group of test takers, the more reliable the test tends to be. If you give a test to a group of grade 3, 4 and 5 pupils, the reliability will tend to be higher than if you give the test to a same size group of grade 4 pupils. The former group is more heterogeneous than the latter group and so will produce a greater spread of scores. Since reliability estimates are based on maintaining the relative position among test takers, when the testees are very similar (i.e., not very heterogeneous) chance factors can easily rearrange relative positions of scores because they are very close together in the first place. On the other hand, for testees who are very heterogeneous, the spread of scores is great and chance factors have less influence on the relative position of the scores and thus the reliability of the test. All things remaining equal then, reliability estimates of a test will tend to be higher when they are based on a very heterogeneous group.

4. Speeded Tests. Speeded tests, in contrast to power tests, have time as a factor, and the items are uniformly easy. That is, they are designed so that most of the testees will not finish the test in the time allotted, although they will get most of what they do correct. When internal consistency methods are used for computing reliability under these conditions, this has the effect of artificially increasing the reliability coefficient. This is because a series of items will be highly consistent in producing results—the last ten items, for example, might be answered incorrectly by nearly all test takers, perhaps because they ran out of time. While speed is rarely a factor in teacher-made tests, it can be an important consideration in standardized tests. Thus, when reliability coefficients are derived by the internal consistency method for standardized tests, you should check carefully if speed was used as a factor. If so, the coefficient is likely to be spuriously high.

5. Test Difficulty. Tests that are too difficult or too easy for the test takers will have poor reliability. The concept of reliability is based on maximizing the variance of the group measured because you wish to detect individual differences as sensitively as possible. When a test is too difficult, most people score poorly and their differences are not detected by the test. Conversely, when a test is too easy, the same result ensues. In norm-referenced test construction then, you should strive to write items of about average difficulty so as to maximize the reliability.

6. Objectivity in Scoring. Essay and short-answer tests cannot be objectively scored as the procedure requires subjective judgments by the scorer. This lack of objectivity will tend to reduce the reliability of these tests. Multiple-choice tests have the advantage that they can be completely objectively scored by anyone in possession of the answer key or indeed, even by a machine such as an optical scanner. Due to validity considerations, however, it is frequently not possible to use objective type items for testing. This might be the case when higher level cognitive outcomes such as synthesis which require the organization and origination of ideas, are measured. Usually only essay type items will suffice in these circumstances. By scoring the responses carefully according to pre-specified criteria, however, the subjectivity can be reduced with the effect that reliability will be improved.

■ Summary and Main Points

Reliability—defined as the consistency of measurement—is a necessary but not sufficient condition for validity. A test which is reliable is not necessarily valid but a test which is valid must be reliable. Reliability is not a single, unitary concept, but rather is several related ideas. There are four basic ways to compute a reliability coefficient, r_{xx}: (1) test-retest, (2) parallel forms, (3) split-half, and (4) internal consistency. Each method focuses on a somewhat different aspect of reliability. Test-retest and parallel forms (administered at different times) both estimate the test's stability over time. Parallel forms (administered both at the same and at different times) estimate form equivalence. Internal consistency—of which split-half is a special case—estimates the degree to which the items of the test "hang together" or measure in the same direction. In the split-half technique, the derived correlation coefficient must be adjusted using the Spearman-Brown prophecy formula which describes the relationship between test length and reliability. While reliability allows for the overall evaluation of a test, the standard error of measurement (S_e) gives an index of the band of error that exists on the total test scale. The S_e is especially useful for determining the band of error around an individual's obtained score and thus estimating the interval of that person's true score. True scores are hypothetical entities which can never be measured directly but only inferred within a specified range on the test scale at a particular confidence level. Three confidence levels are generally used: 68%, 95%, and 99%. As the confidence level increases, the interval within which the true score falls also increases thereby losing precision. Confidence is gained at the expense of precision. Both precision and confidence can be increased by improving the reliability of the test.

A number of factors influence the reliability of the test. These include the length of the test, the heterogeneity of the testees, the length of the time interval in test-retest and parallel forms at different times, whether or not the test is speeded, the difficulty of the test, and objectivity of scoring of the test. There are a number of strategies that teachers can use to increase the reliability of their tests.

1. Reliability is a necessary but not sufficient condition for validity. A test can be reliable but not valid. A valid test, however, must be reliable.
2. Reliability is measured by an index called the reliability coefficient, r_{xx}.
3. There are four basic methods for deriving r_{xx}: test-retest, parallel forms, split-half, and internal consistency. Each method focuses on a somewhat different aspect of reliability.
4. The test-retest method involves administering the exact same test to the same group on two different occasions. The scores are then correlated to derive r_{xx}. This method is quite impractical for classroom use as it is inefficient, subject to practice and learning effects, and is wasteful of limited classroom time.
5. Parallel forms requires that two or more forms of the test be constructed. Each form is thought to measure the same thing and they can be given at the same time or at different times. In the former situation, the second form is administered immediately after the first form is completed. The correlation between the scores on the two forms yields an index of form equivalence. When the forms are administered with a time interval, the resulting r_{xx} combines both form equivalence and stability over time. All things remaining equal, this is the most rigorous method of deriving reliability. Like the test-retest method, parallel forms has shortcomings (wasteful of time, requires that a very large number of items be constructed, is inefficient) that make it impractical for classroom use. It is a widely used technique, however, for standardized testing.
6. The split-half method is more practical for classroom use than either of the above methods. A single test is given and two separate scores are derived subsequently, usually one for the odd numbered items and one for the even numbered items. These scores are correlated to derive a coefficient which then must be adjusted with the Spearman-Brown prophecy formula to produce r'_{xx}.
7. The Spearman-Brown prophecy formula in its most general form (Equation 9.1), describes the relationship between test length and reliability. Thus once you know the reliability of a particular test, you can "prophesize" the effect on the reliability by either increasing the test length or decreasing it. To adjust the correlation coefficient in the split-half method, the specific version of the Spearman-Brown prophecy formula

is used (Equation 9.2) since you always want to know the results when the test is doubled (i.e., the ratio increase is two).

8. The most practical and simplest method of determining reliability for classroom use is the Kuder-Richardson formula 21 (KR21) which is a general internal consistency method. The KR21 method only requires that you know the number of items on the test, the mean of the test and its variance. While KR21 is not as accurate an internal consistency measure of reliability as some other methods (e.g., KR20, Cronbach's alpha), its simplicity of computation makes it the most preferred for classroom use.

9. The standard error of measurement, S_e, translates the test's reliability (Equation 9.5) onto the actual test scale to estimate the error involved in actual scores that pupils receive. The S_e is most useful for interpreting an individual's performance on the test.

10. The score a pupil actually obtains on a test is composed of true score plus error of measurement. True scores are hypothetical entities estimated by the use of the S_e and a particular confidence interval. Thus the true score falls within a band of error as circumscribed by the S_e with a specific degree of confidence.

11. By convention, three confidence intervals are commonly used: 68% ($\pm 1S_e$), 95% ($\pm 2S_e$), and 99% ($\pm 3S_e$). Notice that as the degree of confidence of the interval containing the true scores increases, precision decreases as the error band encompasses more of the test scale. Increasing the test's reliability will increase both confidence and precision.

12. There are several common factors that directly influence a test's reliability. These include the test's length, the heterogeneity of the test takers, whether or not the test is speeded, the length of the time interval in test-retest and parallel forms at different times, the difficulty of the test, and the objectivity of the scoring of the test.

■ Further Readings

Anastasi, A. (1989). *Psychological testing* (6th ed.). New York: MacMillan. See especially Chapter 5, "Reliability".

Crocker, L., and Algina, J. (1986). *Introduction to classical and modern test theory.* New York: Holt, Rinehart and Winston. This is an advanced treatment—see Unit II (Chapter 6, 7, 8, 9).

Cronbach, L. J. (1984). *Essentials of psychological testing* (4th ed.). New York: Harper & Row. See Chapter 6, "How to Judge Tests".

Popham, W. J. (1990). *Modern educational measurements* (2nd ed.). Englewood Cliffs, N.J.: Prentice-Hall. See Chapter 6, "Reliability".

■ Laboratory Exercises

Part A: Methods of Estimating Reliability

1. What are the limitations of test-retest methods for determining the reliability of classroom tests?

2. Describe a measuring instrument and a situation in which test-retest would be appropriate. Be sure to discuss why this method would have to be used and how you would implement it.

3. Briefly discuss why parallel forms techniques of determining reliability are impractical for classroom use.
4. Under what conditions and how is it appropriate to use parallel forms methods to derive reliability.
5. The following set of data is an odd-even split of test results from a 20 item test.

Student	Odd Score	Even Score
1	10	9
2	8	8
3	7	4
4	10	8
5	4	6
6	8	8
7	9	9
8	9	7
9	6	6
10	5	5
11	7	9
12	6	4
13	3	4
15	7	8
16	8	7
17	5	6
18	4	3
19	9	8
20	7	7
21	4	2
22	5	4
23	6	8

a. Compute the correlation between the odd and even halves.
b. Using the correlation from a) determine the reliability of the test (i.e., adjust r_{oe} with Spearman-Brown prophecy formula).
6. Using the Science data from Chapter 7, compute the KR21 reliability for Quiz1, Quiz2, Quiz3, and the Final.
7. Compute S_e for the test data in #5 above. (Hint: you will need the standard deviation of the *total* test scores in addition to r_{xx} you calculated in #5.)
8. Compute S_e for Quiz1, Quiz2, Quiz3, and the Final from the Science data from Chapter 7.
9. For the test in #5 above, calculate the true score intervals for all 23 students at the 68%, 95% and 99% level of confidence.
10. Select any standardized test that you have access to (e.g., IQ tests, Achievement tests, Affective tests, etc.) and review it on the following: (1) reliability (What reliabilities are reported? Are these appropriate given the test's use? In what way is the test reliable? Are the reliabilities adequate given the intended use of the test?), (2) error associated with the test scores (i.e., S_e), and (3) the score reporting system (Are error bands drawn around raw score to indicate the S_e?).

11. The following letter appeared in *The Seattle Times* (July 5, 1990, p. A 11):

In West Germany, children's educational goals are decided around the fourth grade. Depending upon the country's needs, and various other factors, the students are sent through one of three systems translated roughly as high school-bound, trade school-bound, or university-bound.

Can you imagine having your educational goals determined by the fourth grade?

Most Americans couldn't. We like to think our system is superior by the mere fact that it is "equal", democratic even. Anybody can be "all they can be". However, in discussions about what's wrong with our system, it would be prudent to examine exactly how undemocratic it really is.

For the first 12 years, everybody gets the same watered-down education. We mainstream the masses, and forget about individual needs, or unique talents. At the college level we, too, have our own "gates": the SAT, the ACT, the GRE, etc. Americans assume that these are a reliable measure of a student's ability to do well in college. Yet the reliability and statistical measures range between 10 to 15 percent. Yet, poor kinds, minorities, and others have trouble with these tests.

I am one of those cases. I squeaked my way through college and graduate school by way of the back door. Now, I've taught college for the past five years, and I wonder why money and class background played such a factor in my homogeneous group of students. Rarely do I find disadvantaged students, or minorities. You hardly ever hear about poor kids who didn't make it because they couldn't answer the GRE question: an apple is to an orange like: (a) a banana is to a pear. (b) a tree is to a donut, etc.

I think again of West Germans and of Americans. They call an apple by its right name, whereas Americans like to call an apple an orange, when it is really an apple. Somebody, please give me the right answer.

—Page Mordecai, Seattle

    a. What is the writer's main complaint about the American educational system?
    b. What does the author of this letter mean by "the reliability and statistical measures range between 10 to 15 percent"? What in fact is the reliability of the SAT and GRE?
    c. Do you think the writer understands reliability? Why or why not?
    d. In what ways are reliability and validity confused in the above letter?

Notes

1. The number of combinations of n objects taken r at a time is given by the following equation:

$$\frac{n!}{r!(n-r)!}$$

The number of combinations of 4 objects taken 2 at a time therefore $= 4!/2!(4-2)! = 4 \times 3 \times 2 \times 1/2 \times 1(3 \times 2 \times 1) = 6$. To calculate the possible number of split-halves for a test, the number of items (k) is treated as n in the equation while r is half the number of items (k/2).

Chapter

10

Evaluating, Scoring and Analyzing the Test

Overview

Valid classroom testing begins with a test plan and table of specifications that describe in detail both the content areas to be tested and the level of understanding of each question as well as the relative emphasis of both (see chapters 3 and 8). The item-type (e.g. multiple-choice, essay) should also have been determined based on the level of understanding to be measured. The use of the appropriate item-type together with the table of specifications enhances the content and face validity of the test and thus increases the chances that the test will serve its intended purpose. Much effort has gone into the planning of the test and writing the items as well as making the test (see Chapter 3 for details of these steps). In addition, careful attention is required in scoring, analyzing and evaluating the test. Each of these steps play a vital role in effective testing.

In this chapter we will examine each of these vital steps in turn. In scoring tests, you must first prepare a key and decide how to handle guessing on objective tests. Once the test has been scored, it must be analyzed. This involves computing the central tendencies, variability and reliability of the test. Each item must be analyzed using item analysis. This involves deriving the item difficulty, discrimination and distractor effectiveness. Finally, the test must be evaluated based on these data.

Evaluating the Test Before It Is Given

A preliminary evaluation of the test should be done before it is given. This evaluation is based on the adequacy of the test plan, of the items and of the format and directions of the test. Gronlund and Linn (1990) developed a 20 point checklist which is helpful in evaluating the classroom test under these categories. This checklist is summarized in table 10.1.

Table 10.1. A Checklist for Evaluating Teacher-Made Tests

A. Adequacy of Test Plans
1. Does the test plan adequately describe the instructional objectives and the content to be measured?
2. Does the test plan clearly indicate the relative emphasis to be given to each objective and each content area?

B. Adequacy of Test Items
3. Is the format of each item suitable for the learning outcome being measured (appropriateness)?
4. Does each test item require pupils to demonstrate the performance described in the specific learning outcome it measures (relevance)?
5. Does each item present a clear and definite task to be performed (clarity)?
6. Is each test item presented in simple, readable language and free from excessive verbiage (conciseness)?
7. Is each test item of appropriate difficulty for the type of test constructed (ideal difficulty)?
8. Does each test item have an answer that would be agreed upon by experts (correctness)?
9. Is each test item free from technical errors and irrelevant clues (technical soundness)?
10. Is each test item free from racial, ethnic, and sexual bias (cultural fairness)?
11. Is each test item independent of the other items in the test (independence)?
12. Is there an adequate number of test items for each learning outcome (sample adequacy)?

C. Adequacy of test Format and Directions
13. Are test items of the same type grouped together in the test (or within sections of the test)?
14. Are the test items arranged from easy to more difficult within sections of the test and the test as a whole?
15. Are the test items numbered in sequence?
16. Is the answer space clearly indicated (on the test itself or on a separate answer sheet), and is each answer space related to its corresponding test item?
17. Are the correct answers distributed in such a way that there is no detectable pattern?
18. Is the test material well spaced, legible, and free of typographical errors?
19. Are there directions for each section of the test and the test as a whole?
20. Are the directions clear and concise?

Reprinted by permission of Macmillan Publishing Company from *Measurement and Evaluation in Teaching* (6th ed.) by N. E. Gronlund and R. L. Linn (1990). Copyright 1990 by Macmillan Publishing Company.

The adequacy of the test plan focuses on the instructional objectives and the content area while the adequacy of the test items deal with their appropriateness, relevance, clarity, technical soundness, and so on. Finally, the adequacy of test format and directions focus on item grouping, legibility, clarity of directions and so on. Notice that each of these points in Table 10.1 is posed as a question. You should answer ''yes'' to each of these questions to satisfy yourself that the test meets criteria of adequacy. Once you are satisfied with your test, you should make enough copies and administer it to your pupils. The next step is to score the test.

Scoring the Test

Procedures for scoring both objective and essay tests were described in previous chapters. A key should be used for both essay and objective tests to make the scoring most efficient (quick and error free). The pupils' final score on the test is the sum of the points awarded for individual items. For objective items, the simplest procedure is to award one point for each correct answer. For essay tests, each item will have a maximum value that pupils will achieve some (or all) points on. The practice of awarding differential point values for different items on objective tests, makes the scoring procedures unnecessarily complex and arbitrary. It provides no real advantage and, therefore, should be avoided. On objective items, you should decide on how to handle guessing.

Dealing with Guessing

Pupils' proclivity to guess or "set to gamble" is a stable individual difference. Some pupils will guess at an answer no matter how remote the possibility is of selecting the right answer while others will not respond unless they feel certain about the correct answer. Teachers have developed a number of strategies in an attempt to deal with guessing including penalties, instructions *not* to guess, and using correction formulae.

In an attempt to reduce or eliminate guessing, some teachers institute a penalty system such as subtracting the wrong from the right. This is based on the flawed assumption that every wrong answer reflects a guess (the pupil may be truly confused) and can result in absurd results such as negative scores and zero scores. Such procedures should not be used in classroom tests.

Instructions and exhortations *not* to guess do not work very well either. Pupils who have a proclivity to gamble will not be deterred by instructions, while those who are reluctant to guess will be made even more wary. It is virtually impossible to eliminate guessing on classroom tests either through the use of penalties or instructions.

Another procedure for handling guessing is to apply a correction for guessing formula:

$$\text{Score} = \text{Right} - \frac{\text{Wrong}}{n-1} \qquad\qquad \text{Equation 10.1}$$

Where n is the number options in the item. For a four option item (n = 4) then, the formula simplifies as follows:

$$\text{Score} = \text{Right} - \frac{\text{Wrong}}{3}$$

To use this formula you must count both the right and wrong items. Blank items are not included. Suppose that on a fifty item four-option multiple-choice test, Amy, for example, correctly answered 30 items. When you analyze the test you find that she left 5 items blank and answered 15 items incorrectly. Applying equation 10.1 then,

$$\text{Score} = 30 - \frac{15}{3} = 25$$

You would assign a score of 25 to Amy.

This formula (as well as other correction for guessing formulae) are based on the assumption that pupils guess blindly when they do not know the answer. Such guessing rarely occurs in classroom tests. On multiple-choice items, pupils can generally eliminate at least one option thus improving the chances of selecting the correct answer. Even when a pupil answers incorrectly, it may be due to misinformation, confusion or very plausible distractors. Because of these factors, any correction for guessing formulae will introduce error into the scoring and distort scores in unknown ways.

The only time that the use of Equation 10.1 can be justified is in highly speeded tests. On these tests, pupils are generally working so quickly that incorrect responses do reflect blind guesses especially when they rapidly and blindly respond to the remaining items before the time expires. Generally, you should not use any correction for guessing for ordinary classroom tests.

The best procedure for dealing with guessing on objective tests is to have all pupils answer all questions. Thus any advantage which may accrue from guessing will do so uniformly across all pupils rather than just for those who have a set to gamble. You should do this with both instructions ("If you don't know, then guess") and teaching test-taking strategies. On a norm-referenced test, such guessing makes no difference in any case, as in the overall results a constant will have been added to the mean. Since the mean can be arbitrarily set (depending on the test difficulty or number of items on the test) the effect of adding a constant through uniform guessing will not alter the outcome. Teachers, therefore, should encourage all students to respond to all items. To determine the effectiveness of the test you must compute the central tendency, variability and reliability of the test in order to analyze it.

Analyzing the Test

A full test analysis requires that you compute measures of central tendency as well as variability and derive an estimate of reliability and finally, an item analysis (described in the next section).

Central Tendency

On classroom tests, you should generally compute all three measures of central tendency (mean, mode, median). If you are using a computer programme this is a routine matter. You can easily compute all three measures. One of the first questions you might want to ask, is about the nature of the distribution.

Compare the values of the mean, mode and median. If they are approximately equal (within 5 percentage points of each other), the underlying distribution is approximately normal. If the mode is greater than the median which is greater than the mean, then you have a negatively skewed distribution. The reverse—mean greater than the median greater the mode—indicates that you have a positively skewed distribution (see Chapter 7 for a detailed explanation). A negative skew suggest that the test was too difficult, a positive skew means the test was too hard and a normal distribution that the test was about right in the level of difficulty. For a norm-referenced test, 68–72% is an ideal level of difficulty.

Variability

The degree of variability in test scores is best reflected by the variance and standard deviation. The range—derived from minimum and maximum scores—also gives a rough index of the variability in test scores. If you computed the measures of central tendency using a computer programme, you will also have computed all the variability statistics (variance, standard deviation, range, minimum, maximum).

In norm-referenced tests, generally the greater the variability the better. This is because the greater the variability, the higher the reliability of the test. Intuitively this makes sense because there is considerable variability or heterogeneity in a "normal" class. The variability in test scores, therefore, reflects the true heterogeneity in the class. If the variance is very small, this suggests one of two possibilities: (1) your class is very homogeneous, or (2) your test is flawed and it is artificially producing low variability. How large should be the variance? To answer this question, we must consider the standard deviation because the variance cannot be directly interpreted this way.

The standard deviation, of course, is the square root of the variance and represents true scale points on the test. Ideally, the value of the standard deviation should be 10–12% of the total test scale. A test with 50 items, therefore, should have a standard deviation of approximately 5 or 6. A small standard deviation may alternatively indicate that the test-takers are quite homogeneous. A reading test given to only grade 5 pupils in the first instance, and grades 4, 5, and 6 in the second instance, will result in a larger standard deviation with the second instance than the first because greater heterogeneity in reading exists among grades 4, 5 and 6 pupils than just grade 5 pupils. Employing the same reasoning, the test should have a range of 50% of the total scale with the maximum score at or near the total possible score and the minimum score in the bottom half of the test. For a 50 item test, then, the range should be approximately 25 with the maximum score around 46–50 and the minimum score 20–25. A minimum score significantly greater than or less than 20 would not necessarily indicate poor range: outliers are unpredictable and can fluctuate easily.

Reliability

An overall analysis of the test must employ a reliability estimate (which is affected by the means and variance). For most classroom tests, you will probably use an internal consistency estimate of reliability such as Kuder-Richardson formula 21 which is easily computed (see Chapter 9 for reliability). For our current purposes, the size of the reliability coefficient (r_{xx}) is more important than how it was computed. The question that concerns us for the moment is, "How large should the reliability coefficient be?"

To answer this question, remember that r_{xx} represents the consistency of measurement of the test. Therefore, the larger the coefficient, the higher the degree of consistency. A coefficient of $r_{xx} = 1.0$ represents perfect reliability and any value less than that indicates that there is error of measurement involved. In a test with $r_{xx} = .75$, for example, 75% ($.75 \times 100$) of the variance in test scores is due to true score differences among pupils (see Chapter 9). This implies that 25% of the variation in test scores is due to error of measurement.

Consider a test with a reliability of $r_{xx} = .50$. This means that 50% of the variation in test scores is due to true score differences (real differences in achievement) among pupils, while the other 50% is due to error. When the reliability of the test is less than $r_{xx} = .50$, more than half of the variation in test scores is due to error of measurement. For a classroom test with $r_{xx} = .40$, 60% of the variance in test scores is due to error of measurement rather than real achievement differences (i.e., true scores) of the pupils.

Different standards for reliability apply for standardized tests and teacher-made tests. Many standardized IQ, achievement, and reading tests, have r_{xx} greater than .90. This means that less than 10% of the variation in scores is due to error. Conversely, this suggests that more than 90% of the variance is due to true score differences. It is unrealistic, however, to expect the same standards to apply to teacher made tests. Tremendous resources, time and effort usually go into building, refining and perfecting most standardized tests like the WISC-R and SAT which have reliabilities greater than r_{xx} of .90.

Most teacher made tests are constructed from new items and perhaps some previously tested items. The test is usually intended to be given only once. Therefore, if reliabilities of greater than r_{xx} of .75 are achieved, this is excellent. Reliabilities ranging between .60–.75 are good to very good while .50.–.59 are acceptable. Reliabilities of less than $r_{xx} = .50$, however, are poor.

This, of course, is because in such circumstances, more than half of the test score variance is due to errors of measurement. For classroom purposes, therefore, you should aim at reliabilities of at least .50 or greater. Test scores resulting from tests with reliabilities smaller than this should be regarded with suspicion and interpreted very cautiously.

Item Analysis

The measures of central tendency, variability and reliability are overall summary indices of the properties of a test. But a test is composed of a number of items, each of which can be analyzed individually to evaluate its efficacy. Thus a complete analysis of a test also requires an item-analysis. There are three essential features of items that constitutes an item analysis: (1) difficulty of the item, (2) item discrimination, and (3) distractor effectiveness. All three properties are relevant to selection type items (e.g., multiple-choice), while only the first two apply to open-ended or supply type items (e.g., essay). Obviously, there are no distractors in essay items so the third element is irrelevant.

The difficulty of an item has to do with the percentage of pupils that answer the item correctly for a selection-type item, or the mean performance on an item on an essay question. If in a multiple-choice item, all the testees get the item correct, then it is very easy. Alternatively, if no one gets the item correct, then it's very difficult.

Item discrimination has to do with the extent to which an item distinguishes or "discriminates" between high test scorers or low test scorers. Suppose that a test item had a difficulty of 50% (half the testees selected the correct answer). We might very well ask, which half got it correct? Was it the high achievers or the low achievers? Clearly, depending on which of these two groups disproportionately answered the item correctly, the item is discriminating or distinguishing between them. This is called item discrimination. For essay tests, item discrimination refers to the correlation of item performance to the total test performance across all testees.

Distractor effectiveness refers to the ability of distractors in multiple-choice items in attracting responses. A distractor which attracts no responses is not effective; it begins to become effective when it attracts some responses. There are some preparatory steps in conducting an item analysis which differ slightly for essay and multiple-choice tests.

Preparing for an Item Analysis. Items analyses occur after the test has been scored. The procedures are somewhat different for supply and selection type tests so each will be discussed in turn.

For multiple-choice tests, you must identify a high scoring group and a low scoring group in order to conduct the item analysis. After the test is scored then, you must rank-order the test papers from lowest score to highest. Thus you will literally have a pile of test papers with the top ones being the highest scores and the bottom ones being the lowest. We usually wish to compare and contrast performance on each item of the top 25% of the scorers with bottom 25% of the scorers and omit the middle 50% for item analysis. In a classroom of 100 pupils, therefore, the top 25 scorers would be selected to form the upper group and the lower 25 scorers form the lower group. Most classrooms, of course, have far fewer pupils than this so we generally ignore the "25% rule". Because it makes the arithmetic computations involved so much easier, we generally select the top 10 scorers to form the upper group and the lowest 10 scorers to form the lower group. In a class of 27 pupils, therefore, only the middle seven scorers are omitted from the analysis as 10 form the upper group and 10 form the lower group. If the class size is less than 20, the upper group consists of the top half of the scorers and the lower group is the bottom half. If a class consists of 16 pupils, 8 will be in the upper and 8 in the lower group.

For essay tests, it is unnecessary to form upper and lower groups as they will not be compared and contrasted. All that is required is that each item be scored and that a total test score be computed. It is not even necessary to rank-order the tests. Once this preliminary work has been done, the actual item analysis can be conducted.

Item Difficulty. The item difficulty for a multiple choice test is computed with the following formula:

$$P_{mcq} = \frac{R \times 100}{T} \qquad \text{Equation 10.2}$$

Where

P_{mcq} = percentage who got the item correct on an MCQ (multiple-choice question),
R = number who get the item correct,
T = number who tried the item.

If 12 pupils got the item correct, for example, employing Equation 10.2

$$P = \frac{12}{20} \times 100 = 60\%$$

(Remember that we are working with the upper and lower 10 and, therefore, T = 20 assuming all answered this item).

In an essay test, P_{ess} is defined as the percentage mean performance on that item. If, for example, you gave a 5 question essay test to your class of 24 pupils, you would compute the mean on each question and then employ the following:

$$P_{ess} = \frac{Mean \times 100}{Total} \qquad \text{Equation 10.3}$$

Where

P_{ess} = percent mean score on an essay question,
Mean = mean on the item,
Total = maximum possible score on the item.

Suppose that for item 1, the mean performance for your 24 pupils was 3 and the total value of the question was 5. Then employing Equation 10.3

$$P_{ess} = \frac{3}{5} \times 100 = 60\%$$

Item Discrimination. For essay tests, item discrimination is derived for each item by correlating each item performance with total test score performance. Use the Pearson-product moment correlation (r) to derive the discrimination, D. For an essay test then,

$$D_{ess} = r_{it} \qquad \text{Equation 10.4}$$

Where,

D_{ess} = Discrimination of an essay item,
r_{it} = correlation between the item performance and total test score.

For D_{ess} = 0 (no correlation) the item fails to discriminate between low and high scores on the test. If D_{ess} = .2–.5, the item shows good discrimination while values in excess of .5 is excellent. Negative values of D_{ess} indicate a problem with that item as the low scorers overall are performing better on this item than the overall high scorers. Depending on the values of D_{ess} then, each item can be evaluated for its efficacy.

For multiple-choice items, the discrimination coefficient is given as follows:

$$D_{mcq} = \frac{R_u - R_1}{\frac{1}{2}\,T} \qquad\qquad \text{Equation 10.5}$$

Where

D_{mcq} = discrimination of multiple-choice item
R_u = number who got it right in the upper group
R_1 = number who got it right in the lower group
T = number who tried the item

The results from an item are summarized below in Example 1:

Item #10	A	B	C*	D
Upper 10	1	1	8	0
Lower 10	3	3	2	2

In this example, R_u = 8 (C is the keyed response) while R_1 = 2 and T = 20. Therefore,

$$D_{mcq} = \frac{8-2}{\frac{1}{2} \times 20} = \frac{6}{10} = .6$$

Employing Equation 10.2, the difficulty P_{mcq} is given as:

$$P_{mcq} = \frac{10}{20} \times 100 = 50\% \ (R = R_u + R_1)$$

Here is Example 2:

Item #26	A*	B	C	D
Upper 10	6	2	2	0
Lower 10	6	3	1	0

$$P_{mcq} = \frac{12}{20} \times 100 = 60\%,$$

$$D_{mcq} = \frac{6-6}{\frac{1}{2} \times 20} = \frac{0}{10} = 0$$

This item therefore has a difficulty of 60% but a discrimination of 0.

Example 3 follows:

Item #6	A	B	C	D*
Upper 10	0	7	2	1
Lower 10	0	4	2	4

$$P_{mcq} = \frac{5}{20} \times 100 = 25\%$$

$$D_{mcq} = \frac{1-4}{\frac{1}{2} \times 20} = \frac{.3}{10} = -.3$$

Example 4:

Item #73	A	B*	C	D
Upper 10	4	5	0	1
Lower 10	4	3	0	3

$$P_{mcq} = \frac{8}{20} \times 100 = 40\%$$

$$D_{mcq} = \frac{5-3}{\frac{1}{2} \times 20} = \frac{2}{10} = .2$$

Distractor Effectiveness. This refers to the ability of distractors to attract some responses. A distractor which attracts no one is obviously not working. Conversely, a distractor which attracts too many respondents is difficult to distinguish from the keyed-response and therefore is not working either. The way to determine the effectiveness of a distractor is to examine how many testees selected it.

In the above example (1), for instance, 4 testees selected A, 4 selected B and 2 selected D. This indicates that all distractors are working well. In example 2, however, 5 testees selected B and 3 selected C. No one selected option D. Therefore, D is not working and perhaps B is too attractive—possibly both options B and D need to be revised in this example. Example 3 presents a serious problem. The most likely flaw here is that it is mis-keyed and that the true keyed response should be B. Anytime a discrimination is negative as in this example (D = −.3), it suggests a mis-keyed item. If the item turned out *not* to be mis-keyed, then option B is far too attractive and option A is not working at all. Finally in example 4, C is not working and A is too attractive. These results indicate a need to revise the item for future use.

Putting it Together. The three basic elements of item analysis (difficulty, discrimination, effectiveness) must be considered together. What are the ideal values of these elements? Table 10.2 summarizes ranges and values of these elements together with comments on each one.

In interpreting the overall efficacy of an item, all three item characteristics must be considered together. An item, for example, which has a difficulty of 100% (everyone answered it correctly) will by necessity have a discrimination of zero and none of the distractors will be effective. Does this mean that this item is necessarily poor? No. There are at least two reasons for this. First, the item may provide a motivational function such as at the beginning of the test (i.e., the first or second item) and therefore we wish to have such an easy item in this position. The final item on the test may also have the same properties for the same reasons. Second, the item may measure a critical concept or fact which should have been mastered by all pupils. An

Table 10.2. Item Characteristics and Associated Values

Item Characteristic	Value	Comment
1. Item Difficulty	less than 45%	Too difficult
	46–69%	Ideal
	70–80%	Good
	81–90%	Fair
	91–100%	Too easy
2. Item Discrimination	Negative	Mis-keyed
	0–.09	Poor
	.10–.19	Fair
	.20–.29	Good
	.30–.39	Very good
	.40 and up	Ideal
3. Distractor Effectiveness	0% of respondents	Poor (too few)
	5% of respondents	Fair (too few)
	10% of respondents	Good
	11–25% of respondents	Very Good
	26–35% of respondents	Fair (too many)
	36% and up	Poor (too many)

item which is too easy, however, (P = 91% and up) may indicate that it is measuring below the level of understanding for which it was intended. Alternatively, it may mean that the concept or knowledge was very well taught and learned.

An item which has a difficulty of 45% or less may mean that it is misleading or confusing. Alternatively, it may be possible that the item is measuring at a higher order level of understanding than was intended. Finally, it is possible that the item is measuring concepts or knowledge which was not directly taught and therefore lacks content validity.

Items with difficulties in the ideal or good categories (see Table 10.2), should produce discriminations of .20 and up. If this is not the case, there may be some problems with at least one distractor. Distractors which attract no one should be discarded or revised for future use of the item. When all distractors are working well, a good item generally results. Example 1 above shows an ideal item with a difficulty of 50%, a discrimination of .60 and all of the distractors are working well. A test composed of mostly items of this sort will result in a high reliability and produce near ideal psychometric results (i.e., central tendency, variability, reliability, standard error of measurement). The key to producing items of this sort is to include plausible distractors. With the help of an item analysis, items can be revised for future use.

Machine Scoring and Item Analysis. Conducting an item analysis by hand is very time consuming and tedious. With recent developments in micro-computer technology and optical scorers as well as software innovations, however, conducting an item analysis is a simple and routine matter (see Chapter 13 for a detailed discussion of the role of computers in testing). To conduct an item analysis this way, you need to have an optical scorer interfaced with a micro-computer and the appropriate software. Then it is simply a matter of machine scoring pupil response sheets and saving the data on a computer file. These data can then be analyzed to result in item difficulties, discrimination and patterns of responses to items (distractor effectiveness) as well as descriptive statistics and reliability estimates. Tests from a class of 25 pupils can be easily scored and analyzed in 10–15 minutes with such a procedure. The results from such a machine produced item analysis for a large class of 158 are summarized in Table 10.3. The total time for scoring and analyzing this test was less than one-half hour.

Note that the summary sheet indicates the item numbers together with the response patterns as well as difficulty and discrimination indices. You can easily evaluate the efficacy of each item from this output.

Today most schools have micro-computers widely available so all that is generally required is the purchase of an optical scorer and appropriate software. With decreasing costs of this equipment and software recently, an optical scorer and the software can be purchased for a cost in the range or $1,000–3,000, certainly within the budget of most schools. This equipment can be shared among all the teachers in the school and thus make it highly cost effective compared to many other things that schools purchase. These optical scoring facilities and supporting software which until recently were mainly restricted to main-frame and mini-computers, are now widely available to the everyday classroom teacher.

Interpreting the Item Analysis and Evaluating the Test

Once a test has been scored, fully analyzed and an item-analysis has been conducted, the educational interpretations can be made.

There are two possible types of ambiguity of an item: (1) intrinsic, and (2) extrinsic. Intrinsic ambiguity refers to the ambiguity internal to the item which results from confusing questions, trick items, irrelevant information, indistinguishable options, use of inclusive (all of the above) or exclusive (none of the above) options and so on. Intrinsic ambiguity is bad and we wish to avoid it. Extrinsic ambiguity on the other hand, is external to the item. The ambiguity is perceived by the testee because of the testee's flawed understanding, partial knowledge only, or ignorance about the concept tested. Extrinsic ambiguity is good and we wish to strive for it but avoid intrinsic ambiguity.

It is very common for pupils to assert that an item is ambiguous. The question of course is whether the item is intrinsically or extrinsically ambiguous. The only way to determine this is to conduct the item analysis. An item which has a difficulty of 60% and a discrimination of .5 with all distractors working, may still appear ambiguous to some pupils. This ambiguity is extrinsic and due to pupils' confusion. The likely sources of extrinsic ambiguity in this instance are confusion about the concepts, partial and flawed knowledge, a more primitive level of understanding than the item requires, and so on. Nevertheless, such pupils may insist that the question is ambiguous.

An item which has a difficulty of 20% and discrimination of 0 with one distractor attracting too many respondents (e.g., 40%) while others attract no one, is clearly intrinsically ambiguous. Such an item almost certainly contains misleading information, unclear questions, indistinguishable options or some other flaw in it. Even the high scoring pupils were not able to select the correct answer to this question.

The results from the item analysis can be used for educational benefits. The teacher can get precise information about which concepts and knowledge need to be reviewed or studied by the whole group, which are well understood, which pupils need to work on some particular concepts, and which pupils may have persistent problems in some specific subtopics. Finally, an

Table 10.3. An Item Analysis Conducted with an Optical Scorer and Microcomputer

Item	Correct	Pct	A	B	C	D	E	High	Low	Diff	Disc
1	158	93.67	149*	9	0	0	0	42	37	0.92	0.12
2	137	86.71	3	2	137*	14	0	40	30	0.81	0.23
3	99	62.66	99*	12	37	9	0	38	14	0.60	0.56
4	141	89.24	1	3	141*	11	0	42	32	0.86	0.23
5	117	74.05	30	117*	4	6	0	36	25	0.71	0.26
6	129	81.65	23	129*	3	2	0	40	26	0.77	0.33
7	138	87.34	2	0	17	138*	0	43	27	0.81	0.37
8	107	67.72	34	10	6	107*	0	33	24	0.66	0.21
9	97	61.39	1	55	4	97*	0	38	16	0.63	0.51
10	141	89.24	141*	12	0	4	0	42	31	0.85	0.26
11	142	89.87	9	142*	3	3	0	41	38	0.92	0.07
12	101	63.92	101*	20	8	28	0	33	18	0.59	0.35
13	152	96.20	2	3	0	152*	0	42	39	0.94	0.07
14	98	62.03	6	38	98*	15	0	35	13	0.56	0.51
15	115	72.78	115*	29	11	2	0	38	20	0.67	0.42
16	118	74.68	7	118*	11	21	0	40	23	0.73	0.40
17	108	68.35	108*	44	2	3	0	40	17	0.66	0.53
18	130	82.28	23	2	130*	2	0	42	29	0.83	0.30
19	124	78.48	124*	3	16	14	0	42	22	0.74	0.47
20	103	65.19	32	11	103*	12	0	41	14	0.64	0.63
21	131	82.91	131*	7	18	1	0	41	29	0.81	0.28
22	108	68.35	36	108*	9	5	0	39	17	0.65	0.51
23	153	96.84	1	0	3	153*	0	43	40	0.97	0.07
24	133	84.18	12	133*	9	3	0	43	35	0.91	0.19
25	113	71.52	115*	42	1	1	0	33	28	0.71	0.12
26	64	40.51	65*	18	19	58	0	27	9	0.42	0.42
27	106	67.09	16	18	106*	17	0	38	17	0.64	0.49
28	80	50.63	80*	4	47	27	0	31	13	0.51	0.42
29	119	75.32	6	31	1	120*	0	38	27	0.76	0.26

Item	Correct	Pct	A	B	C	D	E	High	Low	Diff	Disc
30	125	79.11	4	26	125*	2	0	42	24	0.77	0.42
31	98	62.03	46	10	99*	3	0	32	21	0.62	0.26
32	139	87.97	5	141*	3	10	0	40	37	0.90	0.07
33	113	71.52	32	2	10	113*	0	33	23	0.65	0.23
34	62	39.24	80	12	62*	3	0	24	14	0.44	0.23
35	108	68.35	9	108*	36	3	0	39	14	0.44	0.23
36	63	39.87	27	63*	14	53	0	29	10	0.45	0.44
37	125	79.11	21	0	125*	11	0	42	26	0.79	0.37
38	142	89.87	1	0	14	143*	0	43	35	0.91	0.19
39	120	75.95	17	10	120*	9	0	41	23	0.74	0.42
40	95	60.13	11	41	96*	9	0	32	21	0.62	0.26
41	48	30.38	32	53	48*	24	0	24	4	0.33	0.47
42	82	51.90	47	26	2	84*	0	33	16	0.57	0.40

Variance	35.02
Standard Deviation	5.92
Average Difficulty	0.71
Average Discrimination	0.33
K-R Form 21 Reliability	0.76

item analysis may give precise diagnostic information about errors depending on which distractor the pupils selected. A full test analysis, then, should be used to review, diagnose and plan educational remediation.

■ Summary and Main Points

Valid classroom testing begins with a test plan and table of specifications. Once a test has been constructed, reproduced and administered, there are a number of steps that should be taken to ensure the validity of the results. These include scoring accurately and guessing on objective tests, computing the descriptive statistics and reliability as well as conducting an item analysis. The latter requires the determination of item difficulty, item discrimination and distractor effectiveness. These item characteristics can inform the teacher about the relative extrinsic and intrinsic ambiguity of items. Such information can help the teacher in making sound classroom and educational decisions.

1. The test should be examined for flaws before it is administered. A 20-point checklist focusing on the adequacy of the test plan, the adequacy of test items, and the adequacy of test format and directions is provided in Table 10.1.
2. Attention to proper procedures in scoring is crucial for both objective and subjective tests. A carefully prepared detailed key is vital in arriving at valid results from the test.

3. The problem of guessing can seriously affect scores on objective tests. A number of "correction for guessing" procedures and formulae have been suggested and employed. In most non-speeded tests, however, the basic assumptions necessary to apply these procedures and formulae are not met and therefore, make their application inappropriate.

4. A procedure which is preferred to "correction for guessing" is to encourage all pupils to answer all questions even if required to guess. In this way, chance scores are randomly distributed across pupils and do not confer advantages on those with a proclivity to guess.

5. Once the test has been scored, a full test analysis begins with the computation of central tendencies (mean, mode, median), variance, standard deviation, and range.

6. Skewed distributions with substantially different values of the central tendencies may suggest that the test was too easy or too difficult. Distributions approximating the normal suggest that the difficulty was appropriate.

7. A very small variance and standard deviation may suggest that the pupils were very homogeneous or, more likely, that the test failed to detect the individual differences which existed.

8. Ideally the standard deviation should be greater than 10% of the test scale and the range should encompass at least 50% of the scale.

9. The reliability coefficient (r_{xx}) of the test indicates the degree of consistency of measurement. For teacher-made test, r_{xx} should generally exceed .50 as this indicates that 50% of the variability in test scores are due to true score differences. Reliability coefficients exceeding .60 and .70 are considered to be very good and excellent.

10. For standardized tests, the reliability should generally exceed .90. Standardized tests with reliabilities of less than .90 are considered problematic.

11. An item analysis requires the computations of item difficulty and discrimination for both essay tests and objective tests and distractor effectiveness for multiple-choice items in addition.

12. The ideal range for item difficulty is between 45–70% and for item discrimination it is greater than .20. For distractors to be effective, they should attract at least 5% of respondents but preferably 10–25%. The ranges and evaluation of the three item properties are summarized in Table 10.2.

13. Optical scorers interfaced with microcomputers are now becoming widely available and within the budget of virtually all schools. A full test analysis—including item analysis—can be conducted routinely and easily with this set-up.

14. Based on all of the data available, the test should be completely evaluated and each item should be evaluated for its intrinsic and extrinsic ambiguity.

■ Further Readings

Anastasi, A. (1988). *Psychological testing* (6th ed.). New York: Macmillan, Chapter 8.

Gronlund, N. E., and Linn, R. L. (1990). *Measurement and evaluation in teaching* (6th ed.). New York: Macmillan. Chapter 10. *Measurement and evaluation in psychology and education (6th ed)*.

Thorndike, R. M., Cunningham, G. K., Thorndike, R. I. and Hagen, E. P. (1991). New York: Macmillan, pp. 241–251.

Wainer, H. (1989). The future of item analysis. *Journal of Educational Measurement, 26,* 191–208.

■ Laboratory exercises

1. Identify as many factors as possible that may interfere with the functioning of an item as intended. Discuss the possible reasons for this.
2. Discuss various strategies for handling the problem of guessing on selection-type items. What are the strengths and weaknesses of each?
3. Ms. Morrow gave a 100-item social studies test to her grade 6 class with the following results: mean = 68, median = 75, mode = 85. What is the likely nature of the distribution of this test? Discuss possible reasons for this result.
4. Mr. Percival gave a 40-item test to his grade 4 class with the following results: mean = 28, mode = 26, median = 29. What is the probable nature of the underlying distribution?
5. Mr. Johnson gave the same 50-item test to both his morning and afternoon grade 10 science classes. The following results were obtained.

Morning Class

mean = 33, median = 32, mode = 32
variance = 32.5
min score = 19, max score = 47

Afternoon Class

mean = 34, median = 33, mode = 32
variance = 18.3
min score = 27, max score = 41

   a. What are the nature of the distributions?
   b. How does the morning class compare to the afternoon class?
   c. Discuss the adequacy of the test.
6. How adequate is a teacher-made test with a reliability of r_{xx} = .36? What is the problem with this test?
7. Compute the KR21 reliabilities for both test results in Mr. Johnson's classes in number 5 above. Discuss reasons for any differences.
8. Why do different standards of reliabilities apply for teacher-made and standardized tests?
9. Ms. Swalwell gave her grade 12 history class a 3 question essay test with the following results:

Student	(Max=10) Item 1	(Max=10) Item 2	(Max=10) Item 3	Student	(Max=10) Item 1	(Max=10) Item 2	(Max=10) Item 3
Bill	3	4	3	Efrem	9	9	8
Mary	5	3	4	Deborah	7	8	9
Jason	6	5	7	Jennifer	6	7	5
Jarrod	5	5	5	Angela	8	9	8
Alison	3	2	4	Robert	5	5	7
Nicole	6	7	6	Anthony	4	4	5
Emilio	9	9	8	Matthew	6	7	7
Noemi	8	9	9	Ivana	7	5	4

a. Compute the descriptive statistics of this test.
b. Compute the reliability of this test.
c. Calculate the item difficulties and discriminations of this test.
   Based on the overall results, evaluate this test.
10. Below are results from a test. Conduct an item analysis for the items and complete the following table.

Item		Option			
		A	B	C	D
1.	U10	0	2	0	8*
	L10	3	3	0	4
2.	U10	0	9*	1	0
	L10	0	7	1	2
3.	U10	7*	1	1	1
	L10	7	1	1	1
4.	U10	0	10*	0	0
	L10	2	2	3	3
5.	U10	0	3	4	8*
	L10	2	1	6	1

Item	Difficulty	Discrimination	Distractor Effectiveness	Revision (Yes or No)
1				
2				
3				
4				
5				

11. Evaluate the test that is fully analyzed in Table 10.3.
12. Evaluate the distractor effectiveness of each item in Table 10.3.
13. Discuss internal and external ambiguity of multiple choice items.
14. Evaluate the internal and external ambiguity of each item in the test in Table 10.3.

Chapter

Standardized Tests for the Classroom

Overview

Standardized or published tests, the focus of this chapter, differ from teacher-made tests in several important ways. They are more formal, involve standard administration and interpretation procedures, and have known psychometric properties. It is important that teachers know about standardized tests since they play a vital role in classroom instruction as well as decisions about individual pupils. There are several types of standardized tests including norm and criterion-referenced ones, test batteries and single-subject tests. Besides teachers, various people such as school counsellors, administrators, psychologists and pupils and parents use standardized test results. Published tests are usually administered by the teacher according to standardized procedures. The interpretation of these tests is also usually done by the teacher employing standard scores, percentile ranks, age and grade equivalents, and score profiles. Norms play a crucial role in the understanding and interpretation of standardized tests. When selecting these tests teachers must attend to the test's relevance, technical quality and usability. Since taking standardized tests involves considerable test-taking skill, teachers should teach these to their pupils to make the resulting scores as valid as possible.

What Are Standardized Tests?

The term ''standardized tests'' refers to a wide range of measures which include aptitude, intelligence, achievement, personality and measures of other attributes. Standardized tests are assessment devices developed by test-construction specialists. These are also sometimes referred to as published tests. The construction of a single published or standardized instrument frequently involves testing experts working with curriculum experts, teachers, and school administrators. The test is then given to a trial group, analyzed and revised accordingly. Uniform instructions and scoring procedures are used and tables of norms for score interpretation are developed.

Eventually, the test will be published together with a technical manual that contains the relevant psychometric information such as validity and reliability coefficients.

This chapter will focus on standardized achievement tests since they are the most frequently used instruments in schools. Moreover, the classroom teacher is almost always involved in some aspect of its administration or interpretation. Intelligence and aptitude tests are other important types of standardized measures but are not given primary focus in this chapter since they play a secondary role for the classroom teacher.

Standardized and Teacher-made Tests

The term **standardized** refers to the fact that the tests are administered and scored according to standardized procedures. These include standard instructions to the testees, controlling testing time, and standard scoring procedures. Also, the results from these tests are interpreted based on norms (see Chapter 7) to result in standard scores for the testee. These tests have been administered previously and, therefore, have known psychometric properties such as reliability and validity estimates. Accordingly, these tests are more formal than teacher-made tests and have much more stringent reliability and validity requirements.

The content validity of standardized tests must be specified in greater detail in tables of specifications or scope and sequence charts than it is for teacher-made tests for example. Similarly, reliability coefficients for standardized tests generally must exceed .90 while for teacher-made tests these coefficients are acceptable in the range .60–.70. Standardized tests may also have known validity coefficients (e.g., criterion-related) which are reported in the technical manual. Teacher made tests will not have such information.

Unlike the teacher-made test, standardized tests have been developed to measure a wide range of pupil's characteristics including intellectual ability, personality factors, attitudes, and creativity. Teacher-made tests primarily focus on achievement in specific subject areas. Also in contrast to teacher-made tests which typically cover a relatively small unit of work, standardized tests generally cover a very broad range of objectives and content. Finally, the administration of a standardized test is a very formal event with test administrators following a uniform set of instructions.

Why Teachers Should Know About Standardized Tests

Standardized tests are administered very widely in Canadian and American schools. Tens of millions of these tests are given to elementary, junior, and high school pupils annually. The results of these are usually kept in pupil's cumulative records and come frequently to teachers' attention. Indeed, teachers are frequently called on to interpret the results of these to pupils and parents.

Results from standardized tests can be instrumental in diagnosing pupils' learning difficulties. They can help pinpoint the root of a problem and perhaps even indicate its solution. Teachers are frequently involved in this diagnosis and remediation and, therefore, benefit accordingly from understanding standardized tests.

Instructional decisions for groups or a whole class may also be improved by information from a standardized test. The class as a whole may show strength in vocabulary but deficits in mathematics problem solving skills for example. Based on this information the teacher may revise her instructional plans to include a greater emphasis on math problem solving in future instruction and thus address the math deficit problem.

Standardized tests frequently play an instrumental role in the identification of exceptional learners. In addition, decisions about programming can be informed by results from these instruments. A child with very low scores on a standardized language development test, for example, may be placed for special help with the speech and language therapist. Conversely, a child with exceptionally high scores on a test of creativity, may be recommended to the gifted center.

Standardized tests receive very widespread support from the general public (Ellam, Rose & Gallup, 1991). Typically, 70% to 80% of the general public support the use of standardized tests as one of the criteria for passing and failing children. Moreover, these tests are supported for use not only in specific subject areas such as language arts and mathematics, but the public generally (84%) also wishes to use them to assess writing ability, problem solving and creativity. More than half (58%) of the general public are in favour of failing pupils based solely on standardized national achievement test performance. This is even a broader mandate for the use of these tests than is currently the case. Based on this information, standardized testing is more conservative than the general public would support.

Many administrators, legislators and evaluators also support the use of standardized tests. Their primary concern is to determine the performance of various schools, school districts and other jurisdictions in order to gauge the effectiveness of educational programmes and policies. Particulary effective reading programmes (as determined by high scores on standardized tests by pupils in the programmes), for example, may receive political and administrator support for continuation and expansion. Conversely, ineffective programmes may be modified or replaced. Decision and policy makers frequently employ standardized test scores, then, to determine and modify educational policy.

Types of Standardized Tests

There are several ways of categorizing standardized tests including norm-referenced, criterion-referenced, test batteries and single-subject tests. Norm-referenced tests are designed to compare performance of individuals or groups with a norm (national, state or provincial, local), whereas criterion-referenced tests are designed to assess pupils' achievement of specific tasks and knowledge (Holmes, 1982). A test battery is a set of subtests that survey a broad range of subject matter. Single-subject tests, as the name implies, measures achievement in one content area. A closer examination of these types of tests follows below.

Norm-referenced Tests

The most widely used standardized tests are norm-referenced measures of academic achievement. Typically, such tests are used to assess progress in language arts, science, social studies and mathematics.

Holmes (1982) has summarized a number of criticisms and potential benefits of norm-referenced tests. The most frequent criticism of such tests centers on the actual content of the tests themselves. Frequently norm-referenced test assess a rather narrow range of objectives in order to maintain high reliability. Moreover, some of these instruments contain content which is easiest to measure but does not reflect the most important aspects of the skill or the curriculum. Tests which are described as measures of writing ability, for example, but focus exclusively on the student's understanding of grammar, clearly fail to adequately sample the relevant domain.

Similarly, standardized measures of reading which focus on word decoding rather than reading comprehension have similar problems: both lack content validity.

A second source of criticism of norm-referenced tests is that they focus too much on reliability at the expense of validity. While these tests have high reliability, they are not the best predictor of future pupil performance (i.e., predictive, criterion-related validity). The best predictor of math in grade 10, is performance in math in grade 9. Nevertheless, many educators might use standardized tests to make this prediction and thus lead critics to question the validity of the tests (Holmes, 1982).

A third source of criticism is that norm-referenced tests have national norms by which all pupils are judged. Many educators believe that it is harmful to judge all pupils by the same criteria as it leads to the false expectation that all children should learn the same things at the same rate.

Despite the limitations of norm-referenced tests, there are a number of legitimate uses of these instruments. First, norm-referenced tests provide the public and school administrators with an indication of some aspects of student learning across schools and other jurisdictions. Second, norm-referenced tests can be used to assess common educational objectives across pupils, schools, school districts, and so on. While many educators strongly support the use of tests for assessing these common objectives, others fear that such practices place severe constraints on what happens in a classroom. Specifically, some educators worry that standardized tests and not teachers actually determine the content that is taught. Still others are concerned that the administration of standardized measures at the end of the school year promotes "teaching to the test".

The concern here is that the teacher is forced to focus on material that is covered by the test at the expense of other more important, timely and relevant material. At first glance such worries that this practice undermines good teaching seem valid. Holmes (1982), however, has argued that it is sensible for teachers to teach to the test if in fact the test reflects important educational objectives. If the tests do not assess relevant, important, and timely objectives, then the problem lies with the content validity of the test and not with the fact that teachers are forced to teach to the test. Indeed, this "teaching to the test" is beneficial since it forces teachers to teach important, basic and common objectives. Without the accountability of the norm-referenced test, some teachers may earnestly teach the basic common material, while others may drift aimlessly.

The third benefit of using norm-referenced standardized tests is that it allows for an assessment of individual pupil performance against a peer group nationally and locally. Such information can allow for a fuller evaluation of performance since not only are teacher-made test results available, but a pupil can also be compared to her peers locally, across the state and nationally. Educational decisions about a particular pupil can thus be based on more complete and therefore more valid information.

Criterion-referenced Tests

These tests (sometimes called domain-referenced or objective-referenced) are measures in which scores are expressed in terms of skills or behaviors achieved (Lyman, 1991). Criterion-referenced tests were developed to fill educational needs that were not fulfilled by norm-referenced survey tests such as mastery learning, prescriptive teaching, and individualized instruction. Thus the pupil is not compared to the performance of other pupils (as in the case of norm-referenced testing) on these tests, but to a set of identified units of knowledge or skills. Using such an evaluation approach the teacher can determine criteria for passing which frequently ranges from

75 to 80 percent correct. While the cut-off score for mastery is usually left up to the teacher, some publishers suggest mastery level performance. If the student can score at this level they are permitted to move on to the next unit of study.

This approach encourages greater teacher emphasis on individualized instruction and pre-scriptive teaching, thereby responding more sensitively to the varying learning rates in the class-room. A fundamental assumption underlying criterion-referenced testing is that pupils' achievement differs not so much because of differences in intelligence, but because of the speed with which they acquire facts, skills, and knowledge. Thus criterion-referenced testing, because it facilitates individualized instruction, allows pupils to work at their own pace and more readily achieve mastery of the subject.

Notwithstanding the potential advantages of criterion-referenced tests over norm-referenced ones, the former also suffer from problems. First, many criterion-referenced tests have objectives or skills that are assessed by too few items, thus compromising reliability. Second, the cut-off score for passing is rather arbitrarily set. Some teachers, for example, may set 80% as a cut-off but lower this when only a few pupils manage to pass. Guidelines recommended by the publish-er are equally arbitrary. Third, strict criterion-referenced interpretations provide no basis for inter-individual comparisons as is the case with norm-referenced tests. Sometimes it is of interest to know how a pupil's performance compares to his peers at a local, state and national level.

Today many standardized achievement tests make provisions for both norm and criterion-referenced interpretations. More detailed and rich information can thus be extracted about a pupil's performance. Not only can the performance be compared to the pupil's peers (norm-referenced), but it can also be evaluated against an absolute standard of performance (criterion-referenced) based on specific tasks, skills an objectives (domain referenced). Undoubtedly, in the future, more standardized achievement tests will provide for both norm and criterion-referenced interpretations.

Test Batteries

Test batteries contain several subtests (from 2 to more than 10) that cover a wide range of skills and knowledge. These tests survey subject matter and therefore do so quite superficially. The interpretation of the results can be either norm or criterion-referenced or both.

The number of items on each subtest may range from as few as a dozen to more than 100. The subtest may take as little as a few minutes to complete to more than one hour. Test batteries like the **Metropolitan Achievement Test** (MAT) and the **Canadian Tests of Basic Skills** (CTBS), for example, can take up to five separate testing sessions.

Elementary school test batteries focus on basic skills which usually include reading (decod-ing skills, vocabulary, comprehension), language (mechanics, spelling), mathematics (computa-tions, concepts, problem solving), and study skills (library and reference skills, reading maps, tables, charts). To account for increasing difficulty across grade and different emphasis, test bat-teries come in several forms. At the primary level, each form covers one or two grades and two or more beyond grade four.

Basic skills batteries have been less widely used at the high school level than they have been at the elementary school level because of the greater variety of courses and educational objectives in high school. Nevertheless, these test batteries are becoming more common in high school and will likely continue to do so given the current emphasis on basic skills. The **School and College Abilities Test** (SCAT) and the **Sequential Tests of Educational Progress** (STEP) both developed by ETS, attempt to assess not only the basic skills than do the elementary tests, but attempt to assess analytical and evaluative skills as well. Some batteries like STEP and **Stanford Achievement Test Series** cover all of the grade levels from K to 12. These tests batteries are an attempt to provide coordinated measures of the whole educational sequence from beginning to end (pre-college).

Single-subject Tests

The main disadvantage of test batteries is that because they **survey** a broad range of areas, by necessity they assess each somewhat superficially. When an assessment that is more thorough in some particular subject area is required, a single-subject test is more appropriate than the test battery. Generally, the single-subject test will contain more total items, more items per objective or skill, and higher level measurement items than will a corresponding subtest from a test battery. While the test battery is used to describe an individual's or group's relative achievement, a single-subject test is used to make a specific decision. This might include decisions about a pupil's readiness (e.g. Reading Readiness Tests), proficiency for graduation (e.g., graduation competency tests), or vocational and educational decisions (tests of musical, artistic or mechanical ability). When an important specific educational decision is to be made, then the single subject test is desirable over the test battery.

Uses of Standardized Tests

As we have already seen, standardized test results in schools are used for a variety of purposes. Moreover, the purpose that the results are used for will depend on who is using the information. Teachers, counsellors, psychologists, administrators, pupils and parents all will use the same test results somewhat differently. This of course stems from each party's function and interests.

Teachers use standardized test scores primarily for instructional purposes. Results from such a test, for example, may be used for diagnostic purposes. The teacher may be attempting to identify the specific area of mathematics with which the pupil is having difficulty. Is it, for example, computations, numeration, measurement, concepts or problem solving? Subtest scores from a mathematics standardized test may help in the diagnosis. An evaluation of curriculum, materials and specific lessons may also be done with standardized test scores. A series of prescriptive teaching lessons on arithmetic computations, for example, may be evaluated with a criterion-referenced arithmetic test.

Teachers also use standardized test scores to supplement and maintain a pupil's cumulative record folder. These data collected over time, can provide a longitudinal assessment of a pupil's progress over a series of grades and thus gauge the pupil's rate of educational growth. Future teachers of the pupil will also benefit from the data as it gives a reliable and valid indication of the pupils' achievement in at least one area. Finally, results for groups can also be used to measure growth and inform instructional decisions about curriculum selection and so on.

Counsellors can use standardized test scores for educational and vocational decisions. Scores which indicate that a high school pupil shows particular aptitude and achievement in science, for example, can be used by to counsel the pupil to pursue studies in this area in college. Another pupil who attains high achievement on an art test, may be counseled to pursue admission to an art school.

Psychologists can use standardized test scores to assist in the diagnosis of deficit areas and learning problems and thus recommend remedial instruction, treatment or intervention. If the learning problem is clearly indicated by scores on a test, this may even clearly point to the possible remediation of the problem.

Administrators are generally less interested in individual test scores as they are in group results. Based on group scores, administrators may evaluate a program, curriculum, a textbook, or even a whole school's performance in some specific area. At an even broader level, administrators and government officials may evaluate a whole districts or even a nation's performance based on standardized test results. It is frequently asserted, for example, that American schools do not teach mathematics as well as schools in many other countries such as Germany and Japan. This evaluation is based on results from internationally administered standardized mathematics tests.

Pupils and their parent's use standardized test scores for individual assessment and educational decision making. Parents may encourage their daughter to pursue a literary course of studies because of her high scores on a standardized literature test, for example. Similarly, based on results from a standardized arithmetic test, parents may hire a tutor to help their elementary school son improve at arithmetic. Finally, a pupil may re-double his efforts at pursuing a career in science because of high scores on a standardized science test.

A complete assessment of a child usually involves data from many sources in all three domains: psychomotor, affective and cognitive. Table 11.1 is a summary of a psychoeducational assessment that has been abridged from an actual report (which was much longer and detailed than what is reported here). Notice that the report deals with reasons for referral, presenting problems, social-emotional data, psychomotor data, standardized test data (cognitive, achievement and reading), and an evaluation. The report concludes with a series of prescriptions and recommendations. This is an example, then, of how standardized test data is integrated with other data and observations to render a diagnosis and recommendations which are of interest to parents, teachers, administrators, counsellors and psychologists. All of these interested parties may use the report for somewhat different purposes.

Administering Standardized Tests

Standardized tests may be administered to a group or on an individual basis depending on the purpose for which the test was designed. In either case, the classroom teacher has a role to play in preparing both their pupils and themselves for the test. This is particularly true if the teacher is to administer the test as is frequently the case. The following are a set of guidelines to help teachers ensure that the results of standardized tests for their own pupils reflect optimal performance.

(1) The teacher should familiarize herself on how well the actual test items relate to the curriculum the pupils studied. Frequently, standardized achievement tests do not adequately sample the objectives, and therefore reflect the curriculum, of a particular school district. In other words, the test lacks content validity. Such tests produce scores that are not very informative nor are they valid indicators of performance. Under such circumstances, teachers should either question the use of the test because of lack of content validity, or prepare her pupils for the content that the test assesses.

(2) Before the actual administration of a standardized test, the teacher should explain to the pupils why such testing is occurring. Moreover, pupils should be told in what way the results will be used. This is particularly important as pupils subscribe to a wide array of myths about the use of such scores. These range from the beliefs that the scores will not be used in any way, to the belief that the test results will govern the nature of their education from that point on.

211

Table 11.1. Psychoeducational Report

Name: William Smith

Age: 9–10

Assessment Date: 92.02.17

D.O.B.: 82.12.10

Grade: 4

Date of Report: 92.03.21

Reason for Referral

William was referred for psychoeducational assessment in order to help determine what factors are contributing to his behavioural and academic difficulties in school. The referral was initiated by Don Brown (psychiatrist) and Mary White (social worker) both of whom have been providing marital counselling to William's parents.

Presenting Problems

Recent school reports indicate that William is encountering significant academic difficulties. William's parents are concerned that his school problems which first emerged in grade 1 will negatively impact on his self-esteem.

Background Information

William is a 9 year 6 month old boy presently attending a grade four programme at Acme School for the Arts.

Academic difficulties for William first emerged in grade 1, where he displayed difficulties sustaining attention, interacting with peers and developing appropriate work habits. During the grade 2 year weak listening skills and slow work pace were noted. Mr. and Mrs. Smith's concern regarding William's learning problems prompted a referral to Dr. Robert Jones for a psychological assessment in March of the grade 2 school year. Dr. Jones found William to be a young boy of very superior intelligence who nevertheless experience a specific weakness in the area of auditory sequencing which could serve to slow his performance on tasks involving reading and spelling.

Dr. Jones concluded his report by suggesting that William was in need of a school and home learning environment which was characterized by a relaxed and less tense atmosphere.

Comments regarding William's slow work pace were again indicated in his grade 3 report. In addition, teacher comments indicate that William was beginning to find the learning situation increasingly frustrating.

Presently in grade 4, William is encountering a number of school related difficulties. Specific problems have focused on a frequently careless inconsistent work effort. A tendency to be easily distracted is thought to underlie William's poor work habits. At the present time William is encountering serious difficulties in the area of written expression and several aspects of the French programme. In order to help William with his academic difficulties he is currently receiving remedial assistance on a regular basis.

Present Assessment

Test Behaviour

William was seen on two occasions in order to complete the administration of test materials. Throughout the session he was attentive and seemed quite interested in the test materials. It was evident that he was eager to please and responded very positively to reinforcement. On several occasions William initiated conversation with the examiner revealing a well developed vocabulary.

On a few occasions, however, he seemed to become overly tense when overcome by a temporary state of frustration. It was interesting to note that these episodes of discomfort were frequently related to test items involving limits. It may be that time pressure conflict with William's very cautious methodical response style.

In light of William's overall positive attitude toward the testing session, scores reported below appear to be an accurate estimate of his current functioning.

Table 11.1. Psychoeducational Report—Continued

Intellectual Functioning

On the Wechsler Intelligence Scale for Children-Revised, William placed in the superior range (93rd percentile) on measures of verbal and non-verbal (97th percentile) abilities. This means that he scored better than 93% of the children his age on verbal tasks and 97% of same aged peers on non-verbal test items. William's full scale performance placed him at the 97th percentile. Across the verbal measures, relative stronger performance was noted on an index of concept formation. A child who scores high on this task is thought to be a good verbal thinker. In contrast, relatively weak performance was noted on a measure of auditory short-term memory for digits. On a task involving auditory verbal memory for sentences, William's score fell slightly below age expectations. Across the non-verbal measures, particulary strong performance was noted on a task requiring perceptual, conceptual, planning and reasoning ability.

Academic Functioning

On the reading comprehension section of the Basic Achievement Skills Individual Screener (BASIS), William's performance fell at the 72nd percentile which is at the upper end of the average range. A similar performance was noted on a measure of word decoding skills (69th percentile) as measured by the WRAT-R. Incorrect responses on this measure suggested that William was able to apply a phonetic strategy to unknown words.

William's spelling skills on the BASIS fell in the mid-average range (55th percentile). An examination of incorrect responses such that William has not fully consolidated the visual representation of many words should be in his automatic spelling word bank.

On the mathematics section of the BASIS, William placed in the above average range (97th percentile). While this performance clearly represents a high level of achievement, it should be noted that William took at least twice the amount of time typically observed to complete the test items.

Social/Emotional

A number of William's comments made during the assessment period suggested that he is a child who is preoccupied by a number of concerns. The two areas which appear to be of primary concern involve his perception of himself as a leaner and the nature of his home support system.

Observations during the testing period indicated that William was overly sensitive to his test performance. His very cautious non-risk taking response style appeared to be an attempt to avoid the possibility of errors. At one point William stated that he feels very ashamed when he does make an error. This desire for what almost seems perfectionistic behaviour can be a significant barrier to experiencing the learning situation in a more open and adventurous manner. On a more practical level, his fear of making errors may force William to adopt a work pace which is simply too slow to meet the demands of daily classroom work. In failing to do so, William may experience a sense of frustration which would serve to undermine his self-concept as a learner. This situation may be particularly discomforting for William given that he describes himself as "brilliant". It is possible that he is simply repeating descriptions of himself which others have provided. Nevertheless, his frustration in failing to meet the self-imposed or externally imposed demand of excellence across all domains may be a significant area of stress for this young boy.

A second source of concern for William focuses primarily on his mother. A number of comments indicated that he is fearful that his mother "I worry about my mother dying. . . . Who would take care of me then." William stated that his mother had been previously very sick and that he continues to worry about her. William offered a number of comments which suggest that he is concerned about the future. The specifics of his concerns did not emerge but he felt uncertain that there would be a place for him in the future.

Table 11.1. Psychoeducational Report—Continued

Formulation

William is a 9 year 6 month old boy currently enrolled in a level 4 in a school for the Arts. On a measure of intellectual functioning, both verbal and non-verbal abilities fell in the superior range. A relatively weak area was noted on a measure of auditory short term memory for both digits and linguistic material. This finding is consistent with the previous assessment completed in March of 1988.

Academic achievement ranged from mid-average on a measure of spelling skills to the upper end of the average range on measures of reading comprehension and word decoding. On a test of mathematical skills William's performance was well above the average range. Academic scores obtained in the present assessment are notably higher than those obtained in William's daily classroom work. It may be that the structure setting of the assessment process and the absence of time restrictions during academic achievement testing contribute to William's relative strong performance.

While classroom reports have frequently commented on William's poor attention span and high level of distractability often associated with an attention deficit disorder, current assessment findings suggest that emotional and learning problems are the primary contributors to William's present of difficulties. Specific emotional factors appeared related to a preoccupation with his home support system as indicated by his concern regarding the well being of his mother. Comments regarding fears for the future may also be related to issues of security within the family system.

Discomfort with risk taking in the learning situation and frustration possibly related to William's perception that he must meet the demands of being "brilliant" may also being producing stress for this child in the home and school setting. It has been suggested that William's slow work pace may be a byproduct of a possible perfectionistic tendency.

Finally, a specific learning difficulty related to an auditory short memory problem initially identified in a previous assessment may contribute to make the processing of auditory instruction more problematic for William.

Recommendations

1. William would benefit from receiving counseling around issues related to self-concept.

2. Consideration should be given to providing William with an opportunity to function as a tutor for younger children. This should raise his self-confidence as learner. Moreover, this will demonstrate that making errors is a natural part of the learning process.

3. In providing instruction to William, it may be useful to address his persisting short term auditory memory difficulties. For example, divide instructional units into smaller units and present material by combining auditory information with visual reinforcement.

4. It may be helpful to help William develop a greater awareness of time in relationship to classroom demands. For example, the use of a timer set for short intervals and a variety of simple tasks may help him develop a sense of what can be accomplished for specific time periods. The important point to stress in this matter is the value of using time effectively and not simply to increase one's work pace.

5. Contingent on availability, the use of microcomputers should prove a highly motivating and useful device in helping William consolidate basic skills in written language. We would be happy to recommend specific software packages which have proven effective in the learning situation.

While there is variability in how tests results are used, typically the actual use of the results falls midway between the two extreme beliefs. The importance of providing pupils with a clear explanation both for the purpose of the testing, and use of the results, is particulary important if someone other than the regular teacher will be administering the test.

(3) While some anxiety is almost always present during testing, this is particularly true with standardized testing. This is in part because standardized testing tends to be more formal than the classroom teacher-made test. In addition, the importance (or at least perceived importance) that many pupils assign to standardized testing adds to the·tension. As a teacher you have an important role to help your pupils become as comfortable as possible in the testing situation. You can achieve this by helping your students become testwise by teaching them test taking skills. Some of these will be discussed later in this chapter.

(4) Too frequently the physical conditions under which testing occurs are given too little attention. Examination rooms which are too hot or too close to high traffic areas and thus excessively noisy, can contribute to a testee's fatigue and anxiety. In addition, poor seating arrangements and overcrowding can facilitate cheating by some which can be disconcerting for the many who are not cheating. Notwithstanding the room limitations which might exist, it is the responsibility of the test administrator to optimize the testing environment by maintaining a comfortable temperature in the room, arranging suitable seating, and providing low levels of noise.

Understanding and Reporting the Results of Standardized Tests

In understanding and reporting the results of standardized tests, it is important to differentiate between aptitude and achievement tests. A simple explanation is that an aptitude test measures the ability or potential to learn, while an achievement test measures the skills and knowledge the pupil has actually learned. The results of most standardized achievement tests, then, indicate the actual achievement that the pupil has attained rather than the potential for achieving.

It is rare to report raw scores or percentage correct scores obtained by a pupil on a standardized test. These raw scores are transformed into derived scores of two sorts to permit norm-referenced interpretation: (1) standard scores and percentiles, and (2) grade and age equivalents. The former are based on a single reference group while the latter are based on several reference groups across grade and age.

Standard Scores and Percentiles

These scores indicate how a pupil's performance compares with those of others in a single peer group. This norm group might be local, national or even international. Performance is usually expressed as a standard score including T-scores, Z-scores, and stanines. Percentile ranks are also frequently used. These are based on the normal distribution and their properties were discussed in Chapter 7.

In reporting standardized test scores to parents and pupils, it is important to remember that they will be much more familiar with such scores as percentage correct than with the more technical standard scores. On a teacher made test, a pupil's performance is typically reported as a percent correct. A pupil who answered 30 out of 40 questions would receive a score of 75%. On a standardized test, performance is expressed not by what the pupil has achieved relative to some test maximum, but rather how the pupil performed relative to her peers. Percentile ranks are the most frequently used and readily understood of these derived scores.

The primary purpose of standard scores and percentiles is to indicate intraindividual differences in achievement across test batteries. Nicole's percentile rank of 62 on the Math Concepts subtest, for example, compared to her rank of 17 on the Math Problems subtest, indicates a relative weakness. While Nicole is better than average in understanding math concepts (e.g., finding area, volume, etc.), she is substantially below average in solving math problems (usually stated as word problems). This suggests that Nicole has difficulty in applying her conceptual understanding to actual problem solving.

A disadvantage of standard scores and percentiles is that they are not equal unit scales since they are based on the normal distribution. Percentile rank scores (and standard scores) represent small intervals near the middle of the distribution and large intervals at the extremes. As a result it is much easier for a pupil to improve from the 45th to 55th percentile than from the 90th to the 95th even though both are 5 percentile rank intervals. This leads to a second disadvantage of these score types, namely that they mask growth. For a pupil who maintains a percentile rank of 76 across several grades, for example, this might suggest that no educational growth has occurred. Of course it has, as the pupil has grown as much as the norm group by maintaining his same relative standing. Grade and age equivalent scores help to overcome this growth problem.

Grade and Age Equivalent Scores

While grade and age equivalent scores have long been criticized by measurement experts, they nevertheless continue to flourish. These scores indicate how a pupil's performance compares with those of others in a series of reference groups defined by chronological age or grade.

To develop grade equivalent (GE) or age equivalent (AE) scores, a test is given to a large number of pupils at different grade levels such as K through 9. Then the median performance is computed for every grade level. Suppose, for example, that the test had 60 questions and was administered to each of 100 pupils at each grade in a school from K to 9. Suppose further that this testing was done in September and the following medians were computed for each grade: K=10, 1=15, 2=20, 3=25, 4=30, 5=35, 6=40, 7=45, 8=50, 9=55. Henceforth, a raw score of 30 would be assigned a grade equivalent of 4.0. Grade equivalent scores are expressed to the nearest tenth which reflects each of the 10 months of school from September through to June. If the above results were obtained in a December testing, for example, a raw score of 35 would be assigned a grade equivalent of 5.4 (5 represents the grade and 4 represents the month of testing). These scores are very widely used to report results from standardized testing but are fraught with problems.

The very name, grade equivalent, has an intuitive appeal to educators. Thinking in terms of what grade levels pupils are functioning in various subject areas is a familiar practice for teachers and school administrators. There is, nevertheless, confusion. Contrary to what the numbers indicate, for example, a fourth-grader with a GE of 7.0 does not necessarily know the same amount or kinds of information as does a ninth-grader with a GE of 7.0. As a second example, an able fourth-grader who does very well on an arithmetic test requiring speed and accuracy, may perform as well as the average seventh-grader and achieve a GE=7.0. A ninth-grader may be poor in speed and accuracy and may perform at the seventh-grade level on a test requiring these abilities. Yet these two pupils who have received the same scores on the arithmetic test, do not know the same things about mathematics in a more general sense. From a very practical perspective a grade five student who scores at grade equivalent of 9.0 on a reading test is not ready for a grade nine reading curriculum. While this seems obvious, it is surprising how frequently teachers and parents interpret such test scores in this manner.

Finally, as another complicating factor, GE and AE norms assume equal intervals of 1.0 across grades or chronological years. These intervals are of course not educationally and cognitively equal even though they are numerically equal. Educationally and cognitively, the differences between a grade 1 and 2 child is not the same as the differences between a grade 7 and 8 child even though the numeric interval is GE=1 in both cases. The fullest interpretation and explanation of standardized test results is to employ both the percentile rank and the GE as the limitations of each will be offset by the advantage of the other. Using score profiles further helps to clarify and explain the test results.

Score Profiles and Error Bands

The profile is a compact, graphical form of communicating test score results. An example of a profile is given in Figure 11.1 based on a hypothetical basic skills test, **The General Tests of Basic Skills.**

The various subtests of the test battery are listed across the top of the profile and the derived scores are given on the vertical axis. These may be t-scores, stanines or GE but are usually percentile ranks as in the present example. The subtest percentiles are plotted as is the total percentile rank and the dots are then connected by lines to produce a profile which is easy to see and interpret. In Figure 11.1, there is substantial discrepancy in Robert's subtest scores although his total percentile rank indicates that he is achieving about "average" for a grade 5 pupil (47th percentile). Robert's Verbal Comprehension and Math Problem scores are quite low (28th and 15th percentiles respectively) while his Vocabulary and Reading scores are above average (72th and 76th percentile respectively). His Math Concepts and Math Computations are about average (46th and 45th percentiles respectively). This pattern of test scores suggests that Robert is scoring well above average in language mechanics but has problems with language comprehension. This is further reflected in his Math Problems subtest which involves language based problems. Robert's math mechanics achievement (concepts and computations) is about average. All of this information is easy to see and the interpretations are simple to understand when presented as a profile in Figure 11.1.

Profiles are useful for identifying individual pupil strengths, weaknesses and needs. Robert, for example, has clear strengths in language mechanics but needs to improve comprehension of language. His math fundamentals are about average but he is having some difficulties with math problems due to his language comprehension deficits. Finally, his study skills are about average compared to his peers.

A second type of graphic presentation that is commonly used is the "error band" profile. This type of profile is used to emphasize that there is error or some uncertainty associated with test scores. Error is due, of course, to the standard error of measurement of the tests (Chapter 9) because the reliability is not perfect. Robert's scores have been plotted on this type of profile in Figure 11.2.

Notice from this profile that rather than a single point, each test result is given as a band around the percentile score. This band represents plus and minus one standard error of measurement (in percentile ranks), much as we estimated the confidence intervals for true scores in Chapter 9. The idea here is to give a visual demonstration of the uncertainty associated with the scores. When bands overlap as Verbal and Reading test results do for Robert, you can conclude that there is no real difference in performance on these tests. Conversely, when the bands do not overlap, you can conclude that the test scores are really different as Math Problems and Math Concepts for Robert (Figure 11.2).

Name: Robert   Grade: 5

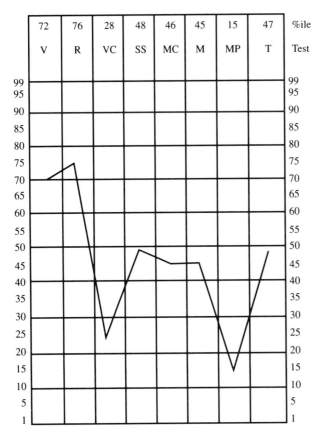

Figure 11.1. Sample student profile

There is a danger of underinterpreting test scores using error band profiles because even minimal overlap may be taken to suggest no differences in scores when there may be a real difference. Therefore, the opposite danger exists with error band profiles than it does with point scores which are subject to overinterpretation. Probably the best strategy to employ, then, is to use both the point profile and the error band profile in combination to arrive at the best possible interpretation.

Guidelines for Interpreting Test Scores

A joint committee of the American Educational Research Association, American Psychological Association, and the National Council on Measurement in Education has prepared a document, *Code of Fair Testing Practices in Education*, which states the major obligations to test takers of

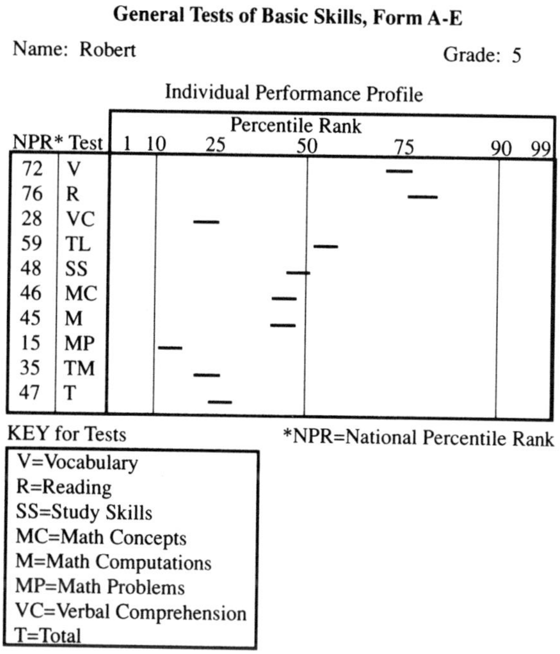
General Tests of Basic Skills, Form A-E
Name: Robert
Grade: 5
Individual Performance Profile
Percentile Rank
NPR* Test
1 10 25 50 75 90 99
72 V
76 R
28 VC
59 TL
48 SS
46 MC
45 M
15 MP
35 TM
47 T
KEY for Tests
*NPR=National Percentile Rank
V=Vocabulary
R=Reading
SS=Study Skills
MC=Math Concepts
M=Math Computations
MP=Math Problems
VC=Verbal Comprehension
T=Total

Figure 11.2. Sample student profile with percentile bands

professionals who develop or use educational tests. *The Code* deals with various aspects of the obligations including the rights of the testee with regard to the test and its results. These guidelines are presented in Table 11.2.

The Code also presents guidelines for both users and developers of tests for interpreting test scores. These guidelines are presented in Table 11.3.

Norms

As we have seen, the interpretation of standardized test results are based on norms. In order to develop norms, the test is given to a large sample of people (many hundreds, thousands or more) and then average or **normative** performance is computed. Generally two averages, the mean and median are often used as synonyms for norms. The reference group who wrote the test is called the norm group. The results from the norm group are published in the technical manuals that accompany the standardized as norm tables. These usually show the correspondence between raw scores on the test and derived scores such as percentiles, stanines, grade equivalents, and so on. The test user, then, merely has to refer to the table to convert a pupil's raw score to the derived score of interest.

For norms to be appropriate and, therefore, valid as a reference group with which to make interpretations they must satisfy the three R's. That is, they must be recent, representative, and relevant.

Table 11.2. Informing Test Takers

Under some circumstances test developers have direct communication with test takers. Under other circumstances, test users communicate directly with test takers. Whichever group communicates directly with test takers should provide the information described below.

Test Developers or Test Users Should:

17. When a test is optional, provide test takers or their parents/guardians with information to help them judge whether the test should be taken, or if an available alternative to test should be used.
18. Provide test takers the information they need to be familiar with the test, the types of question formats, the directions, and appropriate test-taking strategies. Strive to make such information equally available to all test takers.

Under some circumstances, test developers have direct control of tests and test scores. Under other circumstances, test users have such control. Whichever group has direct control of tests and test scores should take the steps described below.

Test Developers and Test Users Should:

19. Provide test takers or their parents/guardians with information about rights test takers may have to obtain copies of tests and completed answer sheets, retake tests, have tests rescored, or cancel scores.
20. Tell test takers or their parents/guardians how long scores will be kept on file and indicate to whom and under what circumstances test scores will or will not be released.
21. Describe the procedures that test takers or their parents/guardians may use to register complaints and have problems resolved.

Code of Fair Testing Practices in Education (1988) Washington, D.C.: Joint Committee on Testing Practices. (Mailing Address: Joint Committee on Testing Practices, American Psychological Association, 1200 17th Street, NW, Washington, D.C. 20036.)

Recency

Because the nature of our society changes over time, norms become outdated. If you were to interpret a pupil's performance on a standardized achievement test in 1992, for example, based on norms that were established for that test in 1972, it is likely that you would get an incorrect interpretation. The reference group from 1972 is no longer meaningful for 1992 since school curricula has changed as has many basic concepts and skills. Many important historical events in the intervening time has also changed society.

The rate at which norms become outdated is in part, related to the content of the test. Norms for tests of basic skills in mathematics, for example, will become outdated more slowly than norms for tests of social studies. In either case, however, the norms will become outdated as the content of the discipline tested changes.

A less obvious way that norms become obsolete is when the nature of the reference group changes. Norms on achievement tests that were established in the 1950s for college students, for example, would not be relevant for today's college students because both the gender and socioeconomic composition of the latter are substantially different from the former. A general rule of

Table 11.3. Interpreting Scores

Test developers should help users interpret scores correctly.	Test users should interpret scores correctly.
Test developer Should:	**Test Users Should:**
9. Provide timely and easily understood score reports that describe test performance clearly and accurately. Also explain the meaning and limitations of reported scores.	9. Obtain information about the scale used for reporting scores, the characteristics of any norms or comparison group(s), and the limitations of the scores.
10. Describe the population(s) represented by any norms or comparison group(s), the dates the data was gathered, and the process used to select the samples of test takers.	10. Interpret scores taking into account any major differences between the norms or comparison groups and actual test takers. Also take into account any differences in test administration practices or familiarity with specific questions in the test.
11. Warn users to avoid specific, reasonably anticipated misuses of test scores.	11. Avoid using tests for purposes not specifically recommended by the test developer unless evidence is obtained to support the intended use.
12. Provide information that will help users follow reasonable procedures for setting passing scores when it is appropriate to use such scores with a test.	12. Explain how any passing scores were set and gather evidence to support the appropriateness of the scores.
13. Provide information that will help users gather evidence to show that the test is meeting its intended purpose(s).	13. Obtain evidence to help show that the test is meeting its intended purpose(s).

Code of Fair Testing Practices in Education. (1988) Washington, D.C.: Joint Committee on Testing Practices. (Mailing Address: Joint Committee on Testing Practices, American Psychological Association, 1200 17th Street, NW, Washington, D.C. 20036.)

thumb for achievement tests is that norms older than five years should be suspect. Of course if there have been rapid curriculum changes or teaching methods in the intervening period, the norms may be obsolete in a much shorter period of time. This may happen even from year to year. In any case, users of standardized tests should be keenly aware of the date when the norms were established and make a determination of their obsolescence (or lack thereof).

Representativeness

A norm group is, technically, a sample. The question arises, then, of how representative the norm group is of the population that it is intended to reflect. There are two crucial characteristics to consider in determining the representativeness of the sample: size and bias.

Size is important because a small sample is unstable. Suppose for instance, a single school involving only 30 pupils in each grade from 1 to 7 for a total of 210 pupils is used as a norming group. The results are likely to be unstable. If we were to repeat the norming with a second school and now compare the results for the grade two's, the results are likely to be very different between the two samples. This is because the original norming group was too small to provide stable results. Generally, many hundreds of pupils are needed at each grade level to provide stable results.

Bias in the norm group has to do with the extent that it reflects the same important characteristics of the subsequently tested pupils. The main characteristics to consider are age or grade, sex, socioeconomic status, race, urban or rural settings, and so on. Norm groups which are heavily biased on any of these dimensions are likely to be unrepresentative. Samples which are predominantly male, from one particular grade and socioeconomic class, are highly biased. The norm developers should use adequate sampling techniques to ensure the representativeness of the norm group and thus minimize bias.

Relevance

This issue deals with the similarity of the tested group to the norm group. In other words, how relevant is the norm group for the pupils you wish to test? A norm group based on a general junior high school sample in a rural working class area, would be completely irrelevant for interpreting test scores for a female from an upper class home who attends an elite private high school in a large city. Perhaps the best way to think of the bias or lack of it in the norm group is that it should be a **peer** group for the testee. If the testee is not really a peer with those in the norm group in some important way, then the norms are likely to lack relevance.

Another important factor to consider in relevance is the type of instruction that the group to be tested has compared to the norm group. If the group to be tested only received 30% as much instruction in mathematics computations as did the norm group, for example, the norms are likely to lack relevance for the intended testees.

A critical aspect of norm-referenced standardized tests, then, is the norms. Remember to judge the validity of the norms on the three R's: recency, representativeness, and relevance. Serious deficits in any of the three areas may render the test invalid for your particular purposes.

Selecting a Standardized Test

The practices for selecting standardized tests vary across school districts. In some districts, testing officers make the decision in consultation with curriculum specialists. In other cases, achievement tests may be selected or developed solely by the state or provincial education branch. In both of these instances there is little or no input from teachers even though it is the teacher who frequently administers and interprets the results of such testing. In many situations, however, teachers play a more direct role in test selection. Special education teachers, for example, frequently determine which tests will be used to monitor performance of pupils receiving remedial services.

Regardless of what process is used for test selection or who is involved in the decision, the following three criteria should be used for making the selection: (1) relevance as evidenced by content validity, (2) technical adequacy as indicated by adequate reliability and norms, and (3) usability, which refers to the practical considerations of testing.

The issue of relevance is particularly important and problematic in choosing a standardized achievement test. You must answer the basic question, "What is the match between the test items and the school curriculum?" Keep in mind that test developers draw from many curricula across the country as the basis for developing the test blueprint and table of specifications. Accordingly, no one school district's curriculum will be accurately represented in the test. Teachers and school officials must review the test items and determine if they are a fair test of what the pupils in their classes studied. While this may seem to be an obvious point, it is remarkable how frequently achievement tests which have little relevance to actual school content are administered to pupils. This of course, is an issue of content validity.

If a test does not adequately represent the skills and knowledge actually taught in school, it lacks content validity. Any educational decisions made on the basis of such an instrument will naturally, be misleading and invalid.

The technical adequacy of any test can be determined by its reliability and its norms. Reliability as you will recall, deals with the consistency with which the test measures whatever it is intended to measure (see Chapter 9). Recall as well that there are three types of reliability: (1) stability, (2) equivalent form, and (3) internal consistency. You must determine which is most relevant to the purposes of the testing that will be done. If testing will be done in September and then again in May to determine pupil growth in basic skills, then stability is the most relevant type of reliability for the test you will choose. The other important element of the reliability is the magnitude of the relevant coefficient. A reasonable expectation is that overall reliability coefficients should exceed, $r_{xx}=.90$ for standardized, norm-referenced achievement tests.

The appropriateness of norms is an issue which is frequently overlooked in selecting a test. Each standardized test has been normed on a particular group of pupils. Use of the test with some other non-similar group will invalidate the norms. For your particular purpose, you must evaluate the norms for recency, representativeness, and relevance as we have seen. Failure to do so may result in derived test scores which lack validity, and may thus lead to poor and even harmful educational decisions.

The final criterion on which the test must be evaluated is its usability, or the practical and financial use value of a test. A test which is most relevant and technically sound for your purposes, for example, may be far too expensive for your school district to use. Its usability, therefore, is low. Similarly, if you simply do not have the people to understand the interpretation of the test, it also has low usability. A test which is ideal on validity and reliability, therefore, may still be inappropriate because it has low usability. A number of guidelines have been published in *The Code* for developing and selecting appropriate standardized tests and are summarized here in Table 11.4. These focus on relevance, technical merit and usability.

In selecting a standardized test, you should always seek an independent evaluation of the instrument besides those provided by the publisher. The most comprehensive source of information about published tests is the *Mental Measurements Yearbook* (MMY) published by the Buros Institute of Mental Measurements. This publication includes such practical information about tests as their costs, time to administer, number of forms available, publication date and scoring services available. In addition, this compendium includes critical reviews of the tests by testing experts. These reviews deal with issues of reliability, validity, usability and other relevant matters. Another similar source of information is *Tests: A Comprehensive Reference for Assessment in Psychology, Education, and Business*. This document has thousands of entries.

Professional journals are another source of information about tests. Major published tests in education, psychology and business are frequently reviewed by testing experts and these are published in professional journals such as the following: *Educational and Psychological Measurement, Journal of Educational Measurement, Measurement and Evaluation in Guidance, Journal of School Psychology, Journal of Special Education, Psychology in the Schools*, and *Alberta Journal of Educational Research*.

Table 11.4. Developing/Selecting Appropriate Tests

Test developers should provide the information that test users need to select appropriate tests.	Test users should select the tests that meet the purpose for which they are to be used and that are appropriate for the intended test-taking populations.

Test Developer Should:

1. Define what each test measures and what the test should be used for. Describe the population(s) for which the test is appropriate.

2. Accurately represent the characteristics, usefulness, and limitations of tests for their intended purpose.

3. Explain relevant measurement concepts as necessary for clarity at the level of detail that is appropriate for the intended audience(s).

4. Describe the process of test development. Explain how the content and skills to be tested were selected.

5. Provide evidence that the test meets its intended purpose(s).

6. Provide either representative samples or complete copies of test questions, directions, answer sheets, manuals, and score reports to qualified users.

7. Indicate the nature of the evidence obtained concerning the appropriateness of each test for groups of different racial, ethnic, or linguistic backgrounds who are likely to be tested.

8. Identify and publish any skills needed to administer each test and to interpret scores correctly.

Test Users Should:

1. First define the purpose for testing and the population to be tested. Then, select a test for that purpose and that population based on a thorough review of the available information.

2. Investigate potentially useful sources of information, in addition to test scores, to corroborate the information provided by tests.

3. Read the materials provided by test developers and avoid using tests for which unclear or incomplete information is provided.

4. Become familiar with how and when the test was developed and tried out.

5. Read independent evaluations of a test and of possible alternative measures. Look for evidence required to support the claims of test developers.

6. Examine specimen sets, disclosed tests or samples of questions, directions, answer sheets, manuals, and score reports before selecting a test.

7. Ascertain whether the test content and norms (group(s) or comparison group(s)) are appropriate for the intended test takers.

8. Select and use only those tests for which the skills needed to administer the test and interpret scores correctly are available.

Code of Fair Testing Practices in Education. (1988) Washington, D.C.: Joint Committee on Testing Practices. (Mailing Address: Joint Committee on Testing Practices, American Psychological Association, 1200 17th Street, NW, Washington, D.C. 20036.)

Table 11.5. Striving for Fairness

Test developers should strive to make tests that are as fair as possible for test takers of different races, gender, ethnic background, or handicapping conditions.	Test users should select tests that have been developed in ways that attempt to make them as fair as possible for test takers of different races, gender, ethnic backgrounds, or handicapping conditions.
Test Developers Should:	**Test Users Should:**
14. Review and revise test questions and related materials to avoid potentially insensitive content or language.	14. Evaluate the procedures used by test developers to avoid potentially insensitive content or language.
15. Investigate the performance of test takers of different races, gender, and ethnic backgrounds when samples of sufficient size are available. Enact procedures that help to ensure that differences in performance are related primarily to the skills under assessment rather than to irrelevant factors.	15. Review the performance of test takers of different races, gender, and ethnic background when samples of sufficient size are available. Evaluate the extent to which performance difference may have been caused by inappropriate characteristics of the test.
16. When feasible, make appropriately modified forms of tests or administration procedures available for test takers with handicapping conditions. Warn test users of potential problems in using standard norms with modified tests or administration procedures that result in non-comparable scores.	16. When necessary and feasible, use appropriately modified forms of tests or administration procedures for test takers with handicapping conditions. Interpret standard norms with care in the light of the modifications that were made.

Code of Fair Testing Practices in Education. (1988) Washington, D.C.: Joint Committee on Testing Practices. (Mailing Address: Joint Committee on Testing Practices, American Psychological Association, 1200 17th Street, NW, Washington, D.C. 20036.)

As a final note to this section, tests that are as fair as possible for test takers of different races, gender, ethnic background, or handicapping conditions, should be sought by test users. Again, a number of guidelines for this have been developed and published in *The Code*. These are summarized in Table 11.5. Teachers can also try to increase fairness for their pupils by teaching them test-taking strategies.

Test-taking Strategies

Test-taking strategies are skills which can be taught and learned. These allow pupils to respond to the test appropriately so that their performance, which should reflect achievement in the content area, is not distorted by a lack of skill in taking tests. If the pupil's performance is influenced negatively because of poor test-taking skills, the information communicated by their test score will lack validity. Any interpretations of these scores are likely to be misleading. As well, you will not have accurate information to inform decisions about your teaching. You should, therefore, teach your pupils test-taking strategies. These which follow will help to improve your pupil's test-taking skills and thus, result in more valid test scores. These test-taking skills are particularly important when taking published tests but apply equally to teacher-made tests. Some test-taking skills are summarized below for the two major question formats that are used on standardized tests, the forced choice item (e.g., multiple-choice) and the open ended item (e.g., short answer or essay).

Multiple Choice Test Items

The multiple-choice item is the most widely used testing format on standardized tests. Increasingly, even pupils at the elementary, and certainly at the secondary level, are encountering the multiple-choice (MC) item on published and teacher-made tests.

Unfortunately, many pupils, particulary those with learning problems, do not perform well on MC tests. These pupils frequently report that such tests cause them to become very anxious and as a result, their performance suffers significantly. Observations of unsuccessful test-takers have revealed at least two sources of difficulties. First, poor test-takers do not generally spend sufficient time reading the question component or stem of the MC item. The stem frequently contains information which the test-taker can use to eliminate the incorrect options. Reading the stem too quickly results in missing such information and thereby, adds unnecessarily to the difficulty of the item. Second, racing through the stem in order to choose an option, creates a frenzied pace for the pupil which adds to their already high anxiety.

The following strategy has been suggested (Marini, 1991) to assist these pupils in slowing their pace and thus read the stem more carefully and thoroughly. The strategy also gives the test-taker a greater feeling of control and accordingly, reduces their anxiety somewhat. These should be given as specific instructions to pupils.

Stop   reading at the end of the stem and cover the options with your hand.

Reflect   on what information the stem provides and what you know about the specific content area of the question.

Respond   silently to the question with what you believe might be the correct answer. After completing this task, uncover the options.

Confirm   your tentative response with one of the options.

This is called the SRRC strategy. Many pupils, particularly those experiencing anxiety during an MC exam, have reported that this strategy has helped them to feel more in control during examinations and has helped to maximize their performance.

Devine and Meagher (1989) have suggested additional strategies for approaching an MC test item. These are presented below, and will be helpful to pupils in both elementary and secondary grades.

(1) Turn the stem into a question. For some pupils, a stem such as "The field of chemistry is concerned with" is more difficult to respond to than the question, "What is chemistry?" While the reasons for this are not completely clear, there is evidence that converting open stems into complete questions does increase test scores (Violato, 1991). One possibility is that converting the incomplete stem to a question, more clearly focuses the problem and thus reduces the ambiguity of the question.

(2) Try elimination. Pupils frequently perceive the task of selecting the correct answer in a four option item as selecting one from four possibilities, it is likely that through the process of elimination, the choice can be reduced to one in two options. Even for questions which are very difficult, pupils usually have *some* knowledge about the item making the elimination of one or more options possible.

(3) Watch for qualifiers. Options which contain absolutes such as never, only, always, certainly or all are frequently incorrect responses. Test constructors sometimes use such options to easily render the option incorrect thus reducing the need to develop other plausible distractors. Therefore, they are rarely meant to serve as correct responses and more often simply provide evidence of poor test construction. Conversely, options which equivocate with the use of words like sometimes, frequently, in most cases, usually and so on, are generally correct options. Identifying these options and responding accordingly, will allow pupils to capitalize on poorly constructed tests rather than be penalized by them.

(4) More words tend to be right. In any well designed MC item, there is only one correct option. In order for this to be true, test writers construct the correct option to be complete and to account for all the possible information. On occasion, the need to construct a valid correct option results in too little attention to the construction of the distractors. Consequently, the distractors may be considerably shorter than the correct answer. Long complete options, therefore, frequently represent the correct answer.

Essay Tests

Compared to the multiple-choice test, the essay test is a much more ambiguous task. This is because the pupil must construct the answer rather than select it. Test wiseness or test-taking strategies are even more important on essay tests, than on multiple-choice tests. There are a number of critical strategies in taking essay tests.

(1) Ensure that you understand the general instructions. Pay particular attention to the time allotted for the total test and how many questions you must answer. Note the value of each question. Spend twice as much time on a question that has twice the value of another one. Does the test require full sentence and paragraph responses? Is point form allowed? If there are optional questions, have you selected ones from the appropriate lists?

(2) Read carefully. The first thing you must do is understand the question. Do not begin writing the instant you have read the question. Allot about 10% of the total question time to (1) understanding the question, and (2) developing an outline for the answer. Suppose, for example, that you will spend 20 minutes answering question #2. Spend the first 2–3 minutes *reading* the question and writing an outline. As you are reading, underline key terms and ideas. If the question asks you to "compare and contrast", do not simply describe. It is amazing how many "brilliant" essays receive poor marks because they failed to answer the question that was asked.

As you are developing your outline, jot down key ideas. Ensure that you have an introduction, a body of the essay, and a conclusion. Your outline should provide both an overview of the answer and enough detail on which you will expand.

(3) Write carefully. Write in full, comprehensible sentences. Do not use jargon, or unnecessary verbiage. Write clearly. Nothing will annoy (and hence negatively dispose) a marker more than not being able to (1) read your answer because it is too messy, or (2) understand what you mean. Pay attention to spelling, grammar, punctuation and the other mechanics of language. Avoid writing an answer that is too long and too flowery.

(4) Answer every question that is required. Even if you feel that you can't provide a full answer to a question, write honestly what you know. You will almost certainly receive partial marks for partial answers. It is the rare pupil who knows **nothing** at all about a question.

(5) Use all of the allotted time. There is no advantage to finishing an essay test early. No one is impressed by early completers. Rarely are prizes given for the first one finished.

(6) Use point form as a last resort. If you are very pressed for time, jot down in point form something for the remaining questions. You may receive some marks.

■ Summary and Main Points

Standardized or published tests differ from teacher-made tests in several important ways. They are more formal, involve standard administration and interpretation procedures, and have known psychometric properties. It is important that teachers know about standardized tests since they play a vital role in classroom instruction as well as decisions about individual pupils. There are several ways to classify standardized tests: norm and criterion-referenced, test batteries and single-subject. Various people besides teachers use standardized test results. These include school counsellors, administrators, psychologists, pupils, and parents. Published tests are usually administered by the teacher according to standardized procedures. The interpretation of these tests is also usually done by the teacher employing standard scores, percentile ranks, age and grade equivalents, and score profiles. Norms play a crucial role in the understanding and interpretation of standardized tests. When selecting these tests teachers must attend to the test's relevance, technical quality and usability. Since taking standardized tests involves considerable test-taking skill, teachers should teach these to their pupils to make the resulting scores as valid as possible.

1. Standardized or published tests are instruments which are developed by testing and curriculum experts. These instruments come with norms, standard administration procedures, and known psychometric properties.
2. Teacher-made tests are less formal than standardized tests since they typically are given only once to assess specific classroom achievement.
3. Teachers should know about standardized tests because they usually are the ones administering them to their pupils and interpreting the results.
4. Standardized tests can be classified in several ways: norm and criterion referenced, test batteries and single-subject tests. Test batteries or single-subject tests, of course, can be interpreted as either norm-referenced or criterion-referenced.
5. Standardized test results can be used by various people for different purposes. Psychologists, teachers, counsellors, administrators, pupils and parents all use them for different purposes.
6. Teachers should take special care in preparing their pupils for taking standardized tests since it is usually a very formal event which can make pupils very anxious.
7. The results from standardized tests are reported as derived scores. These include standard scores and percentile ranks as well as grade equivalents and age equivalents. Graphical forms of reporting such as a point profile and error band profiles, are useful forms of presenting the results.

8. Standard scores, percentiles, grade equivalents and age equivalents all have some limitations as reporting systems. Used in isolation, they can be very misleading. Perhaps the best combination to use for reporting is the percentile rank and grade equivalent score.
9. Norms are a critical element of standardized tests. Users should always evaluate norms on the three R's: recency, representativeness, and relevance.
10. When selecting a standardized test, the user should evaluate not only the norms, but the test's content validity and usability as well.
11. Teachers can help improve the validity of pupils' scores on standardized tests by teaching them test-taking strategies. There are specific skills that can be taught and learned for both multiple-choice and open-ended questions.

■ Further Readings

Lyman, H. B. (1987). *Test scores and what they mean* (3rd ed.). Englewood Cliffs, N.J.: Prentice Hall.
This is a small book that is worth reading from cover to cover because it is particulary useful for understanding standardized tests.
Mehrens, W. A. (1987). *Using standardized tests in education.* New York: Longman.
A comprehensive and authoritative text on this topic.
Salvia, J. and Ysseldyke, J. E. (1991). *Assessment* (5th ed). Boston: Houghton Mifflin.
A comprehensive text in general assessment in special education but is excellent in explicating standardized tests.

■ Laboratory Exercises

1. Compare and contrast standardized tests and teacher-made tests.
2. Why should teachers know about standardized tests?
3. How are standardized tests classified? Describe each type.
4. Who uses the results of standardized tests? Identify the major uses that each of these people might make of standardized tests.
5. Why is it important that teachers take special care in preparing their pupils to take standardized tests?
6. Compare and contrast the use of percentile ranks, standard scores and grade equivalents for interpreting test results.
7. What are point and error band profiles?
8. Describe the limitations of each derived score in reporting test results and how these might be mitigated.
9. What are norms?
10. What are the 3 R's for the evaluation of norms?
11. Which technical features should you examine when selecting a standardized test for a school testing program?
12. What does "relevance" mean when selecting a standardized test?
13. What is the importance of usability in selecting a test?

14. Summarize the basic test-taking skills that teachers can teach their pupils for taking multiple-choice tests.
15. Summarize the basic test-taking skills that teachers can teach their pupils for taking essay tests.

Chapter

Grading and Reporting

Overview

Grading and reporting, the topic of this chapter, is a necessary function of all educational enterprises for them to be most effective. The chapter begins with a discussion of the functions of grading and reporting and then several grading systems are described. Each grading system has advantages and disadvantages. A number of symbols including letter grades and numeric systems are commonly used to assign grades. Each of these have strengths and weaknesses. Procedures for determining grades by weighting components differentially are necessary so as to control the effect of different variances of each component. Grading homework and assignments present special problems for grading. Problems of reporting systems and examples of several are presented in this chapter and some guidelines for developing sound reporting systems are summarized. The chapter concludes with some guidelines for conducting the parent-teacher conference and explaining the meaning of test scores to parents and pupils.

The Purpose of Grading and Reporting

Some form of grading and reporting is part of virtually every educational enterprise from nursery to graduate school. Grading and reporting provide several functions including feedback, accountability, directing pupil effort, as well as rewarding and motivating effort.

Grades (also called marks) provide feedback on performance to the pupil, parents, future teachers and prospective employers. This information is usually provided via report cards and parent-teacher conferences. Grades and other data communicated in this manner can be used by the pupil, parents and teachers to monitor the educational progress of the pupil and thereby facilitate decisions about educational plans. Such information can indicate areas of strength, weakness or deficit that require attention. Based on this feedback, appropriate action may be suggested and taken to improve the teaching and learning that the pupil is engaged in. Parents are thereby also kept informed and involved in the education of their child.

Grading and reporting also provides a form of accountability. Since periodic reporting is done, this holds the teacher, school and pupil accountable for their educational activity. These reports provide analogous functions in education that financial statements play in business. Without such formal reporting systems, there would be no mechanism to hold all those involved in the educational enterprise accountable for their actions. Such accountability ultimately helps to improve education as it requires planning, thought and review of the outcomes of education.

Weaknesses, deficits and strengths are identified by grades and are communicated by reporting. This helps to direct future efforts and interests. Efforts may be directed to correct deficits and strengths may be further developed and interests shaped accordingly. Exceptional achievement in mathematics, for example, may be identified by grading and therefore affect decisions about future efforts in mathematics. Deficits in reading may also be identified by grading and the reporting to parents may help the child direct their efforts to overcome the problem.

Grades can motivate pupils to work hard. Receiving high grades can motivate further effort by pupils and may stimulate keen interest in the subject. High grades also serve to reward hard work and effort. Conversely, poor grades can motivate effort to improve performance.

There are, however, a number of real or perceived problems with grades. The main problem lies in the meaning of grades. Marks may have different meanings across teachers, schools, and school districts. Performance that received an A in one school may produce only a B in another school. Even within the same school, one teacher may assign a C to a pupil while another teacher might give the same pupil a D for the same work. This lack of universal meaning for grades is a problem that can be at least partially solved by more valid assessment procedures.

The discrepancy of grading among teachers, schools and school districts, is directly due to the lack of universal objective evidence for assigning grades. While it is common for most schools to have adjective descriptors associated with letter grades such as "excellent" for A, "good" for B, "fair" for C, "poor" for D, and "fail" for F, the objective evidence for assigning these letters and thus the adjective descriptors for individual pupils is lacking. There is no universal scale to which teachers can refer to assign these letter grades. Thus teachers are left to their own judgment to what is the meaning and the evidence for assigning the marks. While this problem can never be completely solved, it can be mitigated by using as reliable and valid measuring instruments as possible.

Another criticism is that pupils are motivated to work for grades rather than for significant educational outcomes or important learning. This is more a perceived problem than a real problem with grades. In fact it is a criticism of the validity of the grades than of the inherent nature of them. If grades do not reflect important learning it is because they have not been adequately tied to important educational outcomes. The solution to this problem is make the grades more valid and thus reflect important learning outcomes. Then the pupil will work for both grades and important learning.

Teacher assigned grades have been shown to be notoriously unreliable (Educational Testing Services, 1963; Starch & Elliot, 1912, 1913). When the grade is assigned largely or wholly on subjective grounds, numerous irrelevant factors such as pupil appearance, politeness, gender, attractiveness, honesty, and so on influence the grade. This problem, of course, is not that grades are inherently flawed, but rather that the data used to compute the grades are too subjective and therefore unreliable. The solution to the problem is to use data (e.g. test scores) which is objective and reliable.

A final problem which is frequently identified with grades is that they are responsible for a variety of detrimental side effects like anxiety, self-concept problems, hostility, cheating, and produce negative attitudes towards learning and education when low grades are received. That some pupils have low self-concepts, are anxious, cheat and are hostile to learning, is undeniable. These problems, however, are not caused by grades. They are a result of more fundamental factors. Even at the elementary school level, children readily know how well (or poorly) they read, whether or not they are competent pupils, how attractive they are, and how competent they are in athletics. All of these factors are far more important in pupil anxiety, self-concept problems, hostility and so on, than are teacher assigned grades.

Grading and Marking Systems

There are a number of systems that can be used to assign grades and marks. These together with their strengths and weaknesses will be discussed in turn.

Norm-referenced Grading

This system is frequently called grading on the curve. Here it is assumed that final achievement of a class is normally distributed and that marks can be derived based on the standard deviation and the mean of the distribution. The most commonly used technique for this is the Cajori method (Cureton, 1971) which sets +1.5 standard deviations and above for A's (7% of the class), +.5 to +1.5 for B's (24%), −.5 to +.5 for C's (38%), −.5 to −1.5 for D's (24%), and below −1.5 for F's (7%). Essentially, grading on the curve amounts to determining **a priori** the numbers of A's, B's, C's, D's and F's that there will be in any given class.

There are some assumptions underlying this method which are rarely met in practice. First, it is assumed that the underlying distribution is normal. This is rarely the case because typical classes are too small to produce data which even approaches a normal distribution. Moreover, few classroom tests are sufficiently reliable and valid to result in a normal distribution even with large classes. Second, it is assumed that educational performances of less than 1.5 standard deviations below the mean represent a failure. There are no good pedagogical or measurement reasons to make this assumption and it is quite arbitrary. Third, there is little reason to assume that any given class is "normal" and thus assumptions of the normal distribution cannot be applied. If the distribution is highly skewed either way, it may result in failure to assign any of the extreme grades (i.e., A or F). If the scores are positively skewed, none may fall below −1.5 standard deviations and thus no F's would be assigned.

It is rarely advisable to apply grading on the curve strictly to any situation. Perhaps it may be most defensibly used with very large enrollment classes such as freshman history classes of 300 or more students. Even here, however, it is assumed that the measurements were sufficiently reliable and valid to result in a normal distribution. Teachers should thus maintain final discretion over the method used to assign letter grades.

Criterion-referenced Grading

This method is an attempt to overcome the relativistic nature of norm-referenced grading by setting absolute standards called criteria. Using a criterion for evaluating pupil performance is an attempt to address the concern that children should be graded against an absolute standard of performance and not against each other. On the surface of it, this seems like a very sensible idea. In practice, however, this method is generally unworkable because it is very difficult to set meaningful criteria against which to judge performance.

In the past it was common practice to use percentage cut-offs as though they were meaningful evaluation criteria. It is still common, for example, to consider 50% as the cut-off for pass-fail but there are no good pedagogical, measurement or theoretical reasons to use this figure. Nor are there defensible reasons to use 90% as a cut-off for an A, 80% for a B, and so on. Even if such a universal system was employed, it is obviously rather arbitrary. It is easy to imagine where one teacher gives an easy test and therefore most of the pupils surpass the cut-off of 90% and receive A's. Another teacher may give a more difficult test and even though his pupils may achieve just as well or better than the first class, few would receive A's. It is rarely possible to establish absolute standards by some systematic method that is defensible.

Perhaps the best way of establishing such cut-offs is based on the performance of previous pupils. This is a combination of criterion and norm referenced grading. The absolute standards are established based on the normative performance of previous students. This method combines the advantages of both criterion and norm-referenced marking while avoiding the problems of each. The main drawback of this system, however, is that the teacher must have reliable and valid data on large numbers of previous pupils. Most teachers probably use an "intuitive" method of setting standards as they develop a "feel" for what their pupils are capable of or should be capable of. Obviously, such subjective approaches result in questionable standards of performance that are quite arbitrary.

Notwithstanding the above cautions, a percentage cut-off system that may be used as a general **guideline** is provided here for you. The guidelines should be used only as suggestions subject to change and revision by the teacher based on individual needs and circumstances. They should not be regarded as immutable standards.

A (A+, A–)	=	85–100%
B (B+, B–)	=	70–84%
C (C+, C–)	=	59–69%
D (D+, D–)	=	50–58%
F	=	49% and less

Improvement or Individual Growth Based Grading

This approach is an attempt to evaluate pupil performance against themselves. That is, the improvement that the pupil shows in a specified amount of time (e.g., between report card one and report card two), should be the bases for assigning the grade. Thus a pupil who shows marked improvement from September to December should receive an A even if her actual performance is average compared to her peers or an absolute standard. While such a system has appeal, the technical difficulties associated with this method are immense.

Measuring educational change involves the use of gain or growth scores. Even with highly reliable and valid instruments such as some standardized tests, gain scores are highly unreliable (Crocker & Algina, 1986). Furthermore, when attempting to assess student growth, most teachers use informal, unsystematic and subjective methods. Grading based on such procedures would become rather arbitrary and have little validity.

Even if some workable measurement system could be devised for reliably and validly assessing individual growth, there is no sound reason to grade an individual's performance based solely on their improvement or change. How can you justify assigning an A to a pupil who has improved substantially but whose performance is average compared to his peers? Conversely, how can you justify assigning a C to a pupil whose performance might be the best in the class but who has not improved since the beginning of the year?

In the individual growth system you must also consider that it is very much easier for a pupil to improve when their initial performance was poor than one whose initial performance was good. The pupil beginning poorly has nowhere to go but to improve while this is much more difficult for the pupil giving a good initial performance. Finally, if pupils begin to recognize that you are using this "growth" method of assigning grades, they may purposefully perform poorly initially in order to easily improve subsequently. Obviously, this would invalidate the entire system. The individual improvement method is so fraught with problems that it is generally unworkable and not recommended as a system of assigning grades.

Effort Based Grading

In this method, pupils who expend great effort in their studies are assigned high grades while those who put in little or no effort are assigned poor grades. This system, however, confuses the primary purpose of grading which is to summarize and communicate achievement in a subject matter or content area. While effort is an obviously important educational objective, it should be assessed and reported separately from achievement. The grade should reflect achievement **per se** and not other extraneous factors such as effort, attitude, and study habits. Indeed, grading systems are most meaningful and valid when these elements are reported separately. There are no pedagogical, measurement or theoretical basis on which to base a grading system on effort.

Achievement and Aptitude Based Grading

In this system, there is an attempt to judge pupil's academic attainment based on their aptitude or potential. Pupils who are performing up to their potential might receive marks in the average to good range (C, B), those working below their potential might receive marks in the poor to fail range (D, F), and those above their potential receive marks in the excellent to outstanding range (A). This system has appeal for teachers and others alike because it avoids the criticisms of the other grading systems (criterion-referenced, norm-referenced, growth, effort). Proponents of this system argue that each pupil should be judged according to what they can do instead of what others do or based on some external standards of performance.

As appealing as this idea is, it is completely unworkable in practice. The main problem is that the teacher must know the pupil's aptitude or potential in order to judge the merit of their performance. The only valid way that a pupil's potential might be estimated is through standardized test scores and IQ scores. These data are frequently not available for most pupils. Moreover, estimating potential requires different test scores for different subjects as aptitude varies across subject matter. Even with valid test scores available, the technical difficulties in judging achievement relative to potential are large. Teachers who attempt to use such a system frequently "intuit" or guess at a pupil's potential. The resulting grading system, of course, lacks any validity whatsoever.

Types of Symbols Used in Grading

There are numerous grading and marking symbols that have been used with varying degrees of success. Some of these have been used for a long time while others are quite new. Despite the symbol system used, however, their main purpose is to communicate in a simple and understandable way, the achievement of the pupil. Various grading symbols are discussed in turn below.

Letter Grades

The most widely used symbol system is the traditional letter grade (A, B, C, D, F). Here a letter grade is assigned for each subject to indicate the pupil's achievement. While this system is concise, readily understandable, and familiar, it does have some difficulties. First, as we have seen, these letter grades lack universal meaning from teacher to teacher and from school to school. Second, the letter grade alone tells us nothing about other important educational matters such as effort, attitude and interests. Third, the letter grade may have different meanings across subject matter itself. A B in history, for example, may not reflect the same achievement as a B in mathematics.

Numerous attempts have been made to improve the shortcomings of the traditional letter grade. This usually takes the form of using different symbols and reducing the number of categories. One system employs four categories, first class, second class, pass and fail. Another attempt at improvement has been to use E (excellent), G (good), S (satisfactory) and U (unsatisfactory). Still another attempt at simplification has been to employ only two categories, S and U.

These attempts are not really improvements over the letter grades as they have the same problems and introduce new ones as well. Parents and pupils tend not to like these systems as they are not as familiar as the letter grade. As well, the reduction of the number of categories reduces the reliability of the grades. As we saw in the discussion of reliability (Chapter 9), the reliability of an assessment or evaluation can be increased by increasing the number of items, questions or categories in it. Reducing the number of categories in the grading system from 5 or more (A–F) to 3 or less (S, U), will substantially reduce the reliability of the grading system. For this reason it is important to use a system with several categories (at least 5). So despite the shortcomings of the traditional letter grade system, it is likely to continue to be widely used in the foreseeable future.

Numerical Grades

There are two generally used numerical grading systems (1) percentages, and (2) numerals between 1 and 10. In the percentage system, the total achievement scores for the reporting period are summed and converted to a percentage value. This single number is then reported to indicate the quality of performance. To increase meaning, percentage ranges are frequently assigned adjective descriptors (90–100 = excellent, 80–89 = very good, etc.). In the second numerical system, a number between 1 and 10 is assigned with 1 indicating very poor and 10 indicating outstanding.

The main problems with these systems is their lack of familiarity and their deceptive nature. These numerical systems have not been used as widely as have the letter grade and therefore are not as widely known. Moreover, they are deceptive because on the surface of it they would indicate some absolute scale of performance when in fact this is not the case. Does 100% indicate a complete knowledge of the subject matter? Does 50% indicate half knowledge? What does 7 mean? These numerical grades obviously offer no advantage over the letter grade especially when adjective descriptors are required to interpret them.

Pass-Fail System

This system provides only two categories of grading, namely either a pupil passes or fails a course. While there was some initial enthusiasm for this system in the 1960s and 70s, and it became used at various levels of education from elementary to graduate school, it never really became widespread for at least three reasons. First, it is not as familiar as the letter grade system which is generally preferred by pupils and the public. Second, it reduces substantially the information communicated to the pupil. Did the pass indicate a borderline performance or an outstanding one? Did the pupil who failed do so by a clear margin or was the performance within a standard error of measurement of the cut-off? How was the criterion for pass-fail established? Third, as we saw above, the system would be quite unreliable since it reduces the number of categories to the bare minimum (2).

For the above reasons it is unlikely that this will ever become the preferred grading system although it has found some accepted use in specialized applications. Courses which are taken as electives, for example, and are not to be included in the grade point average calculation might profitably employ this system. As well, courses which are taught strictly as mastery learning could employ this grading system.

Anecdotal Records

Anecdotal records or narrative reports are detailed reports that contain statements about effort, attitudes, behaviour and achievement of each pupil. Narrative descriptions have the advantage of allowing for the teacher to include much more information in reporting the pupil's performance than would otherwise be possible. Moreover, it allows the teacher to maintain a detailed daily description of important educational events of the child. These reports also tend to reduce norm-referenced comparisons and focus instead on a more comprehensive picture of the child.

Anecdotal records have a number of problems associated with them. First, while parents generally favour them as do teachers and school administrators, they still want the traditional letter grades in the reports. Second, the collection of information and composing of the reports represents a tremendous amount of work for the teacher. If a teacher maintained a daily anecdotal record for each child in a class of 20, a great deal of time would be required to do this task. Also the amount of information that would accumulate over the course of a month or two would make summarizing and compiling the actual narrative report a huge undertaking. Third, most teachers have little or no training in making and recording behavioural observations. The reliability and validity of the information on the anecdotal record is accordingly poor. Generally these records tend to be high interpretive rather than strictly observational and thus lack validity. Fourth, at the secondary and even upper elementary level, teachers generally have many more pupils and generally tend to know them less well than primary teachers know their pupils. For the upper division and secondary teachers, the data collection and reporting is such an onerous task that it is unworkable.

Perhaps narrative reports alone could be justified for the primary grades if parents are given a convincing rationale for the lack of letter grades. The anecdotal report could also be useful with special education groups that might otherwise receive persistently low grades and thus discourage pupils. Finally, the anecdotal record is probably most useful as an addendum to letter grade (or other) reporting systems. Here it would enrich and elaborate the traditional mark. As a sole reporting system, however, it is doubtful if anecdotal records have much use beyond the primary grade.

Checklists of Objectives

In this scheme, a checklist of objectives or educational outcomes is used and each pupil is rated indicating the degree of performance on the objective. Figure 12.1 is an example of a modern large school district report using the checklist of objectives for language learning and mathematics.

INDIVIDUAL STUDENT GROWTH

The process of learning is continuous throughout the life of and individual. In this report we recognize that no two children are alike and that they develop at different rates. **This assessment indicates your child's growth in these areas as an individual.**

Demonstrates exellence   Demonstrates success   Demonstrates success with support   Encounters difficulty

REPORTING PERIOD	2					3					4				
LANGUAGE LEARNING — *The Learner*	Demonstrates exellence	Demonstrates success	Demonstrates success with support	Encounters difficulty	Additional considerations	Demonstrates exellence	Demonstrates success	Demonstrates success with support	Encounters difficulty	Additional considerations	Demonstrates exellence	Demonstrates success	Demonstrates success with support	Encounters difficulty	Additional considerations
1. Extracts information from print															
2. Extracts information from non-print															
3. Reads for meaning															
4. Responds to ideas and feelings of others															
5. Writes/illustrates to convey meaning															
6. Edits and revises work															
7. Develops and organizes information and ideas															
8. Listens to explore and construct meaning															
9. Uses talk to explore, construct & communicate meaning															
MATHEMATICS — *The Learner*															
1. Describes, creates and solves mathematical problems															
2. Understands and applies mathematical concepts															
3. Uses and understands mathematical language															
4. Knows the basic facts															
5. Computes accurately															

Figure 12.1. An example of a checklist of objectives

This method has the advantage of providing very specific and informative reports about the pupils behaviour and what they can and cannot do. Such information has obvious use for educational decision making and for undertaking remedial action. Moreover, it assesses pupil progress on specific and relevant educational objectives rather than against peer performance or some numerical standard. Objective number 6, ''edits and revises work'', in language learning in Figure 12.1, for example, communicates very specific information about pupil behaviour as does objective number 4, "knows the basic facts", in mathematics. This performance is not norm-referenced or based on some letter grade. It thus can be very useful for undertaking educational action if the pupil is rated as "encounters difficulty" on this objective. By contrast, a C– on language learning might suggest that the pupil is not doing well but would not provide any guidance or direction on remedial action.

Despite their obvious advantages, checklists of objectives have not flourished as the sole method of grading. The main reason for this is that parents still want to know the letter grade performance that meeting the objectives represents. A parent may be gratified that their child mastered 17 of the 20 objectives but will still want to know if this is an A or B performance. A second difficulty with checklists of objectives is that they can become so long and extensive with very specific objectives in every subject matter, that evaluating every objective for each pupil can become an onerous and unworkable task for teachers. Checklists of objectives are most useful and informative when they are used in conjunction with traditional letter grade systems. Here they can be used to enrich and elaborate on the letter grade and communicate very specific information. These checklists work best when only a few of the most important objectives are included and evaluated.

Letters to Parents

Letters to parents in lieu of other more traditional grading systems have also been tried. These are similar to narrative reports that were described above. They are only useful if the descriptions of pupil performance are based on extensive and valid information. As sole methods of grading, however, this system suffers from the same flaws as do anecdotal records and narrative reports. They are best used as addenda to letter grade systems for communicating additional information or elaborating the grade.

Determining Grades

A final grade is usually a composite of a number of components. Several quizzes, tests, lab assignments, reports and so on may be combined to arrive at a total composite score which is used to determine the grade. It is usual for the teacher to want some components of the grade to count more heavily than others in the final total. On the surface, it appears that the component with the largest maximum score will receive the greatest weight when the components are summed but this is not the case. In fact, if several components are merely summed, it is the standard deviation or the variance of the component that will result in differential weighting: the larger the variance the greater the influence of the component.

If four components with equal maximum scores and means are summed, for example, they may not contribute equally to the final total. The component with the largest variance will count most heavily. Ideally in order to weigh each component equally, you should multiply each score in the distribution with the smallest variance by a ratio of the largest variance to the smallest. If two tests, for instance, both with means of 30 and maximum scores of 50 are summed, they may not weigh equally in the total. Suppose that Test 2 has a variance of 30 and Test 1 has a variance of 15. In order for Test 1 to contribute equally to the total, you should multiply each score in Test 1 by 2 (variance of Test 2 divided by variance of Test 1; 30/15 = 2). Obviously this procedure is very time consuming and would not generally be done by most teachers.

A less precise but acceptable approximation to the variance ratio equating is to use the range. In this case the range is taken as an index of variability and even though it is quite a crude index for this purpose, it is acceptable for most classroom use. Suppose that in the above example the minimum score on Test 1 was 20 and the maximum was 40 (range = 20), while on Test 2 the minimum was 7 and the maximum was 47 (range = 40). The multiplier for each score on Test 1, then, is the ratio of the two ranges (40/20 = 2). While in this method things are somewhat simplified because the range is much easier to compute than the variance, it still requires that every score be multiplied by some factor, in this case 2.

This weighting problem is avoided if each component is first converted to letter grades and then these are combined. The problem with this procedure is that it tends to reduce the reliability of the final grade because information is lost in determining letter grades for each component. Two children may both receive a B, for instance, although one may be at the top of the range and the other at the bottom of the range. This loss of information tends to reduce the reliability of the final grades.

There is no definitive and yet simple method with which to combine components for a grade. You should be aware, however, that a simple adding up of the various components may not weigh them equally because of the different variances of scores. You may wish to specifically weigh the scores by some weighting scheme based either on the variances, range or some other predetermined values such as twice the value for the final exam compared to the mid-term test.

Grading Assignments and Homework

Assignments such as reports, essays, arithmetic problems, book reviews and other homework activities are not primarily assessment activities. Their primary purpose is for teaching and learning. That is, they have been assigned with the intention that pupils should learn some important knowledge and skills as a consequence of doing the assignments. As we have seen, tests and other assessments are intended primarily as measurement instruments. It is these that should be used as the components for deriving grades. Assignments ideally should not be included as components in the grade.

If assignments and homework are not assigned a value or a mark, however, it is unlikely that pupils will consistently do them and work as hard as the teacher would like. If the assignments "don't count", they are not likely to be taken seriously by the pupils. It is necessary therefore, to assign some value to assignments and homework. As a rule of thumb, assignments and homework should account for no more than 25% of the total value of the grade. This is because these are likely to lack reliability and validity for grading since they were not designed for that purpose. Keeping the value of these components which are low in validity and reliability to a maximum of 25%, will tend to limit the extent to which they can reduce the reliability and validity of the final grade.

The primary problem with grading assignments and homework is that the expectations of the teacher and the criteria by which the assignment will be evaluated are not clearly laid out and communicated before the assignment is done. Scoring criteria, just as in scoring essay tests, should be developed and guide the evaluation of the assignments.

Preparing and using a scoring guide can result in a number of benefits. First, grading can be done more efficiently because of a clear-cut set of criteria and expectations. Second, the feedback to students can include diagnostic statements indicating specific problems and deficiencies. Third, extraneous factors such as the halo effect, penmanship, and so on are less likely to influence the scoring since clear criteria are specified. Fourth, when the expectations and criteria are presented to the pupils at the same time of the assignment, there is less possibility of

SCHOLARSHIP REPORT

	Oct. Test	Mid-Year Exam	Easter Test	Misc. Test	June Test
1. Health					
2. Science					
3. Social Studies					
4. English Language					
5. Literature					
6. Spelling					
7. Arithmetic	A	A	A		A
8. Reading Comprehension	A	B	B		C
9. Oral Reading					
10. French					
11. Writing					
12. Physical Education					
13. Music					
14. Art					
Average	A	B	A		B
Teaching Days	33	55	42		54
Days Absent	0	2	2		2
Times Late	—				

Test Average .... A .... (Oct.—Easter—Misc.)
Grading Average .... A .... (Mid-Yr.-Test Av.—June)

A-Very Good B-Good
C-Average D-Passed E-Failed

Appraisal of Daily Work	Oct.	Mid-Year	Easter	May
In danger of not grading				
Inattentive				
Capable of better work				
Shows improvement			✓	•
Satisfactory	✓	✓	✓	✓
Interview with parent desirable		✓		

NORTHWOOD PUBLIC SCHOOL

Grades 1-6

PERIODICAL and REPORT of

.... Fena ....

September, 1961

to

June, 1962

Grade.... 1 ....

Teacher Mrs. Wilcox

Figure 12.2. A grade one pupil's report card from 1961

misunderstanding and the nature of the assignment is made clearer. Expectations for the final product can be clearly indicated. Just as it is very important to prepare students about the nature of an upcoming test, it is important to prepare students about the requirements of the assignment.

Putting It All Together—The Report Card

Modern report cards include multiple marking systems involving achievement, effort, skills and checklists of objectives. That is, they attempt to evaluate in all three educationally relevant domains, cognitive, affective, and psychomotor. Current report cards tend to be very detailed, extensive and multifaceted in marked contrast to report cards of even 30 years ago that were perfunctory and global. A typical report card for a grade one pupil from 1961 is summarized in Figure 12.2.

Notice that the ratings are global and an overall global rating is given for the pupil. This also represents a generic report card which in this case has been used for a grade one pupil so that many subjects remain blank. The pupil was evaluated only on arithmetic and reading comprehension. There is also provision for "appraisal of daily work" which is an attempt at a global evaluation in the affective domain (effort, attitudes, interest, etc.). This pupil faired satisfactorily except for mid-year where an interview with parents was indicated. Written comments were also intended to elaborate further on the affective domain although this particular example is not very informative.

By contrast, one page of a five page document, is shown in Figure 12.3 as an example of a modern day report card. This is a 1992 report card for a grade 7 pupil in a large city school district. On this single page, notice the detail as each subject area is broken down into subcomponents. Each of these are evaluated on the three point scale (proficient, satisfactory, needs improvement) and the subject is given an overall grade as well. The top section of this page is a summary of "personal development" (affective domain) and each of the 10 items are rated as satisfactory or needs improvement. The teacher further elaborated these ratings by indicating on the written comment that the child "tends to socialize a little too much in the classroom".

The next two pages of the report were anecdotal comments dealing with both achievements and efforts in specific subject areas. The fourth page summarized Kim's musical achievements followed by more anecdotal comments, while the final page was a glossary of band musical terms. This particular report card did not include it, but it is also common to have checklists of objectives to further elaborate on the report card. The example shown in Table 12.1 is a checklist of objectives from a modern day big city school district report card.

The tendency in the last several decades has been to make report cards more and more detailed, complex and multifaceted to the point of incomprehensibility to many parents. While past reporting practices may be criticized for extreme brevity, modern day ones are engaging in overkill of detail. Good reporting practice includes a balance of simplicity, succinctness, and detail. A number of propositions about good grading practices are summarized in Table 12.1.

No grading and reporting system is likely to be satisfactory to all school districts. Nevertheless, report cards should include multiple reporting systems with enough information to fully and accurately report pupil progress. The amount of detail and information, however, should not be so complex or extensive that it overwhelms and thus frustrates and confuses the parents. The key is to achieve a balance between completeness of reporting and succinctness.

Parent-Teacher Conference

The parent-teacher conference is generally used to complement the report card. Indeed, it is common for schools to request or schedule these conferences immediately following a reporting period.

The parent-teacher conference offers a number of advantages. First, it enhances communication between the parents and the teacher. Second, it provides for the opportunity of some personal contact between parents and teachers. Third, matters that are not reported or cannot be reported on the report card can be discussed during the conference. Fourth, it provides an opportunity for the teacher to show parents some of their child's work and to comment on it. Fifth, it can enhance parent's participation in their child's education.

Notwithstanding the above strengths, there are a number of disadvantages with the parent-teacher conference. First, they are difficult to schedule for both teachers and parents. This is

SCHOOL DISTRICT ELEMENTARY REPORT CARD Year <u>1991-92</u>

Grade <u>7</u>

Name: <u>Kim</u> School: <u>Brooks</u> Teacher: <u>Mrs. B. All</u>

Reporting Period

	1st	2nd	3rd
		X	

PERSONAL DEVELOPMENT

(This section of the Report Card is completed on the basis of the teacher's observation and judgement)

S-Satifactory   NI-Needs Improvement

	S	NI		S	NI
Shows courtesy and respect to others.	✓		Works neatly and carefully.	✓	
Accepts responsibility.	✓		Contributes to class discussions.	✓	
Listens attentively.	✓		Organizes and uses materials and equipment.	✓	
Follows directions accurately.	✓		Completes assignments on time.	✓	
Works independently.	✓		Works cooperatively with others.	✓	

COMMENTS:
Kim has shown steady improvement in all subject areas. She completes her assignments as they are presented to her; although she tends to socialize a little too much in the classroom.

ACADEMIC ACHIEVEMENT

P-Proficient   S-Satisfactory   NI-Needs Improvement

★ | Letter grades provided at 7 only. | Items not checked are not applicable at this time.

LANGUAGE ARTS B ★	P	S	NI
Understand and uses skills of:			
Listening	✓		
Speaking		✓	
Writing	✓		
Spelling	✓		
Handwriting	✓		
Reading: Vocabulary	✓		
Reading: Comprehension	✓		
Reading: Oral Fluency	✓		
MATHEMATICS B ★			
Numeration	✓		
Basic Facts	✓		
Computation		✓	
Problem Solving	✓		
Data Analysis			
Measurement			
Geometry			
Calculator Use (Int. only)			
Fractions	✓		
Decimals	✓		
SOCIAL STUDIES B ★			
Locates Information		✓	
Interprets Information	✓		
Presents Information	✓		
Demonstrates Knowledge	✓		
SCIENCE A ★			
Uses Scientific Methods	✓		
Reports Information	✓		
Knows Scientific Facts and Concepts	✓		

FRENCH (Gr. 6 & 7 only) A ★	P	S	NI
Understand and uses skills of:			
Listening	✓		
Speaking	✓		
Reading	✓		
Writing	✓		
Demonstrates enthusiasm through involvement	✓		
MUSIC A ★			
Demonstrates enthusiasm through involvement	✓		
Demonstrates skills and technical ability	✓		
Demonstrates critical and sensitive responses			
ART B ★			
Demonstrates enthusiasm through involvement	✓		
Demonstrates skills and technical ability		✓	
Demonstrates critical and sensitive responses			
PHYSICAL EDUCATION A ★			
Demonstrates development in:			
Motor Skills	✓		
Manipulative Skills	✓		
Gymnastic Skills			
Dance Skills			
Applies Rules, Techniques and Concepts	✓		
Demonstrates Fitness			

COMMENTS: French— Kim participates in all classroom activities.
Mrs. W. Good

Figure 12.3. One page from a five page report card in 1992

Table 12.1. Guidelines for Multiple Grading and Reporting Systems

1. Involve all users in the development of the report cards and grading system. This should include parent groups, teachers, counselors, pupils and administrators. This will allow each group to feel "ownership" of the system and it will increase the likelihood that all will understand it.
2. Keep the various components of the reporting separate. Report achievement separately with a letter grade, and supplement these with checklists of objectives, assessment of effort, work habits, and personal and social development.
3. Make the central focus of the reporting on the school and course objectives.
4. Ensure that the reporting is based on reliable and valid data, test scores, and information. If pupil aptitudes are to be assessed and reported, then valid instruments must be employed for this purpose. This cannot be based simply on teachers' subjective judgment.
5. Strike a balance between detail and comprehensiveness of information and simplicity and brevity. Too much information and detail can confuse and overwhelm even the most earnest and dedicated parent.
6. There should be sufficient information on the report to indicate whether a parent-teacher conference is warranted. The conference can then supplement the information summarized on the report.

---

especially true for parents who work during the day. Second, the conferences are very time consuming. They can take up a great deal of valuable teacher and classroom time. Third, some parents, for a variety of reasons, will not attend. These are frequently the parents of the children who would benefit most from such conferences. Fourth, in order for the conference to proceed well and to be productive, teachers require considerable counseling skills. Teachers are rarely directly trained in counseling either in their undergraduate education or by inservice courses.

There are a number of simple guidelines, however, that can be used to make parent-teacher conferences effective. These guidelines summarized below have been abridged from Hopkins, Stanley and Hopkins (1990, p. 327).

Do:

Use a structured outline to guide the conference
Review the pupil's cumulative record
Listen
Maintain a positive and professional attitude
Describe the pupil's strengths but be honest about the problems
Accept some responsibility for both achievements and problems
Provide samples of the pupil's work to discuss
Write down questions to ask parents but don't be unnecessarily nosy
Conclude with a summary of the conference
Reiterate what action all parties have agreed to take
Keep a written copy of the conference; send a copy to the parents

Don't:

Criticize other teachers, parents, students or the school
Play amateur psychologist
Discuss the conference with others except for relevant school personnel
Gossip
Do all the talking
Argue or blame parents
Behave condescendingly

Explaining the Meaning of Test Scores

Either during the parent-teacher conference or on some other occasion, teachers are frequently called on to interpret standardized test score results to parents and pupils. Some school districts may even include these on report cards. As you saw in Chapters 7 and 11, standardized test results produce several standard scores: z-scores, t-scores, stanines, percentile ranks, age equivalents and grade equivalents.

Most parents have little understanding or appreciation of the meaning of standardized scores. Most lay people tend to think of test results as a percentage correct on the test. The teacher is faced with a difficult task, therefore, in helping parents and pupils understand standardized test score results.

Generally the scores that are reported and interpreted are percentile ranks, age equivalents and grade equivalents. The other three types of scores, z-scores, t-scores and stanines are too abstract and difficult for most reporting to lay people. Probably the single most preferred score by both parents and teachers is, unfortunately, the grade equivalent. The grade equivalent which is just a variation of the age equivalent, is very misleading. This is because the scale of grade equivalents is not equal along its whole distribution; the intervals along some of its scale are not equal to others (see also Chapter 11). The difference between reading at a grade 6 and 8 level represents 2 grade equivalents as does the difference between reading at a grade 1 and 3 level. The differences in reading performance as represented by these two grade equivalents are not the same. A child in grade one reading at a grade equivalent of 3 is much more advanced than his peers than is a child in grade 6 reading at a grade equivalent of 8. Technically, teachers and parents treat grade equivalent scores as though they are based on an equal interval scale which they are not.

To further compound the problem, parents frequently think that their child can perform the work of the grade which his grade equivalent indicates. Some parents, for example, believe that their daughter in grade three should be advanced because she has a reading grade equivalent of 7. First, the parents may not realize that half of grade sevens score higher than the daughter in grade 3. Second, there are many other factors to consider when accelerating a child. These include physical maturity, sociability and psychological maturity. This child who is producing test scores at the grade equivalent of seven would most likely be completely incapable of functioning in a grade 7 or even grade 4 classroom.

Ideally, grade (and age) equivalents should be eliminated from reporting systems because of their many flaws and misleading information. This is unlikely to happen, however, because of their widespread use and intuitive appeal. Teachers should therefore interpret grade equivalents cautiously and with great care. Moreover, they should always be interpreted with at least one other system, preferably percentile ranks. While the grade equivalent is based on a reference group across grades, the percentile rank is based on a reference group within age or grade. The two systems used together, then, tend to provide a more valid indication of the pupil's true standing.

■ Summary and Main Points

This chapter dealt with grading and reporting, an important element of any educational enterprise if it is to remain effective. Grading and reporting have several purposes including feedback and accountability. Several types of marking systems are employed each representing some strengths and weaknesses. There are also several types of symbol systems used in reporting each having some advantages and disadvantages. The determination of the final grade involves weighting components differentially depending on the variance of the scores that they produce. Homework and assignments, while they are usually graded, should not figure heavily in the final grade since they are not primarily assessment devices and therefore lack reliability and validity. The report card brings all of the components together in an attempt to balance the detail of information required to report educational performance in the cognitive, affective and psychomotor domains, with the need for brevity and understandability. The parent-teacher conference can be an extremely useful activity to accomplish a variety of things including enhancing communication between teacher and home. The teacher may also have to interpret standardized test scores for parents employing considerable skill and finesse.

1. The main purposes of grading and reporting is to provide feedback to the pupil and parents, act as a source of accountability, and to reward and motivate pupil efforts. The main problem with grades is that they lack universal meaning across teachers, schools and school districts.
2. Grading systems can be based on norm-referenced (grading on the curve) or on criterion-referenced bases. In addition, some schools grade pupils on the basis of effort, individual improvement, and the extent to which they perform up to their potential. All of these systems have some problems associated with them.
3. The main and historically oldest symbols for grading is the letter grade, usually ranging from A to F. Substitutes have been attempted but have achieved little success because these usually involve reducing the number of categories (e.g., good, satisfactory, unsatisfactory).
4. Numerical grades (percent or 1–10) have also met with limited success as have pass/fail systems, checklists of objectives and letters to parents.
5. A recent proposal which is gaining popularity is the anecdotal record or the narrative report. Because of the various problems associated with this system, it is likely to find only restricted and specialized use.
6. In order to determine final grades, various components must be combined in some fashion. Measurements which produce the highest variance in the scores will tend to influence the final grade disproportionately unless some weighting system is employed.
7. Homework and other assignments are primarily intended as pedagogical devices and are not intended as measurement instruments. Their reliability and validity is likely to be low. Therefore they should figure as little as possible in the total for the final grade

as they will tend to reduce the validity of it otherwise. In order for pupils to do homework and other assignments, however, it is necessary to assign them some value so that "they will count". Homework and assignments in total should not exceed a value of 25% of the total course grade.

8. The report card should employ multiple reporting systems dealing with the cognitive, affective and psychomotor domain. There should be provisions for reporting pupil achievement, effort, attitudes, interest, social and personal development and other noteworthy outcomes. The wealth of information on the report card, however, should be balanced against the need for brevity and simplicity so that it can be readily understood by lay people.

9. The parent-teacher conference has a number of advantages in that it allows for enhanced communication between parents and teacher, and may involve the parents further in their child's education. Scheduling and time problems are the biggest disadvantages of parent-teacher conferences.

10. Teachers are frequently called on to interpret standardized test score results to pupils and their parents. While grade equivalents are a very popular method of reporting these test scores, they have serious limitations which can provide very misleading information. When grade equivalents are used, they should always be interpreted in conjunction with another system such as percentile ranks.

■ Further Reading

Gronlund, N. E. and Linn, R. L. (1990). *Measurement and evaluation in teaching.* (6th ed). Macmillan: New York. See Chapter 17, "Marking and Reporting", for a good discussion of some grading and reporting techniques.

Hopkins, K. D., Stanley, J. C. and Hopkins, B. R. (1990). *Educational and psychological measurement and evaluation.* (7th ed). Prentice Hall: Englewood Cliffs, N.J.
See especially Chapter 12, "Grading and Reporting".

Meherens, W. A. and Lehman, I. J. (1991). *Measurement and evaluation in Education and psychology.* (4th ed). Holt, Rinehart and Winston: Toronto. Chapter 20, "Marking and Reporting the Results of Measurement", is a good treatment of some of the issues at the heart of grading.

■ Laboratory Exercises

1. Summarize the main functions and purposes of grading and reporting.
2. What are some of the main problems of grading and reporting?
3. What are the main advantages and disadvantages of the various grading systems? Discuss at least four grading systems.
4. Notwithstanding attempts with substitutes, letter grades have remained the predominant mode of marking. What are the reasons for this?
5. Describe the limitations of the various reporting systems that have been used as substitutes for the letter grade (i.e., numerical grades, pass/fail, narrative reports, letters to parents, checklists of objectives).

6. How should various components be combined into a total score with which to assign some final grade?
7. How should a teacher handle homework and other assignments in the final grade? What are the reasons behind these decisions?
8. Design an ideal report card. What are the main reporting systems that should be employed?
9. What are the main functions of the parent-teacher conference?
10. Summarize the do's and dont's of the parent-teacher conference.
11. What are the pitfalls that a teacher should be aware of in interpreting standardized test scores for pupils and parents? How should these be handled?

Chapter

13

Microcomputers and Educational Measurement

Overview

As a teacher you will spend a great deal of time in test construction and student recordkeeping activities. Gullickson (1982) for example, found that 95 percent of the teachers he surveyed gave tests at least biweekly, and the majority of these teachers were solely responsible for the construction, analysis and scoring of their examinations. More recently, Borg (1986) reported that the ability to analyze and improve classroom tests was identified by 479 classroom teachers as one of the most important aspects of the assessment process.

In this chapter you will examine the many ways microcomputers and educational measurement and evaluation software can assist the classroom teacher with their student evaluation activities. While the measurement process is complex, it may be reassuring to note that the availability of microcomputers makes it possible for teachers to receive assistance at each stage of the activity.

The typical configuration of required hardware includes a microcomputer, monitor, disk drives, printer and desktop scanner. While the cost of such a system may have been prohibitive just a few years ago, the decreasing cost of computer technology presently makes such a setup well within the budget of most schools. In fact, microcomputers have become quite common-place in schools. On the other hand, desktop scanners which are required for automated scoring of test response sheets are more slowly finding their way into educational institutions. As the price of these units continues to drop and teachers begin to see the advantages of such devices, scanners will come to play a fundamental role in student recordkeeping, test construction and test analysis activities.

This chapter begins by examining one of the fundamental components of computer assisted test construction, the **item bank.** Subsequently, you will move through all the stages involved in constructing, analyzing and recording the results of classroom tests. In addition, a selection of presently available test construction software will be reviewed and guidelines for selecting the most useful software will be provided.

What Is an Item Bank?

An item bank is a collection of test items which have been organized in a systematic fashion to permit easy retrieval. In its simplest form, the item bank may be a set of index cards on which the specific test item is found along with a number of identifying characteristics. Typically, such information might include the item's format (i.e., multiple choice, short answer, essay, and so on) the general and subordinate taxonomic category under which the item would be classified, and the cognitive complexity of the item along with the correct response. For example, the following item found in educational measurement item bank dealing with the concept of validity might classify as follows:

Item: You have just devised a new instrument called the Acme Test of Mathematical Creativity and correlated this new instrument with an existing Mathematical Creativity Measure. What type of validity would be of greatest interest in this case?

    a. concurrent validity
    b. construct validity
    c. predictive validity
    d. content validity

Item format—multiple choice
General category—Validity
Subordinate category—concurrent
Level of cognitive complexity—comprehension
Correct response—a

More elaborate item bank systems often include additional information such as the location in the test which refers to the question and technical data regarding the item's previously established difficulty and discrimination levels. In the case of our card item bank, you need only select the appropriate index cards and submit them to your school secretary for typing of the test. This procedure, while relatively simple, has a number of disadvantages. First, it is time consuming to manually select the items and reorganize the item bank each time. Second, the security of the items is at risk in that the actual production of the test might involve a number of people. Third, the time delay in obtaining the test may make test revisions impractical.

In contrast, computerized item banks offer a number of advantages. First, the teacher is in total control of the entire process from item selection to the production of the printed test. Second, the time usually involved in having the test typed by a secretary could be better spent reviewing and fine tuning the test. Third, issues of test and item security are under better control in that the entire testing enterprise is solely in the hands of one person.

As a teacher you will have at least two sources for the development of an item bank. First, commercial publishers frequently provide item banks as ancillary materials with textbooks. Second, you may choose to purchase item banks from software publishers who construct extensive item banks related to specific content areas. For example, software publishers such as *Snowflake Software* offer item disks to accompany their *Test Quest* test generating software in a variety of content areas including high school biology, earth science, physics, American History and Government and European history. Cross Educational Software makes available a number of item bank diskettes each containing over 400 questions on specific subjects areas such as Government, History and Geography. Third, departments of education frequently develop vast item banks both for classroom evaluation and system evaluation uses. These banks are usually developed by a number of specialized individuals. It is quite typical for item banks to be developed by a team, including teachers, curriculum specialists and test specialists.

Developing Your Own Test Bank

While adopting an existing item bank may appear to be the best option, such a decision may result in a number of problems. Specifically, the content of such item banks may not meet your local curriculum objectives. The alternative is to develop your own item bank or perhaps more profitably, to form a group of teachers who are willing to put forth the time and effort to develop a useful and potentially very valuable collection of test items.

In developing an item bank, Baker (1989) suggests that at least three different types of information should be stored for each item. First, the textual and graphical components of the item must be entered. Second, the unique characteristics used to access the item should be included such as keywords related to the item content, its instructional objective and its cognitive complexity. Third, the psychometric data for the item as determined by previous administration of the items should be included (i.e. item difficulty and item discrimination indices). It is important to recognize that the psychometric properties of an item used in the context of very small classes are tentative. Nevertheless, the teacher may still find them useful as a guideline. Storing both the item and item characteristics is but the first step in taking full advantage of a computerized item bank. This is particularly the case when you are trying to determine the quality of items in your bank. For example, if a particular item yields negative discrimination values or simply is too difficult, the item should be revised or deleted. By examining how an item actually performs in the testing situation you will have an opportunity to refine the items in your bank and your item writing skills.

Constructing a Test

Computerized item banks do not typically exist on their own but are usually a component of a test generating programme. These programmes permit the selection of questions from the bank to create the test. In addition to letting you pick the items for your test, test generating software also permits you to edit, add or delete test items.

In the category of test-generating software, *All of the Above, Version 2*, offers a number of useful features, including excellent editing, a variety of formatting features (for example, boldface, underlining and italics), flexible item selection, on-screen test administration and student recording options. This package can also handle a large number of questions, and it accepts alternate answers. Moreover, students who are given on-screen quizzes are provided with immediate feedback regarding their performance. *All of the Above Version 2* is designed to operate on an Apple computer.

Using an 80-column format, *TestWriter* has many features of more expensive test-generating packages. Besides being easy to use, this package permits teachers to load tests into *AppleWorks*, thereby making word processing capabilities available.

A number of test-generating packages also have been developed for the IBM computer. Microsystems Software's *MICRO-PAC Test Bank* is a comprehensive educational testing and authoring system for IBM computers and compatibles. *MICRO-PAC* permits educators to easily create, maintain, and administer a variety of test formats, including matching, true and false, multiple-choice, fill-in-the-blank and essay questions. The teacher may develop a test bank for

1.	TEST	to prepare a test from questions on diskette
2.	MAKE	to transfer questions or test banks electronically
3.	BANK PRINT	for print out of any or all of the test items
4.	BANK EDIT	start a "new" test bank or edit questions
5.	BANK MAINTAIN	display, copy, rename, or delete chapters
6.	TNT	to create student interactive tests and tutorials
7.	EXIT to DOS	

Figure 13.1. Micro-Pac System III—Main Menu

each content area (for example, social studies) and then proceed to enter up to 10,000 test items for that bank. Each test bank may be subdivided into a number of 'chapters' or 'units' with each reflecting some aspects of the test bank's overall theme. Potential test items may be reviewed on screen before selection, and any modifications required are easily accomplished with the program's word-processing features. The program's test-printing functions are easy to follow, and an overall presentation of the test is excellent. Figure 13.1 and Figure 13.2 represent the main and secondary menus of the MICRO-PAC programme. As you can see, the programme provides you with a wide range of options in dealing with the test items. By simply entering a numbered selection, the programme brings you to one of the secondary menus. Through the use of this embedded menu system, working with the item bank and selecting items for the actual test becomes an easy task.

Perhaps two of the most comprehensive packages for assisting educators in student evaluation activities are *Pitt Educational Testing Aids (PETA)* system developed for Apple computer systems by Nitko and Hsa (1984) and *MICROCAT* (Assessment Systems Corporation, 1989) designed to run on IBM and IBM compatible microcomputers. Among the more important distinctions between the two packages is the intended audience. *PETA* was designed to be used by teachers while *MICROCAT* was designed with the testing professional in mind. For a review of the *MICROCAT* system you are referred to Baker (1989). Given that the emphasis in this chapter is on the role of testing for the classroom, we will focus our attention on the *PETA* system.

The *PETA* system, according to its authors (Nitko, & Hsa, 1984) was designed to improve instruction and classroom tests and improve the evaluation and reporting of student learning. The system includes three main components: (a) an item-banking and construction component (b) a test-scoring, analysis, item-evaluation and reporting component, and (c) a student data base component. The item-banking module allows the teacher to enter test items along with some identifying properties similar to those mentioned above. The extensive features of the item banking component of **PETA** and gives the teacher complete control over the imputing, editing and printing of test items.

Perhaps the most innovative component of *PETA* is the item analysis and evaluation module which the authors claim as useful in guiding instruction. Specifically, this component of *PETA* was developed to assist a teacher in making instructional relevant decisions and improve the quality of test items.

BANK PRINT

1. Print out whole chapters or the entire test bank
2. Print out selected questions
3. Print out random questions
4. MENU: Return to the Menu

BANK MAINTAIN

1. Files — To display the question files in each drive.
2. Fastcopy — To copy a chapter onto another diskette.
3. Rename — To rename or renumber a chapter.
4. Kill — To eliminate a chapter from a test bank.
5. Menu — To return to Menu.

BANK EDIT

1. Append — type new questions or create a new bank
2. Change — modify existing questions
3. Replace — supplant a question with another question
4. Insert — add a question any place in the test bank
5. Delete — eliminate a question
6. Review — display a question
7. FILES — display test banks in drive B:
8. MENU — go back to Menu

TEST

1. Print out selected questions
2. Print Out random questions
3. MENU: Return to Menu

Figure 13.2. Micropac System III—Secondary Menus

Analyzing Your Test

Test analysis programs generally combine the grading and analysis of optically scanned multiple-choice test items. One such program available from Classroom Consortia Media, entitled *Test Analysis* requires a Scantron optical reader and provides such information as grade distributions, student and class averages, standard deviations, student choice distribution, and identification of confusing questions. *Teacher's Assistant,* from *MICRO-PAC,* combines both the features of grade management system and a test analysis programme. The programme allows for test responses to be recorded via the keyboard or an optical scanner. In addition to a wide range of descriptive statistics and grade calculations, the program includes a very useful item analysis. Included in the analysis output is information related to the item's difficulty and discrimination. Finally, a Kuder-Richardson Formula 21 reliability coefficient for the entire test is calculated.

Recording Your Grades

Student record-keeping software has long been regarded as a useful and time-saving microcomputer application. While software of this type varies in term of available options, there are several good features that a good grade-keeping application should have. The program should allow for a sufficient number of student records per class. Programs that have a student maximum of forty or less are of limited usefulness for elementary and secondary school classrooms. The ease with which the teacher can modify and delete individual student records or entire class records also plays a critical role in determining the utility of such software. Several currently available programs allow for as many as fifty scores to be entered for each student. Such capacity can provide the teacher with a comprehensive means of determining the student's overall achievement throughout the school year. Perhaps the most time-saving feature of grade-keeping software is the speed with which final grades can be calculated. In most cases, teachers can easily assign the desired weight for each evaluation activity and quickly calculate the final grade.

A variety of student record-keeping or grade book software is currently available for virtually all types of microcomputers. Among the more favourable reviewed are *Grade Busters 1/2/3* and *Scorekeeper* both of which operate on the Apple computer. *Grade Busters* is excellent because of its ease of use. The format of the program involves an eighty-column screen and spreadsheet layout in which student grades can be easily entered and revised. In addition, test-score entry can be efficiently accomplished with the program's optical scanner provisions. Finally, a built-in set of printer drivers permits the teacher to make use of such print enhancement features as bold and double-wide fonts that contribute to the production of attractive student-progress reports. *Scorekeeper* possesses all the standard record-keeping and grading procedures of this category of software, as well as a number of particularly useful functions. Among the most important is customization of grading scales to fit any school policy.

A program that goes beyond the traditional record-keeping functions of most electronic grade books has been developed by faculty members of the Laboratory for Educational Measurement at the University of Calgary. *The Classroom Records and Statistical Package* (CRASP) program, has been designed to help the teacher keep track of student grades and perform various types of data analyses. The record-keeping features of the program allow the teacher to enter class lists and specify the type of evaluation procedure to be employed (for example, quizzes, examinations, papers and projects). The teacher may enter, edit or update test scores at any time. In addition, *CRASP* will sort the test scores either alphabetically by name or numerically by student identification numbers for posting purposes. The statistical features of *CRASP* are numerous and attempt to address a wide range of needs. Basic features include the reporting of descriptive statistics (for example, mean, mode, median and standard deviation), standard scores, and numerical and letter grades. The program also offers the option of assigning a weight to each evaluation procedure and developing a grading criteria specific to the teacher's requirements. Moreover, the program computes the statistical relationship between various evaluation activities as well as the reliability of the various tests and assessments.

The Concept of SHAREWARE

An alternate to the commercially available programs described above, is *Shareware* software. While sometimes incorrectly identified as free software, *Shareware* is software which you preview first to determine if it actually meets your needs. If the software is appropriate, you can purchase a registered copy of the program which includes manuals and update information. What is particulary attractive about Shareware software are the very reasonable prices making the programs available to a large number of potential users. Perhaps the best source of information regarding this type of software is the publication *Shareware*. This magazine both announces and reviews new software packages covering a wide range of applications. A number of **Shareware** programmes are available for assisting teachers with student evaluation procedures. For example, *PC-CAI* offers a complete system for developing interactive tutorials and quizzes. Cross (1990), in a review of *PC-CAI*, suggests that the programme be used with *Exam Bank*, a Shareware item banking programme. *Exam Bank* permits the user to store items in a variety of formats including matching, multiple-choice, true-false, short-answer and essay. Other features of the package include menu-driven selection which makes working with the programme easy, wordprocessing features thus allowing for the entering and editing of items, and a number of printing features (e.g. math symbols, foreign characters) permitting for the development of a wide range of tests.

Among the shareware programmes for student record keeping, a particulary useful IBM compatible application is *The Prograde System* which is designed to meet the grading needs of elementary to college level teachers. The programme permits the teacher to create an unlimited number of classes with up to 45 assignment grades for each student. The one potential limitation of the programme is its 35 student class size restriction, which could be problematic in some settings. Once past this limitation, however, the user has a host of features to call upon. For example, *Prograde* handles numerical and letter grades and permits you to decide on your own letter grade criteria. Entering student scores is permitted in any fashion the teacher deems appropriate including by name or assignment. In addition to the standard features found in most grade book programmes, *Prograde* has an excellent array of student reports. Print and summary reports include date, assignments, maximum score, pupil score, and a weighted average. In addition, printed reports can include comments for a good effort or information regarding remedial suggestions. Overall, *Prograde* is a useful teacher tool which, like many other shareware products, is available at a very modest cost.

Students Testing Themselves

To this point we have reviewed microcomputer software which the classroom teacher would find useful in student recordkeeping and evaluation. Recently, software to help students become their own evaluators has become available. One such product developed for Apple computers is *Studymate: The Grade Booster* (Compu-Tech) which has been designed to be of use for both high school and university students. *Studymate* is similar to many test-authoring systems reviewed above in that it allows for the development and printing of quizzes using the true/false, multiple choice, Question-Response and Fill in the Blanks item formats. The Main Menu includes the following features: Take a Test, Create a New Test, Edit a Test, Review a Test, Print a Test, Delete a Test, Change Directory and exit. Create a New Test is quite straight forward with the program prompting you to select one test format or the multiple format features. For the multiple format feature, you will be prompted for the desired question format (e.g., multiple-choice) for each new question entered. *Studymate* is sold with *Studymate Vocabulary* disks, an eight-page manual, and a book providing suggestions for developing good study habits.

The Future of Computers in Testing

A current interest among educators is the potential of microcomputers for the direct administration of tests. Increasingly, schools have opted for a network configuration of microcomputers which makes group administration of tests possible. With such computer networks, a test could simultaneously be administered to an entire class with student responses being stored on a remote file server.

To date, few studies have investigated the impact of such an approach to classroom testing. Nevertheless, some of the benefits and concerns have already been identified. First, the time involved in constructing the test and providing feedback to students can be greatly reduced. Second, direct references to instructional material may be sorted with each test item thereby providing some direction to specific remedial activities. Third, the computer provides an opportunity to assess student understanding at a more complex level than might ordinarily be possible using paper and pencil tests. For example, computer simulations can be developed to more accurately assess the student's ability to apply his or her knowledge in a more realistic setting.

Bunderson, Inouye, and Olsen (1988) in review of computer assisted testing identified four generations of this testing format which they refer to as computerized conventional testing, adaptive testing, continuous measurement and intelligent measurement. We shall restrict our discussion to the first two types of testing as they are the most likely forms of computerized testing to be used in the classroom setting. Both continuous measurement and intelligent measurement are as Oosterhof (1990) has suggested, futuristic involving comprehensive and continuous monitoring of each student's performance across the school year and requiring, in the case of intelligent measurement, the use of highly sophisticated artificial intelligence within computers. At this level, the computer would be used to evaluate student products such as written essays, computer programmes and even works of art. In the case of computerized conventional testing the computer would simply administer the equivalent of a paper pencil test in an automated fashion. While this may be a necessary first step in employing computers in the testing process, such computer applications may be doomed in that they tend to use the computer as nothing more than an expensive page turning device. While such an application does have the benefits mentioned above, the costs associated with this type of testing outweigh the potential benefits.

A more useful application of computers in the testing process is adaptive testing. In this case, the student responses actually influence the item selection of the test. Specifically, the items administered to the student depend on how the student responded to the previous item. Failure to obtain the correct response on any particular item will result in the subsequent selection of an easier item. Conversely, a more difficult item would follow a correct response. In using this approach, the time involved in assessing an individual student's ability level is significantly reduced resulting in more time for the teacher to address the instructional needs of the students.

To date, studies which have focused on the use of computer assisted testing have typically compared computerized test administration and traditional testing modes (i.e. paper-pencil). The findings generally indicate that students tend to produce the same level of achievement using either method. While this finding is encouraging for continued use of computerized testings, some investigators (Plumly & Ray, 1989) report that students actually prefer paper pencil test formats (See Box Insert 15.1.) The principle complaint of students being tested with computers

Focus on Research

To date, research focusing on computer administered testing has produced inconsistent findings. For example, Sorensen (1985) found that graduate and undergraduate students performed significantly better on a computerized version of four cognitive ability tests. In contrast, Lee, Moreno & Sympson (1984) found that young adult subjects performed more poorly on a computerized test of arithmetic reasoning.

More recently, Plumly and Ray (1989) investigated the equivalency of computer administered versus the traditional paper-and-pencil test with 65 junior level college students. Each test included 10 multiple-choice questions, ten true-false and ten matching questions. The overall findings indicated that student performance was comparable across both testing modes. In the computer testing mode, students greatly appreciated receiving immediate feedback on their performance but were frustrated by the inability to review items or change responses. A key observation of this study was the importance that students attach to a flexible testing

programme. As the authors suggest, a testing program which could accommodate a review feature would have likely minimized the frustration experienced by their subjects. Overall, Plumly and Ray (1989) view their findings as supportive for the further application of computerized testing.

One of the most frequently cited criticisms of computerized testing is its assumed depersonalizing nature. This criticism may be overstated particularly for individuals who are familiar with computers. In addition, a growing body of literature suggests that many individuals are actually more comfortable with computers in what might be regarded as anxiety producing situations. For example, many people tend to provide more accurate and detailed medical histories when responding to computer administered questions than when the source of the questions is another human being. In any case, the growing tendency to use computers for testing will necessitate a need for research into the impact of this potentially useful application.

---

is that frequently the testing programme does not permit them to go back and review or change previous responses. Clearly, this is a serious limitation which could be easily corrected with more sophisticated test administration software.

An example of a software package that includes many of the features necessary to successfully employ computerized testing is the *TnT* module of the *MICRO-PAC* Programme. The programme is designed to create tutorials and tests which are administered by the computer. The questions for the test are selected from the test bank module or can be entered directly via the keyboard. The testing formats include matching, true-false, multiple choice, fill in, or short answer. Tests are graded immediately and the student is able to scan the questions before answering as well as review and change responses at any point. Student test results are stored allowing the teacher to evaluate student achievement at some convenient time.

■ Summary and Main Points

The availability of both microcomputers and testing and measurement software provides an opportunity to greatly enhance the efficiency of classroom evaluation procedures. As the above review indicates, assistance at all stages (for example, item storage, test construction and grade record keeping) of the evaluation process is currently available. As teachers find tools to help with the more mechanical aspects of evaluation, they will free valuable time to further concentrate on the reliability and validity of their testing and measurement activities.

1. Low cost computer technology is making the use of educational testing software a potentially very useful tool to assist teacher with their student evaluation activities.
2. The development of computerized item banks is a very useful method of organizing and refining a collection of test items which can easily be incorporated into a classroom test.
3. A wide selection of affordable test construction software is currently available for the most popular microcomputers.
4. Test analysis software which provides feedback on item difficulty and discrimination is available to teachers who have incorporated an optical scanner into their computer testing system.
5. In the near future, the role of computer administered testing is likely to increase resulting in a significant decrease in test construction and grading time for the teacher and immediate feedback for the student.

■ Further Readings

Baker, Frank B. Computer Technology in Test Construction and Processing. In R. Linn.

Haksar, L. (1983). Design and usage of an item bank. *Programmed Learning and Educational Technology, 20.*

Hiscox, M. D. (1984). A planning guide for microcomputers in education. *Educational Measurement: Issues and Practices, 3,* 28–34.

Hsu, T. & Nitko, A. J. (1983). Microcomputer testing software teachers can use. *Educational Measurement: Issues and Practice, 2,* 15–31.

Nitko, A. J., & Hsu, T. (1984). A comprehensive microcomputer system for classroom testing. *Journal of Educational Measurement, 21,* 377–390.

■ Laboratory Exercises

1. In the preceding chapter, you had an opportunity to review a number of features found in test construction and recordkeeping software. With this information as a starting point, describe the features you would like to have (both software and hardware) in your own computer assisted testing system.
2. The use of computers for administering tests has sparked controversy among educators. Briefly state your position on this issue and indicate both the potential benefits and concerns this computer application might present.
3. Choose a recordkeeping or test construction program you may have access to and evaluate its strengths and weaknesses.
4. State factors which you think are presently hindering the increased use of microcomputers in student evaluation activities and propose possible solutions to these barriers?
5. In what ways could microcomputers be employed to assess student achievement levels in domains other than those typically assessed by classroom tests?
6. In what ways would your teaching activities be enhanced if you had access to both recordkeeping and test construction software?

Appendix

A

Software Resources

(All of the Above)
C & C Software,
5713 Kentford Circle,
Wichita, KS 67220

(Exam Bank)
(PC-CAI)
(Prograde System)
PC-SIG
1030 D East Duane Avenue
Sunnyvale, CA 94086-9543

(Grade Busters 1/2/3)
Grade Busters Corporation,
3610 Queen Anne Way,
Colorado Spring, CO 80917

(MICRO-PAC Test Bank)
Microsystems Software Ltd.
1270 E. Broadway Road, Suite 215
Tempe, Arizona 85282

(Pitt Educational Testing Aids (PETA))
Institute for Practice and Research in
Education,
School of Education
University of Pittsburgh,
SRO2 Forbes Quandrangle
Pittsburgh, PA 15260

(The Scorekeeper)
Stokes Publishing Company,
1125 Robin Way,
Sunnyvale, CA 94087

(Statistical Processing and Record Keeping
(SPARK))
Laboratory for Educational Measurement
and Evaluation
Department of Teacher Education and
Supervision
University of Calgary

(Studymate: The Grade Booster)
Compu-Teach Corporation;
78 Olive Street
New Haven, CT 06511

(Teacher's Assistant)
Microsystems Software, Ltd.
1270 E. Broadway Road, Suite 215
Tempe, Arizona 85282

(Test Analysis)
Classroom Consortia Media, Inc.,
57 Bay Street,
Staten Island N.Y. 10301

(Test Quest)
Snowflake Software
8 Cedar Heights Road
Rhine Back, N.Y. 12572

(Test Writer)
K-12 Micro Media Publishing,
6 Arrow Road,
Ramsey, N.J. 07446

Optical Scanners

SCAN-TRON Corporation
3398E 70th Street
Long Beach, CA 90805

Bibliography

Ahmann, J. S., and Glock, M. D. (1975a). *Evaluating pupil growth* (5th ed.). Boston: Allyn and Bacon.

Ahmann, J. S., and Glock, M. D. (1975b). *Measuring and evaluating educational achievement* (2nd ed.). Boston: Allyn and Bacon.

Aiken, L. R. (1987). Testing with multiple-choice items. *Journal of Research and Development in Education, 20,* 44–58.

Alker, H. A., Carlson, J. A., and Herman, M. G. (1969). Multiple-choice questions and students' characteristics. *Journal of Educational Psychology, 60,* 231–243.

Allan Nairn and Associates (1980). *The reign of ETS: The corporation that makes up minds.* Washington, DC: Ralph Nader.

Ammons, R. B., and Ammons, C. H. (1962). The Quick Test (QT): Provisional manual. *Psychological Reports, 11,* 11–161.

Anastasi, A. (1982). *Psychological testing* (5th ed.). New York: Macmillan.

Ausubel, D. P., Novak, J. D., and Hanesian, H. (1978). *Educational psychology: A cognitive view* (2nd ed.). New York: Holt, Rinehart and Winston.

Baker, F. (1989). Computer technology in test construction and processing. In R. L. Linn (Ed.), *Educational Measurement* (3rd ed., pp. 409–428). New York, NY: American Council on Education and Macmillan.

Benbow, C. P., and Stanley, J. C. (1983). Consequences in high school and college of sex differences in mathematical reasoning ability: A longitudinal perspective. *American Educational Research Journal, 19,* 598–622.

Bloom, B. S. (Ed.). (1956). *Taxonomy of educational objectives, the classification of educational goals. Handbook I: Cognitive domain.* New York: David McKay.

Bloom, B. S., Madaus, and G. F. Hastings, J. T. (1981). *Handbook on formative and summative evaluation of student learning.* New York: McGraw-Hill.

Borg, W. R. (1986). Teacher's perception of the importance of education measurement. *Journal of Experimental Education, 54,* 9–14.

Bouchard, J. T. and McGue, M. (1981). Familial studies of intelligence: A review. *Science, 212,* 1055–1059.

Bunderson, C., Inouye, D., and Olsen, J. (1988). The four generations of computerized educational measurement. In R. Linn (Ed.), *Educational Measurement* (3rd ed., pp. 367–407). New York, NY: American Council on Education and Macmillan.

Burgess, T. C., and Wright, D. D. (1962). Seventh-grade evaluation of the Ammons Quick Test (QT). *Psychological Reports, 10,* 791–794.

Bushway, A., and Nash, W. R. (1977). School cheating behavior. *Review of Educational Research, 47,* 623–632.

Campione, J. C., Brown, A. L., and Ferrara, R. A. (1982). Mental retardation and intelligence. In R. J. Sternberg (Ed.), *Handbook of human intelligence* (pp. 392–492). Cambridge: Cambridge University.

Carlisle, A. L. (1965). Quick Test performance by institutional retardates. *Psychological Reports, 17,* 489–490.

Chapanis, A. (1961). Men, machines and models. *American Psychologist, 16,* 113–131.

Chase, C. I. (1986). Essay test scoring: Interaction of relevant variables. *Journal of Educational Measurement, 23,* 33–41.

Ciula, B. A., and Cody, J. J. (1978). Comparative study of validity of the WAIS and Quick Test as predictors of functioning intelligence in a psychiatric facility. *Psychological Reports, 42,* 971–974.

Coffman, W. E. (1971). Essay examinations. In R. L. Thorndike (Ed.), *Educational measurement* (2nd ed., pp. 271–302). Washington, DC: American Council on Education.

College Entrance Examination Board (1980). *Undergraduate admissions.* New York: CEEB.

Cornehlsen, V. H. (1965). Cheating attitudes and practices in a suburban high school. *Journal of the National Association of Women Deans and Counsellors, 28,* 106–109.

Crocker, L. and Algina. J. (1986). *Introduction to classical and modern test theory.* Toronto: Holt, Rinehart and Winston.

Cronbach, L. J. (1951). Coefficient alpha and the internal structure of tests. *Psychometrika, 16,* 297–334.

Cronbach, L. J. (1984). *Essentials of psychological testing* (4th ed.). New York: Harper & Row.

Cronbach, L. J., Glesser, G., and Rajaratnam, N. (1972). *The dependability of behavioural measurements: Theory of generalizability for scores and profiles.* New York: Wiley.

Cronbach, L. J., and Meehl, P. E. (1955). Construct validity in psychological tests. *Psychological Bulletin, 52,* 281–302.

Cross, J. (1990). Tools for teachers. *Shareware Magazine, Sept.–Oct.,* 9–11.

Crouse, J. (1985). Does the SAT help colleges make better decisions? *Harvard Educational Review, 55,* 195–219.

Cureton, L. W. (1971). The history of grading practices. *NCME Measurement in Education, 2,* 1–8.

De Cecco, J. P., and Crawford, W. R. (1974). *The psychology of learning and instruction: Educational psychology* (2nd ed.). Englewood Cliffs, NJ: Prentice-Hall.

Devine, T. G., and Meagher, L. D. (1989). *Mastery study skills: A student guide.* Englewood Cliffs, New Jersey: Prentice-Hall.

Dizzonne, M. F., and Davis, W. E. (1973). Relationship between Quick Test and WAIS IQs for brain-injured and schizophrenic subjects. *Psychological Reports, 32,* 337–338.

Dubois, P. H. (1970). *A history of psychological testing.* Boston: Allyn and Bacon.

Dudycha, A. L. and Carpenter, J. B. (1973). Effects of item format on item discrimination and difficulty. *Journal of Applied Psychology, 58,* 116–121.

Ebel, R. L., and Frisbie, D. A. (1986). *Essentials of educational measurement* (4th ed.). Englewood Cliffs, NJ: Prentice-Hall.

Eccles, J. S., and Jacobs, J. E. (1986). Social forces shape math attitudes and performance. *Signs, 11,* 367–389.

Educational Resource Information Center. (1987). Thesaurus of ERIC descriptors (11th ed.). Phoenix, AZ: Oryx.

Educational Testing Services. (1963). *Multiple-choice questions: A close look.* Princeton, NJ: ETS.

Elam, S. M., Rose, L. C. and Gallup, A. M. (1991). The 23rd Annual Gallup poll of the public's attitudes toward the public schools. *Phi Delta Kappan, 73,* 41–56.

English, H. B. and English, A. C. (1958). *A comprehensive dictionary of psychological and psychoanalytic terms: A guide to usage.* New York: David McKay.

Estes, W. K. (1982). Learning, memory, and intelligence. In R. J. Sternberg (Ed.), *Handbook of human intelligence* (pp. 170–224). Cambridge: Cambridge University.

Feingold, A. (1988). Cognitive gender differences are disappearing. *American Psychologist, 43,* 95–103.

Foos, P. W., and Fisher, R. P. (1988). Using tests as learning opportunities. *Journal of Educational Psychology, 80,* 179–183.

Furst, E. J. (1981). Bloom's taxonomy of educational objectives for the cognitive domain. *Review of the Education Research, 51*(4), 441–453.

Gage, N. L., and Berliner, D. C. (1979). *Educational Psychology* (2nd ed.). Chicago: Rand McNally.

Gagne, R. M. (1970). *The conditions of learning* (2nd ed.). New York: Holt, Rinehart and Winston.

Gagne, R. M. (1986). *The conditions of learning* (4th ed.). New York: Holt, Rinehart and Winston.

Gardner, H. (1984). *Frames of mind.* New York: Wiley and Sons.

Glaser, R. (Ed.). (1965). *Teaching machines and programmed learning II.* Washington, DC: National Education Association.

Glaser, R. (1963). Instructional technology and the measurement of learning outcomes: Some questions. *American Psychologist, 18,* 519–521.

Good, C. V. (Ed.). (1959). *Dictionary of education* (2nd ed.). New York: McGraw-Hill.

Good, T. L., and Brophy, J. E. (1990). *Educational psychology* (4th ed.). New York: Longman.

Graham, J. R. (1987). *The MMPI: A practical guide* (2nd ed.). Toronto: Oxford University.

Gronlund, N. E. (1985). *Measurement and evaluation in teaching* (4th ed.). New York, NY: Macmillan.

Gronlund, N. E., and Linn, R. L. (1990). *Measurement and evaluation in teaching* (6th ed.). New York: Macmillan.

Gullickson, A. R. (1982). *The practice of testing in elementary and secondary schools.* (ERIC Document No. ED 229 391).

Haney, W. (1981). Validity, vaudeville, and values: A short history of social concerns over standardized testing. *American Psychologist, 26,* 1021–1034.

Hanford, G. H. (1985). Yes, the SAT does help colleges. *Harvard Educational Review, 55,* 324–331.

Hills, J. R. (1991). Apathy concerning grading and testing. *Phi Delta Kappa, 73,* 540–545.

Hoffman, B. (1962). *The tyranny of testing.* New York: Macmillan.

Holmes, M. (1982). *What every teacher and parent should know about student evaluation.* Toronto: Ontario Institute for Studies in Education.

Hopkins, K. D., Stanley, J. C., and Hopkins, B. R. (1990). *Educational and psychological measurement and evaluation* (7th ed.). Englewood Cliffs, New Jersey: Prentice-Hall.

Hughes, D. C., and Keeling, B. (1984). The use of model essays to reduce context effects in essay scoring. *Journal of Educational Measurement, 21,* 277–281.

Hughes, D. C., Keeling, B., and Tuck, B. F. (1980). Essay marking and the context problem. *Educational Research, 22,* 147–148.

Husband, S. D., and DeCato, C. M. (1982). The Quick Test compared with the Wechsler Adult Intelligence Scale as measures of intellectual functioning in a prison clinical setting. *Psychological Reports, 50,* 167–170.

Huttenlocher, J. (1962). Some effects of negative instances on the formation of simple concepts. *Psychological Reports, 11,* 35–42.

Hyde, J. S., and Linn, M. C. (1988). Are there sex differences in verbal abilities? A meta-analysis. *Psychological Bulletin, 104,* 53–69.

Joesting, J., and Joesting, R. (1972). Quick Test validation: Scores of adults in a welfare setting. *Psychological Reports, 30,* 537–538.

Joreskog, K. G., and Sorbom, D. (1988). *LISREL 7, A guide to the program and applications.* Chicago: SPSS.

Kane, M., and Wilson, J. (1984). Errors of measurement and standard setting in mastery testing. *Applied Psychological Measurement, 8,* 107–115.

Kibler, R. J., Barker, L. L., and Miles, D. J. (1970). *Behavioral objectives and instruction.* Boston: Allyn and Bacon.

Kibler, R. J., Cegala, D. J., Barker, L. L., and Miles, D. T. (1974). *Objectives for instruction and evaluation.* Boston: Allyn and Bacon.

Krathwohl, D. R., Bloom, B. S., and Masia, B. B. (1964). *Taxonomy of educational objectives, the classification of educational goals. Handbook II: Affective domain.* New York: David McKay.

Krathwohl, D. R., and Payne, D. A. (1971). Defining and assessing educational objectives. In R. L. Thorndike (Ed.), *Educational measurement* (2nd ed., pp. 17–45). Washington, DC: American Council on Education.

Lambrith, T. T., and Panek, P. E. (1982). Comparison of the Quick Test and the Stanford-Binet, Form L-M for institutionalized mentally retarded adults. *Psychological Reports, 51,* 1065–1066.

Lee, B. N., and Merrill, M. D. (1972). *Writing complete affective objectives: A short course.* Belmont, CA: Wadsworth.

Lee, J., Moreno, K., and Sympson, J. (1984). *The effects of mode of test administration on test performance.* Paper presented at the annual meeting of the Eastern Psychology Association, Baltimore, Maryland.

Lubin, B., Larsen, R. M., and Matarazzo, J. D. (1984). Patterns of psychological test usage in the United States: 1935–1982. *American Psychologist, 39,* 451–454.

Lyman, H. B. (1991). *Test scores and what they mean* (4th ed.). Englewood Cliffs, NJ: Prentice-Hall.

MacCorquodale, K., and Meehl, P. E. (1948). On a distinction between hypothetical constructs and intervening variables. *Psychological Review, 55,* 95–107.

Mager, R. F. (1962). *Preparing instructional objectives.* Belmont, CA: Fearon.

Marini, A. E. (1990). Concurrent, criterion-related validity of the Quick Test based on a sample of gifted students. *Psychological Reports, 67,* 1007–1010.

Marini, A. E. (1991). *A strategy for reducing Test Anxiety while writing multiple choice exams.* Manuscript submitted for publication.

Marshall, J. C., and Powers, J. C. (1969). Writing neatness, composition errors, and essay grades. *Journal of Educational Measurement, 6,* 97–101.

McCall, R. B., Hogarty, P. S., and Hurlburt, N. (1972). Transitions in sensorimotor development and the prediction of childhood IQ. *American Psychologist, 27,* 728–748.

McDaniel, M. A., and Masson, M. J. (1985). Altering memory representations through retrieval. *Journal of Experimental Psychology: Learning, Memory and Cognition, 11,* 371–385.

McGuken, W. J. (1932). *The Jesuits and education.* Milwaukee: Bruce.

McKnight, C. C. (1987). *The underachieving curriculum.* Champaign, IL: Stipes.

McMorris, R. F., Brown, J. A., Snyder, G. W., and Pruzek, R. M. (1972). Effects of violating item construction principles. *Journal of Educational Measurement, 9,* 287–295.

Mednick, M. T. (1967). Relationship of the Ammons Quick Test of intelligence to other ability measures. *Psychological Reports, 20,* 523–526.

Mednick, M. T. (1969). The validity of the Ammons' Quick Test of intelligence. *Psychological Reports, 24,* 388–390.

Mehrens, W. A., and Lehmann, I. J. (1973). *Measurement and evaluation in education and psychology.* New York: Holt, Rinehart and Winston.

Melton, R. F. (1978). Resolution of conflicting claims concerning the effective of behavioral objectives on student learning. *Review of Educational Research, 48,* 291–302.

Metfessel, N. S., Michael, W. B. and Kirsner, D. A. (1969). Instrumentation of Bloom's and Krathwohl's taxonomies for the writing of educational objectives. *Psychology in the Schools, 6,* 227–231.

Morgan, C. T., and Deese, J. (1957). *How to study.* New York: McGraw-Hill.

Morris, V. C., and Pai, Y. (1976). *Philosophy and the American school: An introduction to the philosophy of education* (2nd ed.). Boston: Houghton Mifflin.

Niedermeyer, F. C., and Sullivan, H. J. (1972). Differential effects of individual and group testing strategies in an objectives-based instructional program. *Journal of Educational Measurement, 9,* 199–204.

Nitko, A. J., and Hsu, T. C. (1984). A comprehensive microcomputer system for classroom testing. *Journal of Educational Measurement, 21*(4), 377–390.

Norton, L. S., and Hartley, J. (1986). What factors contribute to good examination marks? *Higher Education, 15,* 355–371.

Ogilvie, R. D. (1965). Correlations between the Quick Test (QT) and the Wechsler Adult Intelligence Scale (WAIS) as used in a clinical setting. *Psychological Reports, 16,* 497–498.

O'Malley, P. M., and Bachman, J. G. (1976). Longitudinal evidence for the validity of the Quick Test. *Psychological Reports, 38,* 1247–1252.

Oosterhof, A. C. (1990). *Classroom applications of educational measurement.* Columbus, OH: Merrill.

Owen, D. (1985). *None of the above: Behind the myth of the Scholastic Aptitude.* Boston: Houghton Mifflin.

Owen, D. (1983). The last days of ETS. *Harpers, 266*(1596), 21–37.

Pless, B., Snider, M., Eaton, A. E., and Kearsley, R. B. (1965). A rapid screening test for intelligence in children. *American Journal of Diseases of Children, 109,* 533–537.

Plumly, W. L., and Ray, H. N. (1989). Computer administered testing in a classroom setting: An alternate. *Journal of Research on Computing in Education, 22*(1), 326–338.

Popham, W. J. (1965). *Systematic instructional decision making.* Los Angeles: Vimcet Associates.

Popham, W. J. (1968). Probing the validity of arguments against behavioral goals. In R. J. Kibler, D. J. Cegala, L. L. Barker, and D. T. Miles (Eds.), *Objectives for instruction and evaluation* (pp. 9–17). Boston: Allyn & Bacon.

Popham, W. J. (1988). *Educational evaluation* (2nd ed.). Englewood Cliffs, NJ: Prentice-Hall.

Posner, R. (1987). Life without Scan-Tron: Tests as thinking. *English Journal, 76,* 35–38.

Quattlebaum, L. F., and White, W. F. (1969). Relationship between two quick screening measures of intelligence for neuropsychiatric patients. *Psychological Reports, 24,* 691–693.

Rice, J. M. (1897). The futility of the spelling grind: I. *Forum, 23,* 163–172.

Sadler, D. R. (1983). Evaluation and the improvement of academic learning. *Journal of Higher Education, 54,* 60–79.

Scarr, S. A., and Carter-Saltzman. (1982). Genetics and intelligence. In R. J. Sternberg (Ed.), *Handbook of human intelligence.* (pp. 792–896). Cambridge: Cambridge University.

Schomaker, J. H., and Knopt, R. C. (1982). Generalizability of a measure of visitor satisfaction with outdoor recreation. *Applied Psychological Measurement, 6,* 173–183.

Siegler, R. S. and Richards, D. D. (1982). The development of intelligence. In R. J. Sternberg (Ed.), *Handbook of human intelligence.* (pp. 897–974). Cambridge: Cambridge University.

Simpson, E. J. (1972). The classification of educational objectives in the psychomotor domain. In *The psycho-motor domain: A resource book for media specialists* (pp. 43–56). Washington, DC: Gryphon.

Snow, R. E., and Yalow, E. (1982). Education and intelligence. In R. J. Sternberg (Ed.), *Handbook of human intelligence.* (pp. 493–585). Cambridge: Cambridge University.

Sorensen, H. B. (1985). The equivalence between paper-and-pencil versions and computerized versions of cognitive ability tests. *The Monitor, 24,* 22–26.

Stalnaker, J. M. (1951). The essay type of examination. In E. F. Lindquist (Ed.), *Educational measurement* (pp. 495–530). Washington, DC: American Council on Education.

Stanley, J., and Hopkins, K. D. (1981). *Educational and psychological measurement and evaluation.* (6th ed.). Englewood Cliffs, N.J.: Prentice-Hall.

Starch, D., and Elliot, E. C. (1912). Reliability of grading high school work in English. *Scholastic Review, 20,* 442–457.

Starch, D., and Elliot, E. C. (1913). Reliability of grading high school work in Mathematics. *Scholastic Review, 21,* 254–259.

Sternberg, R. J. (1985). Reasoning, problem solving, and intelligence. In R. J. Sternberg (Ed.), *Handbook of human intelligence.* (pp. 225–307). Cambridge: Cambridge University.

Stiggins, R. J. (1988). Revitalizing classroom assessment: The highest instructional priority. *Phi Delta Kappan, 70,* 363–368.

Stiggins, R. J. (1991). Assessment literacy. *Phi Delta Kappan, 73,* 534–539.

Stiggins, R. J., and Bridgeford, N. J. (1985). The ecology of classroom assessment. *Journal of Educational Measurement, 22,* 271–286.

Terman, L. M. (1916). *The measurement of intelligence.* Boston: Houghton Mifflin.

Thorndike, R. L., and Hagen, E. P. (1977). *Measurement and evaluation in psychology and education* (4th ed.). Toronto: Wiley and Sons.

Townsend, M. A. R., Kek, Y. K., and Tuck, B. F. (1989). The effect of mood on the reliability of essay assessment. *British Journal of Educational Psychology, 59,* 232–240.

Traub, G. S., and Spruill, J. (1982). Correlations between the Quick Test and Wechsler Adult Intelligence Scale-Revised. *Psychological Reports, 51,* 309–310.

Tyler, R. W. (1950). *Basic principles of curriculum and instruction.* Chicago: The University of Chicago.

Violato, C. (1984). Effects of Canadianization of American-Biased items on the WAIS and WAIS-R Information Subtests. *Canadian Journal of Behavioural Science, 16,* 36–41.

Violato, C. (1986). Canadian versions of the information subtests of the Wechsler Tests of Intelligence. *Canadian Psychology, 27,* 69–74.

Violato, C. (1990). Social and communication issues in testing. In R. A. Fiordo (Ed.), *Communication in education* (pp. 147–160). Calgary: Detselig.

Violato, C. (1991). *A structural equation model of the relationship between intelligence, creativity and achievement in gifted children.* Laboratory for Educational Measurement and Evaluation. University of Calgary, Calgary, AB.

Violato, C., and Blank, S. (1982). An evaluation of a programme for the gifted. *B.C. Journal of Special Education, 6,* 323–341.

Violato, C. and Harasym, P. H. (1987). Effects of structural characteristics of stem format of multiple-choice items on item difficulty and discrimination. *Psychological Reports, 60,* 1259–1262.

Violato, C. and Marini, A. E. (1988). *Educational measurement and evaluation: A laboratory and exercise manual.* Calgary: Detselig.

Violato, C. and Marini, A. E. (1989). Effects of stem orientation and completeness of multiple-choice items on item difficulty and discrimination. *Educational and Psychological Measurement, 49,* 287–295.

Violato, C. and Odhiambo, K. (1990). The social ecology of literacy and achievement in primary schools of Kenya. *Canadian and International Education, 19,* 50–60.

Violato, C. and Travis, L. D. (1985). Sex as a moderator variable in the academic achievement of elementary school children: A structural analysis. *B.C. Journal of Special Education, 9,* 215–230.

Violato, C. and Travis, L. D. (1988). An application of generalizability theory to the consistency—specificity problem: The transsituational consistency of behavioural persistence. *The Journal of Psychology, 122,* 389–408.

Violato, C., White, W. B., and Travis, L. D. (1984). Some concurrent criterion-related data on validity for the Quick Test based on three Canadian samples. *Psychological Reports, 54,* 775–782.

Wallace, W. L. (1972). College Board of Scholastic Aptitude Test. *Seventh Mental Measurements Yearbook,* (pp. 648–650). Highland Park, NJ: Gryphon.

Wason, P. C. (1961). Response to affirmative and negative binary statements. *British Journal of Psychology, 52,* 133–142.

Weiten, W. (1983). *Psychology applied to modern life: Adjustment in the 80's.* Monterey, CA: Brooks Cole.

Wesman, A. G. (1971). Writing the test item. In R. L. Thorndike (Ed.), *Educational measurement* (2nd ed., pp. 81–129). Washington, DC: American Council on Education.

Zastrow, C. H. (1970). Cheating among college graduate students. *Journal of Educational Research, 64,* 157–160.

Zern, D. (1967). Effects of variation in question-phrasing on true-false answers by grade-school children. *Psychological Reports, 20,* 527–533.

Zimmermann, R. R., Schroll, E. F., Ackles, P., Barrett, R., and Auster, M. (1978). Performance of institutional retardates on standard and new forms of the Quick Test. *Perceptual and Motor Skills, 46,* 263–266.

NOTES

NOTES

NOTES

NOTES

NOTES

NOTES

NOTES